JESUS, LORD AND SAVIOR

JESUS, LORD AND SAVIOR

A THEOPATHIC CHRISTOLOGY

AND SOTERIOLOGY

William M. Thompson

PAULIST PRESS
New York/Ramsey

Library of Congress
Catalog Card Number: 80-81052

ISBN: 0-8091-2306-1

Published by Paulist Press
Editorial Office: 1865 Broadway, New York, N.Y. 10023
Business Office: 545 Island Road, Ramsey, N.J. 07446

Printed and bound in the
United States of America

CONTENTS

for my Mother
Rosa Maria Eugenia Uberuaga Thompson

Asko dakik bizitxen baldin ba dakik.
You know much if you know how to
live.

Jakiteko artzen ikasi zazu ematen.
To learn to receive, first learn to give.

—*Basque Proverbs*

FOREWORD

A book such as this must be a collaborative effort, since it draws on the aid of one's friends and inevitably carries one into concerns that far transcend the command of any one person. The lofty realms of historical hermeneutics, philosophy and theology of history, metaphysics and systematic theology, the historical faith of the Christian churches—these are but some of the areas into which the author was carried, and my debt to experts in all of these areas is thankfully registered here. My first thanks, however, is to my wife and friend, Patricia Marie, who has mastered the art of leading me to my desk and yet again drawing me away from it. Secondly, I wish to express a deep thanks to Dr. Francis Kerins, President of Carroll College, who has supported the writing of this work in all the ways such a book demands. His commitment to theological scholarship and to the welfare of Carroll College in general provided me with the basic professional support I needed to complete this work. Thirdly, there are scholars to whom I am especially indebted because of the illumination provided by their works: Karl Rahner, Walter Kasper, Gordon Kaufman, Eric Voegelin, Raymond Brown, Gregory Baum, Peter Chirico, William Johnston, Abraham Heschel, Thomas Merton. This list is by no means exhaustive, but it gives expression to how deeply this work is collaborative. Finally, my personal thanks to friends who have continued to challenge and support me in the day-to-day exchange enjoyed by college professors, especially Clayton Meyer, Francis Kromkowski, Eugene Peoples, Thomas Flynn, Richard Lambert, Jeremiah Sullivan, Mary Frances Jeske, Frank Cooney, the Carroll faculty and my former and present students. The typists were Annette Mannix and Cheryl McNurlin, and my sincere thanks can end with them.

PART ONE

METHODOLOGY, INTRODUCTION

I

APPROACHING CHRISTOLOGY:
INTRODUCTION

Because the question of Jesus Christ has so penetrated the conscious and unconscious convictions and motivations of Western man, it seems important from the outset to grapple with the issue of how to approach Christology. For us Westerners there can be no "neutral" approach to Jesus, and I suspect that this is as true of the Western nonbeliever as it is of the most ardent Christ-follower. Our observations here on "approaches to Christology" are not written with the hope of finding some pure, totally neutral approach. Rather we want to raise to the level of conscious awareness the approaches one can take, and thus foster some measure of awareness of and responsibility for their limits and adequacies.

Perhaps the dominant approach to Christology until recent times in Roman Catholicism and Eastern Orthodoxy—and until the Enlightenment in Protestantism—has been the dogmatic approach. This takes as the starting point for Christological reflection the great dogmatic symbols of the councils of Nicaea, Ephesus, Chalcedon, and Constantinople I, II, III. As is well known, the dogmatic formulae of these Councils still operate on the basis of the presupposed theocentric framework of ancient times. Thus they formulated a Christology "from above," from the divine point of view, and took as their paradigm the Johannine model of "God's becoming flesh" (Jn. 1). Under the pressure of the various Christological disputes, the Johannine insight was then translated into the abstract terminology of Hellenistic metaphysics. The *Logos* becomes man; he can be differentiated into a divine and human nature; he is one divine "Person."

The great importance that the churches give to these dogmatic symbols does not derive from any superstitious or unintelligible belief in the efficacy of ecclesiastical Councils. It ultimately derives from two sources. On the one hand, it derives from an insight into man as not just an isolated individual, but a being-in-community who comes to self-knowledge through relationships with others. Thus, the great Councils bring to expression the

3

collective wisdom of the Christian community about its founder, Jesus of Nazareth. On the other hand, it derives from the experience of God as a God-with-her-people, and not an isolated Being to be sought in the privacy of esoteric religious experience. The dogmatic symbols thus express and deepen the collective identity of God's people, and only an unthinking individualism would denigrate their historic importance. In our own times, the individualism stemming from the Enlightenment runs the danger of severing Christology from the collective beliefs of the historic churches.[1] For example, attention tends to focus on Rahner's, Pannenberg's, Kasper's, or Cobb's Christology, rather than on the Christology of the Church. The best insurance against this "privatizing" of Christology is the historic beliefs of the faith, preserved in a concentrated way in the dogmatic formulae of the Councils.

But if the individual today runs the danger of "privatizing" Christology, so the churches run the danger of "ossifying" it by forgetting that the great dogmas exist only to cement the collective identity of God's people and thus to give God praise in this way. History amply demonstrates that the churches can use the historic dogmas to their own ends. Christology then becomes a "possession" of ecclesiology, rather than its font and origin. The way out of this difficulty is neither individualism nor dogmatism, but a rethinking of Christology on our own terms, just as the Councils sought to rethink it in their own terms.

I think we are far enough along in our research today to recognize that the charge of the Hellenization of dogma—leveled against the historic formulations of the Councils—is not entirely adequate. There is, of course, a "weak" and a "strong" form of this accusation of Hellenization. In its weak form the charge would maintain that the Councils translated the biblical affirmations into the foreign categories of Hellenic metaphysics. While this may have obscured the meaning of the biblical affirmations, it did not destroy them. Even in this "weak" form, the Hellenization theory can be inadequate if pushed too far. For it would presuppose that the biblical affirmations are not themselves "metaphysical," implying a world view, but only a species of functional and practical thought.[2] Further, this view could overlook that we, too, are metaphysical beings, perhaps not in the theoretical sense, but at least in the pretheoretical. We simply have and need some world view and orientation, and because we do we must, like the great Greeks, probe the "metaphysics" of Christology.[3] The "strong" form of the Hellenization thesis goes further and maintains that the historic formulae were a corruption of the biblical faith that turned the man Jesus into a Hellenistic cultic deity. This process is thought to begin with Paul, reach a biblical apex in John, and become cemented and institutionalized by the ecumenical Councils. But this view simply does not come to terms, as we shall try to show, with the profound Christianization of Hellenism that begins even with Paul and continues to the Councils. The Johannine "God became flesh" would have been impossible for the Hellenist. The evidence, in the end, suggests that Christianity and Hellenism stood in creative tension with each other, at least in the Councils and among the recognized spokesmen for Christian orthodoxy.[4]

The limitation of the dogmatic approach is not, then, its supposed Hellenization. It is rather the same limitation that we should level against ourselves: its historic conditioning. Two features of the dogmatic approach especially merit mention. First, its predilection for the static, unhistorical point of view. Our modern consciousness of history had not yet sufficiently differentiated itself. With this goes the second feature, a theocentrism, a tendency to view the world from the divine point of view. Reality was viewed as a divinely "predetermined" reality. Hence the tendency to underplay the historicity of being human, in reality at large and in Christ in particular. This unhistorical theocentrism shows up in the incarnation-view of Christology that characterizes the dogmatic symbols. It is sufficient here that God became man. But no clear, conscious attention is focused on Jesus' life, death, and resurrection—the historical "mysteries" of Jesus' life. These realities are not viewed in a truly historic way: they are an "unfolding" of the predetermined Divine Will, and not yet clearly a truly historical human response to the Divine Will. What I am saying, then, is that it is too simplistic to restrict the Christological task to simply an articulation of the Church's dogmatic faith. For this overlooks the way that the Church's dogma is embedded in and to some extent tied to the society and culture from which it emerged. Thus the Christologian cannot accept, without question, the dogmatic standpoint. Because it is culture-bound, it is open to questioning. Further, because these great dogmas are culture-bound, we cannot simply assume that we know their meaning. There is a cultural distance that we must traverse first by grasping them on our own terms.

It is partly a dissatisfaction with the underplaying of human historicity in the dogmatic symbols that has led to our second approach, a biblical Christology. Partly the return to a biblical focus was the result of a positivistic, antimetaphysical attitude, and in that sense it was doomed to failure. For while it thought it was substituting the outmoded metaphysics of the dogmatic symbols for the a-metaphysical approach of the scriptures, it was really committing itself to the even more ancient biblical "metaphysics" or view of reality. But more basically the return to the scriptures was motivated by a desire to reappropriate the historical point of view that so characterizes the Judaeo-Christian tradition, and in this way it was a necessary corrective to the dogmatic approach. But, of course, the biblical Christology is historically conditioned too. There simply is no "pure" and inspired biblical Christology, uninfluenced by the presuppositions of the ancient world and ancient man. Very few would accept everything the scriptures say, both about reality at large and about Christ in particular. This fact is enough to indicate that some extra-biblical norm is operative, causing them to accept now one aspect of the biblical Christology, to reinterpret another, and to discard another. In other words, while recognizing the historic importance of the scriptures as our main link to Jesus of Nazareth, we also recognize that we approach those scriptures, consciously or unconsciously, from our contemporary point of view. As with the dogmatic approach, the Christologian cannot accept the biblical approach without question. We would again be simplistically overlooking the way it is embedded in the culture from which it sprang, and our need to grasp the scripture in a way intelligible to us.[5]

At this point, let me clarify somewhat. By claiming that our Christological search cannot begin without further question with the Church's scripture and dogma, I am not denying that Christology has its final basis in God's own revelation. Our concern here is how best to approach Christology, how to begin our reflection on the Christ in a theological manner. Theology is and always has been a human work of reflection. Because it is we cannot simply presuppose that we humans of the twentieth century understand the terms and concepts to be found in the scriptures and dogmas. We first have to understand how these terms and concepts can be made meaningful in the light of our own contemporary experience and understanding. Thus we cannot simply begin with God's revelation, but that does not mean that we cannot end with it. Clearly the Christian theologian would want to say that our knowledge of Christ is God's revelatory gift to which we respond in faith. With Kaufman[6] we can usefully fall back upon the distinction between the "order of being" and the "order of knowing." From the perspective of the "order of being," all that we can come to know of the Christ is God's gifted revelation to us. But this is not the order in which we come to know the Christ. That revelation needs to be grasped and understood first through and in the light of our contemporary self-understanding.

In the light of the above, I am led to the conclusion that we must admit that a study of Christology begins with the Christologian's own present self-understanding. It is here that each of us begins, insofar as we approach what the tradition has to tell us of Christ from the perspective of our own present level of development. Despite what some may have claimed in the past, Christology never was a study that simply began with scripture or dogma without further question, as if the data of scripture and dogma were simply facts in the positivistic sense waiting to be plucked by the Christologian. To be sure, there are data pertaining to Christ (scripture, dogma, New Testament history, etc.), but it is out of these data that the Christologian constructs what he considers the "facts" of Christ to be. As I will try to show in my next chapter, this clearly implies that the Christologian selects and makes judgments of many kinds. And on what basis does he/she do this? Ultimately on the basis of her own present level of self-understanding. This is, of course, true of every Christian from the Pope to the pious believer to the theologian. But it is the Christologian's task, it seems to me, to be conscious that she is doing this, to spell out the implications of what this might mean, and to take responsibility for these implications.

Doing just that will be the goal of our next chapter, but by way of introduction I should indicate that this fact—that we begin our Christological work with our own present level of understanding—means that there is a heavily theoretical dimension to Christology. We approach the data relevant to a study on Christ with a consciousness already preformed and mediated by values, interests, and even, I would claim, by an implicit worldview, however inconsistent it may be. The Christologian's task is not to lament this theoretical "preformation," but to take responsibility for it by articulating its consequences clearly. It is the Christologian who is conscious of his starting point, after all, who has the best chance of transcending its limitations. I will also argue in the next chapter that it is this consciousness of our starting point that insures our capacity for self-transcendence, for entertaining other points of view, for expanding our consciousness, and then for avoiding Christological relativism. The great task for the Christologian, then, is not to try to "escape" the fact that he begins theologizing with his own limited consciousness, but rather to "expand" one's consciousness. There are, of course, many theories that propose criteria by which we might discern whether one's consciousness is being expanded. In a preliminary way, I will follow Lawrence Kohlberg's criteria of evaluative discrimination and evaluative integration. That is, "an interpretative frame of reference enjoys greater adequacy if it allows me to think about things that are either ignored or only vaguely perceived in a different reference frame, and if it allows me to grasp relationships among discriminated elements in experience that were previously either ignored or only vaguely felt."[7]

The fact that the Christologian always begins with her own present consciousness also enables us to grasp, by the way, why there is a pluralism of Christologies present in the contemporary Church. There was, of course, always a pluralism of Christologies, even in the scriptures. The recovery of this truth is one of the most important discoveries of contemporary biblical and patristic research,[8] and throughout this book we will be reviewing this early Christological pluralism. This pluralism stems from the different experiences and traditions that have shaped the consciousness of the Church's early theologians. But this was a less radical form of pluralism than we experience today. Today's historical consciousness, and the fact that ours is an increasingly planetary world, made such through intercommunication, has radicalized the phenomenom of pluralism, in theology and elsewhere. The consciousness of the contemporary theologian has greatly complexified in modern times, and this will probably increase rather than lessen. While this surely brings confusion and frustration, it is also a necessary condition for the expansion of the theologian's consciousness.

We can illustrate this expansion of the theological consciousness by dwelling, for a moment, on the varieties of Christology available today. Starting from an analysis of the contemporary person, one might attempt an anthropological Christology, which would seek to make sense of Christological affirmations by showing how they are rooted in the experience of being human. Thus Christ might be viewed, with Karl Rahner, as the "perfect instance" of what it is to be human. Or we might attempt a cosmological Christology, in the manner of Teilhard de Chardin, beginning with our contemporary understanding of evolution or process and attempting to show how the Christ realizes and completes the evolutionary process. Or further, one might attempt a socially responsible Christology, which might take as its starting point modern society's struggle for human emancipation and liberation and thus attempt to translate Christological assertions into the terms of a critical and liberating praxis. In each case, Christological data are related to particular dimensions of our contemporary experience, dimensions we have become increasingly sensitized to under the pressure of our complexifying experience and understanding. The Christological task is then one of describing and analyzing that particular dimension of contemporary experience as carefully as possible and showing how Christology can be illuminated in its light.

My point is not to say that we should accept any of these Christologies as a whole, but only to indicate that they are a result of an "expanding" theological consciousness. Few there are who would deny that these Christologies have been able to lay bare, under the pressure of our more complexified experience, essential elements for a truly contemporary Christology. The Christologian's task is one of building upon these insights, refining them, and in this truly collaborative way developing his own theological consciousness. Hopefully this book will more than once manifest its debt to many Christologians.

Of course, the Christologian ultimately cannot accept everything that has been written in the area of Christology. Pluralism not only potentially expands the theologian's consciousness, it also causes disagreements among competing points of view. There is no need here, however, for settling for a Christological relativism. For, first, such a position would ultimately deny the Christologian's capacity for self-transcendence, for moving to a different point of view; for expanding her consciousness, in other words. Further, as I have said, and as I will try to spell out more clearly in my next chapter, there are ultimate theoretical presuppositions that we do and must bring to any study such as this. The issue is whether we have adequately rendered ourselves conscious of them, whether our consciousness has sufficiently expanded through evaluative discrimination and integration.

In the end, I would describe the Christological task in the way in which Eric Voegelin described the classical search for truth, what the ancients called a *zetema*.

> It is . . . a search for truth both cognitive and existential. Definitions in the course of a *zetema*, however, are cognitive resting points, which articulate the view of reality that has been gained at the respective stage in the existential advance toward truth. As a consequence, the validity of the definitions has two dimensions. In the one direction, they must be tested against the data of reality to which they purport to refer; in the other direction, they must be measured by the existential level

reached in the search for truth. Moreover, the two dimensions of validity are related to one another, insofar as the question which is a datum of reality depends for its answer on the existential level reached. What is relevant on a lower level may become irrelevant on a higher level, and vice versa. Hence, the definitions that articulate the view of reality achieved in earlier stages of the *zetema* are liable to be superseded by definitions reached at higher existential levels. In an existentially authentic *zetema* we are faced, therefore, with a series of definitions, the later ones qualifying and superseding the earlier ones; and under no circumstances must they be pitted against one another on the level of a logic of the external world which ignores the logic of existence.[9]

Voegelin is saying, in his own classicist terms, what I have been attempting to maintain. We approach a study of the Christ from the perspective of our own "preformed consciousness"—"the existential level reached in the search for truth." We are caught, then, in a kind of circle, the famous "hermeneutical circle," for we begin with the fact that the only Christ we know is the Christ available to our consciousness. But it is not a vicious circle. For that consciousness has a capacity for self-transcendence, for "expansion." This is but another way of saying simply that a study of Christ calls for "conversion."

By way of outline then, and in consistency with my view that Christology inevitably begins with my own level of existential development, I begin this book with an exploration of the hermeneutical question in Christology (Chapter 2). This is my own attempt to become conscious of, and take responsibility for, the presuppositions that I bring to this study. Thus I engage in a kind of review of the hermeneutical methods currently in use, investigate and analyze their inevitable presuppositions, and propose my own. I would like to think that this is a collaborative study building upon and perhaps nuancing somewhat the insights of others. For while it is true that this study begins with my own present level of consciousness, it is also true that my consciousness was not self-made but indebted to many others. Basically I propose that Christological hermeneutics is a very sophisticated praxis in need of a more adequate theory, and that the first step toward this entails firmly accepting the proposal that all historical reconstruction involves, at every point along the line, the imaginative capacities of the historian/Christological critic. This is neither a cause for lamentation nor a lapse into subjectivism in our view of Jesus, but a summons to articulate how good historical reconstruction occurs, the conditions on which the critic can develop his own capacities for self-transcendence and thus appreciatively appropriate the historical data pertaining to Jesus. I am led to the conclusion that both the Old and the New Quests, in their respective ways, have assumed too naïvely that the "bare" and uninterpreted Jesus could be recovered through historical research. There never was a "bare portrait" of Jesus, but only an interpreted Jesus, and the key issue is not whether "Jesus" should be so interpreted, but how best to interpret and thus to continue the work already begun in the scriptures. I close this chapter with some observations on the hermeneutical distinction between the "Jesus of history" and "Christ of faith." I cautiously propose that it was always a mistake to think of the first as a pure, uninterpreted reality and the latter as the faith-influenced interpretation of the early Church. Both are "interpretative" realities created by the critic, and the issue is not to play the Christ of faith off against the "solid" core of the Jesus of history, but to ask whether the "Christ of faith" stems from a more differentiated experience and understanding, calling for a new interpretation of Jesus. The issue is not whether the kerygma is an "interpretation" of Jesus, but what kind is it, how did it occur, and, if it represents a more differentiated understanding of Jesus, how might we appropriate and continue it today?

Chapter 3, "The Genesis of the Christ-Belief," is an attempt to defend the proposal that the kerygma represents a more differentiated comprehension of Jesus under the pressure of the resurrection experience. The kerygma, in other words, is neither a "distortion" nor simply an alternative comprehension of the historic Jesus, but a deepened comprehension of Jesus. The resurrection experience is treated as an epistemological factor, deepening the consciousness of the apostolic Church. This elevation of the kerygma as the central concern of my book does not devalue the pre-Easter Jesus. It rather brings out the deeper implications—the "depth dimension"—of the Jesus of history.

Quite naturally, then, my book turns to the central concerns of the kerygma. Chapter 4, "Toward a Christic God-Concept: God as *Pathos* and Lord," is my attempt to grapple with the very central affirmation of Jesus' divinity. It is the book's "central nervous system" upon which all else depends. This confession summons us to a new—in terms of the history of religious thought—understanding of God and spiritual praxis. Such a confession, again I cautiously propose, is of course quite different from the Hellenistic notion of the Divine as isolated and unrelational. Divine transcendence must be reformulated in terms of divine immanence, in terms of relationality, historicality and human involvement. The Divine is *Pathos,* not *apatheia,* to borrow Heschel's profound term. Yet this is a truly divine form of *Pathos,* and so I am led to register my reservations with schools of thought that tend to reduce God to one among many other finite influences in this world of ours. Ultimately I propose that theopathy is a way of imagining God which is an authentic alternative to both the Hellenistic "God" of "coercion and apathy" and the more contemporary "God" of simple "persuasion."

Chapter 5 moves us into the difficult terrain of Christian reflection on the "self" of Jesus. This is, of course, already a central concern of the kerygma, as the very existence of the scriptures manifests. Some might feel that this chapter is too speculative and interpretative, yet I would maintain that the only other alternative is to leave the affirmations of the scriptures and Councils, at the best, mere propositions of notional rather than real assent and, at the worst, residues of superstition. The key insight into the "person" of Jesus stems from the Christic view of God, already explored. Because the Divine, and thus the ultimate ground of reality, is relational, so too is the "person." Personhood is a living relationship, to God and to man, and this chapter explores how the entire being of Jesus was so "poured" into this Divine-human relationship that we can still truly affirm: Jesus is God and man.

The remaining chapters simply probe the implications for humanity of belief in the Christian God of relationship and involvement. The nature of man and his response to the Divine corresponds to his experience and apprehension of God. Heschel had already noted this in his superb study of the prophets: "When the Divine is sensed as mysterious perfection, the response is one of fear and trembling; when sensed as absolute will, the response is one of unconditional obedience; when sensed as pathos, the response is one of sympathy."[10] Similarly, then, the new experience of God in Christ grounds a new experience of being human. Chapter 6, "Exploring the Christ-Experience: Foundations," probes this new experience on the individual level, primarily through a study of the paradigmatic example of Paul's Christ-mysticism. The deepened personal and dialogical experience of God through Christ heightens one's self-and-world consciousness. Chapter 7, "Exploring the Christ-Experience II: Reflections on Soteriology," extrapolates from the individual's Christ-experience to history at large, to explore how the Christ grounds a new experience of human history, of human community and freedom, and of overcoming human and social alienation. This is my attempted reformulation of the doctrine of soteriology.

The remaining Chapters 8 and 9 simply prolong our exploration of the Christ-experience. Both of these chapters will appear elsewhere,[11] although they have been revised and expanded for this book. "A Study of Bérulle's Christic Spirituality" is my attempt to introduce and renew interest in the remarkable Christocentric spirituality of Pierre de Bérulle and the seventeenth-century French school of spirituality. Bérulle has come to be known as the "apostle of the Incarnate Word," and not without cause, for he is one of the few figures in Christian history to explore systematically the Christ-experience, quite consciously attempting a living synthesis between Christology and spirituality. Like St. Paul, Bérulle's Christ-mysticism is paradigmatic, for not only does he consciously integrate the major themes of Christology into his spirituality, but he also lived at the turning point of the emergence of Western secularism and attempted a Christian alternative. I have been attempting a similar reformulation of spirituality in my chapters on the "Christ-Experience," and hopefully the inclusion of this study on Bérulle manifests my continuity with the tradition.

Our final study, "Thomas Merton's Transcultural Christ," is perhaps the most "experimental" of all the studies in this work. I say this because the next task confronting humanity at large and Christianity in particular is that of planetization. Our planet has already become "one" in the minimal sense made possible through intercommunication. But this is not yet an integrated planetization; we are only at the critical edge of this crucial development. Just what will happen to Christianity as it penetrates and is penetrated by the venerable religious traditions of the Orient is not yet clear. Yet some Christians have made this journey of the spirit, and their reflections merit thoughtful consideration. I have selected as my paradigmatic sojourner Thomas Merton. Remarkable with him is the fact that he was able to experience planetization not in spite of, but precisely because of his Christ-experience. Merton's Christ-mysticism is one in which Christ is experienced as the ground of planetization, drawing mankind from self-absorption to cosmification and universal love. I find this not only very suggestive but also an experimental confirmation of my view that in Christ God is experienced as the relational Being of Love who "draws" mankind into participation into the fullest depths of the divine, universal, and cosmic Love. Because this study is experimental and a task yet to be completed, it is fitting that we end our Christological search here.

This book marks the partial completion of my earlier *Christ and Consciousness: Exploring Christ's Contribution to Human Consciousness.*[12] In that work I studied how Christianity is related to the larger phenomenon of the evolution of human consciousness in general. My intent was similar to and inspired by Erich Neumann's *The Origins and History of Consciousness* and Eric Voegelin's monumental *Order and History* and *Anamnesis.* Like Voegelin I sought to explore "man's consciousness of his humanity as it differentiates historically," through analyzing "the history of experiences and their symbolization."[13] For the most part I concentrated on the epochal advances in human consciousness associated with the first millennium, a period I saw reason to call "axial," with Karl Jaspers. I proposed that the phenomenom of Christ fostered an epochal advance in human consciousness—a leap in the history of the differentiation of human consciousness—insofar as through Christ and his resurrection mankind became aware of God and himself in a new way. God was experienced as an "Empowering Presence" in man's psyche, and this enabled the Christian self to define its identity in terms of a transcendent source of personal identity. As I put it, the Christian psyche "experienced the presence of a transcendent spiritual source, co-constituting its very self, empowering it to transcend all forces threatening to destroy the self."[14]

What remained only partially explored in that earlier work was, if you will, the "objective pole" of mankind's and Christianity's evolving/developing consciousness. This work on Christology now seeks to complement my earlier work by more carefully exploring the ontological ground of the phenomenon of Christian consciousness. What was the experience of God through Christ as "Empowering Presence" is now further spelled out in the terms of God as Relationality, as Divine *Pathos.* This further development, by the way, is a good example of how our theological work is a *zetema,* a search, whose insights are hopefully deepened at higher existential levels of advance toward the truth. My earlier *Christ and Consciousness,* however, remains an essential propaedeutic to this newer one. Not only does it present the necessary historical presuppositions for a study on Christology—without the emergence of a Christian consciousness no one would have ever thought to write a Christology. It is also the necessary experiential and existential propaedeutic, for without the appropriate Christian consciousness, the experiential reference for an understanding of this book would be missing.

Inevitably the question will arise as to what is the cognitive status of the major insights I will propose throughout this work. The notion of God as Divine Relationality—as Divine *Pathos*—is essentially a hypothesis attempting to articulate the necessary ontological ground for the phenomena of Christ and Christian existence. As the "ground," it is not directly available to experience and thus cannot be tested by the ordinary methods of correspondence. One simply cannot check one's notion of the Divine as Sovereign *Pathos* against some particular object within the world, since this is the very ground of the world itself. But this does not mean that no such "ground" exists. There are many realities that cannot be tested by the criteria of correspondence, and yet they are utterly real. The notion of "world," for example, is not directly experienced; only objects and events within it. Yet few would dispute that the notion of "world" gives expression to a necessary ontological presupposition for the objects and events we do experience. So, too, with the notion of God as Divine *Pathos*. As the ultimate ground of reality, such a notion can only be verified indirectly, by asking to what an extent it makes sense out of human reality and human history. Such an indirect method of verification holds for all high-level, metaphysical abstractions/notions.[15]

Before concluding, let me say something about the kind of expression such a high-level notion as the "Divine *Pathos*" might be. This issue is of some importance, for throughout this book the reader will come across key notions, additional to "Divine *Pathos*," whose precise nature will be puzzling; viz., "kingdom of God" (in the preaching of Jesus); "resurrection/exaltation" (in the kerygma), etc. Basically the question comes down to whether we have to do here with "myth" or with "concepts," and so some explanation of how I would understand these categories seems appropriate at this point.

Despite the controversy that rages over the precise nature of myth and concept, for the sake of clarity I will simply present my own view. Both myth and concept are modes/media of human experience and perception. If we consider human perception as a broad continuum ranging from the most concrete to the most abstract, we might say that myth is human perception in the concrete mode, that concept is human perception in the abstract mode, and that between the two is a broadly gray area where concrete shades into abstract, myth into concept. For example, "being raised" is a concrete image; "eternity," abstract; and "resurrection," somewhere in between the two.

What gives rise to myth? If myth is a concrete mode of human perception, it would seem that it arises from the concrete, from basic patterns of our human experience. Myth is replete with images deriving from our profound ties with this concrete, bodily universe of ours. Skies, clouds, air, breath, fire, water, ocean—these are but some of the recurring images found in myth. The fact is that we are all linked in a rather patterned manner to this universe of ours, and it is this linkage that furnishes the imagery of myth. But besides the pattern of our physical linkage to the universe, there are also basic psychic/human patterns that we experience: our sexual drives and orientations; our need for protection and triumph over fear; our need for love; and our need for ultimate meaning and unconditioned love, from which arises the religious dimension of being human.[16] The imagery found in myth, then, has the capacity not only to express our linkage with this physical universe, but also to operate on our psychic/human level, and thus to stir us to ever deeper levels of meaning. For example, a "cloud" is simply a natural phenomenon, a basic human experience shared by all. It is something seen and yet not fully penetrable by the eye, near and yet distant, disclosed and yet hidden, sometimes powerful and often unpredictably dangerous. Now this physical pattern has the capacity to evoke all such facets of our linkage to the universe, and when employed as an image in myth the cloud sometimes does just that. But because of our patterned psychic/human make-up, the image of the cloud can also operate on this further level. For example, as a religious image the cloud can evoke at once the self-disclosure and yet mystery of God, his presence and yet his distance, his blessings and yet his anger. As such, the image finds its place in Yahweh's revelation at Sinai (Ex. 19.9), in the prophets (Ez. 1.4–2.7; 10.1–8), at Jesus' transfiguration (Mk. 9.2–8), at the ascension (Acts 1.9), and most prominently in the book of Revelation as an image at once of God's mysterious presence and yet distance (Rev. 1.7, 10.1, 11.12, 14.15–16).[17] Now there are many kinds of images, deriving from our very varied human experiences, but images deriving from basic patterns of human experience, shared by many or all across the times, such as the cloud, have the capacity to become symbols, disclosures of near-universal or universal significance. Place these symbols into a story form, and we have what can be called "myth" in the full sense of the term.[18]

Myth most fundamentally, then, is a mode of perception, and this in no way determines the truth or falsity of its claims. The difficulty is in penetrating the pattern of experience giving rise to the myth, adequately grasping the reality being pointed to imaginatively and symbolically in the myth. This wasn't even a question for archaic man, to be sure. But as the human person has become more and more critical, down to our own highly critical epoch, we can no longer avoid the critical, factual questions. Which brings me to concepts/conceptualization. For it is our own critical mind that gives birth to concepts, which are simply an attempt to generalize facets of our human experience, only now literally rather than pictorially. Where mythical thinking works with the imagination, concepts work with dissection and analysis, always seeking a literal correspondence between concept and empirical reality.

While there is presently an active controversy on the question of whether modern, rational man should or should not outgrow the use of myth, preferring the literal and testable conceptual mode of knowing, I would argue for a complementarity between the mythical and the conceptual modes of knowing. The justification of conceptualization perhaps needs little comment here. On it is based our entire modern, critical, historically conscious society. But the mythical mode of knowing also has its own justification. For, as we have pointed out, myth has the capacity to stir the entire person, physically and psychically, intellectually and emotionally. Particularly in the religious sphere myth has the capacity to evoke the transcendent without claiming to master and dominate it. It further has the capacity to stir the individual to commitment to the transcendent. I see no reason to doubt that concepts can also carry us to the awareness of the transcendent, by pushing us to the furthest reaches of human speculation. But when they do, they too are no longer to be understood literally, but rather analogously, as Aquinas understood it. With this in mind, it should be clear that the notion of the "Divine *Pathos*" is then a concept, but a concept used analogously.

Yet both myth and concept have their dangers. Myth, by its very nature, while a true mode of knowing, is uncritical—it does not even ask such critical questions as to whether what is evoked is true, how it is true, with what limits, etc. As such, it can easily lend itself to fanaticism, and one needs little proof of the fanatic happenings empires have perpetrated upon one another in the name of their myths. Thus, myth, at least for us moderns, cries out for rational exegesis, for the counterbalance of conceptualization. Concepts can lead to fanaticism too, for the analytic and dissective mentality undergirding concepts is a mentality that wants to possess and conquer. In the religious sphere this dissective mentality can easily lead to a forgetfulness of the analogical and extended use the concept has in theology. Thus the theological concept cries out for the religious myth.

Throughout this work, then, the reader will come across notions whose precise nature is certainly mythical as I have defined it; viz., "kingdom of God," "being raised/exalted to God's right hand," "appearances" of the risen Jesus, the heavenly "Abba," etc. Yet this in no way argues against any reality that these mythic notions attempt to evoke. The difficulty is precisely the attempt to penetrate those images/symbols and grasp the experiential correlate undergirding them. Certainly in our critical age this rational exegesis of myth is a necessary and valid enterprise, despite the obvious advantages of myth over concept in the religious realm. Particularly is this a valid enterprise because of the historical nature of Christianity, which indeed is full of mythic images, but whose images are attached to a concrete, historical person, Jesus of Nazareth.[19] Throughout this work I will be endeavoring to penetrate the experiential correlate underlying many of the great mythic symbols of Christianity. I may not adequately penetrate, but in our critical age the attempt must at least be made.

By way of conclusion, let me note briefly how the Christology presented in these pages differs from others presently available to the Christian community. In accordance with general usage, and by way of a typology (individual Christologians do not necessarily fall into simply one category), we can differentiate three general "styles" of doing Christology.

The classical Christology has come to be known as a Christology from above. As Pannenberg writes, "For christology that begins 'from above,' from the divinity of Jesus, the concept of the incarnation stands in the center."[20] This has its origins in the Johannine incarnation of the *Logos*, and as we shall see throughout this book, is solidified as the Church's doctrine at the great Christological Councils. Whether in its Alexandrine variation of the *Logos-sarx* model or in the Syrian variant of *Logos-anthropos* model, this view presupposes the trinitarian doctrine. Its only question is how did the *Logos* become human?

A Christology from below, as Pannenberg tells us, rises "from the historical man Jesus to the recognition of his divinity, is concerned first of all with Jesus' message and fate and arrives only at the end at the concept of the incarnation."[21] For this view the notion of the Trinity is not presupposed. Historically one might perhaps trace this view to the adoptionist Christology of the New Testament (the man Jesus is "adopted" as God's son), trace it further through Paul of Samosata, Luther, and eventually the Christologies of nineteenth-century Protestant Liberalism. Modern echoes of this man-centered approach can be found in both Protestantism (Bultmann, Tillich, New Questers) and Catholicism (transcendental Christology).

Recently a third school has arisen, which can be called a Christology from before *(von vorn)*. It is difficult to characterize this school, but a few generalizations seem possible. Pannenberg, for example, bases himself on an evolutionary philosophy, partly indebted to Hegel. History is constantly moving into the future, and God is seen as essentially that Future, the Where-unto of human history. Others, influenced by modern critical theory, take as their major insight man's consciousness of his ability to overturn the past and create the future. For these too, God can be meaningfully said to be man's absolute Future. In any case, this experience of the future is the horizon in the light of which to approach Christology. Jesus is the one through whom the absolute Future-God proleptically breaks into history.

The difficulties with the Christology from above are well known. Most importantly, it takes for granted the divinity of Jesus, and this is just the issue that modern man can no longer presuppose. Further, if one assumes the divinity of Jesus, one may be basing himself already on an a priori view of what God is, rather than on learning through Jesus something about the divine reality. Finally, a concentration on the divinity of Jesus has historically tended to devalue Jesus' historical humanity, viewing it as only an "instrument" of the *Logos*.

On the other hand, a Christology from below encounters its own difficulties. So far as I can tell, this generally begins with a view of man or his world (anthropology, cosmology, evolution, process, etc.), and seeks to make sense out of Christology from this prior point of view. As Peter Hodgson puts it, however, such a Christology "tends to perpetuate the same dualism in which Christology 'from above' operates," but it "merely reverses the direction or movement: not 'from above below' (the descent of the divine Redeemer, the *Logos,* into human flesh) but 'from below above' (as Pannenberg puts it, a 'rising from the historical man Jesus to the recognition of his divinity')."[22] If a Christology from above tends to be excessively theocentric, this tends to be excessively anthropocentric and subjectivistic, and hence Hodgson's charge of a dualism between God and man. A further difficulty is this approach's tendency never to get beyond its a priori anthropology or philosophical view. The historical figure of Jesus is viewed more as a datum to be interpreted in the light of a theory, rather than as itself a source of one's theory.

The Christology from before, to my mind, shares in both of the difficulties of the above two schools. With the Christology from above, it starts off from an assumption that simply cannot be taken for granted. Instead of assuming the *Logos* doctrine, now we are to assume the Future, but this too transcends our presently accessible knowledge. Hodgson put this well: "Just as it is not clear how a concept of the Son of God can be established apart from the concrete historical figure of Jesus, so also we must ask how the future can provide the hermeneutical horizon for interpretation when access to the future is first had through that which is to be interpreted, namely, Jesus of Nazareth the Messiah."[23] With the Christology from below, Jesus tends to be interpreted simply in terms of a prior theory, rather than being seen as a source of one's theory.

My own search for Jesus Christ, my *zetema,* has led me to the conclusion that none of the above Christological types is adequate to the reality of Jesus. As will become evident as we proceed, the theopathic Christology in this work implies that the alternatives from above, from below, and from ahead are false alternatives. More than anything else, we simply need new categories that transcend the dualisms implied by all the above views and do not perpetuate them. As I hope to show, a theopathic Christology necessarily leads to the conclusion that to talk about God's descent to man from above is to talk about man's ascent to God (from below), that the absolute Future is also historically present now. Jesus, in other words, teaches us a new way to think about God and man, a way that transcends the old dichotomies and dualisms. Our Christological categories have not yet caught up with this fact. Hence my choice of the term theopathic Christology. Christ reveals that the Divine *(Theos),* the ultimate Lord of man and the future, is *Pathos,* not apathy, and thus to be encountered in man, and in the present. There are perhaps good historical reasons for why each of the above Christological types has emerged. The Christological task for the future, however, lies in the direction of developing categories more adequate to the reality of Christ.[24]

Notes

1. For an overview of the nature of the magisterium and dogma, see my "Authority and Magisterium in Recent Catholic Thought," CHICAGO STUDIES 16 (1977), 278–298.

2. See Eric Voegelin, *Order and History* 1, *Israel and Revelation* (Louisiana: Louisiana State University Press, 1956), for a superb articulation of the biblical world view.

3. On this, see Bernard J. F. Lonergan, "Dehellenization of Dogma," THEOLOGICAL STUDIES 28 (1967), 336–351.

4. Cf. Richard A. Norris, Jr., *God and World in Early Christian Theology* (New York: Seabury, 1965).

5. This is true for either a "kerygmatic" approach to Christology or the so-called quest for the historical Jesus.

6. Gordon D. Kaufman, *An Essay on Theological Method* (Montana: Scholars Press, 1975), p. 4.

7. Donald L. Gelpi, *Experiencing God: A Theology of Human Emergence* (New York: Paulist, 1978), interpreting Lawrence Kohlberg, "The Claim to Moral Adequacy of a Highest Stage of Moral Judgment," THE JOURNAL OF PHILOSOPHY 70 (1973), 630–646.

8. Cf. James M. Robinson and Helmut Koester, *Trajectories through Early Christianity* (Philadelphia: Fortress, 1971).

9. Eric Voegelin, "Toynbee's *History* as a Search for Truth," in Edward T. Gargan, ed., *The Intent of Toynbee's History* (Chicago: Loyola University, 1961), pp. 183–184.

10. Abraham J. Heschel, *The Prophets* 2 (New York: Harper Torchbooks, 1971), p. 87.

11. The Bérulle piece: "The Christic Universe of Pierre de Bérulle and the French School," THE AMERICAN BENEDICTINE REVIEW 29 (1978), 320–347; the Merton piece will be in a volume edited by the Vancouver School of Theology.

12. William M. Thompson, *Christ and Consciousness: Exploring Christ's Contribution to Human Consciousness* (New York: Paulist, 1977). What yet remains is a study of the emergence of mysticism in general and Christian mysticism in particular. On p. 47, n. 40, I indicate the basis for a theory of mysticism that I hope to explore more fully in a work to come.

13. Voegelin, *Order and History* 4, *The Ecumenic Age* (Louisiana: Louisiana State University, 1974), p. 302; cf. p. 242 and 2, *The World of the Polis* (1957), p. 159. Cf. also Eugene Webb, "Eric Voegelin's Theory of Revelation," THE THOMIST 42 (1978), 95–122.

14. Thompson, *Christ and Consciousness*, p. 71.

15. Kaufman, *op. cit.*, p. 71, falls back on criteria of *coherence* and pragmatic *usefulness*, rather than correspondence; that is, how adequate is this ontological theory when it comes to accounting for every dimension of human experience; to what an extent does it enable us to sustain and realize our full and authentic human potentialities? There is some question, further, as to what to name such high-level ontological notions. Some prefer the terms "symbol" or "myth," since we are referring to realities that transcend and ground empirical experience. There is a long historical precedent for this, going back to Plato. "Myth" here does not mean "unreal" but only what transcends our finite reach and thus can only be pointed to. "Myth" and "symbol" do tend to connote to the modern mind the "un-

real" and "merely symbolic," and thus some speak of "historicized myth" or "broken myth." To avoid ambiguity, I would argue that "myth" or "symbol" more properly appeals to the imagination through evocative images and in this manner evokes the ontological in a way that corresponds to the suprarational, intuitive, and emotive dimension of man; "ontic notion" as a term attempts to evoke the ontological by appealing to the critical, rational mind. Cf. Avery Dulles, *Myth, Biblical Revelation, and Christ* (Washington, D.C.: Corpus Papers, 1969), pp. 1–27; Thomas Fawcett, *The Symbolic Language of Religion* (Minneapolis: Augsburg, 1971); and Lee W. Gibbs and W. Taylor Stevenson, eds., *Myth and the Crisis of Historical Consciousness* (Montana: Scholars Press, 1975).

16. See C. G. Jung's analysis of these basic patterns giving rise to myth in Joseph Campbell, ed., *The Portable Jung* (New York: Viking, 1971), pp. 23–46. Jung's particular contribution is in the discovery of modern man's recurring need for myth.

17. For an excellent analysis of the cloud symbol see Paul S. Minear, *I Saw a New Earth: An Introduction to the Visions of the Apocalypse* (Washington, D.C.: Corpus, 1968), pp. 279–285.

18. On the formation of myth, and the various kinds of myth, see Gerald A. Larue, *Ancient Myth and Modern Man* (Englewood Cliffs, N.J.: Prentice-Hall, 1975).

19. I would argue very strongly the thesis that historically conscious persons cannot engage in mythical thinking in the same manner as their precritical ancestors. The emergence of rational thought in the evolution of humanity meant an emancipation from myth, not in the sense that myth was completely negated, but in the sense that its absolute power was broken. This trend has been heightened by our historical consciousness. We use myth, like the ancients; but unlike them, we *know* it is myth. Cf. my *Christ and Consciousness,* especially pp. 22–44, on the relativization of myth. I still continue to think that one can gain an excellent insight into how a precritical person employs myth from Lévy-Bruhl, despite his tendency to deny any logic in myth. Cf. Lucien Lévy-Bruhl, *How Natives Think* (New York: Alfred A. Knopf, 1925).

20. Wolfhart Pannenberg, *Jesus-God and Man* (Philadelphia: Westminster, 1968), p. 33.

21. *Ibid.*

22. Peter C. Hodgson, *Jesus-Word and Presence: An Essay in Christology* (Philadelphia: Fortress, 1971), pp. 68–69.

23. *Ibid.,* p. 64.

24. The work of Walter Kasper, *Jesus the Christ* (New York: Paulist, 1976), seems to be moving in this direction.

II

ON HERMENEUTICS IN CHRISTOLOGY

The Problem of History: From Innocence to Self-criticism

Few would dispute the observation that our contemporary understanding of history poses a fundamental challenge to traditional orthodox Christianity. Gordon Kaufman considers it the fundamental issue in modern theology, and has accordingly attempted a complete historicist revision of systematics in its light.[1] Others, like Mircea Eliade,[2] even speak of the terror of history, and consider our contemporary view of history not only the basic challenge to theology but to the survival of humanity itself. Although our aim here cannot be to examine the full scope of this problem, any careful reconsideration of Christology must confront the historical question, asking (and tentatively answering) how and to what extent historical consciousness challenges the traditional portrait of Jesus Christ.

By way of entry into this question, I would propose that we view the emergence of historical consciousness as the shift from "innocence/naïveté" to self-criticism. It will become apparent as we go on that this is not necessarily a shift from falsity to truth. A child might be said to be "innocent," but this assuredly does not mean that the child is always wrong. Similarly the archaic individual of earlier times might be said to be "innocent," but that cannot mean that all access to truth was barred from him/her. Probably the best way to describe this development is as one from an undifferentiated to a more differentiated understanding of reality. Further, I do not intend to indicate that every individual in modern society has undergone our shift to self-criticism. Every teacher knows how truly difficult it is to lead her students to self-criticism, and the theologian especially knows how strong the hold of "original innocence" can be in areas purporting to deal with "supernatural revelation." I am only speaking of a shift that has occurred in principle and is at least a relevant possibility for the contemporary individual.

Several important turning points had to be traversed on the road to historical consciousness. The most basic was the emergence of rationality itself, that basic ability to "test" understanding in the light of experience, which occurred roughly in what is called the "Axial Period" of the first millennium. Writing was probably a great incentive to this. As John Dunne puts it, writing "had to be invented; it could not be discovered like a natural process."[3] Thereby man gained some appreciation of his own self-creative abilities. But it was probably early man's urbanization, and the consequent need for planning and regulation, which intensified man's use of his rational capabilities. But while it may be said that at least some people became rational by the first millennium, we do not thereby claim that they were fully aware that they were rational. This further awareness would require the recording of history and the availability of those records to the men of later ages. The study of these, leading to an awareness of how man's views and accomplishments have varied, gradually promoted the self-awareness of oneself as radically historical. This self-awareness of oneself as able to test her views in the light of experience—and consequently the ability to alter and change one's views and the results of those views—is what I most fundamentally mean by historical consciousness.

Historians of thought differ as to the precise date of the emergence of historical consciousness. I am inclined to view the twelfth and thirteenth centuries as the beginning of the great turning point. Medieval Christendom was a fertile soil for the emergence of a new historical awareness. The Judaeo-Christian view of God as a God-who-acts-in-history and even changes the course of history's events predisposed Christian thinkers to pay serious attention to history.[4] The emergence of a new and educated middle class meant a greater democratization of rationality and thus a more widespread self-critical ability. Added to these were the new curiosity in nature—the attempt to probe the "secondary causes" of nature's reality—and the beginnings of an historical and scholarly approach to sacred and revered Christian texts.[5] All of this, however subtly, promoted man's awareness of his ability to test his views in the light of experience. However, no doubt exists that the new historical consciousness was beginning to clearly make its claims by the time of the eighteenth-century Enlightenment. In Peter Gay's terms:

> The historians of the Enlightenment . . . at least . . . freed history from the parochialism of Christian scholars and from theological presuppositions, secularized the idea of causation and opened vast new territories for historical inquiry. They went beyond tedious chronology, endless research into sacred documents, and single-minded hagiography, and imposed rational, critical methods of study on social, political, and intellectual developments.[6]

What the Enlightenment philosophers brought to awareness, at least in principle, was a new dimension of time, as Norman Hampson[7] put it. This awareness emerged in both the physical and human/historical sciences. In the physical sciences, Montesquieu, from his geological studies, questioned the accuracy of the biblical six-thousand-year chronology of the world. Later proven correct, this meant that the Bible itself came to be seen as the result of a human, time-conditioned view of reality. Maupertuis, from his biological studies, developed a theory of genetic transmission, even hinting at the existence of dominant and recessive characteristics in the human organism. Clearly all of this was pointing to the historically conditioned makeup of nature, and indirectly of man himself. A parallel happening occurred in the human and historical sciences. In fact, historians usually date the emergence of history as a science from this period. Helpful for this new awareness of time was the quest for discovery and travel, which enlarged European horizons beyond Europe with its Christian world view and helped to reveal the historically conditioned nature of European and indeed of all cultures. As a result of his own travels Voltaire would say, referring to China: "Authentic histories trace this nation back . . . to a date earlier than that which we usually attribute to the Flood."[8] Thus the scriptural chronology was beginning to be viewed as only one among many culturally conditioned views of human history. Coupled with this was the new use of historical texts coming into prominence during the Renaissance and Enlightenment periods. While few ages knew such a return to the writings of classical antiquity, yet this return was not motivated by a kind of nostalgia or archaism. In part this was an expression of the desire for freedom from the binding dogmatism of the classic texts of Christianity. In part and more importantly even these texts of classical Greece and Rome were no longer appealed to as authoritative sources, but rather as sources to be critically evaluated by historical methods. Vico began to envision history as "the developing self-knowledge of societies, which became increasingly aware of their ability to control their material environment and to influence the complex of assumptions and attitudes which is misleadingly described as 'human nature.'"[9] Clearly the individual was becoming aware of herself as historical, a self-creator of herself and of historical institutions. This insight was further consolidated by the events of the French Revolution, which poignantly brought home how transient the most established of human institutions can be.

For our own purposes what is important to note is the development in human consciousness fostered by these events of the Enlightenment. Basically man was becoming self-conscious, aware of himself as the creator of his views, his ideals, and his institutions. This need not entail a radically anti-religious stance, although some of the philosophers, most notably Voltaire, took this step. For example, Newton and his followers saw the new complexified scientific knowledge of the cosmos as an argument for God. Roger Cotes, the editor of Newton's *Principia,* could say: "He must be blind who from the most useful and excellent contrivances of things cannot see the infinite wisdom of their Almighty Creator, and he must be mad and senseless who refuses to acknowledge them."[10] Yet, the nineteenth and twentieth centuries have confirmed and even radicalized the nascent historical consciousness of the Enlightenment. With this has inevitably gone a radical anti-religious attitude. Some scholars view these later developments as so radical that they prefer to speak of a "later" Enlightenment.[11]

In the physical sciences we can, most importantly, point to developments in geology and biology that called into question the established view of nature's order and indirectly, God's role within that order.[12] James Hulton and Charles Lyell confirmed that the biblical six-thousand-year chronology needed to be replaced by a time-period spanning aeons of time. Similarly Divine Providence, at least as regards nature, needed to be replaced by a notion of the uniform laws of change: "All former changes of the organic and inorganic creation are referable to one uninterrupted succession of physical events, governed by the laws now in operation. . . ."[13] Darwin took the further step of applying Lyell's principles not only to nature but also to man. For him all forms of life were temporary, transient and the result of chance, to be understood "in terms of random mutations and subsequent natural selection of the fittest among those mutations."[14] While, at this early phase of the late Enlightenment, theologians did their best to discover lacunae in Darwin's theories—hoping to find some role for Divine Providence, if only now in more "natural," this-worldly terms— nonetheless the major insight remained unchallenged: the historicity of the forms of life.

While there was a tendency at this early stage in the physical sciences to foster an ethos of "progress"[15]—after all, nature seems to improve through the survival of the "fittest"—the founders of the new human sciences of the late Enlightenment brought out the most radical implications of natural and human historicity by calling into question any role for Divine Providence. H. Stuart Hughes,[16] in his masterful analysis of the generation from 1890–1930—a period that he calls "the reorientation of European social thought"—has shown how such varied thinkers as Freud, Marx, Durkheim, Pareto, Croce, Sorel, Bergson, Dilthey, Troeltsch and Weber have both confirmed the historical character of man and more importantly brought to light the "irrational" factors constitutive of human self-making.

In the shifting, transitional world of ideas in which they dwelt, the problem of consciousness early established itself as crucial. Another way of defining their intellectual epoch would be to suggest that it was the period in which the subjective attitude of the observer of society first thrust itself forward in peremptory fashion. . . . Earlier it had commonly been assumed that this attitude presented no serious problem: rationalists and empiricists alike agreed on an identity of view between actor and observer in the social process, and on assuming this common attitude to be that postulated by scientific investigation or utilitarian ethics. All other standpoints, it had been argued, could be dismissed or discounted as intrusions of irrelevant emotion. Now rather suddenly a number of thinkers independently began to wonder whether these emotional involvements, far from being merely extraneous, might not be the central element in the story. By slow stages of reorientation—and often against their original intention—they were led to discover the importance of subjective "values" in human behavior. Man as an actor in society, they came to see, was seldom decisively influenced by logical considerations: supra- or infra-rational values of one sort or another usually guided his conduct.[17]

Freud, of course, began the uncovering of the irrational, unconscious motives and mechanisms conditioning human behavior. Man was not only historical in the sense of being the rational self-creator of his subjectivity, but he was historical in the further sense of being at the mercy of irrational historical factors, over which, to some extent, he has no control. Marx, and the founders of sociology, extended this insight to social institutions by uncovering the hidden ideologies constitutive of human societies themselves.[18]

In the end, a quite new human consciousness was fostered by all of these events. It had been brought home to the individual to what an extent she herself gives shape to and indeed creates her own humanity and the social institutions in which she dwells. Langdon Gilkey puts it this way: "Although the 'historical consciousness' has . . . greatly increased the human sense of immersion in history, it has also engendered, paradoxically but understandably, the sense of the transcendence of human freedom and creative praxis over the forms of history."[19] For, if nature and society are eternally predetermined by permanent forms given once for all, then at most the individual experiences his freedom through fostering the right conditions for the emergence of these forms. However an historical consciousness recognizes that the forms of nature and history are themselves relative. Human freedom actually creates its social forms, and this is a much more radical experience of human self-transcendence. It is for this reason that Gilkey extends his analysis of historical consciousness into ontology itself and speaks of "the temporalizing of Being." "Prior to the decision of freedom as to what we are to be and do, there is ahead of us only possibility; with that decision the new entity and the new event become formal, definite and actual."[20] This is, of course, what Whitehead grasped, and his entire *Process and Reality* is one of the few attempts to explore the ontological implications of being-as-process-or-temporal. Thus I have spoken of historical consciousness as the shift from "innocence" to self-criticism. For the qualitatively new experience of human transcendence and creativity brings home to us our need to take responsibility for our actions and ideals in history.[21] The innocence of being simply nurtured by a predetermined cosmos is ruptured.

Christology Becomes Historically Conscious

Obviously theology could not remain untouched by our new historical consciousness. The history of theology, Protestant and Catholic, since the Enlightenment is actually the story of the gradual appropriation of historical consciousness on the part of theologians.[22] For our purposes, though, we are interested in how the new historical, self-critical attitude manifested itself in Christology. To understand this story we must distinguish two meanings to the word "history."[23] On the one hand it can refer to the actual course of historical events themselves, the locus in which historical beings dwell and come to be. Studies that analyze this and attempt to discuss the possible structure, meaning and goal of the historical process give rise to the philosophy and theology of history. In the classic Christian and Western past, such great names as Augustine, Aquinas, Bonaventure, Calvin, Kant, Hegel, Toynbee, Freud, should come to mind. Contemporary philosophies/theologies of history have been contributed by Von Balthasar, Löwith, Jaspers, Berdyaev, Voegelin, and now Gilkey, etc.[24] On the other hand history can refer to the sort of inquiry historians engage in when they study historical events: what sort of knowing is historical knowing, is it objective or purely subjective, what might be the criteria necessary to adjudicate adequate historical judgments, etc.? The study of this field is called variously "critical history," historiography, historical epistemology, or hermeneutics (in the widest sense). It should be noted too, at this point, that history in this latter sense could not become "critical" until historians became historically conscious. For critical history presupposes the ability of the historian to question to what an extent historical inquiry is itself the result of human self-making. In any case it is history in this second sense—critical history—that has had the greatest influence on contemporary Christology. In summary, one may venture the generalization that it is the progressive application of critical history to the classic Christian texts on Christ that has created the, by now, famous distinction of the Jesus of history and the Christ of faith and thus spawned the movement of radical questioning of the traditional Christian understanding of Jesus. We shall see later that critical history inevitably leads to questions that ultimately can only be adjudicated by a philosophy/theology of history. If Gilkey[25] is correct in his assertion that this latter, more speculative brand of history has been largely out of favor in our positivistically oriented culture, we may well have here one of the main reasons for the seeming lack of consensus on the historical reality of Jesus.

Since the story of the application of critical history to biblical Christological texts is a well known one, I can content myself here with a sketch of the three great turning points in its evolution. A more detailed analysis can be had by consulting the many studies detailing this history.[26] I think it can safely be said—and this is our first turning point—that really critical biblical history began when the German professor of Oriental languages, Herman S. Reimarus (d. 1768), issued his summons: "Back from the Christ of dogma to the real Jesus."[27] Thus was born the inchoate recognition that the New Testament portrait of Jesus was largely the result of generations of dogmatic interpretation. Such an insight would not have been possible without the appropriation of an historical consciousness, and thus the ability to grasp to what an extent the history individuals—including the biblical authors—write is the result of their own self-making. Heinrich Julius Holtzmann classically expressed the new venture in 1863:

> We are here simply concerned with the question, whether it is now still possible to describe the historical figure of the One from whom Christianity derives its very name and existence and Whose person it has made the centre of its own particular religious view of the world, in such a way as to satisfy all just claims of a scrupulous historical-critical investigation. Is it possible to discover the character of the founder of our religion, the true, natural features of His person, by the application of the sole legitimate means of scientific historical criticism, or must we once and for all abandon any hope of achieving such a goal?[28]

David Strauss further consolidated this new position. In his *Life of Jesus Critically Examined*[29] he ventured the observation that the individual sayings and stories of Jesus as reported in the gospels are "like a necklace of pearls without a string, fragments that had received an artificial order from the evangelists." What led him to this observation was a highly negative view of myth, a great deal of which he found in the gospel. On Strauss's criteria, indications of myth are (1) the "rational" unthinkability of a particular biblical narrative and (2) the inconsistency present between two or more biblical narratives of the same event. For example, Strauss reasoned, the "high Christology" of the New Testament—those passages, especially found in Paul and John, which portray Jesus in particularly exalted and deified terms—is "mythical," rationally unthinkable and best understood as the result of the "natural religious tendency" to glorify the founder of a religion. But this kind of Christology was not simply fabricated or invented. It was the natural and slow result of a mythical attitude that really believed that Jesus was the Messiah. If he was, then "such and such things happened to him."

Liberal Protestant theologians, seeing in Strauss's program the continuation of the Reformation ideal of returning to the original Jesus, a Jesus freed from the accretions of ecclesiastical dogmatizing, began what has come to be known as the "Old Quest for the Historical Jesus." Differing with Strauss's skepticism of ever piercing through the embellished overlay of the gospels, they felt that the new hypothesis of the two-source theory[30] could put them in touch with the original Jesus and enable them to peel away the later layers of embellishment found in the gospels. Thus, as Dulles phrases it, "a vast progeny of lives of Jesus was spawned."[31] Jesus was portrayed, unfortunately, in a way all too congenial to the positivistically minded intellectuals of the nineteenth century. He was a supremely ethical and moral figure, perhaps the greatest in history, but nothing more. As George Tyrrell put it quite early in the discussion, referring to one of the earliest representatives of this position: "The Christ that [Adolf] Harnack sees, looking back through nineteen centuries of Catholic darkness, is only a reflection of a Liberal Protestant face seen at the bottom of a deep well."[32] Albert Schweitzer's *On the Quest of the Historical Jesus* (1910) is generally considered the death-knell of the "Old Quest." As he put it, "The historical investigation of the life of Jesus did not take its rise from a purely historical interest; it turned to the Jesus of history as an ally in the struggle against the tyranny of dogma." But Schweitzer saw this as a necessary stage on the way to an adequate appropriation of the original Jesus: "The dogma had first to be shattered before men could once more go out in quest of the historical Jesus, before they could even grasp the thought of His existence."[33] To drive home his point of how different the original Jesus was from the sophisticated liberal Protestant, Schweitzer's studies led him to portray Jesus as a somewhat fanatical, at least deeply passionate, apocalypticist.

The second great turning point flows from the steady stream of studies that decisively put an end to the optimism undergirding the "Old Quest." First, Wilhelm Wrede's *Das Messiasgeheimnis in den Evangelien* (1901) used the critical method against the "Old Questers." Mark, the basis of the two-source theory, he claims, far from being an historical picture of Jesus, represents a profound theological interpretation. His thesis is that the real Jesus never made any claim to be the Messiah; the evangelist read this back into his life and created the so-called "messianic secret" (Mk. 1.34, 8.30) to account for Jesus' Messiahship not being known during Jesus' life. While Wrede's thesis is still debated today, it did demonstrate, against the old questers, that although Mark may be the earliest source for a life of Jesus, still it, too, represents a highly original theological interpretation.

Secondly, the nascent history of religions school[34] further seemed to bring home the impossibility of arriving at the original, historical Jesus. By comparing the biblical narratives with nonbiblical parallels of religious history, this school hypothesized that the high Christology of the New Testament manifests much interreligious borrowing. At this stage of our story this was a likely hypothesis, although biblical scholars today are much less apodictic in their citation of parallels. In any case, this school could point to the possible gentile origins of much of the New Testament and argue for borrowings and influence from pre-Christian gnosticism, and the various cults of the mystery religions (Eleusis, Osiris, Tammuz, Marduk, Adonis and Atis). Paul's view of Christ as dying and rising (Rm. 6.1–11) was especially thought to represent a particularly close parallel to the redeemer myth current in some forms of pre-Christian gnosticism.

Thirdly, the nascent science of form criticism further complicated the issue by pointing to even further evidence of active interpretation in the biblical texts. This science was originally developed in the early nineteen hundreds as a technique of Old Testament interpretation by Herman Gunkel of Berlin. Martin Dibelius and Rudolf Bultmann, Gunkel's pupils, would refine it and apply it to the New Testament. Form criticism went beyond the two-source theory—the so-called "source criticism"—used by the Old Questers and asked whether one can get "behind" the written documents ("sources") to the period between the events and the written records. They proposed, first, that the determinative factor in preserving a particular tradition about Jesus was the needs and interests of the local Christian community. Thus, they postulated, varying views of the Christ would have been preserved in primitive Christianity's period of expansion (30–65; viz., Paul), the period of conflict (65–90; viz., Mk., Mt., Lk., 1 Pt., Heb., Rev.), and the period of consolidation and apologetic (90+; viz., Jn., the pastoral letters, Jude, 2 Pt, James, Acts). Secondly, they proposed that the gospels are composed of many smaller pericopes that originally circulated as separate units ("forms") in early Christian communities before the gospels were actually written. Dibelius's *From Tradition to Gospel* (1943) well illustrates this trend; it argued that the synoptics were actually designed for popular consumption, and that they evidence more the compilation of pre-existing material than true authorship in our modern sense of the term.

Finally and most difficultly, Rudolf Bultmann represents both the climax of the reaction against the Old Quest and, paradoxically, the beginning of what has come to be called the "New Quest." Bultmann is an enormously complex figure and interpretations of him still vary today. As Schubert Ogden put it, "Bultmann's friends as well as his enemies have pretended to more of an understanding of his thought than they actually possess."[35] Nonetheless, we can indicate the main directions of his thought. First, Bultmann accepts the major hypotheses of Strauss, Wrede, the history of religions school and form criticism—at least as methodological tools, but his individual use of each may be unique. This leads him to draw a radical distinction between the Jesus of history and the Christ of faith. Secondly, basing himself on the Lutheran tradition of *sola fide,* he is able to maintain that though, for the most part, we cannot know the historical Jesus, overlayed as it is by the faith (kerygmatic) interpretation of the New Testament authors, still faith does not depend upon the acquisition of historical information in any case, but upon the redemptive power of Christ's cross as preached in the present. Finally, although a good deal of the redemptive message of the New Testament is expressed mythologically, in the primitive mind-set of the first century, it remains possible to reinterpret this material existentially and thus recover its power for man's understanding of his own existence and possibilities. This is his famous program of "demythologization," which is not accurately described as a process of eliminating myth but rather as one of restoring to the myth its existential power for contemporary man.[36]

The focus, then, for Bultmann is on what the Christ-event can do for us existentially. Hence his view that the crucifixion "is not the saving event because it is the Cross of Christ, rather it is the Cross of Christ because it is the saving event." The same reticence on the historical Jesus shows up in his *Jesus and the Word* (1926). "I do indeed think that we can now know almost nothing concerning the life and personality of Jesus, since the early Christian sources show no interest in either, are moreover fragmentary and often legendary; and other sources about Jesus do not exist."[37] Bultmann did initially qualify this historical agnosticism somewhat in his various writings. For instance, what the New Testament presupposes is the "that" and not the "what" of Jesus, he maintains. A perceptive reading of his *Faith and Understanding* presupposes that there was a Jesus "who was nothing for Himself and knew no desire to count for something, whom surrender and love brought to the cross. . . . "[38] Further, his *Kerygma and Myth* presupposes the fact that "We are set free to give ourselves to God because he has given himself for us."[39] Yet, in the end, as one of Bultmann's interpreters put it:

> The kerygma, the Gospel is that in Christ God meets man here and now and offers him a new possibility of understanding his own existence. That, and not a set of historical data, is for Bultmann, rightly or wrongly, the centre of Christianity.[40]

Our third great turning point can be said to appear when both Bultmann's own pupils and a host of other biblical scholars began to question Bultmann's tendency to radically dehistoricize the gospels. I say "tendency" because Bultmann nowhere unequivocally denies the possibility of *Jesu-Forschung;* he just questions its relevance given the Lutheran *sola fide* against a *"solo facto."* Some justification for this already existed in Bultmann himself, for in a 1959 lecture he had said of the historical Jesus: "Characteristic of him are ritual purifications, polemic against Jewish legalism, fellowship with outcasts such as publicans and harlots, sympathy for women and children; it can also be seen that Jesus was not an ascetic like John the Baptist, but gladly ate and drank a glass of wine."[41] Any number of scholars pursued this lead and eventually their collective investigations gave birth to what has been called "the new quest for the historical Jesus." The so-called Marburg school—including especially Ernst Käsemann, Ernst Fuchs and Günther Bornkamm—might be said to be the real beginning of the New Quest. Ernst Käsemann, in his "The Problem of the Historical Jesus,"[42] argued that scholars must attempt to recover the historical Jesus. On the one hand this is a matter of fidelity to the gospels, for if the early Church were as disinterested in Jesus' history as Bultmann contends, then why were the gospels written at all? On the other hand it is a matter of theological principle, for without access to the historical Jesus Christianity quickly degenerates into an unhistorical myth, as much of later Christianity demonstrates all too well. Käsemann proposed a development of form criticism into what he called *Leben-Jesu-Forschung.* That is, by eliminating all gospel material having a "kerygmatic" (post-Easter) tone, by excluding anything that can be paralleled in Judaism and gentile thought, and by searching for sayings of Jesus that reflect Aramaic features, Käsemann felt that a genuine but limited recovery of the historical Jesus would be possible.[43] In the main, Käsemann's program remains the standard one of the New Questers, though various individuals have refined it in their own way. For example, Ernst Fuchs and Franz Mussner[44] think that New Questers have concentrated too heavily on the "words of Jesus," and that his deeds—for example, his attitude towards Jews and Essenes—might reveal more of his real nature. Similarly Bornkamm will emphasize Jesus' *exousia*—his overwhelming sense of authority—as radically new in religious history and thus unique to Jesus.[45]

Additionally to the Marburg school, a large number of exegetes have provided evidence that "while the nineteenth-century quest of the historical Jesus did not succeed, a more modest venture of the same order might be feasible in our own day."[46] Joachim Jeremias first deserves mention. Few are the exegetes who have been untouched by his highly scholarly and spiritually refreshing studies on Jesus' use of the term "Abba."[47] Jeremias thinks that a number of new factors now make it possible for us to detect the earliest strata of the gospel tradition—that of Jesus' *"ipsissima vox"* and of his earliest companions. He points especially to new techniques of literary analysis like the New Quest's *Jesu-Forschung;* archaeological discoveries (viz., Qumran), which make it possible to grasp Jesus' Palestinian environment with more accuracy; and the growing knowledge of Galilean Aramaic, making possible a greater knowledge of the Aramaic elements in the gospels. He remains quite optimistic about *Jesu-Forschung:* "The multiplication of examples yields ever the same result: if, with utmost zeal and conscientiousness, using the critical resources at our disposal, we occupy ourselves with the historical Jesus, the result is always the same. . . . A Man has appeared; those who heard His message were indeed aware that they had heard the word of God."[48] Further, scholars such as T. W. Manson, Vincent Taylor, Oscar Cullmann and C. H. Dodd have argued convincingly that a solid core of historical data is recoverable from the gospels, and indeed must be so, since the object of New Testament faith is the historical Jesus of Nazareth himself.[49] As Taylor put it, "The first narrators felt that it was enough to relate the events, without commenting upon them, and without making Jesus the mouthpiece of their doctrinal views."[50] Dodd, through analyzing the content of the earliest Christian preaching as practiced by Peter and Paul in Acts, contends that it always entailed a brief summary of the main facts of Jesus' life, death and resurrection. "If we lose hold upon that historical actuality, the Gospels are betrayed into the hands of the Gnostics, and we stand on the verge of a new Docetism."[51]

In a class apart, yet confirming the basic historicity of the gospels, are the studies of certain Scandinavian Lutherans, called collectively the "traditio-historical" school. These scholars believe that a careful study of the methods of oral transmission as practiced by Palestinian Jews of the first century might not only reveal a larger core of historical material in the gospels than the New Questers admit, but also illustrate the accuracy of the biblical, post-Easter kerygma. These scholars hypothesize that Jesus taught as a Jewish rabbi and that his disciples came from rabbinic Judaism. Jesus would therefore, they maintain, have used the rabbinic methods of instruction, which involved a highly refined ability to remember, facilitated by fixed verbal formulae, solemn symbolic actions, and repeating back to the rabbi his instructions. After Pentecost the apostles continued this instructional rabbinic process, building up a skilled corps of "reciters" of the words of the rabbi Jesus: the gospels are a somewhat edited version of this "rabbinic tradition." As Harold Riesenfeld states it, "the essential point is that the outlines, that is, the beginnings of the proper genus of the tradition of the words and deeds of Jesus, were memorized and recited as holy word. We should be inclined to trace these outlines back to Jesus' activity as a teacher in the circle of his disciples."[52]

Allied with this new recovery of the historical Jesus is a new concept of history, at least for the Marburg New Questers. Basing themselves on a kind of intentionality-oriented or existential view of history, stemming from Wilhelm Dilthey and R. G. Collingwood,[53] they would maintain that although there is a "factual" dimension to history, still the element of greater interest to the historian is the "inside" or the "meaning" of past events. Through a process of sympathetically entering into the thought and action of a historical figure, an "existential" relation is created between the past and the historian. As Raymond Brown put it, "This type of historical research can view the kerygma (what Jesus meant to the primitive Church) and its appeal (what Jesus should mean for us) much more sympathetically than could the scientific historiography of the nineteenth century."[54] Unlike the Old Quest, which sought to move from the kerygma to the historical Jesus, the New Quest recognizes a greater continuity of intentionality and meaning between the Jesus of history and the Christ of faith. Perhaps Bultmann was led to undervalue this continuity-in-meaning because of a more "positivistic" (fact-oriented) view of history. Just as Jesus issued a call for "authentic self-existence," so the kerygma presents Jesus as the bringer of God's redemption to man. Intentionality-history would see the continuity between Jesus and the kerygma precisely in this element of "authentic self-existence." Although differences increasingly surface among the New Questers, James M. Robinson holds that

> There are now two ways of gaining knowledge about the person of Jesus: (a) the *via kerygmatica:* the church's kerygma presents an understanding of Jesus which it presupposes to be a continuation of his own understanding of himself; (b) the *via historica:* modern historiography uses the nonkerygmatic material of the Gospel to reconstruct the self-understanding of the historical Jesus. Obviously, the kerygma offers to those who accept it the possibility of authentic existence; but, if history is approached from the Dilthey-Collingwood philosophy, so does the *via historica. . . .* the selfhood of Jesus is equally available to us as a possible understanding of our own existence in the two ways.[55]

One will notice in our sketch of the application of critical history to the New Testament that nothing has been said about Roman Catholic scholarship. This stems from the fact that Protestant scholarship early entered into dialogue with the newly emerging historical sciences since the Enlightenment, unlike Catholicism, which early stalled the nascent biblical scholarship of the so-called "modernists" at the turn of the century,[56] from approximately 1800–1940. The official Roman congregations of the Curia, unfortunately, "made little distinction between the possible intrinsic validity of biblical criticism and the theological misuse of it by the Modernists."[57] Thus the Pontifical Biblical Commission in Rome issued decisions between 1905–1915 which forced Catholic scholars to absent themselves from critical biblical scholarship. Pope Pius XII's encyclical *Divino Afflante Spiritu* (1943) is generally considered the turning point in Catholic studies, allowing as it did the "scientific study" of the Bible. Rather spectacularly, in 1955 the Pontifical Biblical Commission, without completely reversing its earlier decisions of 1905–1915, did substantially alter their importance:

> ... as long as these decrees propose views which are neither immediately nor mediately connected with truths of faith and morals, it goes without saying that the scholar may pursue his research with complete freedom and may utilize the results of his research, provided always that he defers to the supreme teaching authority of the Church.[58]

This decree even speaks of the "narrowness and constraint which prevailed fifty years ago," although understandably so. Perhaps for our interests the most important document of the Biblical Commission is "The Historical Truth of the Gospels" (1964), occasioned as a result of the defeat of the "conservative" schema on Revelation at the Second Vatican Council and actually issued with the approval of Pope Paul VI.[59] This decree states that "the interpreter should pay diligent attention to the three stages of tradition by which the doctrine and the life of Jesus have come down to us." As Raymond Brown explains it, the decree differentiates (1) the stage of Jesus, in which even Jesus himself "followed the modes of reasoning and of exposition which were in vogue at the time";[60] (2) The stage of the apostolic preaching, in which it is admitted that the New Testament view of Christ is post-resurrectional and read back into Jesus' ministry; and (3) the stage of writing by the evangelists who "selected some things, reduced others to a synthesis, [still] others they explicated as they kept in mind the situation of the churches." Brown thinks this comes close to an official endorsement of form and redaction criticism and adds: "Note that the Roman Catholic Church has gone on record stating that the Gospels are not literal or chronological accounts of the words and deeds of Jesus."[61]

I am not sure that John Kselman's judgment is still true that "overall, modern Catholic New Testament scholarship has consisted in a judicious selecting and combining of acceptable elements in Protestant scholarship; it is not yet following its own new paths."[62] At least the Catholic exegete and theologian Raymond E. Brown manifests a systematic hermeneutical program and is clearly following his own paths.[63] While it is difficult to classify Brown, since he "judiciously" uses all the methods of biblical criticism currently available, his methodology comes closest to that of the Marburg New Questers, since he does employ the techniques of *Jesu-Forschung*. However, he does employ additional working criteria in his study of the New Testament Christ, and a sketch of these will be helpful, since they seem representative of more recent Catholic scholarship in general.

First Brown questions, against Robinson, whether the *via historica* is on a par with the *via kerygmatica*. "If full Christian faith is possible only after Easter, then the *via historica,* valuable as it may be for self–understanding, cannot be put on a par with the *via kerygmatica.*" He thus surmises, " The whole concept of a twofold way to Jesus may yield to that of a single way to Jesus in which historical research helps to enrich the contact possible only through the kerygma."[64] Brown questions whether the by-passing of the kerygma through existential history does not represent a restlessness with regard to the Church and with belief in a divine faith given us through the kerygma. To be sure, the *via historica* "should make possible the same type of faith in Jesus that was possible during the public ministry," but that faith cannot "be equated with the divine faith in Jesus made possible by the kerygma."[65] Brown views the Resurrection in epistemological terms as a new factor in the understanding of Christ, granting a superiority to the *via kerygmatica:*

> If there is a new dimension, a difference, in the resurrected Jesus, what would it consist in? Is it something positive that has been added, or is it simply an unveiling of what was already there? Certainly there was one positive factor present in the resurrected Jesus that was not present during the public ministry: a glorified body. And perhaps it is in this direction that a solution may be. It is through His humanity that Jesus made an impact on men; could it not be that after the Resurrection a new dimension was given to the humanity of Jesus which first made it possible for men to believe in Him as Lord?[66]

Secondly, Brown contends—and here he aligns himself with *Jesu-Forschung*—that critical history can recover more of the historical Jesus than the modest results of the New Quest have thus far brought to light. He first contends that the New Quest downplays the role of "facts" in favor of existential meaning. "It may not save my soul, but I for one still very much want to know if Jesus was born at Bethlehem, if He had a many-year ministry, if He made more than one trip to Jerusalem, if He actually spoke to God as His Father and spoke of Himself as Son of Man."[67] Here Brown sees the need to temper Marburg research by the kind of historiography practiced by Jeremias, Cullmann and Taylor. Further, the minimalist rules for recovering the authentic Jesus "would be applicable if the Gospels were written to deceive."[68] Clearly the New Questers do not deny that more of the gospel portrait of Jesus may be authentic than their techniques indicate. In fact an excessively rigid adherence to their criteria would leave us with a Jesus who shared nothing in common with either the Jews or the gentiles of the first century. But what Brown contests is the need to adopt such minimal criteria as a hermeneutical principle. "It seems far more probable to me that Jesus' statements took on new meaning after the full revelation of His lordship than that a large body of sayings never uttered by Him were placed on His lips to bring out this revelation."[69] Finally, in line with this, Brown thinks it may be possible to take the gospel of John much more seriously as a primary source of the life of Jesus, rather than as simply a late, post-Easter theological reflection.

Foundational Hermeneutical Presuppositions

1. Difficulties in Contemporary Biblical Criticism: One cannot help but gain the impression that, despite the enormous sophistication of contemporary biblical criticism, it still has not adequately dealt with the complex problem of the interrelation between the objective and the subjective in historical research. It strikes me as a very sophisticated praxis in search of a more adequate *theoria.* A survey of the science as currently practiced reveals that it is much more presuppostion-laden than its practitioners "openly" admit, and I think this observation is as true for the New Quest as it is for the Old Quest. Biblical scholars are themselves more frequently admitting this,[70] and perhaps some more specific indications of what I mean would be in order.

As currently practiced,[71] mainline biblical criticism embraces the following specializations: (1) Source and (2) form criticism; (3) *Redaktionsgeschichte;* (4) *Tendenzkritik;* (5) *Theologiegeschichte,* and (6) *Religionsgeschichte.* We have already treated source and form criticism; the difficulty I would want to signal here is the questionable (not necessarily rigidly incorrect) subjective assumptions upon which they are based. Source and form criticism employ a number of working criteria in order to recover the earliest texts of the New Testament and to discover the "local" social interests coloring the preservation of the biblical traditions, respectively. Yet these criteria represent only "selective hunches" on the part of the biblical critic that can be called into question. Aramaisms, for example, can no longer be simply considered as indications of an earlier tradition, since we now know Aramaic continued to be spoken after the fall of Jerusalem (A.D. 70). The greater complexity of a document, we now know, can indicate both earlier and later—we have examples of both. Assigning traditions to a pre- or post-Easter origin is to argue circularly, since it presupposes that the critic has already determined what characterizes the "kerygma." Allied with this is our lack of knowledge of early rabbinism[72] and perhaps too great an acceptance of the two-source theory. There seems no reason why the patristic priority accorded to Matthew should not be more thoroughly considered. Now, since *Redaktionsgeschichte* (the recovery of the redactor's contribution) itself depends on form criticism, we can surmise that our critical argumentation grows even more circular. Were there such a thing as "audience criticism"—but history usually records the exceptional and not the common—even more caution would have to be employed here.

Tendenzkritik seeks the larger cultural trends influencing the thought patterns of the first century, a sort of *Zeitgeist*-research,[73] whose aim partly is to ascertain to what extent the historical Jesus may be unique when set against the backgrounds of first-century Judaism and Hellenism. But again, here too we encounter a kind of circular argumentation, for who knows pre-70 Judaism well enough? Perhaps if we knew more of this period, Jesus would appear to share much more in common with first-century man. Jesus may not be so radically antipharisaic if the research of Neusner and Ruether is correct.[74] *Religionsgeschichte* and *Theologiegeschichte* seek to give more specificity to *Tendenzkritik* by uncovering the larger religious and theological tendencies influencing the first century. For example, the widespread assumption of a first-century expectation of an immediate end of the world and an imminent arrival of God's kingdom is a basic hypothesis of *Religionsgeschichte,* which leads many to attribute this to Jesus. But Ruether has uncovered evidence that this tendency does not apply to the Pharisees—in fact their opposition to it is a key factor in their emergence as the normative Jewish party[75]—and it can be asked whether Jesus might not have shared this view in common with the Pharisees. After all, his interest in the problems of this world does not bespeak a kind of world-amnesia. In this light James Mackey's view strikes common sense as more sound: "No man who has the kind of faith in God the Father which Jesus had could be without the firm expectation that God would work to rectify the wrongs of the world, nor would he be without the strongest hope that God would sustain and enrich himself and his fellows in a creative act that could overcome even the tragedy of death."[76] Similarly *Theologiegeschichte* detects a universalism in Jesus' message that seems unique to him. Yet, again, a similar universalism can be found in the prophets and in Pharisaism.[77] Does not this force us to moderate our judgments about the recovery of the historical Jesus?

I am not arguing for the demise of contemporary biblical criticism, only for a greater recognition of the subjective assumptions operative in research. Only in this way can we achieve some measure of control over and responsibility for them. The complex interrelation between the objective and the subjective in historical criticism simply needs more recognition, and I think this judgment equally applies to the new Dilthey-Collingwood historiography practiced by the Marburg New Questers. True enough, this latter biblical historiography rightly objected to the nineteenth-century quest for Jesus on the grounds that it was based too heavily on the scientific and positivistic model, seeking to reconstruct the "past as it really was." Hence its predilection for "external facts": names, occurrences, dates, causes, etc.[78] The New Quest, under the influence of Dilthey and Collingwood, sought to return to a more humane view of history, stressing the recovery of human intentionality, as James Robinson especially understands it:

> The dimension in which man actually exists, his "world," the stance or outlook from which he acts, his understanding of his existence behind what he does, the way he meets his basic problems and the answer his life implies to the human dilemma, the significance he had as the environment of those who knew him, the continuing history his life produces, the possibility of existence which his life presents to me as an alternative—such matters as these have became central in an attempt to understand history.[79]

Arguing that the "self" most deeply leaves its imprint through its commitments, and that it is just precisely this which endures throughout human history and thus establishes a continuity with the past, the New Quest believes it possible to reconstruct with great plausibility the selfhood of Jesus, as we have seen. But over and above the question of whether history is primarily concerned with intentions rather than facts—we will examine this later—I believe Van Harvey is correct in his contention that the New Quest "puts the heaviest weight on just those kinds of historical judgments which, from a logical point of view, are the least capable of bearing it." And he adds: "The general presumption is that the more a decision touches the deepest springs of motivation and conduct, the more tentative our claims about it ought to be."[80] Recently Robinson has argued that not only must the fact-oriented tendency of positivistic historiography be critiqued, but also "the traditional static, substantival, essence/accidence-oriented metaphysics which gave our inherited categories their most basic form."[81] This has led to a tendency to reify and immobilize the religious world of the first century in categories such as rabbinic Judaism, Gnosticism, Oriental cults, mystery religions, etc., as if these were static rather than developing realities. Yet recent advances (Qumran, Nag Hammadi) make it imperative to move beyond "such mocked-up backgrounds." They "must be reconceptualized in terms of movements, 'trajectories' through the Hellenistic world."[82] And further:

> What has been said with regard to Jesus is equally true of the New Testament and of early Christianity as a whole. The interaction between the modern understanding of reality from which scholarly categories are derived, and the results of scholarly study which in turn modify the understanding of reality, is both inescapable and legitimate. Progress takes place when the modern categories employed are sufficiently illuminating that they lead to a more adequate understanding of the data, and thus are relatively validated by the successful research itself.[83]

Here Robinson places greater weight on the subjective factors operative in the historian's judgment, and, as I hope to show, I think this moves him beyond the Collingwood style of history.

Finally, before ending this sketch of contemporary biblical criticism, something should be said of the newly developing science of literary criticism. As used by some, literary criticism seeks to complement the above historically oriented methods of interpretation through more properly textual and semantic methods.[84] As used by Paul Ricoeur,[85] it tends to become a total hermeneutical program, seeking to replace the above methods of interpretation. Its methodological starting point is the distinction between "speech-event" and "textual meaning." While the concentration of historical hermeneutics is the attempt to retrieve the "speech-event" or "performance" of the past authors of the biblical texts, literary criticism concentrates on the meaning that resides in the text precisely as text. The text has meaning precisely because it transcends the original speech-event by fixing the meaning intended. As Tracy succinctly puts it:

> What we write is the meaning, the *noema* of our speech-events, not the event itself. Once I write, it is my text alone which bears the meaning; not my intention in writing it; not my original audience's reaction to it.[86]

The text's meaning, thus, is ideal (noematic): "What happens in writing is . . . the detachment of meaning from the event."[87] As such, it becomes distanciated[88] from just those factors that are of primary interest to a historical hermenuetics: the local factors influencing the author (form criticism); the author's original psychic intentions *(Redaktionsgeschichte);* the larger cultural factors "behind" the author *(Tendenzkritik).* Thus the method of retrieval of meaning shifts from the historical and psychological methods used by historical criticism to the semantic methods used in literary criticism:[89] the nature of symbol, metaphor, parable, myth, narrative, religious language, etc.

Literary criticism further distinguishes between a text's "sense" and its "reference." The former is, of course, the *noema* or ideal meaning, found only in the words of the text itself, requiring only semantic methods of retrieval, and not requiring any further historical or psychological investigations. Yet Ricoeur adds to this the hermeneutical need to comprehend the text's "reference," that aspect of reality which the text opens up before the reader. "What has to be appropriated is nothing other than the power of disclosing a world that constitutes the reference of the text."[90] But this further task does not imply a return to psychologizing hermeneutics: ". . . it is not the inner life of another ego, but the disclosure of a possible way of looking at things, which is the genuine referential power of the text."[91] Ricoeur wants to eliminate all psychologizing:

> Are we not putting the meaning of the text under the power of the subject who interprets it? This objection may be removed if we keep in mind that what is "made one's own" is not something mental, not the intention of another subject, presumably hidden behind the text, but the project of a world, the pro-position of a mode of being in the world that the text opens up in front of itself by means of its non-ostensive references.

> Far from saying that a subject already mastering his own way of being in
> the world projects the *a priori* of his self-understanding on the text and
> reads it into the text, I say that interpretation is the process by which
> disclosure of new modes of being . . . gives to the subject a new capacity
> for knowing himself.[92]

Surely no doubt could exist that this literary enterprise will contribute
greater clarity to our understanding of the complex role that myth, narratives, symbols, metaphors, allegories, parables, etc., play in the New Testament texts. Further, it concentrates the hermeneutical task on texts and
makes a strong case for this being the primary aim of interpretation. I
would agree that the interpreter has most certainty here and least certainty
when he hypothesizes about the condition's "behind" or "implied by" the
text. As complementary to historical hermeneutics it can only be welcomed, but with respect to its being a total hermeneutics, eliminating the
need for historical criticism, I, at this point, would want to register several
objections. First, from the side of the text itself, I would agree that what is
written is the meaning as "idealized," and not the speech-act itself, obviously. But what I would question is whether this *noema* is fully recoverable through semantic and literary methods. For while myth, for example,
is to be found in most of the classic texts of the religions, it is patently not
true that the literary form "myth" means in the same way in the archaic
religions and, say, in the New Testament. The form of the myth is present
in both the archaic religions and the New Testament, but the meaning of
the form has changed.[93] There is simply no way to adjudicate the differences in meaning of literary forms in different ages without an attempted
reconstruction of the presupposed world views of different epochs. When
Ricoeur tells us the "metaphor implies a tensive use of language in order to
uphold a tensive concept of reality,"[94] this may be true wherever metaphor
is to be found, but it does little to clarify for us the specific "concept of reality" held by, say, a precivilizational and a post-industrial intellectual. My
problem is not with the text's idealization of meaning, but with the sufficiency of semantic and literary methods of retrieval. Secondly, from the
side of the interpreter, when Ricoeur tells us that we must allow the text to
open up a world before us to comprehend its reference—he speaks, with
Gadamer, of a "fusion of horizons *(Horizonverschmelzung)*[95]—by his de-
historicizing of the text he makes it impossible for the text-as-a-*past*-world
precisely to challenge us in the present world. It is not just the interpreter's
task to allow the text-as-text to appear before us; for its textual aspects,
perhaps, semantic analysis suffices. At least the biblical interpreter is dealing with a *past* text precisely-as-*past,* with to some extent a different world
view, and something like *Tendenzkritik* seems called for. Further does not
Ricoeur presuppose that a sufficient knowledge of literary forms and semantic expertise frees the interpreter from his own cultural presuppositions? But how can the interpreter know this unless he attempts something
like a cultural—and thus psychological—critique of himself? What I find

most problematic here is the pretense that the interpreter need not raise to explicit consciousness his own presuppositions; does not this set the conditions for eisegesis? Here again we seem to meet the problem of the objective and subjective in hermeneutics.

2. *The Need for a Consensus on the Problem of the Objective and Subjective in Critical Biblical Research:* Just as, to my mind, contemporary biblical research has not adequately worked through the complex interrelation of the objective and subjective in New Testament interpretation, neither has contemporary historiography in general. But our purpose here, in alluding to this debate as it occurs in historiography, is simply to heighten our consciousness about the issues involved. First, then, we have what the historians are divided over: (1) the nature of historical explanation and (2) the issue of objectivity in history.[96] With respect to the nature of historical explanation, the "dispute" between Carl Hempel and Karl Popper is instructive.[97] Hempel would argue that the historian can really explain a historical event in terms of general laws: "A set of events (the initial conditions) can be said to have caused the event to be explained only if general laws can be indicated which connect 'causes' and 'effects' . . ."[98] Of course Hempel realizes that many historians do not provide us with such a cause-effect explanation, thus promoting the impression that history is merely accidental. But his point is that the general laws of psychology and sociology are at least implied and presupposed in the writing of history. Popper, while agreeing with Hempel that all true theory achieves a cause-effect explanation, denies that history is such a theory-oriented enterprise. In Gilkey's words, for Popper "writing history is a mode of selective interpretation, viewing the series of events from an interesting but partial and ultimately arbitrary perspective, the one perspective being no 'truer' than the other, since, none being testable, none are theories in that sense."[99] Popper, of course, makes room for historical contingency, but by doing so he lands us in a radical historical subjectivism.

As might be expected, historians have responded to the Hempel-Popper debate, and at least the following seem to represent a reasonable assessment of the continuing dispute.[100] First, one must recognize that the goal of history is not simply the explanation of general or universal laws, but the understanding of unique, unrepeatable events. Thus we cannot experimentally test historical hypotheses. The mistake of both Hempel and Popper was to assume that scientific *theoria* is the only true form of knowledge. This led Hempel to argue that true historical explanation uncovers laws; it led Popper to deny of history any genuine cognitive claim because of history's contingency. Secondly, the only way to explain historically a unique, historical event is not to appeal to some universal law but to assess the relevant conditions giving rise to the event. This is what Popper overlooked: if general laws cannot be invoked, it does not follow that no explanation is forthcoming, for there are relevant conditions, and relevant conditions are in principle limited. Thirdly, beyond the relevant conditions, the historian must recognize that an event might not have happened or at least that it could have happened otherwise. In other words, there is a contingency in history stemming from the reality of human response and freedom. Thus Gilkey's comment: the historian is led "inevitably beyond the initial conditions, the context or destiny, of an event to the actors, to considering disposition and character, goals and desires, intentions and purposes, the understanding or the misunderstanding of a situation by its actors—the whole 'inward,' 'human' side of history, or ingredient, to his explanation."[101] The discovery of this dimension of historical inquiry was, of course, primarily Collingwood's. Yet, and this is our fourth conclusion, the "inward" or "meaning" aspect of an event is not the only goal of historical inquiry, against Collingwood. For not only are the inward intentions of past actors partially the result of prior societal and cultural values, trends, and institutions, but the actual results of an agent's intentions are often different from what that agent intended, given the interplay of other contingent events. Finally, then, it is clear that historical explanation involves a great amount of "imaginative reconstruction" on the part of the historian of the complex whole termed "historical event": (1) The relevant conditions, (2) the inward intentions and motivations of historical agents, and (3) the constellation of societal, cultural, and institutional factors both "pre-shaping" inward intentions and sometimes altering the outcome of those same intentions. What is important to note is that in this imaginative reconstruction the historian must inevitably rely upon his entire intellectual and personal formation: his scientific, philosophical, and theological understanding of nature, man, society and history. As Gilkey puts it, "it is clear that historical inquiry is not devoid of a crucial theoretical component."[102] If that is the case, we are inevitably led to consider our second question, that of "objectivity" in history.

If should now be clear that there is a strongly "theoretical"—or if you will "subjective"—element in historical reconstruction. At least minimally this would mean something like the following. "Bare facts" are not to be had by the historian. To be sure, there are data (in the case of the New Testament, documents, records, archaeological artifacts, letters, etc.). But it is out of these data that the historian reconstructs what he considers the "facts." In Leff's terms:

> There is not a part of history which is objective—the facts—and another part—the historian's interpretation or judgment—which is subjective. Judgment and interpretation are equally inherent in deciding what are the facts, which are the relevant ones in a certain context, and how significant they are.[103]

Further, the historian selects, obviously. What conditions he deems relevant, what inner motivations seem most important, what larger cultural and institutional factors are most influential on a particular historical agent—all of this must come from the historian's hopefully informed judgment. As many have put it, thousands have had long noses in human history, but historians have selected Cleopatra's as having significance! Finally, the historian either makes or implies moral judgments. She makes them when she tells us a particular epoch was a breakthrough or a decline in human history, or just simply neutral. She implies them when she singles out certain factors as either helpful or detrimental to a period's or a person's existence. These judgments clearly presuppose values and norms of the historian's own consciousness as to what is the nature of the good, the helpful, the creative—in short, morality.

What validity, if any, can then be given to the historian's reconstruction? Speculators like Bernard Lonergan and Van A. Harvey propose a modified form of "perspectivism" as a way of dealing with this problem. Van Harvey's argument with the sheerly relativist position—what he terms "hard perspectivism"—is threefold.[104] First, as we have already argued, a relativist like Popper presupposes that the only valid knowledge is a strictly scientific one, based on universal laws. Then, discovering that history does not simply admit of this, he countenances relativism. But this is a *non sequitur.* For he overlooks the limited and relevant conditions giving rise to a historical event. Secondly, the hard relativist presupposes "that selection always involves distortion, that interest and purpose are necessarily antithetical to objectivity."[105] But this again is a *non sequitur,* for it can plausibly be argued that interest/selectivity is a condition for all knowledge. And the relevant issue can only be, not whether selection should be operative, but what data warrant the historian's selectivity. Hence the importance of our articulating above the multiple factors that enter into a reconstructed "historical event." By bringing them to conscious awareness, there is less likelihood of an important element being overlooked. Finally, Van Harvey argues that hard relativism involves "the denial of self-transcendence, the ability of human beings to enter imaginatively into possibilities of understanding and evaluation not their own, to appreciate alien claims, to evaluate and assess them, and to commit oneself to them."[106] The telling argument against the hard relativist is that, on his view, the historian would never be able to rise above his own interests and biases. But in fact he does and thus he achieves some measure of self-transcendence. Yet what should be added to Van Harvey's program is Gilkey's view that, at the deepest level, the historian will be ultimately influenced by an at least implicit philosophy/theology of history—and I might add, a metaphysics and ontology—and that therefore this more speculative brand of history is a necessary condition of historical research. This is not to argue that every historian need be a philosopher, nor that every exegete be a speculative theologian. It is to argue that every historian and exegete should strive to be aware of this level of his presuppositions and thus gain some measure of control over them. It is this deepest level that determines what a historian thinks is possible at all in history, whether history has a structure and a possible goal worth explaining, and indeed whether the historical enterprise is worthwhile at all.[107]

Gilkey speaks of "imaginative reconstruction"; Van Harvey speaks of the historian's capacity for "self-transcendence"; Gadamer speaks of a "fusion of horizons"; Lonergan speaks of the historians' capacity to "rid themselves of biases, undergo conversions, come to understand the quite different mentalities of other places and times, and even move towards understanding one another, each in his own distinctive fashion"[108]—each in his own way rests his case on the quality of the experience and self-understanding of the individual in the hermeneutical task. As we know, it was Collingwood who perhaps most forcefully took his stand on the capacities of the historian's subjectivity. He claimed that the historian actually reenacts the thought of the past. Speaking of Plato, he said: "Yet, if I not only read his argument but understand it, follow it in my own mind by re-arguing it with and for myself, the process of argument which I go through is not a process resembling Plato's, it actually is Plato's, so far as I understand him rightly."[109] Yet, besides Collingwood's reduction of history to intentionality, it can be questioned whether the historian's mind can be so radically free of its own historical conditioning, and whether it needs to be. Although I personally owe a great deal to Collingwood for bringing me to some measure of historical consciousness and forcing me to think through the complex questions of historical reconstruction, I think the historian's continuity with the past and his consequent ability to reconstruct that past can be more moderately expressed.

It is, of course, "self-transcendence" that enables the historian to retrieve the past, but what ultimately ensures that the historian's self-transcendence can at least ideally reconstruct the complex whole known as an historic event is a basic commonality between the world of humanity of the past and that of the present. Both men of the past and those of the present share to some extent a common objective world and common capacities, though the first can be differently understood and the latter differently developed. It is this commonality in objective world and human capacities that grounds our continuity to the past. We are of course speaking in the ideal, for men can somewhat close themselves to their world and refuse to develop their capacities. And so it is not Plato's world but my world that I live in, and to some extent that world has changed. But common to both Plato's and my world are conditions relevant to the way we can act and a basic constellation of societal, cultural, and institutional factors. To the extent that the historian knows what these are in his own experience he can attempt to discover what they were in Plato's. And it is not Plato's thought but my thought that I actuate, but common to us both is a capacity to think. Because the historian knows what thinking is in his own life, what it is to entertain ideas, he can attempt to entertain Plato's ideas, his intentions, his motivations. As someone once put it, the opposite of the past is not the present but the absent. For it is precisely absence to the world and to our capacities that renders historical retrieval impossible. Perhaps what ultimately makes some afraid to accept the proposition that hermeneutics rests on the enlightened subjectivity of the individual is that they think this lands us in an unsolvable solipsism. But that would only be the case were the subject an isolated monad. In fact, the subject is a subject with a world and with capacities for self-transcendence made possible by that world and its past artifacts and data.[110]

If we have learned something, then, from the historians, it is that both the Old and the New Quests for the historical Jesus assumed too naïvely that the "bare reality" of Jesus could be recovered through their methods of biblical research. It makes no difference that the New Quest argues for a recovery of meaning rather than facts. For both "fact" and "meaning," intertwined as they are, are imaginative reconstructions on the part of the historian. As should be evident, I do not think this makes the historical recovery of Jesus an impossible task. It only forces the exegete to render more conscious his operative assumptions and to take some measure of responsibility for them. Further, as I shall try to argue later, the recognition of the inevitable role of interpretation on the exegete's part turns the exegete's attention to the nature of interpretation itself, especially to the nature of the post-Easter kerygma as our earliest instance of an interpretation or reconstruction of the historical Jesus. The key issue in biblical research would then become, not whether the early disciples interpreted Jesus in the light of their post-Easter experience, but what kind of interpretation is it; what implicit philosophy and theology is operative in that interpretation; whether the disciples' "selectivity" in interpretation, under the impact of the Easter experience, necessarily hampered their understanding of Jesus or enriched it; whether, through the Easter experience, their interpretation shows the signs of falling into some sort of "illusion" or whether the Easter experience fostered some measure of self-transcendence in the disciples, causing them to rise above their own interest and biases.

3. A Differentiated Consciousness Grounds Differentiated Hermeneutical Functions: Just as all historical reconstruction is an imaginative reconstruction on the historian's part, so the reconstruction of the historical events recorded in the New Testament will flow from the exegete's and theologian's imaginative capacities. And it seems possible to establish the axiom: the more differentiated the interpreter's consciousness, the more differentiated becomes the hermeneutical task. At least a minimum for interpreting the biblical texts would be the interpreter's ability to attain the same level of understanding exhibited by the biblical texts themselves. And while I by no means think even this minimal level of understanding was commonly reached in Christianity's past, given the phenomenon of mass political "conversions" and the large numbers of barely educated Christians, it was in principle the level of understanding open to people before the emergence of critical history. Critical history, however, marks a turning point, in that now one becomes more conscious of his cultural conditioning and thus able to inquire into the cultural and theological factors "implied" in the New Testament texts.

Given the emergence of critical history, it becomes possible to differentiate, with Peter Chirico,[111] the following hermeneutical functions. First, then, is the task of interpreting what the text itself "ideally" says. This involves, of course, the ability to reconstruct the text as carefully as possible from the available manuscripts, the grasp of the literary genres, and thus primarily the methods of literary and source criticism. Insofar as the interpreter will have to employ historical hypotheses to reconstruct the text, he will be moving into our other levels of interpretation. Secondly—and critical history has especially given this importance—the interpreter can seek to grasp what is implied by the text. It could be that the text's author consciously implied certain elements and simply left them unexpressed, or that he was not even aware of these larger implications. In either case, critical historiography can ask about this level and attempt to reconstruct the elements implied by the historic events of the New Testament. As we have said, this will involve the interpreter in asking about (1) the conditions relevant to the particular episode(s) of the New Testament under consideration, (2) the inward intentions and motivations of the historical agents involved, and (3) the larger constellation of societal, institutional, and cultural factors operative. In short, this is the level at which form criticism, *Redaktionsgeschichte,* and *Tendenzkritik* operate. For example, the commonly accepted distinction between the "Jesus of history and the Christ of Faith" is a complex, imaginative construction on the part of the biblical interpreter. It is not a distinction clearly stated by the biblical text (first task) but one that is thought to be "implied" by the text (second task). And this distinction is terribly complex, involving hypotheses about the conditions relevant to such a distinction (something called the resurrection happened); the inner intentions of the agents (the disciples became people of faith); and that larger constellation of conditions (the times were susceptible to belief in the supernatural), etc. One should also notice at this point that as one moves from task one to task two the interpretation becomes less probable, simply because the interpreter's imaginative capacities are more forcefully at work. But, thirdly, critical history forces upon us a third philosophical and theological hermeneutical task. It is this final level that involves us in the philosophy/theology of history, ontology and Christology. And while I do not think it necessary for every exegete to be expert at this task, I think it important for him to be aware of the role of this task, for it is the presuppositions operative at this level that in part determine what the interpreter will consider a possible "historical event." Beyond reconstructing what the text either says or implies, this level adjudicates differences in understanding between the text's "world" and the contemporary "world" of the interpreter. Real or apparent conflicts in the understanding of nature, man, history and religion need some resolving. This is obviously the function of philosophy and theology, but it is also a genuine hermeneutical function, for assumptions operative here will influence, sometimes decisively, the reconstruction of historical events. For example, the issue of the resurrection, the meaning the interpreter gives it, will clearly influence her reconstruction of the historic events of the New Testament. Chirico speaks here of the interpreter's call "to complement and correct that aspect of the text which reflects the *ex se* unintelligible aspect of the author's experience."[112] He points, for example, to Paul's evident acceptance of the institution of slavery and the interpreter's ability, from his own deepened experience, to correct Paul. But I would add that interpretation can work the other way, too. That is, it can challenge and enrich the interpreter's own experience and understanding, and thus the "past" can enlarge the present. In any case, as Gilkey has so well pointed out, if such a strong theoretical component is operative in historical interpretation, and if that theoretical component ultimately derives from an at least "implied" philosophy and theology, then it makes good sense to raise this level to explicit consciousness and take responsibility for our assumptions. If the first two tasks are more past oriented, this task is more future oriented. For here the text and its implied historical "depth" becomes a catalytic agent that challenges, partially confirms and enriches present self-understanding. Its appeal is to our contemporary imagination, insofar as it forces us to imagine alternative world views.[113]

4. Hermeneutical Observations on the Distinction Between the "Jesus of History" and the "Christ of Faith": Before beginning our exploration of Christology, it is necessary to probe the implications of our hermeneutical theory for a major category operative in both critical biblical and critical theological study: the "Jesus of history" and the "Christ of faith." First, it should be clear that we are not dealing in this category with one element that is purely objective and free of interpretation—the "Jesus of history"— and another element that is subjective and purely the result of interpretation—the "Christ of faith." The entire category is a complex abstraction or imaginative reconstruction created, hopefully with sufficient warrants from the data, by the critical exegete. Perhaps the mistake of both the Old and the New Quests was to assume too easily that the "Jesus of history" was a sheerly "objective reality" and not an imaginative construct. But what is of most importance is to examine how this major category can function in the works of exegetes and theologians. There seem to be three possibilities. First, the exegete can seek, much as the Old Questers, to use the "Jesus of history" as a norm for determining the validity of the "Christ of Faith." Reimarus's slogan, "Back from the Christ of dogma to the real Jesus," was just such a use of this category. Here the Christologian's task becomes one of recovering as exactly as possible the "original" Jesus and then "playing this" off against the Christ of faith. For example, because the exegete hypothesizes that the original Jesus was radically Father-centered while the later kerygma (the Christ of faith) presents us with a Jesus-centered proclamation, the former is the "real" historical reality and the latter is to be seen as a Church-influenced dogmatizing of Jesus. In part, as we recall, the Old Questers failed to recognize to what an extent their "original Jesus" was their own imaginative reconstruction. And it was just this failure that enabled them to project their own nineteenth-century "liberal" view of man back onto this Jesus. Hence their tendency to write off the kerygma as a supernaturalistic dogmatizing. This failure to note and take responsibility for one's own presuppositions is also, by the way, the chief problem with all "fundamentalist" readings of scripture too. Refusing to admit one's presuppositions enables one unknowingly to allow them to influence one's historical interpretation.

Secondly, the exegete and theologian can seek, not to "play off" the Jesus of history against the Christ of faith, but to discover a strict continuity between them. One gains the impression that this is what the New Quest is up to by its use of a Collingwoodian, meaning-oriented historiography. It feels confident in establishing a continuity of meaning between the Jesus of history and the Christ of faith, insofar as both, though in different terms, proclaim the summons to a new radical self-understanding in the light of God's offer of grace. In Robinson's terms: "Thus the deeper meaning of Jesus' message is: in accepting one's death there is life for others; in suffering, there is glory; in submitting to judgment, one finds grace, in accepting one's finitude resides the only transcendence. It is this existential meaning latent in Jesus' message which is . . . finally codified in the church's kerygma." But this is a matter of strict continuity between the Jesus of history and the Christ of faith: "The identity in existential meaning between Jesus' eschatological message and the church's kerygma could not be made more apparent. . . . "[114] I have already argued that the New Quest believes too naïvely in its ability to recover the "bare intentionality" of Jesus. And one might construct a case that it is this refusal to admit to what an extent their "inward Jesus" is their own imaginative reconstruction that permits them to draw such an "existential" portrait of Jesus and the kerygma. But my greater problem with both the Old and the New Quests is their failure to entertain our third possibility that the "Christ of faith" stems from a development in experience and understanding on the part of the apostolic Church. The Old Quest assumes that the kerygma was a mistake; the New, that it is identical with the Jesus of history. Neither comes to terms with the possibility of real development on the part of the apostolic Church. This failure leads them to presuppose that what is earliest (the "Jesus of history") is what is "best" and solely valid, and thus to be used as the norm for interpreting the Christ of faith. Here we see to what an extent the interpreter's presuppositions color his reconstruction of historical reality. One must thank the New Quest for granting a greater validity to the kerygma, but one must question why it refuses a priori to grant to it what it grants to itself: development in experience and understanding. If this third possibility were to be taken seriously, then the Christologian's task would not be that of playing off the Jesus of history against the Christ of faith, nor that of establishing a strict identity between them, but rather investigating the possible factors involved in the development of the apostolic Church and the theological validity of the apostolic interpretation of Jesus. As we have seen, Raymond Brown grants the resurrection event epistemological status as a key factor in the development of the apostolic Church. I am convinced that this observation needs pursuing.

A preliminary expression of what I mean might be as follows. All interpretation of historic events proceeds from the enlightened subjectivity of the interpreter. If this hermeneutical observation applies to contemporary interpreters, it equally applies to our earliest "interpreters" of Jesus, the constructors of the apostolic kerygma. A further observation that seems warranted is that the more "enlightened" or differentiated the subjectivity of the interpreter, the more enlightened will be his interpretation. This is a truism at work in all historiography. For what enables the historical studies of contemporary historians to advance is precisely their more nuanced understanding of nature and man. It is precisely development in contemporary experience and understanding that increases our ability to reconstruct the past. Certainly this further observation might apply to the constructors of the kerygma too; namely, that here we are dealing with an interpretation of Jesus that stems from a development in their experience and understanding. Were this the case, then the Christologian should not only not ignore the kerygma (Old Quest), nor simply identify it with the "Jesus of history" (New Quest), but he should grant it an epistemological priority. The only ultimate test of whether this might be true is for the contemporary interpreter to apply to the kerygma the same norm that he applies to his own historic reconstruction: the more developed one's understanding, the more profound is one's interpretation.

Clearly the question turns on what counts as a genuine "development" in consciousness. To what extent, then, can the kerygma be considered a genuine development in consciousness, enabling the disciples to grasp more profoundly the "historic reality" of Jesus? Clearly the kerygma is not simply an instance of logical development on the part of the disciples. While undoubtedly the construction of the kerygma assuredly involved "logic," it cannot be reduced to it. I think the Jewish "no" to Jesus clearly illustrates this, unless we wish to take the untenable view that first-century Judaism was incapable of logic. Avery Dulles put this well:

> Whence did the apostles derive their conviction that Jesus was Lord over all creation, sharing with his Father in the government of the universe [the kerygma, in other words]? If we wish to accept the apostles' own account of their faith, we shall have to say that it was not simply a matter of assenting to what Jesus had expressly said of Himself in His earthly existence. Still less was it a logical inference.[115]

Perhaps here one might speculate that both the Old and the New Quests are implicitly under the influence of logical development. The Old Quest stresses the lack of logical continuity between the Jesus of history and the Christ of faith, and moves to the conclusion of the invalidity of the kerygma. The New Quest, under the influence of Collingwood's meaning-oriented history, stresses the continuity in meaning between Jesus and the kerygma, but then it must downplay just those elements that seem logically most discontinuous with the original Jesus: the kerygma's centering of attention on Jesus rather than the Father, the confession of Jesus' divinity, the role of the resurrection, etc. The New Quest eliminates the "sting," so to speak, of the kerygma. The difficulty with the logical theory of development is precisely its emphasis on logic and its consequent failure to highlight the role of experience in the development of understanding. This is something that contemporary historians know well, for it is precisely the contemporary experience of historical consciousness that enables the historian to ask more complex questions about the events of the past and to explain more accurately those events. The possibility remains, in other words, that the constructors of the kerygma have undergone some enlightening experience that has deepened their understanding of the historic Jesus.

A further alternative is to argue, as the modernists at the turn of the century are supposed to have argued, that in the kerygma we are not encountering continuity at all with the historical Jesus. The kerygma is simply discontinuous, a result of the evolution of the Christian community under new and differing circumstances. Perhaps Jan Walgrave is correct in his assertion that the logical theory's stress on continuity probably generated its opposite: a new stress on discontinuity.[116] Apart from the question of whether human development is ever simply discontinuous in this manner, one might raise the question of to what extent this discontinuity theory was still operating from an implicit acceptance of the logical theory. That is, because one was looking for logical continuity and could not find it, one simply acquiesced in no continuity at all.

Yet a third possibility,[117] and the one that I will explore in this work, is to argue that the kerygma represents that form of development which moves from the undifferentiated to greater differentiation and clarity. We are, I think, familiar with this kind of development in our own experience. Childhood, for example, is largely a phase of undifferentiated experience and understanding. As our experience widens, becoming more complex, we find ourselves capable of clarifying and differentiating aspects of ourselves and insights we had entertained that earlier remained only obscurely known. The child's cognitive capacities, for example, are still undifferentiated. They express themselves in vague imagistic thinking, in dreams, in fantasy, etc. Under the pressure of more complex experience—entrance into school, the imposition of societal and familial tasks, etc.—the child gradually is forced to discover her hitherto vaguely experienced cognitive capacities. This in turn promotes a clearer, more differentiated awareness of them. The route of this model of development moves, then, from the undifferentiated to a complexification of experience—this promotes the more differentiated awareness.

It is important to indicate that, on this model, development is never purely logical, although it is rational and may include elements of logic. The young child, for example, cannot simply logically deduce its cognitive capacities. Their discovery can only occur through experience, through the increasingly more complex demands that experience will make upon him. But neither, on this model, is development a quantum leap, the emergence of simply "new" capacities by mutations and a kind of natural selection. Perhaps the best, although clumsy, way to put this is to say that human development is a process of complexification in experience and differentiation in consciousness in which deepened experience can bring to the surface, through a process more complex than logic, new data incapable of being deduced without that deepened experience.

What I will propose throughout this work is that the passage from the Jesus of history to the kerygma's Christ can more adequately be explained on this model of development—I am calling this the "historical and human model"—rather than on the logical or simple discontinuity models. It is already apparent that the kerygma is not a simple logical deduction from what Jesus said and did in his ministry. It will also become apparent that the kerygma's Christ cannot adequately be explained as a mutation stemming from the new Hellenic influences of the apostolic Church. The passage from the Jesus of history to the Christ of faith rather seems to be an example of our passage from the undifferentiated to the differentiated. On this view, there is real continuity between the Jesus of the ministry and the kerygma, for the undifferentiated reality of Jesus is truly presented in the kerygma, only now in more differentiated terms. There is discontinuity, for under the pressure of the new and more complex experience of the resurrection, the disciples have come to a deeper, more differentiated understanding of Jesus. The key event is the reality of the resurrection—without this the disciples would never have broken through to the more differentiated understanding of Jesus with which we are presented in the kerygma.

Notes

1. Gordon D. Kaufman, *Systematic Theology: A Historicist Perspective* (New York: Charles Scribner's, 1968).

2. See any of his many works, but esp. *The Myth of the Eternal Return* (New Haven: Yale, 1971). Helpful on Eliade is Guilford Dudley III, *Religion on Trial: Mircea Eliade and His Critics* (Philadelphia: Temple University, 1977).

3. John Dunne, *The Way of All the Earth* (New York: Macmillan, 1972), p. 145. I have traced the emergence of rationality in my *Christ and Consciousness,* pp. 19–47.

4. Of course, humans have always been historical, coming to be only in time and through historical events; but that is something different from the self-reflective consciousness of being historical.

5. Most helpful for the medieval awareness of history are Étienne Gilson, "The Middle Ages and History," in his *The Spirit of Medieval Philosophy* (New York: Charles Scribner's, 1940), pp. 383–402; M.-D. Chenu, "Nature and Man: the Renaissance of the Twelfth Century," and "Theology and the New Awareness of History," in his *Nature, Man, and Society in the Twelfth Century* (Chicago: University of Chicago, 1968), pp. 1–48, 162–201; Joseph Ratzinger, *The Theology of History in St. Bonaventure* (Chicago: Franciscan Herald, 1971); Johannes Baptist Metz, *Christliche Anthropozentrik: Über die Denkform des Thomas von Aquin*

(München: Kösel, 1962); and Max Seckler, *Le Salut et L'Histoire: La pensée de saint Thomas d'Aquin sur la théologie de l'histoire* (Paris: Cerf, 1967), esp. pp. 101–141.

6. Peter Gay, *The Enlightenment: An Interpretation* (New York: Vintage, 1966), p. 37.

7. Norman Hampson, *The Enlightenment* (Baltimore: Pelican, 1968), pp. 218–250; cf. also Stephen Toulmin and June Goodfield, *The Discovery of Time* (Baltimore: Pelican, 1967).

8. *Ibid.,* p. 26.

9. *Ibid.,* p. 235.

10. Charles C. Gillespie, *Genesis and Geology* (New York: Harper Torchbooks, 1959), p. 7.

11. Cf. H. Stuart Hughes, *Consciousness and Society: the Reorientation of European Social Thought 1890-1930* (New York: Vintage, 1961).

12. Cf. Langdon Gilkey, *Reaping the Whirlwind: A Christian Interpretation of History* (New York: Seabury, 1976), pp. 203–208.

13. Charles Lyell, as cited by Gillespie, *op. cit.,* p. 126.

14. Gilkey, *op. cit.,* p. 205.

15. Cf. the classic, J. B. Bury, *The Idea of Progress* (New York: Dover, 1955).

16. Cf. Hughes, *op. cit.,* among others.

17. *Ibid.,* pp. 15–16.

18. Cf. Robert Nisbet, *The Sociological Tradition* (New York: Basic, 1966).

19. Gilkey, *op. cit.,* p. 193.

20. *Ibid.,* p. 200.

21. This is why Gilkey, *op. cit., passim,* speaks of the ontological polarity of freedom and destiny in history. The new experience of human self-transcendence brings home the dimension of freedom in history; the heightened sense of autonomy increases man's experience of self-responsibility, his need to insure the triumph of order/law over chaos/anarchy, and hence his experience of destiny in history.

22. Cf. my *Christ and Consciousness,* pp. 109–127.

23. See the helpful comments of Gilkey, *op. cit.,* pp. 91–114, and Bernard J. F. Lonergan, *Method in Theology* (New York: Herder and Herder, 1972), pp. 175–234.

24. Cf., for overviews, Patrick Gardner, ed., *Theories of History* (New York: Free, 1959); C. T. McIntyre, *God, History, and Historians* (New York: Oxford, 1977).

25. Gilkey's comment, *op. cit.,* p. 92: "In the contemporary Anglo-Saxon world this sort of speculative approach to history, seeking to uncover its basic patterns and possibly its goal as a whole, has been out of fashion."

26. Cf. John S. Kselman, "Modern New Testament Criticism," in *The Jerome Biblical Commentary* (Englewood Cliffs, N.J.: Prentice-Hall, 1968), II, pp. 7–20 (whose helpful outline I am following); Raymond E. Brown and Joseph P. Cahill, *Biblical Tendencies Today: An Introduction to the Post-Bultmannians* (Washington, D.C.: Corpus, 1969); and Dulles, *op. cit.*

27. Dermot A. Lane, *The Reality of Jesus* (New York: Paulist, 1975), p. 20.

28. H. J. Holtzmann, *Die synoptischen Evangelien, ihr Ursrung und geschichtlicher Charakter* (Leipzig, 1863), p. 1, as cited by Dulles, *op. cit.,* p. 30.

29. David Friedrich Strauss, *The Life of Jesus Critically Examined* (Philadelphia: Fortress, 1972).

30. This, of course, refers to the well known view that Mark and a hypothetical "Q" are the earliest sources of the narratives and sayings of Jesus.

31. Dulles, *op. cit.,* p. 31.

32. George Tyrrell, *Christianity at the Crossroads,* reset edition (London, 1963), p. 49, as cited by Dulles, *ibid.,* p. 53.

33. Albert Schweitzer, *The Quest of the Historical Jesus* (New York: Macmillan, 1961), p. 4, p. 3.

34. For a critical examination of this school, see Günter Wanger, *Pauline Baptism and the Pagan Mysteries* (Edinburgh: Oliver and Boyd, 1967).

35. Cf. Schubert Ogden, *Christ without Myth* (New York: Harper, 1961), p. 99.

36. Bultmann claims to find demythologization at work in the New Testament itself; for example, in Paul's understanding of "body" there seems to be an evident demythologization of the gnostic notion of the same. Whereas for the gnostics evil happens to the body by evil powers, for Paul evil comes from the self (Paul's demythologized notion of "body"). Cf. Rm 7. Not everything in the New Testament is mythological, however, For example, Bultmann will speak of God's act in Christ as "analogical" and not in need of demythologization.

37. Rudolf Bultmann, *Jesus and the Word* (New York: Charles Scribner's, 1958), p. 8.

38. Cf. Ian Henderson, *Rudolf Bultmann* (Richmond, Virginia: John Knox, 1966), p. 47.

39. *Ibid.*

40. *Ibid.*

41. As cited by Brown, *op. cit.,* p. 30, n. 48.

42. Ernst Käsemann, *Essays on New Testament Themes* (London: SCM, 1964), pp. 15–47. Cf. also "Is the Gospel Objective?" *ibid.,* pp. 48–62.

43. As we will see, the rigorous criteria proposed by the New Questers, by which the historical Jesus might be retrieved, have been criticized as leading us to a Jesus who shared nothing in common with the world of his own day.

44. Cf. Ernst Fuchs, *Studies of the Historical Jesus* (London: SCM, 1964); and Franz Mussner, *Die Wunder Jesu* (München: Kösel, 1967).

45. Günther Bornkamm, *Jesus of Nazareth* (New York: Harper and Row, 1960).

46. Dulles, *op. cit.,* p. 36.

47. Joachim Jeremias, *The Prayers of Jesus* (London: SCM, 1967), esp. Chapter One, "Abba," pp. 11–65.

48. Joachim Jeremias, "The Present Position in the Controversy Concerning the Problem of the Historical Jesus," EXPOSITORY TIMES 69 (1958), 338.

49. Relevant bibliography can be found in Dulles, *op. cit.,* pp. 59–60.

50. Vincent Taylor, *The Life and Ministry of Jesus* (Nashville: Abingdon, 1955), p. 183.

51. C. H. Dodd, *History and the Gospel* (New York: Charles Scribner's, 1938), p. 37.

52. Harald Riesenfeld, *The Gospel Tradition and Its Beginnings* (London: A. R. Mowbray, 1961); Birger Gerhardsson, *Memory and Manuscript: Oral Tradition and Written Transmission in Rabbinic Judaism and Early Christianity* (Uppsala: C.

W. K. Gleerup, 1961); see also the critical studies of J. A. Fitzmyer, THEOLOGICAL STUDIES 23 (1962), 442–457, and W. D. Davies, "Reflections on a Scandinavian Approach to 'the Gospel Tradition,' " NEO-TESTAMENTICA ET PATRISTICA (Supplement to NOVUM TESTAMENTUM, 6), Leiden, 1962, 14–34.

53. Cf. H. A. Hodgson, *The Philosophy of Wilhelm Dilthey* (London: Routledge, 1952); Wilhelm Dilthey, *Pattern and Meaning in History* (New York: Harper and Row, 1962); R. G. Collingwood, *The Idea of History* (London: Oxford, 1946).

54. Brown, *op. cit.,* pp. 5–6.

55. *Ibid.,* p. 7. See James M. Robinson, *A New Quest of the Historical Jesus* (London: SCM, 1968), pp. 106–107, who disagrees with Käsemann and Bornkamm on this matter. These latter give a primacy to the *via kerygmatica.* See Brown, *op. cit.,* pp. 7–9, for differences among the New Questers.

56. Modernism scholarship is only now coming into its own and we are being compelled to revise many of our simplistic judgments on the matter. Cf., among others, John Ratté, *Three Modernists* (New York: Sheed and Ward, 1967) and T. M. Schoof, *A Survey of Catholic Theology 1800-1970* (New York: Paulist, 1970).

57. Raymond E. Brown, *Biblical Reflections on Crises Facing the Church* (New York: Paulist, 1975), p. 6.

58. Cited by Brown, *ibid.,* p. 111. A complete translation will be found in CATHOLIC BIBLICAL QUARTERLY 18 (1956), 23–29, with the Latin and German originals.

59. For translation and commentary see J. A. Fitzmyer, THEOLOGICAL STUDIES 25 (1964), 386–408.

60. Brown, *Biblical Reflections on Crises Facing the Church,* p. 112, notes: "Stage one recognizes a limited world view on Jesus' part, even if it delicately attributes this to accommodation. Most Catholic scholars would speak more openly of Jesus' own limited knowledge rather than of his accommodating himself to the limited knowledge of his time."

61. *Ibid.,* p. 112.

62. Kselman, *art. cit.,* p. 19.

63. Cf., for example, his "Hermeneutics," *Jerome Biblical Commentary* II, pp. 605–623.

64. Brown, *Biblical Tendencies Today,* p. 17.

65. *Ibid.,* pp. 15–16.

66. *Ibid.,* p. 17.

67. *Ibid.,* p. 18.

68. *Ibid.,* p. 20.

69. *Ibid.,* p. 21.

70. Cf. H. Palmer, *The Logic of Gospel Criticism* (London: Macmillan, 1968); E. P. Sanders, *The Tendencies of the Synoptic Tradition* (Cambridge: University, 1969); Walter Wink, *The Bible in Human Transformation: Toward a New Paradigm for Biblical Study* (Philadelphia: Fortress, 1973); and M. D. Hooker, "Christology and Methodology," NEW TESTAMENT STUDIES 17 (1970–71), 480–487.

71. Cf. C. F. D. Moule, "The Techniques of New Testament Research: A Critical Survey," in Donald G. Miller and Dikran Y. Hadidian, eds., *Jesus and Man's Hope* II (Pittsburgh: Pittsburgh Theological Seminary, 1971), pp. 29–45.

72. Jacob Neusner, *From Politics to Piety: the Emergence of Pharisaic Juda-*

ism (Englewood Cliffs, N.J.: Prentice-Hall, 1973), only argues with great caution for the period following A.D. 70.

73. An excellent example is Hans Jonas, *The Gnostic Religion, The Message of the Alien God and the Beginnings of Christianity* (Boston: Beacon, 1972), who postulates a widespread tendency toward dualism in the first century. Eric Voegelin's brilliant *Order and History,* 4 volumes (Louisiana: Louisiana State University, 1956–1974), is also an example of this.

74. Besides Neusner, *op. cit.,* cf. Rosemary Radford Ruether, *Faith and Fratricide: The Theological Roots of Anti-Semitism* (New York: Seabury, 1974).

75. Ruether, *ibid.,* p. 61.

76. James M. Mackey, *The Problems of Religious Faith* (Chicago: Franciscan Herald, 1972), p. 196; cf. p. 129: "The man of disillusionment speaks apocalyptic language, the man of confidence speaks prophetic language, but in times of increasing stress the latter imperceptibly shades into the former."

77. For the prophets, cf. Voegelin, *Order and History* I, pp. 428–515; for the Pharisees, cf. Ruether, *op. cit.,* pp. 55–57, on the Pharisaic notion of the "spiritual Jew."

78. See Van A. Harvey, *The Historian and the Believer* (New York: Macmillan, 1969), pp. 164–203, upon whom I am relying, for a sympathetic critique of the New Quest.

79. Robinson, *op. cit.,* p. 28.

80. Van Harvey, *op. cit.,* pp. 187, 192.

81. James M. Robinson, "The Dismantling and Reassembling of the Categories of New Testament Scholarship," in Robinson and Koester, *op. cit.,* p. 9.

82. *Ibid.,* p. 13. Koester, "The Intention and Scope of Trajectories," *ibid.,* pp. 269–279, argues convincingly for the following: (1) we must recognize a much more intricate relationship between Christianity and its surrounding culture than is usually assumed; (2) the accepted schema of an evolution from Jewish to Christian literature and thence to gnostic thought is unsatisfactory; (3) Judaism, Christianity, and Gnosticism have developed writings of the same genre almost simultaneously; (4) "There is no justification for the division between 'New Testament Introduction' and 'Patrology.' The same credal developments that formed the apologetic literature also created the gospels of the New Testament canon. Conversely, the factors deriving from Jewish and pagan literary productions are no less conspicuous in the earliest gospels than they are in the apologetic writings"; (5) the distinction between "Palestinian" and "Hellenistic" is an oversimplification; (6) there are different and simultaneous kinds of early Christianity: east Syrian, Western, Latin, etc.

83. *Ibid.,* pp. 2–3.

84. See, for example, Norman Perrin, *Jesus and the Language of the Kingdom* (Philadelphia: Fortress, 1976), and David Tracy, "Christian Texts: The Possibility of Their Interpretation," in his *Blessed Rage for Order* (New York: Seabury, 1975), pp. 72–79. Tracy tends to make this his sole hermeneutics in his analysis of Christology, pp. 204–236.

85. Paul Ricoeur, *Interpretation Theory: Discourse and the Surplus of Meaning* (Fort Worth, Texas: Texas Christian University, 1976). Cf. esp. pp. 75–76: "Here perhaps my opposition to Romanticist hermeneutics is most forceful. . . . the Romanticist forms of hermeneutics overlooked the specific situation created by the disjunction of the verbal meaning of the text from the mental intention of the author. The fact is that the author can no longer 'rescue' his work. . . . His inten-

tion is often unknown to us, sometimes redundant, sometimes useless, and sometimes even harmful as regards the interpretation of the verbal meaning of his work. In even the better cases it has to be taken into account in light of the text itself. . . . understanding takes place in a non-psychological and properly semantical space, which the text has carved out by severing itself from the mental intention of its author." Cf., for this approach in rather broad terms, Norman R. Petersen, *Literary Criticism for New Testament Critics* (Philadelphia: Fortress, 1978), which unfortunately does not study Ricoeur's important contribution to this enterprise. Helpful for this is "Paul Ricoeur on Biblical Hermeneutics," SEMEIA 4 (1975).

86. Tracy, *op. cit.,* p. 75.

87. Ricoeur, *op. cit.,* p. 25.

88. For this notion see *ibid.,* pp. 43–44, 89–95, and Paul Ricoeur, "The Hermeneutical Function of Distanciation," PHILOSOPHY TODAY 17 (1973), 129–141.

89. When meaning is "fixed" in writing, it becomes "idealized" in the following ways: (1) the author's meaning becomes a dimension of the text; (2) spoken discourse is local, but a text is potentially universal and even creates its own public; (3) the works of language become as self-contained as sculptures; the text's reference is freed from its situational limits (Ricoeur, *Interpretation Theory,* pp. 25–37).

90. *Ibid.,* p. 92.

91. *Ibid.*

92. *Ibid.,* p. 94.

93. For the notion of how the form of the myth remains, but its meaning changes, cf. G. van der Leeuw, *Religion in Essence and Manifestation* II (New York: Harper Torchbooks, 1963).

94. Ricoeur, *Interpretation Theory,* p. 68.

95. *Ibid.,* p. 93.

96. See Gilkey, *op. cit.,* pp. 92–105, for a helpful summary, upon whom I partly rely. Cf. also Richard E. Palmer, *Hermeneutics* (Evanston: Northwestern University, 1969); and Hans-Georg Gadamer, *Truth and Method* (New York: Seabury, 1975).

97. Cf. Carl Hempel, "The Function of General Laws in History," in Gardner, *op. cit.,* pp. 344–356, and Karl Popper, *The Poverty of Historicism* (New York: Harper Torchbooks, 1969).

98. Hempel, *ibid.,* p. 347.

99. Gilkey, *op. cit.,* p. 93.

100. I find Gilkey's assessment, *ibid.,* pp. 95–98, remarkably reasonable. He relies on Gordon Leff, *History and Social Theory* (New York: Doubleday, 1971). I have been personally influenced by Bernard J. F. Lonergan's chapters on history in his *Method in Theology,* pp. 175–234.

101. *Ibid.,* p. 96.

102. *Ibid.,* p. 98.

103. Leff, *op. cit.,* p. 111.

104. Harvey, *op. cit.,* pp. 204–245.

105. *Ibid.,* p. 209.

106. *Ibid.,* p. 221.

107. It is this deepest philosophical/theological level that seems not fully developed in Van Harvey's work. Yet an implicit philosophy/theology is clearly operating, especially in his view (*ibid.,* p. 281) that the kerygma may not be as intelligible an interpretation of Jesus as a more modern perspectival interpretation

of the historical Jesus. This involves the important question of whether the modern exegete can by-pass the resurrection. Such an issue is clearly one that needs adjudication on the theological level.

108. Lonergan, *op. cit.,* p. 217.

109. Collingwood, *op. cit.,* p. 301.

110. This is the key point of Alfred North Whitehead's "reformed subjectivist principle," in his *Process and Reality* (New York: Macmillan/Free, 1957), pp. 182–194. Cf. also Hans Jonas, "Change and Permanence: On the Possibility of Understanding History," in his *Philosophical Essays: From Ancient Creed to Technological Man* (Englewood Cliffs, N.J.: Prentice-Hall, 1974), pp. 237–260.

111. Peter Chirico, *Infallibility: the Crossroads of Doctrine* (Kansas City: Sheed, Andrews and McMeel, 1977), pp. 3–29. It might be well to indicate here the criteria of Jesus-research that seem valid and useful to me: (1) the criterion of dissimilarity, which eliminates the kerygmatic, and what can be derived from Jewish and Hellenistic sources; this is useful along with other criteria, and bearing in mind that Jesus shared much in common with the world of his day (it goes without saying that the more we know of Jesus' world, the more accurate is our use of this criterion); (2) multiple attestation, which looks for a consistent tradition in primary sources; this needs confirmation from the other criteria; (3) consistency; along with the other criteria, this is important and can argue for authenticity; (4) for the reasons given, I do not accept the linguistic criterion (looking for what is Aramaic). These criteria are widely employed by the exegetes relied upon throughout this book.

112. *Ibid.,* p. 26.

113. Cf. Ray L. Hart, *Unfinished Man and the Imagination* (New York: Herder and Herder, 1968).

114. Robinson, *op. cit.,* pp. 123–124.

115. Avery Dulles, *Apologetics and the Biblical Christ* (Westminster: Newman, 1964), p. 68.

116. For doctrinal views of development, see Jan Hendrik Walgrave, *Unfolding Revelation: The Nature of Doctrinal Development* (Philadelphia: Westminster, 1972) and J. P. Mackey, *Tradition and Change in the Church* (Dayton, Ohio: Pflaum, 1968).

117. I prefer the notion of development as a process moving from undifferentiation to differentiation, rather than as a "meta-logical" process. Development as I understand it is, if you will, reasonable (logical), if not merely that. My *Christ and Consciousness,* pp. 5–47, details my view of human development. Cf. also Eric Voegelin, *Order and History* I, pp. 1–11, for a succinct explanation of the movement from the undifferentiated to the differentiated. It is gratifying to note that Peter Chirico has arrived at conclusions similar to my own in his own critique of Hans Küng's Christology; see his "Hans Küng's Christology: An Evaluation of Its Presuppositions," THEOLOGICAL STUDIES 40 (1979), 256–272.

PART TWO

THE CHRIST

III

THE GENESIS OF THE CHRIST-BELIEF

The New Testament "Shift" [1]

No reputable scholar denies that a historical person named "Jesus" existed at the beginning of our era. The books of the New Testament and the existence of Christianity presuppose as their ground the charismatic founder Jesus. It may be true that Jesus never founded Christianity in the "legal" sense of that term, through a legal and witnessed charter or constitution. But no doubt exists that he is the charismatic founder whose teachings and life "inspired" the Christian movement.[2] Further, Günther Bornkamm tells us that it never occurred to anyone, not even the Christian movement's most bitter enemies, to doubt the existence of Jesus.[3] And thus it is that Tacitus speaks of a Christ executed by Pilate under Tiberius (*Annals*, 15, 4); Suetonius, of a "Chrestus" causing disturbances in Rome (*Claudius,* 25, 4); Pliny, of Christians revering Christ as a god (*Epistola,* 10, 96); and the Jewish historian Josephus speaks of James, the brother of Jesus (*Antiquities,* 20, 200).

Further, although biblical scholars are divided on details, as we have seen there has been a vigorous pursuit of the historical Jesus since the Enlightenment period. I have tried to show that historical research cannot produce for us a Jesus-biography in the strict sense. The New Testament sources, primarily "confessional" in nature, do not admit of such a biography, and our hermeneutics has taught us that the so-called "historical Jesus" is itself a historian's reconstruction. But this need not land us in a kind of historical agnosticism. As critics become more conscious of their presuppositions and more knowledgeable about the world of the first Christian century, we can look forward to a greater consensus in Jesus-research. One may consult the standard works for summaries of the present research on Jesus.[4] What I wish to probe here are the theological bases and implications of what is a major hypothesis of current biblical critical research; namely, that while the Jesus of history presents us with a figure radically centered on the Father and God's kingdom, the New Testament and the normative Christianity of the first five centuries present us with a church-community radically centered on Jesus and his divine prerogatives. To be sure, this is a historical hypothesis, resting primarily on the insight that the New Testament was written some time after Jesus' death and after the early Christian Church had come increasingly to "revere" Jesus. But there are data in the New Testament itself that make no sense without this hypothesis.

We know, for example, that Jesus' teaching on the kingdom is radically Father-centered. The "tone" of Jesus' message on the kingdom is so consistently unself-centered that scholars are led to postulate that Jesus stands out as unique in the religious world of the first century and must have been different from that New Testament portrait that consistently focuses attention on Jesus and tends to "glorify" him. Jesus nowhere clearly tells us what he means by the "kingdom." He presupposes a familiarity with the notion that we can no longer take for granted, especially those of us who live in democratic countries and tend to link terms like "kingdom" and "rule" with monarchies and despotism. Thus, here too the critic must speculate and attempt to reconstruct this notion, taking full account of all the knowable data. On the most general level I would link the notion to a wider movement in the first millennium called by some the "Axial period." As Eric Voegelin views it, the constant collapse and reemergence of the pragmatic empires of the first millennium (Assyrian, Babylonian, Persian, Hellenistic and Roman) had created a spiritual crisis. The various imperial conquests resulted in huge power organizations, but what was lacking was a spiritual basis. In Voegelin's view, what found expression in Jesus was analogous to what occurred in Greece through the philosophers, in China through Lao-tzu, and in India through Buddha; namely, an "outburst of universal spirituality that in turn formed movements in search of a people whose order they could become."[5] Jesus gives expression to this aspiration for universalism through the Semitic concept of the "kingdom" developed by the prophets earlier in Jewish history and especially Isaiah and Jeremiah. It is really man's search for a universal order founded on justice, peace, and love that is expressed by the "kingdom." This is why Paul will speak of "justice" (cf. Rm.) and John of "life" (cf. Jn. and 1 Jn.) rather than "kingdom." This note of universalism is what separates Jesus' views from those of the Zealots, the Pharisees,[6] and the Essenes, who linked their message more precisely to the reestablishment of Judaism as a national entity.

But what is important to note is that it is always God's reign that Jesus preaches, and thus the characteristic unself-centeredness of Jesus' message is apparent in this stress on God the Father. The kingdom is "given" by God (Mt. 21.43; Lk. 12.32); "appointed" by him (Lk. 22.29); thus we can only "inherit" it (Mt. 25.34). In this light, Jesus' speech of God as "Abba"—occurring no less than a 170 times in the gospels—brings home more fully Jesus' deep confidence in and intimacy with this God whose reign is in process of establishment. While Jeremias[7] studies have highlighted how this term expresses Jesus' intimacy with the Father, at the same time it underlines his radical dependency upon the Father, his orientation to the Father rather than toward himself; "Unless you turn and become like children, you will never enter the kingdom of heaven" (Mt. 18.3). With this kind of God-orientation, it becomes clear why Jesus' kingdom is both present and future (Mt. 13.33, etc.). Surely Jesus' radical dependency upon God inspires him with a trust in God's presence now and gives him hope that even in the future this God will triumph.[8]

Jesus' miracles intensify this radical Father-centeredness in Jesus' life. To be sure, critical history has taught us that traditional religious literature tends to elaborate and magnify the miraculous element, and this may be especially true of the nature and punitive miracles recorded in the New Testament. The likelihood of this may even have been increased by early Christianity's contact with the Greek and Jewish legends of the miraculous acts of the rabbis and gods. Yet there are sound reasons for not eliminating the entire miracle-tradition from the gospels. Perhaps the most important reason is that the miracles, far from exalting Jesus, continue Jesus' radical stress on the Father. It is the Father and faith in this Father that heals: "but if it is by the Spirit of God that I cast out demons, then the kingdom of God has come upon you" (Lk. 11.20). Thus the gospels do not use the ordinary term *"terata,"* which tends to place the stress on the prodigious aspect of the miracles, but *dunameis* ("acts of power") and *semeia* ("signs"). In Kasper's terms: "Attention in this process is not directed at nature and its laws. . . . A miracle turns people's eyes upwards, toward God."[9] It is God's kingdom that is expressing itself in the miracles of Jesus. And one might speculate that it is the loss of the sense of God—a "closed" world view in which God has no part—that makes the miraculous problematic for modern man.

Perhaps it is Jesus' death that most clearly and dramatically illustrates the radicality of Jesus' Father-centeredness. The traditional picture of Jesus' being put to death because he proclaimed his own divine status simply fails to agree with what we know of the ministry of Jesus, and as we shall see in our next chapter, really is based on a God-concept quite alien to Jesus. As is well known, the passion narratives of the synoptics are thought to be the earliest written by the early Christian disciples, since the shameful death by crucifixion was perhaps the greatest stumbling block in the world of the first century for potential converts. The amazing elements in these narratives are well known, especially the agreement in the chronology: the journey to Jerusalem, the agony in the garden, the arrest and trials, the execution. But most amazing is the consistent refusal to "exalt" Jesus—except in the case of John, whose theological motives seem quite different from the synoptics—and even the tendency not to play upon the emotions and excite a kind of sympathetic piety toward Jesus. Even in his passion the stress is on the Father: it is God's work coming to fulfillment that is the underlying motif (Mk. 10.33f; 11.12–14; 13.9–13; 14.10; 15.1).

Why was Jesus put to death? I agree with Moltmann[10] that we need to recapture the "public" nature of Jesus' death in order more fully to grasp the factors bringing Jesus to his death. For Jesus did not die as a merely private individual, through old age or disease or suicide. He was put to death by public authorities, and this must surely tell us that his message put him in opposition to the dominant institutions of the time. Undoubtedly the note of universalism in his message—that God's favor shines on the unrighteous as well as the righteous—put him in opposition to the Sadducees, the Essenes, and the Zealots. We are learning that the Pharisees had their own doctrine of universalism; it was perhaps their tendency to view Jesus as the founder of a radical messianic sect that placed them in opposition to Jesus. Ruether seems quite persuasive on this point:

> Although the Pharisees apparently did not take such note of Jesus in his own lifetime that one can say, literally, that they rejected him, they did reject him retroactively, in the sense that they rejected the Christ presented to them by the Church. They did so in the same spirit in which they turned their back on all the messianic activism of this period. For them this development had revealed itself as a false direction, destructive alike to the nation and to the individual religious personality.[11]

But it was just this opposition to Judaism which meant that Jesus could not appeal to the standard Jewish authorities for the legitimation of his claims. He could rest only on his intimacy with the Father, and it was perhaps this direct access to the Father, transcending the commonly accepted modes of access to God, which brought Jewish opposition upon him. Again, it is his stress on God and his kingdom, not a Jesus-centrism, that brings him to his death. In this light, Luke's view, (23.46) that Jesus proclaims on the cross, "Father, into thy hands I commend my spirit," is not just a correction to Mark's and Matthew's "My God, my God, why hast Thou forsaken me?" (Mk. 15.34; Mt. 27.46), but an expression of the real meaning behind Jesus' death.

Yet, Jesus was executed by the Romans, and by means of the political punishment of crucifixion. This forces us to probe what it is that brought him in opposition to these authorities. Perhaps Jesus' radical theocentrism makes sense of the Jewish opposition, but how does it explain the Roman opposition? Here we might have a tendency to see Roman opposition to Jesus in purely political terms, but this would be to project our separation of religion and politics into the world of the first century. At that time a religious claim was tightly interwoven with political implications. The only question can be what was it about Jesus' religious stance that caused the opposition? A possible view would be to say that the Romans thought of Jesus as a Zealot, and indeed we can speculate that there was reasonable cause for this. As Moltmann points out, Jesus shared with the Zealots a stress on the dawning of the kingdom; a tendency to polemicize against the Roman collaborators, the Pharisees (cf. Lk. 13.32); he even had zealotic disciples, and the temple cleansing could be interpreted as a revolutionary act. Yet the differences from the Zealots are too great to sustain this view: Jesus was consistently nonviolent (Mt. 11.12); his universalism transcends the zealotic sectarianism (Jn. 18.36); he appeals to an authority higher than the Torah (Mt. 5); and his disciples counted among them non-Zealots. In the end I would hypothesize that the Roman authorities sensed in Jesus a threat even more radical than that of the Zealots. The key here is Jesus' radical trust in the Father. It is this that frees him from the need to rely upon force and violence, which relativizes the place of power in human life and thus calls into question what seems to be the key value in Roman rule. The Zealots unwittingly manifest power's supremacy; Jesus' radical Father-trust frees him from its dominance.

It is clear, then, that the Jesus of the ministry orients his entire life toward the Father, and yet the New Testament and early Church took the dramatic step of orienting its life around Jesus. In fact the entire New Testament is written from this point of view, even though critical research can hypothetically reconstruct the original ministry of Jesus. The development of this Jesus-centrism has been carefully analyzed by numerous scholars, and after presenting the main finds of their research we will consider the more properly theological meaning of this Jesus-centrism. We are, I think, taken part of the way toward understanding the New Testament's Jesus-centrism by a consideration of what some biblical scholars are calling the "implicit" Christology and soteriology of the pre-Easter ministry of Jesus. We might express this by saying that while it is true that Jesus' entire ministry is oriented to and centered upon God the Father, still it is impossible to separate Jesus himself from his cause and mission. A general consideration of Jesus' preaching and actions shows that it is in the man Jesus that the Father's kingdom is now being initiated in human history. Thus the Church father Origen would take the step of naming Jesus the *autobasileia*, that is, the kingdom in person.[12] The importance of this "hidden" Christological element in Jesus' ministry is to show that the New Testament's kerygmatic understanding of Jesus was not simply created *de novo*, a sort of "bolt from the heavens" that is without foundations in the Jesus of history. It can be said that the kerygma attempts to bring to expression in its Jesus-centrism what was already the case in a more concealed manner in the pre-Easter Jesus. Furthermore, without this hidden Christological element the resurrection event would have been simply unintelligible. Instead of being the confirmation and fulfillment of the man Jesus, which the New Testament claims it is, it would have appeared as only a strange and extraordinary phenomenon, quite unrelated to Jesus himself. Yet there is a danger in speaking of an "implicit" Christology and soteriology, for it could give the impression that the kerygma is simply a *logical* deduction from the pre-Easter Jesus, a sort of mental conclusion to a syllogism. Such an estimate, I think, doesn't sufficiently come to terms with the "concealed" character of this Christological element, nor does it adequately explain the lack of understanding and despondency characteristic of Jesus' disciples, particularly after Jesus' death. Many scholars have written on this implicit element.[13] Here I will follow our general outline, employed above, of Jesus' preaching, his deeds, and his death, indicating the respective Christological elements involved.

We have seen that Jesus preaches the kingdom of God. In what way, then, does this proclamation involve Jesus himself, implying a Christological claim? Reginald Fuller brings us to the heart of the matter:

> There can be no doubt that in Jesus' perspective the kingdom was future—as indeed it had to be, since it was conceived in apocalyptic terms. Yet it is doing less than justice to ἔφθασεν ("has come") in Matt. 12.28 par. to say that there the kingdom is not actually present, but merely casting its shadow before it.... Let us say, therefore, that the message of Jesus proclaims the *proleptic presence* of the future kingdom of God. In Jesus' ministry God is already beginning his eschatological action, and will shortly consummate it.[14]

Here Fuller is pointing to the distinctive twist that Jesus gives to the ancient notion of the kingdom. Rather than simply a future hope, as for the prophets; rather than simply the expectation of a new age to replace the present one, as for the apocalyptic literature (cf. Dn. 2); for Jesus the kingdom is in realization now through his person (Mk. 1.14–15; Mt. 4.17).

A number of elements will perhaps reinforce this presentness of the kingdom in Jesus' message and person. One might point to the remarkable similarities and yet differences between John the Baptist and Jesus. Both John and Jesus stand within the prophetic tradition; for both the plan of God is imminently expected. Both are associated with the wilderness spirituality of the Hebrew scriptures (Lk. 7.33). The fact that Jesus has himself baptized by John must surely be an authentic Jesus reminiscence which shows that Jesus partially identifies himself with John's prophetic ministry of judgment (Mk. 1.2–11; Mt. 3.13–17; Lk. 3.21–22; Jn. 1.29–34). The reminiscence would have been too scandalous for the post-Easter Church to have simply fabricated it: the early Church had difficulty with this subservient posture of Jesus toward John. Perhaps Jesus' cleansing of the temple should be seen as a typical symbolic prophetic act of judgment, very much in the line of the Baptist's message of judgment (Lk. 3.7–9; Mt. 3.7–12). And yet, what is missing in John and present in Jesus' preaching is the note of joy and happiness (Mt. 11.16–19; Lk. 7.31–35), attitudes that characterize Jesus and his followers. Jesus in fact was accused of being an eater and a drinker, one who consorts with sinners; he is not simply a wilderness ascetic like John. Does this point to an experience of the inbreaking of the kingdom already now in Jesus' ministry? How else can all this be explained?

Further, contemporary research on the parables and proverbial sayings of Jesus[15] brings out the note of the dawning of the kingdom in Jesus' proclamation. It is now fairly well recognized that a solid core of the parable material derives from Jesus himself. Characteristic of his parables is their metaphorical nature: their inexplicability, the element of surprise that they contain, their ability to place the hearer in question and bring him to a new level of self-understanding and decision. To some extent this rather original metaphorical use of the parable by Jesus was transformed into allegory by the New Testament (cf., for example, Mk. 4.13–20), explaining it fully and thus weakening its ability to question and surprise.

In any case, as used by Jesus, the parable was a fit instrument, not simply for instruction, as with the rabbis, but for actually proclaiming the kingdom's presence. This is well brought out in the Good Samaritan parable (Lk. 10.30–36), in which a Jew of Jesus' time, who would have despised a Samaritan, is faced with the inexplicable: a Samaritan who is good. It is this very inexplicability that not only instructs the hearer but challenges him, upsets him, and in so doing sets in motion a process of conversion and entry into God's inbreaking kingdom. Dominic Crossan puts it this way:

> The literal point confronted the hearers with the necessity of saying the impossible and having their world turned upside down and radically questioned in its presuppositions. The metaphorical point is that *just so* does the Kingdom of God break abruptly into a person's consciousness and demand the overturn of prior values, closed options, set judgments and established conclusions. ... The hearer struggling with the dualism of Good Samaritan is actually experiencing in and through this the inbreaking of the Kingdom upon him. *Not only does it happen like this, it happens in this.*[16]

Here we see how the parable in the hands of Jesus actually inaugurates the kingdom, a feature somewhat typical of the parables. In line with this, Crossan notes that a constant theme in the parables is that of reversal: the metaphorical and inexplicable character of the parable, by reversing the hearer's accepted prejudgments about God and man, actually begins the entry of God's kingdom in the hearer's life and consciousness. As examples we might point to the reversal of the human situation in the parable of the Rich Man and Lazarus (Lk. 16.19–31); the reversal of accepted human judgment in the case of the Pharisee and the Publican (Lk. 18.10–14); the situational reversal in the case of the Wedding Guest (Lk. 14.7–11). This note of reversal also characterizes the authentic proverbial sayings of Jesus (Lk. 9.60; Mt. 5.39–41; Mk. 8.35; 10.23, 25, 31; Lk. 14.11; Mk. 3.27, 24–26). Unlike the instructive proverbs characteristic of Jewish literature (Sir. 3.2–4) and also employed by Jesus (Lk. 9.62; Mt. 7.13–14, etc.), these proverbs again actually inaugurate God's holy kingdom through the device of reversal.[17]

We come to the heart of Jesus' proclamation in his use of the Aramaic term *Abba* as an address for God. Clearly the Hebrew scriptures know this title of Fatherhood for God, denoting as it does Israel's election as Yahweh's son (Ex. 4.22; Is. 30.1). In the light of the biblical doctrine of creation, the title could also give expression to God's creative and providential guidance over history (Sir. 23.1; Is. 63.15–16). More common, still, was its use in Jesus' time as a titular appellation for God. Yet, as we have noted, this title is extraordinarily common in the New Testament (170 occurrences) and must reflect in its core an authentic Jesus reminiscence, for Jesus is portrayed—and this is unprecedented—as directly addressing God with this word (Mk. 14.36). This address seems to connote intimacy with God, for it was the address of a child to the parent. As such, it manifests that God is now becoming intimate with his people, becoming love for them in Jesus (Mt. 10.29; 6.8; Lk. 12.30). Yet, too, it connotes respect and obedience for God, a readiness to do his will, for the title was also used by older children of authorities and elders. As such it connotes, much as Jesus' parables and proverbial sayings, that God is now issuing a summons to obedience in Jesus, calling for the change of heart. For this reason Fuller can say: "Jesus can call God 'Abba' because he has known him as the one who has drawn nigh in his own word and deed, and he admits to the same privilege those who have responded to his own eschatological message."[18]

A study, then, of the authentic proclamation of Jesus indicates that in his message God's kingdom is now, in the present, being inaugurated in history. Yet this quality of the presence of the kingdom in Jesus goes hand in hand with another series of authentic Jesus sayings that speak of the future coming of the kingdom (Mt. 6.10; Lk. 11.2). As Fuller indicated above, there is a subtle tension between present and future in Jesus' preaching. This tension simply cannot be eliminated without doing violence to Jesus' preaching.[19] I suggested earlier that the Father-centeredness of Jesus leads us to the view that if Jesus trusted in the Father's presence so radically in the present, we can scarcely doubt that he would have confidence in the Father in the future. That is perhaps a nonexegetical assumption, but it is confirmed when we consider the understanding of God characteristic of Jesus. For God in the preaching of Jesus is not an immobile deity removed from history, but a historical God who opens up a new series of possibilities for history. God, in the biblical view, is, if you will, both the power behind the present and he who makes possible a new future for humanity. The tension between present and future in Jesus' proclamation simply reflects this tension between God's present effectiveness in history through Jesus and the realization of the new possibilities that this will create for mankind. It is because of this view of God that Jesus could speak of and expect the imminent coming of God's kingdom in the future. He was not mistaken in this expectation, for the historical God he preached and experienced would in fact change the future course of history by opening up new possibilities now through Jesus.

Turning now to the authentic deeds of Jesus, again I think we will notice a strongly Christological element involved and implied. For example, as we have seen, although Jesus' miraculous works point to the Father, up-

lift humanity to what the Father wants to do for it, still those miracles occur through the man Jesus: "If it is by the finger of God that I cast out
demons, then the kingdom of God has come upon you" (Lk. 11.20). Yet it
is perhaps to Jesus' actions vis-à-vis Judaism that we should look for the
clearer indication of the inbreaking of the kingdom in Jesus' ministry.
Here we come particularly to the difficult question of Jesus' attitude and
stance toward the Law/Torah of Judaism itself.

Apparently the Jewish attitude toward the Torah was somewhat fluid
and pluralistic in Jesus' time. The gospel portrait of the Pharisees as the
dominant authority over Judaism, with their simply legalistic view of the
Law, simply cannot be validated by historical research and must stem
from the anti-Judaic polemics of the post-70 situation. In fact, the Pharisees[20] appear to have been a more "liberal" lay movement within Judaism
who granted equal supremacy to the oral Torah, thus attempting some
measure of delegalizing of the Law through ongoing tradition. On the other hand, the Sadducees were from the aristocratic and priestly class, admitting only the validity of the written Torah, and in general oriented to the
preservation of the status quo. In terms of similarity to Jesus, we would
have to say that the Pharisees were nearer than the Sadducees. For they
"preached penitence and repentance of sin as the way of bringing in the
kingdom of God."[21] They were not interested in mere legalism, but only in
the complete fulfillment of the Law. Here we notice that they, like much of
Judaism, shared the late Jewish hope of the coming of the kingdom too,
something characteristic of their openness to new ways of understanding.
Further, we know that the Jews of Graeco-Jewish Galilee, where Jesus
spent much of his early ministry, tended to interpret the Torah in a more
spiritualized, Hellenistic manner, thus differing from the strict legal method of interpretation characteristic of Judean Judaism. As Schillebeeckx indicates, "Whereas Aramaic Judaism equated the whole Torah with the
expression of the ordering of creation, Greek Judaism sharpened the distinction between that ordering (*torah* proper) and the man-made laws in
the Mosaic *torah* (as in the matter of the divorce law)."[22]

With our knowledge now of this fluidity in Jewish approaches to the
Law, it is no longer possible simplistically to oppose Jesus to Judaism, setting Law against gospel as it were. Jesus' attitude to the Torah would seem
to share much in common with the Pharisaic and Graeco-Jewish Galileean
stance. Yet, even so, there seems to be a marvelous freedom in Jesus' approach to the Law that transcends Judaism. In Matthew 5 Jesus is remem-
bered as going beyond the Law, thus beyond Moses its author, through his
abolishing of the distinction between the righteous and the unrighteous,
through his coupling of the command to love God with that of loving the
neighbor, and through his more daring command to love the enemy. This
much is surely authentic Jesus material which implies that Jesus can speak
for God himself. He does not simply interpret the Law, as the rabbis; neither does he transmit the Lord's word, as the prophet. Fuller put it well:

"God is directly present in the word of Jesus, actually demanding unreserved obedience to his will from those who have accepted the eschatological message and its offer of salvation (Mk. 1.22, 27; 2.10, etc.)."[23]

It is surely in this light—that Jesus speaks and acts for God on behalf of man—that we should understand the radical summons to discipleship issued by Jesus as well as his table fellowship and acting as host. Discipleship, of course, was something known to the Greek world, as a form of instructional pedagogy; and it was known to later Judaism, as a rabbinic manner of studying the scriptures and religious traditions.[24] Jesus, for his part, appears to share many of the traits of the rabbi-disciple *(talmid)* relationship: he teaches in the synagogue and, like the rabbis, he proclaims God's will; he engages in discussions on questions of the Law; and he is even called "rabbi," while his disciples are known as the *talmidim,* the technical term for a rabbi's disciples. Yet, here again, Jesus appears to remarkably transcend the rabbi-disciple relationship, thus, I think, indicating that a new access to God is opening up through him. He does not confine his teaching to the synagogue, but engages in it everywhere, even in the open fields (cf. Mt. 5). His credentials are questionable (Mk. 6.2f; Jn. 7.15), for he does not present himself as the graduate of a famous rabbi. Neither, as we have seen, does he confine himself to simply expounding the Law, for he overturns it in some cases (Mk. 1.22, 10.2–9).

Equally startling is Jesus' relationship with his disciples. The disciple of Jesus will permanently remain such (Mt. 23.8, 10.24f); it is not a temporary position leading to the rank of rabbi. The disciple does not choose Jesus; Jesus summons him (Mk. 1.16f; Jn. 1.35–42) and demands of him radical renunciation and obedience (Mk. 8.34). All must be sacrificed: one's occupation (Mk. 1.18, 10.28); one's family (Lk. 14.25f); even marriage (Mt. 19.11f); personal possessions (Mk. 10.21). One must be prepared to follow the master in suffering, hatred, persecution, and even death (Lk. 9.58; Mt. 8.19; Lk. 21.16; Mk. 8.34–35; Jn. 8.31f). Such a radical summons amounts, I think, to a Christological claim: it is because God is approaching man in Jesus that the disciple must respond with this utmost seriousness, even to the point of death.

The problem of Jesus' fellowship at meals, particularly with outcasts and sinners (Mt. 14.14–21; Lk. 9.11–17; Mk. 8.1–9),[25] also takes on special meaning in the light of Jesus' claim actually to usher in God's eschatological kingdom. To understand properly the meaning which the sharing of a meal carried in Jesus' ministry we must pause for a moment to consider the origin and meaning of Jewish "feasts" in general. Although we cannot be certain, very likely Israel's feasts were originally either nature festivals or borrowed from neighboring religions. Through the genius of its own historical experience Israel gradually historicized these feasts, attaching them to key events in its own past. For example, the Passover, originally a spring festival celebrated by the various nomadic Jewish tribes, was transformed into a celebration of the Exodus. This celebration did not simply "remind" the Jew of the liberation from Egypt. As Marxsen expresses it,

"The distinctive feature of these 'remembrances' is that the time-gap was, as it were, nullified, and these events of the past were now conceived of not as happenings cut off in the past but as experiences shared in the present."[26] Furthermore, this and other Jewish festivals undergo an "eschatologization" when the post-exilic writers begin to develop the eschatological genre. Thus, for example, not only does the Passover look *back* to the Exodus; it looks *forward* to the future realization of God's promises for Israel. It becomes a feast of messianic expectation. Zechariah, in reference to the feast of Tabernacles, brings this note of eschatologization out in his description of the last days: "All who are left of all the nations that came against Jerusalem shall come up year after year to worship the King, the Lord of hosts, and to celebrate the feast of booths" (14.16).

In such a light, it was not a surprising development when the last days were envisaged as a meal at Yahweh's table. Here, for the Jewish mind, it was assumed that Jews could not dine with gentiles nor with the ritually impure or unrighteous. For the meal celebrated the coming of Yahweh's kingdom; it mediated fellowship with God. Now perhaps we can grasp the full force of Jesus' gracious table fellowship with outcasts. In Marxsen's striking words:

> With these ideas as the background we can see what an unprecedented thing it was when Jesus invited sinners and tax-collectors to his table. This was not just ordinary human kindness. It was much more. Jesus re-incorporated these people into the covenant with God, and here and now gave these very people whom strict Jews looked down on a share in the coming kingdom of God. This is an essential feature of the message of Jesus: he offers fellowship with God without attaching conditions which must first be fulfilled. Paul later expresses this as "justification of the sinner without the works of the Law."[27]

More and more, then, the conclusion forces itself upon us that, although the Jesus of history appears before us as radically oriented to the Father, still that Father does not wish to separate himself from Jesus. It is in and through the man Jesus, apparently, that the Father's kingdom and his good works are dawning in history. This insight is terribly important now, as we enter into the difficult terrain of the Christological dimension of Jesus' death. I have already indicated that, if we keep in mind the public nature of Jesus' death, we can plausibly argue that it is Jesus' Father-centeredness and the consequences he drew from that which brought him to his fateful opposition to Judaism and Rome. Our question now is, however, what Jesus' death might tell us about Jesus himself.

Was Jesus' death simply an accidental fate that violently overtook him because of his radical trust in the Father, or does this death reveal something essential about Jesus himself, about *his* role in the coming of God's kingdom into human history? Here, of course, we must be quite careful, for the state of our sources will permit only hypotheses. To my mind, the most plausible explanation is that of Reginald Fuller.[28] We must fully recognize, first, that most of the sayings of Jesus about his death reveal the influence of post-Easter Christology (viz., the passion predictions) or soteriology (viz., Mk. 10.45b and 14.24 on the "cup word"). Yet Fuller, following J. Wellhausen, regards two passages as authentic Jesus material: Lk. 13.32–33 and Mk. 14.25. The first regards Jesus' exorcisms and healings that, as we have seen, are part of God's eschatological action through the man Jesus: "Go tell that fox, 'Today and tomorrow I cast out devils and perform cures, and on the third day my purpose is accomplished. For all that, I must proceed on course today, tomorrow, and the day after, since no prophet can be allowed to die anywhere except in Jerusalem.' "

Here we note that Jesus' death, apparently lacking any post-Easter influence, is seen to be the ultimate outcome of Jesus' eschatological actions. "Jesus goes up to Jerusalem," says Fuller, "not simply in order to die, which as J. Knox has contended, would be morbidly pathological and tantamount to suicide, but in order to continue his eschatological ministry."[29] I am not sure that Jesus goes up to Jerusalem specifically to issue an eschatological challenge at the center of Judaism, as Fuller indicates. It is perhaps not precisely a challenge, as if Jesus were trying to force his death, but a prophetic symbolization of his eschatological vocation, in the line of the prophets (Is. 56.7; Jer. 7.11). But in any case we can plausibly assume that Jesus knew this prophetic act might very well involve the possibility of death. For we must remember that Jesus was very likely aware of the fate of the Baptist (Mk. 6.14–29; 9.13). Further, the gospels all record the increasingly violent opposition Jesus had encountered (Mk. 2.7; Mt. 12.24; Mk. 2.23–24; Lk. 13.14–15; Mk. 3.2, etc.), and it is quite unlikely that someone of Jesus' sensitivity could not have entertained the radical consequences of such opposition. Finally, and possibly most importantly, in some circles "martyrdom was at that time considered to be inherent in the prophetic vocation."[30]

Our second Jesus saying stems from the supper tradition: "I solemnly assure you, I will never again drink of the fruit of the vine until the day when I drink it new in the reign of God" (Mk. 14.25). Although a part of the general, post-Easter supper tradition (Mk. 14.17–25; 1 Cr. 11.23–25)—thought to be post-Easter because of its liturgical stylization—this particular saying was progressively eliminated from this tradition and so can be considered authentic Jesus material. Here Jesus seems to associate his death directly with the eschatological banquet of the end-time. In the light of everything else we know of Jesus' death, we are surely entitled to say that Jesus views his death as a part of God's eschatological action through him.

The question naturally arises at this point as to whether Jesus viewed his death as a salvific action for others. As the scholars put it, does the death reveal an implicit soteriological claim? Certainly if God's eschatological kingdom was indeed being inaugurated through Jesus, then the kerygma was clearly only bringing to expression in its belief in Jesus as the Savior what was already the case in a more concealed and ambiguous manner in Jesus' ministry. Note how the kerygma speaks of the death, possibly under the influence of Isaiah's suffering-servant theme (Is. 53.1–12), as expiatory and salvific (1 Cr. 11.24; Mk. 14.24). One can plausibly argue, I think, that if Jesus regarded his death as God's eschatological action, then clearly this implies a soteriological claim. As Kasper expresses it, ". . . the Kingdom of God is the essence of salvation."[31] But might we go further?

Here we are inevitably speculating, but we can say that the particular form that God's eschatological kingdom takes in Jesus is that of agape and service. The texts that record this facet of Jesus' ministry (Lk. 22.27; Mk. 9.35, 10.28, 8.34–35) are very likely authentic, for the Easter Church had difficulty in passing them on in the tradition. Just as Jesus regarded his death as a prophetic, eschatological action, could we not say that he saw it as a supreme act of service and agape for mankind? This fits the entire tenor of his ministry, surely, and doesn't make of his death the "grand exception" in his life. While this hypothesis does not mean that the last supper sayings or passion predictions are authentic Jesus material, it does at least enable us to argue for an authentic historical core to these traditions.

Against this background of substantial Jesus material indicating what we might call an implicit Christological and soteriological dimension in Jesus' ministry, it is a relatively secondary question as to whether Jesus himself actually self-designated himself by any of the titles later applied to him by the post-Easter Church.[32] It is sufficient to note that these titles are giving expression to what was already entering history in the man Jesus. Furthermore, the fact that exegetes have not been able to achieve a consensus on this issue indicates, I think, the ambiguity that surrounds the historical Jesus, an ambiguity that is only clarified in the post-Easter situation. This ambiguity, indicated by the tradition of the disciples' failing to comprehend Jesus both during his ministry and after his death, must be taken seriously in any reconstruction of the genesis of the Christ-belief. Apparently, what was happening in Jesus simply did not fit the established categories or titles of the time. This is what we mean by the concealed character of the Jesus of history. If indeed God was inaugurating the eschatological kingdom now in Jesus, this was an event unparalleled in Jewish thought. It would mean that the ancient prophetic hope of a future kingdom was in process now. It would also break through the apocalyptic expectation of a transcendent kingdom to replace the present one. Apparently the standard honorific titles for religious figures would first have to be "reworked" in the light of Jesus before they could adequately correspond to the reality that he was. This is the fundamental hermeneutical principle to maintain in any consideration of whether Jesus himself employed titles as a designation for his own person and work.

Among the varied titles possibly used by Jesus as a self-designation— Messiah, Son of David, Servant, Kyrios, Son of Man, and Prophet—so far as I can tell serious debate centers around only that of Messiah, Son of Man, and Prophet. This is not to deny that the other titles do not have some foundation in the historical Jesus which, in the light of the post-Easter situation, would enable the disciples to apply them to Jesus. This is most clearly the case with the title "Son of God," so popular in the gospels, yet never used by Jesus himself. Here we can note how this title gives expression to Jesus' own filial relationship to the Father, his radical Father-centeredness, which finds expression in his speaking of "my Father" (Mk. 14.36, always carefully distinguished from "your Father" [Lk. 6.36] or "your heavenly Father" [Mk. 11.25]).

Any consideration of Jesus' possible use of the title Messiah must begin from the consideration that the gospels never portray Jesus as actually using it; only his disciples apply it to him (Mk. 8.27–33; 14.61f). This surely must be authentic, and we are entitled to draw the conclusion that Jesus refuses this title precisely because of its unclear meaning in the Judaism of his time. From originally referring to the king as Yahweh's "anointed" one *(messiah)* (see 1 Sm. 10.1), and then the king's heir as a future salvific figure (Am. 9, 11; Is. 9.6–7; Jer. 33.15–17, etc.), the title is generalized and can variously apply to a suffering servant of God (Is. 42.1–7), to Daniel's apocalyptic Son of Man (7.13), and even to the two messianic figures written of at Qumran: the king and high priest. Apparently, this title carries either political or apocalyptic connotations that, we can surmise, Jesus wishes to distance himself from.

Yet we must say that when the post-Easter Church begins to attribute this title to Jesus, such an application is not purely without foundation in the ministry of Jesus. Wrede's position, which as we earlier saw regards Jesus' messiahship as purely a fabrication by Mark, is too simple. Albert Schweitzer had already noted this when he maintained that we can only account for Jesus' death on the basis of *some* messianic, eschatological claim.[33] I have already proposed that Jesus was executed, not because he was mistaken for a zealotic, political pretender, but because his message completely overturned and challenged such pretensions. Jesus was, if you will, really experienced already in his ministry as transcending the up-to-then messianic claims. This "new" form of messiahship is sufficient to account for the trial and the title over the cross (Mk. 15.26), without directly attributing the title to Jesus himself. At the same time, the post-Easter Church is able to take the step of naming Jesus Messiah in a way now clarified by the experience of the cross. If you will, a new messianism was breaking into history.

Did Jesus designate himself the "Son of Man"? Perhaps no title has spawned as much controversy as this one.[34] This exegetical interest seems motivated by the fact that the Son of Man sayings are always found to be those of Jesus himself, with the exception of Acts 7.56, and this some eighty times in all. This argues that here we have to do with an authentic Jesus tradition which might well clarify Jesus' own self-understanding, even if many of these sayings have been secondarily added to in the tradition as we know it. Following Fuller, whose approach seems moderate and current,[35] we need to distingush two main problems: (1) the derivation of the term and (2) its use in the gospels. With regard to origin, there is widespread agreement now that we must look to the apocalyptic literature of second and first-century Jewish literature: ". . . there is a body of evidence which, on a plausible interpretation, indicates that the figure of the Son of Man as the pre-existent divine agent of judgment and salvation was embedded in the pre-Christian Jewish apocalyptic tradition" [cf. Dn. 7.13f].[36]

When we turn to the gospels, we find three different kinds of sayings: those referring to (1) a suffering son of man, (2) a present and a (3) future son of man. The suffering sayings (Mk. 8.31, 9.31, 10.33–34, etc.) are missing from the early sayings source "Q" and are all in Mark, who, as we will see, most stresses the suffering dimension of Jesus against a false, exalted view of Christ in the fashion of the Hellenistic cults. This need not argue that Mark has simply fabricated the title, for the element of suffering is certainly a central feature of Jesus' ministry. The other series of sayings, however, are found in both Mark and Q, and never are they in the form of a confession of faith (the mark of a post-Easter development). This would seem to argue for their authenticity.

More difficult is the meaning of the present and future sayings as used by Jesus. While Jesus *seems* to identify himself with the present son of man (Mk. 2.10, 28; 8.20; 11.9; Lk. 17.22, 26), he draws a clear distinction between himself and the future figure (Mk. 8.38; Lk. 12.8). Why this distinction? Presumably Jesus saw some connection between himself and this figure, and yet he could not go so far as to identify himself with him. On the basis of Luke 12.8f Fuller suggests the following view:

> The distinction between Jesus and the coming Son of man corresponds to the distinction between the kingdom as it is breaking through in Jesus and its final consummation. Jesus is not concerned to impart teaching about the future Son of man, any more than he imparts teaching about the future kingdom or indulges in apocalyptic elaboration.[37]

This view has the merit of pointing out just why Jesus should have bothered to speak at all of this mysterious figure, and yet why he could not simply identify himself with this agent. Undoubtedly the term was apt for expressing the tension within Jesus' own experience itself between the kingdom's inauguration and yet its futurity. It corresponds to the tension in Jesus' experience of God as both Lord of the present and the future; the historical God who by acting in history actually opens up a new future for it.

Fuller reluctantly does not accept the authenticity of the "present" sayings, despite the fact that they are in both Mark and Q, mainly because they do not seem to derive from an apocalyptic framework. It is possibly easy to recognize the Marcan sayings as later Church formulations (Mk. 2.10, 28), but the Q sayings (Mt. 8.20, 11.19: "the Son of Man has nowhere to lay his head" and "the Son of Man appeared eating and drinking, and they say, 'This one is a glutton and drunkard . . .' ") seem to fit rather well into what we know of the ministry of Jesus. Despite the fact that this usage cannot be derived from apocalyptic, might one not be permitted to postulate a certain amount of originality on Jesus' part? Most of these sayings concern Jesus' poverty, service, and suffering, and it just this aspect of Jesus' ministry that was most novel, calling for new usages and categories.

The point of view taken here on the Son of Man passages represents what could be called a moderate position. On the other hand, were one to take a more radical position, what might the result be? There is a body of scholarship which would maintain that the Son of Man cannot be said to be clearly a title for a heavenly figure; rather in Daniel 7 it simply refers to the "saints of the Most High." This view would maintain that Son of Man was not then a title at all in Daniel, and because of this it infers that Jesus could not have so employed it. Hence, it looks to the early Church as the originator of its use. Yet, one can say in response that if this is indeed the case, then it seems unlikely that the Church would have invented its use as a title for Jesus. Simply put, no precedent existed for this, and there must have been some catalyst bringing its use into being as a title. Might not this argue for Jesus' own original use of it, at least in the sense that Jesus' usage is the underlying core of its employment in the New Testament? In any case, the issue is far from settled in biblical research.

Finally, the issue of whether Jesus designated himself a prophet—or possibly was thought to be such—has received a renewed emphasis from both Walter Kasper and Edward Schillebeeckx, two prominent Christologians of our day. Kasper simply says: "The best description for him is 'prophet' . . . not just one in the line of the prophets, but the eschatological one: the last, definitive, all-transcending prophet."[38] Schillebeeckx is more forceful, for he regards the title of eschatological prophet as one most likely made prior to Easter and, more basically, as the "matrix of all the other honorific titles and credal strands" in the New Testament. In his words:

> That the link between the earthly Jesus and the kerygmatic Christ is the recognition, common to all credal strands, of the earthly Jesus as the eschatological prophet (who does, it is true, surpass all expectations) and that this identification (at least as question and surmise) was most likely made prior to Easter, has enormous consequences. It points to a considerable continuity between the impression that Jesus made during his earthly days and the apparently "advanced Christology" of the Church's *kerygmata* or affirmation of belief after his death.[39]

Schillebeeckx does not appear to cite Fuller at this point, but this was the latter's contention also: "Take the implied self-understanding of his role in terms of the eschatological prophet away, and the whole ministry falls into a series of unrelated, if not meaningless fragments."[40]

Very likely Jesus was regarded as a prophet by some of his contemporaries. Mark 6.15 and 8.27f report that some of his disciples regard him as "one of the prophets" (εἰς τῶν προφητῶν), a Semitism for one belonging to the general prophetic type. This reminiscence survives in Luke 7.39, 24.19, and Matthew 21.11, 46, although perhaps these latter are post-Easter secondary elaborations. The Q source lacks any reference to this popular estimate of Jesus, but Fuller attributes this to the absence of narrative material characteristic of that source. Further, Mark 6.14f and 8.28 would seem to be authentic reminiscences indicating that Jesus was thought by some to be either a John the Baptist *redivivus* or an Elijah *redivivus*.[41] As Fuller explains it, this means that some thought of Jesus as an eschatological prophet, "not indeed in the sense that the End was breaking through with him, but in the sense that he was the immediate herald of the End."[42] Yet one wonders whether this identification of the eschatological figure with Jesus, who *actually exists* in history, doesn't break through this apocalyptic framework, which thought of Elijah and the Baptist as *symbols* for the future age. Doesn't this indicate that at least some thought that the kingdom was now actually entering into history through this really existing eschatological prophet?

Further, although Jesus never actually designates himself a prophet, he does liken his fate of rejection and possible martyrdom to that of the prophets (Mk. 6.4; Lk. 13.33). And, when one surveys the ministry of Jesus, a great many prophetic traits surface: he uses the prophetic "I came" and "I was sent" (Lk. 12.49; Mk. 2.17); his sense of authority readily reminds one of the prophets' stance of judgment; and if Mark 3.29 is authentic, Jesus then indicates that he considers his baptism by John to be an anointing with the Spirit in the sense of an eschatological-prophetic mission (cf. Is. 61.1). Yet, the collection of sayings in the Q material (Mt. 23.29f, 34–36, 37) goes further: "The finality of the judgments pronounced over Israel at the end of each of these sayings (vv. 31, 36 and 38) indicates that Jesus thought of his mission not only as belonging to the same class as that of the Old Testament prophets, but as representing the final prophetic mission to Israel, and of his own rejection (and possible martyrdom) as the culmination of Israel's rejection of the word of Yahweh."[43] Here we have then, not an explicit, but at least a functional and implicit identity between Jesus and the eschatological prophet.

Thus we are faced with a considerable body of material which indicates that, although Jesus appears in history as a man radically centered on God the Father and what that Father will do for humanity (the kingdom), yet that kingdom is known to be breaking into history now in the person of this man Jesus. God's kingdom and Jesus cannot be separated. The divine kingdom as we encounter it in Jesus "implies" a Christology and soteriology that will later find its formulation in the New Testament's kerygma.

Perhaps we should pause for a moment and consider the meaning of what we have studied so far. Jesus' message of the Father's kingdom can be "historically" illuminated when we consider the horizon of Jewish expectations in his own time. This kingdom-notion originally derives from Jewish belief in Yahweh's dominion over history and nature, something often celebrated in Israel's psalter (Pss. 91.1, 96.10, 97.1, 47.6–9, 145.3). Through the experience of the exiles this kingdom-notion undergoes an eschatologization: Yahweh's great saving deeds of the past no longer seem evident; they become, then, hopes for the future, in which a new covenant and exodus will occur (see Jer. 31). During the later period of Helleniza-tion the notion undergoes a further transformation in the apocalyptic liter-ature: now the hoped for future kingdom will not be a reestablishment of the covenant and exodus, but a wholly new age with truly divine qualities (cf. Dn. 2.34–44). In summary, the kingdom-notion is a conceptual extrap-olation giving expression to a profound trust in Yahweh as sovereign of history. It is an expression of hope and faith.[44]

As we have seen, Jesus chooses this kingdom-conceptuality to give ex-pression to his central message: he, too, trusts that Yahweh is Lord of his-tory who can be counted upon to save humanity. But we must go further and ask ourselves whether we can still find meaning in this proclamation today. No doubt exists that we today do not expect "salvation" in every re-spect in just the way that the biblical ancients did. We are to a great extent historically conscious and so aware that we ourselves make and contribute to history. We "save" ourselves to some extent, and this in many ways: through technology, medicine, learning, social and institutional reform, etc. This has led some to the conclusion that a belief in God's Lordship is mythological, and should be dispensed with. And yet we can still say—at this point only in a preliminary manner—that there still remains the hu-man quest and need for ultimate meaning and hope, and most of all for un-conditioned love. Our very historical consciousness presupposes this more fundamental hope and possibility of meaning; without it, we simply would not "make" history. But these fundamental attitudes which actually "found" our human existence cannot be simply "created" by man; they re-quire a transcendent ground to make them possible and sustain them. Per-haps here we have a point of contact between our own self-understanding and what was being said in the ancient biblical notion of God's holy king-dom. God still founds and rules history; it is still his kingdom.

But we have not yet touched upon the rather radical "twist" that Je-sus gives to his proclamation of this kingdom. For in and through his per-son he, and possibly some of his contemporaries already during his earthly ministry, believe that this hoped for kingdom is now finally breaking into history. It is in this sense that scholars speak of Jesus' bringing to "fulfill-ment" the prophetic kingdom-hope and "breaking through" the apocalyp-tic notion of a future kingdom that will simply replace history as we know it. God's offer of salvation and Jesus cannot be separated, if this Christo-logical claim be taken seriously. This belief, too, needs to be paused over, in view of our current horizon of self-understanding. For we are heirs of the Enlightenment, of the intellectual tradition that proclaims the auton-omy of the individual and of his potential freedom through knowledge. This we have already seen in an earlier chapter. Yet it must be asked whether this is not a too highly individualistic notion of the human person, as if the individual achieved autonomy in an isolated manner, completely on his own. The founders of the so-called "Second Enlightenment"—

Marx, Freud, Durkheim, Weber, etc.—had already seen through this individualism when they recognized to what an extent man's selfhood is co-constituted by the society and institutions in which he finds himself. In other words, the realization of our humanity is always "mediated" through history: through other persons, events, institutions, etc. The crucial question is not whether it should be mediated, but what/who does the mediating? This recovery of the mediated notion of the person—of the person as becoming through relationships in history—is, I think, of great significance for the biblical claim that God's kingdom is mediated through the person of Jesus.[45] Perhaps we can still give meaning, then, to the dawning of the kingdom in Jesus if we regain a thoroughly historical view of ourselves as becoming in and through our historical relations. As I try to indicate in my chapter on soteriology, the doctrine of the mediatorship of Jesus is a corrective to a onesided, a-worldly and nonhistorical view of salvation. Salvation, like all things human, must be humanly mediated. But, as I will also try to show, we must perhaps regain a more historical notion of God, too, of a God who mediates himself through history to humanity. This is the ultimate foundation for the doctrine of the mediatorship of salvation through the Christ.

In any case there can be little doubt that in the expectant, salvation-yearning atmosphere of Jesus' time, Jesus appeared as one offering new hope for men and women. This salvific character of Jesus is undoubtedly what attracted attention to him: Herod thought he was a fool (Lk. 23.6–12); his relatives think him mad (Mk. 3.21); but some, as we have seen, wonder whether he might not be a prophet, and indeed the eschatological prophet (Mk. 6.14–16; 8.28). His message of a God who is for humanity, and that unconditionally and radically—transcending all the known "conditions" of Jesus' time—and of this God breaking into history through himself must be seen as the historical ground and basis for the New Testament's later kerygma. And yet that kerygma cannot be simply logically deduced from this Jesus of history. For Jesus remains ambiguous— "concealed," we have said. One simply cannot eliminate the misunderstanding, doubt, and eventual disowning of Jesus by the disciples from an account of the genesis of the Christ-belief. This disavowal of Jesus by the disciples, after his death, is noted by all the gospels (Mk. 14.50, 51–52; Jn. 16.32; Mt. 13.57, 26.31, 35; Lk. 7.23). Further, there is a tendency in the gospels to be somewhat embarrassed about this and to mollify it, and this is surely a mark of authenticity. For the Marcan rebuke of Peter (14.37–38) undergoes a toning down in Luke 22.45–46 and John 18.8.[46] It seems that Mark especially has a tendency to present the disciples in a bad light, possibly because of his thematic purpose of rebuking a false, Hellenistic view of Christ (viz., the disciples may represent this view), yet the denial of Jesus cannot be eliminated or overlooked; it is too embedded in the tradition.

There is, I think, also a profoundly theological reason for the ambiguity of the historical Jesus. It clearly does not stem from God's or Jesus' desire to trick or deceive. Nor does it simply stem from the incredulity and stubborness of the disciples. Rather does it come from the manner in which God is now entering into history. For God's kingdom is being inaugurated in a man who speaks of a God that should be directly addressed as *Abba,* a God who simply wants to love man unconditionally; a man who says that God wants to free man from the restrictions and conditions imposed by man-made legalisms; a God who wants to spread his table with all, especially outcasts and sinners; and most of all, a God of service, suffering, and the cross. Such a God was simply unexpected in the Judaism of Jesus' time; necessarily he would have to come in the form of concealment and ambiguity. As we will see, a new revelation of God is entering history through Jesus. Yet, the New Testament records that this ambiguity surrounding Jesus was, if not precisely removed, at least seen through; that the disciples' disavowal of Jesus became faith in Jesus.

In the end, the shift to Jesus himself means, as Gordon Kaufman put it, "that the christian Church is a community which explicitly and openly believes that in some decisive fashion God manifested himself in these particular events [of Jesus], that is, it believes its historical ground to be its true ontological ground."[47] But this belief was the result of a rather long reflective process, according to the reconstruction of the biblical critics. Whether this development occurred in a linear fashion, one phase following upon the other, or whether we have to do with simultaneous and moving points of view,[48] is not yet decided among the critics.

Further, biblical scholarship seems now to be in a process of reformulating just how the Christological development that culminated in the New Testament actually occurred. Widely accepted has been the view that we can delineate an early Palestinian, a later Palestinian-Hellenistic, and a very late Hellenistic form of Christological thinking. But evidence is accumulating that this delineation is perhaps too neat, that we must rather think of a constant interpenetration between Judaism and Hellenism throughout all the forms of Christology represented in the New Testament. We have already seen how Hellenism influenced Jewish thought on the Torah in Galilee already during the historical ministry of Jesus, and such Hellenistic influence must be seen as at least an open possibility for the entire New Testament. But the influence works the other way, too: we must think of the possibility of a constant Jewish influence for the entire New Testament. In any case, we must at least recognize that there is a plurality of Christologies in the New Testament, that these Christologies were to some extent the result of a slow and reflective development, and that it is possible to argue that either Palestinian or Hellenistic modes of thought—or both—seem to be the predominant emphases of these Christologies.

According to the biblical witness each of these Christologies is grounded upon a dramatic event called the "resurrection" that set in motion a process of reevaluation of Jesus and converted the early Christian disciples from shocked and fearful men following Jesus' death to believing followers of Jesus.

Among the Jewish/Palestinian Christians the reevaluation of Jesus took a characteristically Jewish point of view. What captured their imagination and turned their attention to the future realization of God's plan for the world was the resurrection belief itself. Jesus' resurrection was seen as a sign of the future and final breaking in of God's kingdom. This was necessarily a Jewish point of view, for Jewish reflection on the afterlife had come to associate a general resurrection of the dead with the end of time (Hos. 6.1–2; Is. 26.19; Dn. 12.1–3; Eno. 51; Bar. 50; 4 Esd. 7.29f). This belief may in part have been influenced by contact with Zoroastrian speculation on the future, but more immediately it was linked to the Jewish trust in Yahweh, a God of promises and fulfillment. As Gerald O'Collins put it, "In the faith of Israel belief in resurrection emerged as a corollary of theism."[49] This belief, held by the Pharisees, is alluded to in the New Testament (Mk. 12.18; Acts 23.8), and Jesus himself may have presupposed it in his preaching (Mk. 12.25; Mt. 8.11–12; 24.30–31; 25.31–32). In any case, the resurrection belief caused the Jewish Christians to associate Jesus with the dawning of the final age, an insight that we gather from the titles used to describe Jesus, especially in the synoptics.

In this light, the Jewish title "Messiah" ("*Christos*" in the Greek), found frequently in the synoptics and Acts (cf. 3.20) became apt for expressing Jesus' role as the bringer of the hoped-for messianic era of the final days, though to be sure the title was freed from the nationalistic and political connotations it carried owing to its roots in Jewish monarchical thinking (the monarch was the "anointed one," i.e., the Messiah). The note of universalism in Jesus' message, and his relativization of the importance of power, demanded this reunderstanding of the Messiah-concept, and it is for this reason that scholars speculate that its application to Jesus must have been the result of a slow reflective process.[50] The important notion of the "Son of Man," associated in Daniel 17 with the final era (cf. also Ez. 2.1; Pss. 8.4, 80.17–18; Eno. 48.2f.; 4 Ez. 13), also became apt as a title for Jesus (Acts 7.55–56), though it, too, has undergone a process of rethinking in the light of Jesus' ministry and death, insofar as this figure is not only the glorious, quasi-transcendent figure spoken of in Daniel, but a suffering servant-like figure (Mk. 8.31, 10.45). Other indications of this Jewish Christology are the titles "Son of David" (Rev. 3.7, 5.5), "Son of God" (Lk. 1.32) and the "New Moses" (Acts 3.12–26). Perhaps too the gospel genealogies (Mt. 1.1–17; Lk. 3.23–38), which situate Jesus in the climactic position in Jewish history, were ways of highlighting Jesus' role as the harbinger of the "final days."

Because elements of this Jewish Christology resurface in Paul (Rm. 1.3–4) and in the circles influenced by him (Phil. 2. 6–11; 1 Pt. 3.18), it is probably best to imagine these Christologies as partially simultaneous and live options throughout the New Testament period. Yet, simultaneous though they are, one can discern a line of progress and development in thinking too. This becomes quite clear in the case of Paul, who initiates another main Christological style of thinking in his use of the title "Lord" for Jesus. Paul spans both the Jewish and the Hellenistic world, raised a Jew as he was yet born in the Hellenistic city of Tarsus. Thus we can infer that Paul's Christology is a fusion of Jewish and Hellenistic elements. Just what caused Paul to prefer the title "Lord" must be inferred by the biblical critic. Surely Paul's own religious experience[51] of conversion fostered in him a consciousness of Jesus' empowering presence in his life. Surely, too, the seeming delay of the "final day" and Paul's non-Jewish, gentile audience must have made the Jewish Christology inappropriate for Paul. In any case, the notion of "Lord," as we shall see, attributed a more active and divine role to the resurrected Jesus in the lives of Christians, and for this reason Dermot Lane says: "This particular confession was a major Christological advance, the implications of which took time to be fully absorbed."[52]

Thus, "Lord" seems to be Paul's preferred designation for Jesus: "For if you confess with your mouth 'Jesus is Lord!' and you believe in your innermost self that God raised him from death, you will be saved" (Rm. 10.9). Sometimes Paul fuses this newer designation with the Jewish Christology: "For we do not proclaim ourselves, but Jesus Christ [Jewish] as Lord [Jewish-Hellenistic], and ourselves as your slaves with respect to Jesus" (2 Cr. 4.5). Originally this title was used in the Greek Septuagint translation of the Old Testament for the Hebrew "Yahweh." By applying it to Jesus Paul was attributing to him Yahweh's task of social governance over his realm. It is not simple identification with Yahweh, but identification with one of Yahweh's functions that Paul attributes to Jesus.[53] The term did not carry the arbitrary and tyrannical connotations of the Greek *despotes,* but linked Jesus to the faithful and caring form of mastery that Yahweh displayed in the forming of the Covenant. The term was apt for expressing Jesus' risen presence among his disciples, despite the delay of the final day. It "exalted" Jesus to God's sphere, as the use of Psalm 110.1 in Romans 8.34, Ephesians 1.20, Colossians 3.1, and especially Acts 32. 34–37 showed: "The Lord [Yahweh] said to my Lord [Jesus], sit at my right hand, till I make Thy enemies a stool for Thy feet."

Dermot Lane has helpfully suggested that, owing to the two poles of Paul's audience—Jewish monotheism and Greek polytheism respectively—the term "Lord" acts as a bridge to the later designation of Jesus as "God."[54] It is not that Paul really wanted to call Jesus "God" but was forestalled by his audience. This would not be a historically conscious view of the matter, for it would lift Paul above the historical conditioning of his own epoch. Rather, Paul had probably not yet moved to the stage when "God" as a title was a live option as a designation for Jesus. Thus Paul does not "subordinate" Jesus to God (despite 1 Cr. 15.28) but likely does not even ask whether Jesus is God. In any case, for Paul's Jewish audience the title "God" always referred to the "Father," given the reality of monotheism. As Lane puts it,

> To call Jesus "God" within this situation . . . would have been too sudden a transition. Furthermore any such designation could easily have appeared to border on blasphemy for early christian Jews. Moreover this strong monotheistic climate was perpetuated by the fact that the first christian Jews continued to frequent the Jewish temple in Jerusalem. This fact alone would have made it an anathema to call Jesus "God."[55]

Similarly Paul's Hellenistic audience would have likened Jesus to one of their many "gods" in the polytheistic pantheon had Paul referred to Jesus as "God" in their presence. Paul seems quite consciously aware of the possibility of regression to polytheistic thinking, and thus is careful to affirm the truth of monotheism while maintaining Jesus' exalted status: "For although there may be so-called gods in heaven or on earth—as indeed there are many 'gods' and many 'lords'—yet for us there is one God, the Father . . . and one Lord, Jesus Christ, through whom are all things and through whom we exist" (cf. also Eph. 4.5; 1 Tm. 2.5; Gal. 3.20). We find this balance between monotheism and Jesus-centrism consistently present in Paul and circles influenced by him: (1) the parallelisms "Spirit of God"—Spirit of Christ" and "love of God—love of Christ" (Rm. 8.9, 35, 39); (2) the varied descriptions of Jesus as God's "agent" in creation (1 Cr. 8.6; Col. 1.16), the "form" (Phil 2.6) and "image" (2 Cr. 4.4; Col. 1.5) of God, reflecting God's "glory" (2 Cr. 4.6), the dwelling of God's fullness (Col. 1.19).

Paul's influence was enormously important in the early Church and undoubtedly both gave expression to the growing faith of the Church and prepared the way for our next, more purely Hellenistic and also most dramatic Christology found in the New Testament: that which attributes "deity" to Jesus. Undoubtedly a number of more immediate factors must have fostered this development. The fall of Jerusalem in A.D. 70 caused Pharisaism to reorganize Judaism and to grow further alienated from the growing Christian movement. This tended to distance Christians from Jewish monotheism, and while Christianity never departed from monotheism, it did gain the distance needed to rethink its meaning in the light of Jesus. Further, Raymond Brown thinks that the central role of Jesus in the Christian liturgy would have lent itself to the confession of Jesus' deity.[56] Finally, one should not overlook the political fact that Christians were increasingly being forced to assert the deity of the Roman emperors—confessing Jesus' deity may well have been a partial attempt to correct this Roman tendency (1 Pt. 3.15; Rev. 17.14).

The "Hellenistic" character of this third Christological style of thought can be inferred in a number of ways. We know, for example, that the problems of fate *(moira)* and death were of key concern in the Greek imagination, rather than the issue of national deliverance, which so occupied the Jewish mind. Thus the tendency of this Christology to portray Jesus as God's mediator (the Greek *Logos*) breaking through the endless cycle of life by leaving his eternal home and entering into the human plight to redeem man. Fuller[57] describes this as a three-stage Christology: Jesus as the (1) pre-existent one, (2) entering into the human plight through an incarnation that is God's epiphany, and (3) saving man through an ascension that breaks through the endless cycle of eternal return (Jn. 1; Phil. 2.6–11; 1 Cr. 8.6; Hb.; 1 Pt. 1.20). Further, this style of Christological thinking is more purely reflective and philosophical; it adds to the "functional" and salvation-oriented Christologies above a more probing analysis of the person of the Savior. The progressive nature of the human intellect, which tends to move from action to being, from experience (salvation) to reflection on the meaning of experience (Christology), may also explain why the New Testament only at this late stage develops this more philosophical style of Christology. In this light Fuller's observation is pertinent:

> It may, of course, be argued that this ontic language is merely the translation into Greek terms (and mythological terms at that) of what the earlier functional Christologies were affirming. This is true, but it is not the whole truth. For it is not just a quirk of the Greek mind, but a universal human apperception, that action implies prior being—even if, as is also true, being is only apprehended in action. Such ontic reflection about Yahweh is found even in the Old Testament, e.g., "I Am" (Exodus and Deutero-Isaiah).[58]

The most distinctive characteristic of this third style of Christological thinking is that it takes the decisive step of naming Jesus "God." Raymond Brown's careful study of the New Testament texts that attribute deity to Jesus discovers only three definite texts which do so, all in the later strata of the New Testament: "In the beginning was the Word: the Word was in God's presence, and the Word was God" (Jn. 1.1); Thomas said in response, "My Lord and my God" (Jn. 20.28); and Hebrews, in reference to Jesus: "You have loved justice and hated iniquity: therefore, O God, your God has anointed you with the oil of gladness" (Hb. 1.9).[59] His own analysis tends to confirm our own, namely that these texts are so few and so late because of the need to gain a creative distance from Jewish monotheism: ". . . in the earliest stage of christianity the Old Testament heritage dominated the use of the title 'God'; hence 'God' was a title too narrow to be applied to Jesus."[60]

Despite the rarity of the title "God" for Jesus—the New Testament also generally uses *ho theos* only for the Father, reserving simply *theos* for the Son—it is not possible to deny that some greater ontological depth has been achieved in this Christological trajectory. While the other Christologies stress Jesus' function as Messiah and Kyrios, functions he attains in the second, risen stage of his life, this one proclaims his divine status throughout his life. We may speak here of "being" and not simply of "function." This is particularly clear in the Johannine prologue and well-known Christological hymns that stress the theme of the preexistence of the Logos. These texts, while they rather creatively speak to Hellenistic concerns—the problem of fate and God's entry into it—do not have as their point a kind of divine "fall" into matter, as with the gnostic savior myths. Matter here is not denigrated; the divine entry into the flesh is gospel ("good news"). We should rather look to the Wisdom tradition of the Hebrew scriptures (Wis. 7.25, 12; 8.4; 9.9–10, 17) that speaks of the preexistence of Yahweh's Wisdom. That these Hebrew texts could be the source of this third Christological view makes sense when we remember that it was largely Hellenistic Jews who brought it about. In this light, the meaning of Christ's preexistence is to highlight that the ultimate and final source of Jesus' existence is God herself.

I do not think that the more "functional" Christologies should be played off against this more expressly "ontic" one. We seem to be dealing here, under the pressure of the Christ-experience, with the biblical understanding of God as outgoing and involving himself in history. As we shall see, Being/God for the Hebrews is not an apathetic deity who does not function in history. The ontic (God) and the functional (God's historical outgoingness) are both entailed in the biblical understanding of God. This is also, of course, why the New Testament does not see any contradiction between its Christ-belief and monotheism. It is not lapsing into ditheism/polytheism (cf. Mk. 10.18; 1 Cr. 3.22f), but trying to come to terms with the Father's outgoing in the Christ event. Ultimately this will lead the Church to a trinitarian view of the Divine.

Attempted Evaluations

How did it happen, then, that this decisive step in the history of religions—adoring Jesus as "God"—was taken by the New Testament? Interestingly enough, this step would not have been possible without the Jewish understanding of God—as I will try to show—though in and of itself the Jewish tradition cannot explain the deity of Jesus. The Jewish "no" to Jesus—a reality that cannot simply be attributed to Jewish obduracy and that deserves more careful attention in Christology than it has so far received—probably stems from monotheism and a fear of regressing to polytheism and a crude form of excited messianism. For this reason even Jesus' own disciples were slow to understand the "depth" dimension of Jesus (Mk. 8.32; 9.32). Thus scholars have not looked to the Jewish tradition for an explanation of Jesus' deity, though I will later attempt to analyze the important contribution of Judaism to the Christian understanding of Jesus.

Perhaps the more common evaluation of this step in our times might be called the "comparative approach," since it has become possible since the nineteenth-century development of the specialization known as comparative religions. Comparative studies have enabled scholars to note a striking similarity between the New Testament and early Christian tendency to gradually "deify" Jesus and similar deification processes at work in the Greek mystery religions and the world's great Oriental religions. For instance, in the mystery religions the initiate undergoes a sort of deification transformation, a kind of divine metamorphosis. In the Roman imperial cult, the emperors were frequently thought to be deified. Most importantly, scholars note a tendency for later disciples to deify the founders of the various religions. We can see this at work in the gradual development from Theravada (early) Buddhism, in which Gautama Buddha preaches a kind of mystical silence in the face of the Absolute, to Mahayana Buddhism, in which Gautama himself has been deified. Herbert Stroup, in his study of the known founders of the world's great religions, has noted this process; we can call it the "deification tendency":

> The founder is assumed to be divine through the process of deification. It is true that the founders of religions have refrained from claiming their own divinity. At times they have specifically asserted that they are thoroughly human. They have even denied the claim of their disciples that they are exceptional, saying that only God is good. But their followers do not accept their views. The followers traditionally respond to the heroic lives and noble teachings of their founders by worshiping them as gods. Even those founders who denied the existence of the gods or God end up becoming gods.[61]

One manner of utilizing this discovery of comparative research is the thesis of "intercultural borrowing." In our particular case, this would hypothesize that as the young Christian movement spread into the Hellenistic world, it inevitably came under the influence of the mystery religions. This brought with it, then, a tendency to ascribe miraculous wonders to Jesus and even, eventually, deity. The dying and rising of Jesus and the Christian described by Paul in Romans is often thought to be a particularly clear parallel between the mystery religions and Christianity.[62] While there can be no doubt that the New Testament has come under the influence of Hellenism, as we have seen, it is also true that the parallels uncovered by comparative research are never exact and that the evidence points more toward a Christian transvaluation of Hellenistic beliefs rather than vice versa. For example, while the New Testament ascribes wonders to Jesus and even tends to elaborate them—much like the Greek legends of Asclepius—the stress primarily falls on God, not Jesus, and on faith, not the prodigious. Similarly, the dying-rising process described by Paul in Romans does not result in a divine metamorphosis, for the humanity of both Jesus and the Christian initiate is constantly stressed by Paul.

But this thesis of intercultural borrowing does not really bring us to the heart of the matter. What Stroup and numerous others[63] have noted is that the "deification tendency," especially in the case of a founder, is a "natural" tendency of the religious consciousness, found internationally and not dependent upon intercultural borrowing. For example, the movement from Theravada to Mahayana Buddhism was a natural—and one might say, almost inevitable—one, irrespective of borrowings from cults that deify founders. The Buddhist scholar Christmas Humphreys sees this as the movement from the dominance of mind/rationality in religion (Theravada) to the increasing dominance of emotion/myth (Mahayana): "Certainly the fundamental distinction seems to be that between the emotions and the mind, of Bhakti yoga as distinct from Jnana or Karma yoga."[64] What is being pointed to is the natural desire to give historical reality to our religious hopes, to bring the distant Absolute close to man, to satisfy not just the mind but the religious heart and feelings too. In this sense, the deification tendency is a kind of *regressus ad uterum,* the suppression of reason by the stronger drive of the religious emotions. Just as the archaic individual lives in a numinous world inhabited by wonders and mythical numinous powers; just as the child lives in the same world before the dawn of reason in his life; just as the adult "returns" to this world in his dream life—so the religious consciousness reestablishes its link with the numinous world by deifying fellow human beings.

In the history of Christian theology it was perhaps Ernst Troeltsch who gave classic expression to this thesis of the deification tendency in Christology. In his still provocative *The Absoluteness of Christianity and the History of Religions,* written in 1901, Troeltsch bravely attempted to come to terms with the implications of the new findings in comparative religion for the Christian faith. His hypothesis is that all religions are "born absolute," for through the founder the followers experience a divine call demanding obedience and belief. This absoluteness is then naïvely attached/identified with the founder. One might say that the more powerful the founder's proclamation is, the greater the tendency to absolutize him naïvely. Out of this naïve absoluteness springs a further "artificial, apologetic absoluteness," stemming from the followers' need to defend themselves against other views. This can then lead to a "supernatural absoluteness," in which all other creeds are negated and one's own is solely identified with the Divine itself. Yet, this will not do, for as the religion becomes more sophisticated it senses in other doctrines a similarity in view and tendency to its own. Thus the emergence of "rational absoluteness," the attempt to explain all other creeds/truths as partial manifestations of one's own. Finally in our own times, under the pressure of the expansion of knowledge, our historical consciousness, and the awareness of other religions, we arrive at the stage of "evolutionary absoluteness," in which we realize that "The absolute is the goal of the human spirit . . . a boundlessness and other-worldliness that transcend all history."[65]

One gains the impression that in our increasingly planetized world, in which we are more exposed to and knowledgeable about the religious world views of others, this comparative approach to Christology will become increasingly more popular. This process of planetization should be welcomed, too, insofar as it will necessarily force us in the West to deabsolutize many of our inherited Western assumptions and enable us to discover the genuinely universal values of our religion. Yet the great temptation of planetization in its early stages is that of syncretism, in which adequate distinctions are not drawn and the differences among the religions are not carefully enough discriminated. We have already seen how the thesis of intercultural borrowing—at least in the case of the New Testament—too quickly found parallels between Christianity and the Greek mystery religions without noting important differences. So, too, in the case of the thesis of the natural tendency of the religious consciousness toward deification, certain distinctions should be drawn.

There can, of course, be no doubt that the notion of a *regressus ad uterum* is a terribly useful one, especially in theology. Just as we know that adult human beings are capable of regression, so, too, *homo religiosus* is capable of the same. In fact, some such notion is absolutely essential, since we simply need some way of distinguishing "healthy" religious behavior from "sick," illusions/fantasies from reality, naïve myth from a more sophisticated and limited use of myth, superstition and idolatry from a genuine adoration of a transcendent God. But surely not every manifestation of the heart and emotion in religion is to be seen as regressive behavior. We know well that psychologists draw a distinction between "regression in the pure and simple sense" and the so-called "regression in the service of the ego." The latter is not really a regression at all, but rather a recapturing of capacities learned at an earlier phase of development—the infantile ability to marvel, fantasize, experience the world as numinous—but a recapturing on a higher level. This latter experience does not result in a loss of reality contact, nor a disintegration of the personality, nor an inability to make distinctions on the basis of sound reason, but rather in an "enlargement" of the personality, a renewing of it, and the release of new energies. So, too, unless one bases himself on a purely rationalistic and abstract notion of religion, the possibility remains open that Christianity is a renewed recapturing of the numinous experience of reality too. That is, that in the Christian experience of God not only the mind but also the heart and feelings experience a renewal and release of new energies, leading not to a loss of reality contact but to an enlargement in the perception of reality. In other words, it could be that the ascription of deity to Jesus is an instance of this latter kind of behavior: a renewal of the personal experience of God in the full sense, not just the mind but also the heart.

The above possibility leads us to the more problematic aspect of the comparative approach; namely, its presupposed and implicit God-concept. Although this will be the subject of our next chapter, one gains the impression that the comparative approach tacitly presupposes a rationalistic and almost deistic view of God as the transcendent One, removed from human history and incapable of intersubjective communication. In this sense, the comparative approach is the victim of its nineteenth-century rationalistic origins. Here we see how an adequate evaluation of the comparative approach brings us to the deepest level of our hermeneutics outlined in Chapter 1: ontology. For in the end it turns on the question of what is the nature of the real, of the Divine itself. For only if God cannot be understood as an historically self-communicative Being, only if history and God are mutually antagonistic, is the issue of the deity of Jesus a priori a regression in the simple sense. This issue ultimately has to be adjudicated on the ontological level, for it deeply involves the metaphysics of love; that is, the issue of how Being (God) remains itself precisely through "losing itself" in the other (man/Jesus). As we will see this issue is a difficult one for Western man to cope with, since the West has steadily stressed the view of being as a self-enclosed monad, independent in himself, who is only "weakened" by losing himself in the other. The notion of the "perfect being" is then easily assumed to be the most independent and self-enclosed monad, and quite obviously on these terms the deity of Jesus can only seem absurd. For the moment, then, the possibility remains open that the deity of Jesus is founded upon a metaphysics of Being-as-love, and on these grounds can make good sense. Later we will see that this was a more likely development for the Jewish tradition than for the Greek-Western. In Walter Kasper's terms,

> In Greek metaphysics from the pre-Socratics to Plato and Aristotle and on to Neo-Platonism, immutability, freedom from suffering and passion *(apatheia)* were always regarded as the supreme attributes of the divine. The God of the Old Testament . . . is known as . . . God of history. God's eternity is something taken for granted in the Old Testament: it does not mean however immobility, unchangeability and timelessness: it means mastery over time, proving its identity, not in unrelated, abstract self-identity, but in actual, historical fidelity.[66]

A further attempted explanation of the deification of Jesus has, since the time of the great dogmatic historian, Adolf Harnack, come to be known as the Hellenization of dogma. To be precise, it is important to distinguish a "soft" and "hard" form of the Hellenization theory. In its "soft" form this theory would maintain that the New Testament's "high Christology" and deification of Jesus has taken its form largely under Hellenistic influence. As we have seen, the Christological thought of Paul and especially of John does show Hellenic influence, and there seems no cogent reason to deny this. The shift from Jewish categories—"Messiah, Son of Man"—to terms comprehensible to the Hellenistic world—"Lord, God"—are instances of such Hellenic influence. But Hellenization was more than a shift in categories; it was also a shift in questions and interests, that is, in one's intellectual horizon. And thus both Paul and John, for example, manifest a greater interest in specifically Hellenistic questions and issues: not a renewed Jewish nation under a Messiah, but how does Jesus save us from death and fate, how does he enter into the human plight, how does he break through the powers of the world (*moria*/fate)?

In its "hard" form, the Hellenization theory would argue that in the process of becoming Hellenized Christianity was progressively de-Christianized. Something of this motivated Reimarus's desire to move away from Paul back to Jesus, but it was perhaps especially Harnack who advocated this view.[67] While we have learned that perhaps the patristic period shows greater signs of Hellenization than the New Testament and that even Christology tends towards a gradual "copying" of the imperial cult,[68] the question at issue is whether Hellenization is in and of itself a sufficient explanation of the deification of Jesus. On this hypothesis the deity of Jesus is seen as a Greek "ontologizing" of Jesus that carries Christianity away from its Jewish roots and away from Jesus' own stress on God the Father. A Jesus-centrism takes the place of Jesus' orientation to the Father and saving interest in man. The way is then prepared for Christianity to become another "cultic" religion, with its stress on ritual and legalisms, and Jesus' stress on the kingdom as the establishment of the reign of justice, freedom and love recedes in the Christian imagination.

While not overlooking the possible tendency toward "culticization," it must be said that the "hard" form of Hellenization overlooks a number of essential factors in its evaluation of Jesus' deity. First it wrongly assumes that ontology is only a Greek possibility and fails to recognize that even the Old Testament involves an at least implicit ontology, when one defines ontology as the universal human tendency to move from action to being in thought. Were this denigration of ontology pushed far enough, it would deny to Christianity the possibility of any intellectual and theoretical development. It too easily assumes that the earliest form of reflection is necessarily the best. Further, as we have seen, it overlooks the Greek concept of God, in which the Divine and the historico-human are mutually antagonistic. This Greek "self-enclosed" God could never have become flesh, as John tells us. Finally, it overstresses the Hellenization of Christian thinking present in the New Testament, overlooking the careful manner in which Greek thought has been "transvalued" in the light of Christ:[69] (1) The New Testament rejects Greek polytheism; against the many gods (Gal. 4.8) there is only one God (1 Cr. 8.6). While there may be other "forces/powers" in the world (Col. 1.16, 20), they have been dedivinized and are under God's dominion. (2) We can find no parallel in Greek thought to the New Testament combination of God's transcendence and his immanent and redemptive action. The Olympian gods were indifferent to man and history; the Stoic creed was one of self-salvation and acceptance of fate, not God's gracious entry into history. Thus, it is possible to speak of a "Christianization of Hellenism"; in any case, the decisive catalyst for the confession of Jesus' deity cannot be traced to the Hellenistic world. This is perhaps why Paul can say, and his Christology is a very "high" one, that he is handing on what he himself has received (1 Cr. 11.23, 15.3); he believes that his thought is in agreement with that of the apostles (Gal. 2.1–10).

The Resurrection as an Epistemological Factor

The inability of either the comparative or the Hellenization approaches to account adequately for the confession of Jesus' deity has increasingly led scholars to reevaluate the possible role of the resurrection event as the decisive catalyst behind such a decisive step.[70] In other words, the resurrection is accorded epistemological status as an event fostering a transformation of the disciples' consciousness, expanding their horizons through deepening their understanding of Jesus. As long as scholars confined themselves to either the comparative or the Hellenization thesis, the resurrection was not taken seriously, but treated as an unhistorical myth either projected by the natural drive of the religious consciousness (for comparativists) or borrowed from the Greek mystery cults (for Hellenists). Many scholars today, however, despite important differences on the question of how best to interpret the details of the resurrection, would agree with Gordon Kaufman that the resurrection "was preeminently an event in the history of meaning"; through it

> ... was born a new awareness of the authentic meaning of human existence and a new hope for the future movement of human history. . . . Understood on the theological level, the resurrection was that event through which the real meaning of Jesus' career and death—and thus of all human history—broke into history. ... it was the event through which it became clear that Jesus' crucifixion was not simply the tragic death of another good man but was the definitive expression of God's being and will.[71]

The resurrection, of course, has been the object of a vigorous pursuit among scholars.[72] For our purposes it will be helpful to separate the historical question from the more properly philosophical and theological questions involved, although our hermeneutics teaches us that these two levels are interdependent.

On the historical level, we must rely heavily upon the sagacious imaginative capacities of the historical critic, for the resurrection narratives, such as they are, are filled with discrepancies in historical details[73] and further complicated by the fact that no one evidently witnessed the event itself. Despite this, however, a marvelous agreement in substance exists between Paul, our earliest source, and the gospels. Features that are common to both Paul and the gospels, when taken collectively, indicate that Jesus is thought to have undergone some transforming experience. Not to be overlooked is the fact that no one actually witnessed the event, for this could be a biblical way of indicating that the resurrection was a "transhistorical" event, not perceptible to our ordinary historical senses. Further, the accounts are careful to distinguish Jesus' resurrection from a simple bodily resuscitation, such as might be imagined in the case of Lazarus (Jn. 11.1–44). Lazarus was, of course, easily recognizable after his revivification for he returned to life as he had earlier lived it. The resurrection accounts, however, are careful to indicate that Jesus did not return back to his prior mode of life but entered into a new modality of existence. This is especially clear in Paul who uses the apocalyptic language of "being raised up" (1 Cr. 15.3) which suggests some decisive transformation (Is. 26.19; Dn. 12.3; Eno. 92.32). He further underscores this element of transformation by his series of contrasts in 1 Corinthians 15.42–44:

> What is sown is perishable, what is raised is imperishable.
> It is sown in dishonor, it is raised in glory.
> It is sown in weakness, it is raised in power.
> It is sown a physical body, it is raised a spiritual body.
> If there is a physical body, there is also a spiritual body.

Paul has apparently invented the notion of the "spiritual body" to describe this transfigured Jesus. But the gospels, too, bring out this aspect of change in Jesus: Jesus is not recognizable to those who stand before him (Lk. 24.16; Jn. 20.14, 21.4); some even doubt that it could be Jesus (Mt. 28.17; Lk. 24.41); Jesus comes and goes in a way impossible to an ordinary earthly being (Lk 24.31; Jn 20.19, 26). Mark sums the matter up: "he appeared in another form" (16.12). Finally, both the gospels (Mk. 8.31, 9.31, 10.33; Mt. 26.60; Jn. 2.19–21) and Paul (1 Cr. 15.4) link the resurrection with a "third-day" motif. Apart from the issue of whether this is a historical reminiscence, it is highly suggestive in meaning. The key phrase is "in accordance with the scriptures," for this indicates to us that the "third day" is an Old Testament motif, and when we turn to the Old Testament we indeed find the "third day" to be expressive of decisive transforming events in the history of salvation. In Exodus it is the day of Yahweh's theophany; in Genesis, Isaac is spared on the third day because of Abraham's faith; and in the prophet Hosea (6.1–2), it is the day of deliverance and liberation by Yahweh.

What further suggests that in the resurrection we have to do with a transforming experience of Jesus is that, additionally to "resurrection-language," we find alternate modes of expression for what has occurred in Jesus. We know, for example, that the New Testament also describes Jesus as being "exalted" or "enthroned" at God's right hand. This image of "exaltation" is important, for it highlights slightly different elements than the "resurrection" language. The image is more "vertical"—Jesus is lifted "from the world" to God's glory—while the resurrection image necessarily implies that Jesus has first died, and thus carries with it a more earth-centered reference. It is even possible that this exaltation terminology was a later New Testament attempt to distinguish the resurrection from a mere bodily revivification.[74] O'Collins[75] thinks that the two traditions—resurrection and exaltation—were originally independent and only eventually came to be interchangeable. He traces the following pattern in the texts: (1) death followed by resurrection (1 Cr. 15; Mk. 9.31); (2) death followed by exaltation (Phil. 2.8f; Mk. 14.62) or glory (Lk. 24.26); (3) death followed by both a resurrection and exaltation (Rm. 8.34; Aa. 2.32f.) or enthronement (Rm. 1.4); (4) resurrection and exaltation as interchangeable explanations for what has occurred to Jesus (Lk. 24.26–46; Mt. 28.16f). The deeply theological interests of John, in which Jesus is viewed as dwelling in the Father's glory, perhaps explain John's preference for the exaltation terminology (3.14, 6.62, 8.28, 12.32). In fact, for John the death is the exaltation. Luke even adds the terminology of "ascension" (Aa.1.9–11), which further gives a note of completion and finality to what has occurred in Jesus. In any case, these alternate expressions bring home the point "that the resurrection was no return to earthly life and transcended any mere resuscitation of a corpse."[76]

Scholars are quite divided on how to evaluate the one element missing in Paul and present in the gospels: the discovery of the empty tomb. Kaufman, arguing that the gospels are later elaborations while Paul is our earlier and safer guide on the question of the resurrection, views the empty tomb as a crude, physicalist extrapolation from the earliest preaching about the risen Lord: ". . . it was only natural that most of the unsophisticated early Christians understood the resurrection to have been of Jesus' physical body—and the obvious conclusion to be drawn from this was that the tomb where that body had been laid was now empty."[77] O'Collins, while opining that the greater problem with this tradition is theological rather than historical, thinks good evidence exists to support its historicity. He especially points to the role of women as witnesses; legend-makers would have chosen male witnesses in a society not admitting female witnesses. Further, Christian opponents in Jerusalem assume that the body is missing, and one wonders how the preaching of the resurrection could have long endured were it not. Finally, it is incorrect, *pace* Kaufman, to view the gospels as crudely physical while Paul is highly sophisticated in his view of the resurrection. We know from *Redaktionsgeschichte* that the evangelists were highly skilled theologians, and even Paul seems to presuppose a somewhat physicalist view of the resurrection. He speaks of a "transformation of our mortal bodies, not the . . . substitution of brand-new risen bodies."[78]

How might we evaluate this empty-tomb tradition? The gospels themselves give us a decisive clue by telling us that in and of itself the empty tomb is ambiguous. In Mark the women "went out and fled from the tomb" (16.8), while Luke is even more to the point: to the apostles the women's report "seemed . . . an idle tale and they did not believe them" (24.11). Even John, who clearly views the empty tomb as sufficient for faith (20.8), admits that it is ambiguous (20.2, 13–15). The fact is, many reasons exist for why the tomb could be empty. It is simply best to hypothesize that only in the light of the appearances of the risen Jesus could the ambiguity of the empty tomb be removed. We might further speculate that if our reconstruction of the evidence so far indicates to what an extent Jesus has been "changed/transformed" by the resurrection, the empty tomb, through its "physicalism," indicates the continuity between the historical and the risen Jesus. Jesus is not a completely new Being but a transformed Being. Thus, this tradition warns us against a completely "spiritualistic" interpretation of the resurrection. We have already seen how Paul emphasizes this continuity-within-discontinuity; the gospels further indicate this by dramatically telling us that the risen Jesus actually "touches" (Jn. 20. 27), eats (Lk. 24.41–43), and speaks (Jn. 21.15f), albeit without the normal limitations that we historically experience.

But because no one actually saw the resurrection event, and because of the ambiguity of the empty-tomb tradition, it is primarily the significance of the appearances of the risen Jesus that are decisive for any reconstruction of what has occurred to Jesus. There are, of course, discrepancies in the appearance traditions,[79] but common to both Paul and the gospels is the belief that the appearances brought them to a new understanding of Jesus. Paul, in 1 Corinthians 15.5, uses the term "he appeared" *(ophthe),* which in the Greek Old Testament is used for divine epiphanies (Gn. 12.7; Ex. 3.2 f/LXX). The term highlights the idea of Jesus' "becoming visible," and this visibilization depends both upon the initiative of the one revealing and the subjective dispositions of the recipient, for in the Old Testament God's manifestation is always gratuitously given, yet not arbitrarily, but to those subjectively disposed. Some scholars even detect a pattern in the gospel accounts of the appearances, a movement from (1) despondent hope (Lk. 24.21; cf. Jn. 20.19) to (2) an initiative on Jesus' part to appear ("Jesus came and stood among them" [Jn. 20.19; cf. Lk. 24.15; Mt. 28.9, 18]), followed (3) by a greeting from Jesus (Jn. 20.19; Mt 28.9), a (4) moment of recognition by the witnesses ("It is the Lord" [Jn. 21.7; cf. Jn. 20.20; Mt. 28.9, 17]) and (5) a commissioning for a mission (Mt. 28.19, 10; Jn. 20.21, 21.15f; Lk. 24.26f).[80] Recognition, of course, presupposes a movement from startling discontinuity (Jesus is different) to a grasping of the familiar or underlying continuity (it is the same Jesus "we" had known). Pousset suggests that these appearances again underline the continuity between the pre-Easter and risen Jesus and that they occurred only to the disciples because only they actually knew this pre-Easter Jesus and thus were in a position to grasp this continuity.[81]

As we might expect, these "appearances" have led to various scholarly interpretations. To begin, and for the sake of simplicity, we can speak of a purely "subjectivist" view that accounts for the resurrection on the basis of the subjective dispositions of the disciples themselves. The "appearances," then, would be a kind of outward "projection" of an interior state, although this is explained variously. Some have said the disciples simply gained the conviction that the cause of Jesus still goes on today; others, that the life of Jesus continued to inspire them, despite his death.[82]

There are, of course, more properly philosophical questions here, having to do with the reality of God and the divine ability to initiate the radically novel in history. One might opine that modern-day acceptance of the subjectivist view largely stems from a secularistic or deistic world view, and this simply illustrates our view of how deeply the theoretical component is present in historical reconstruction. But apart from this, there are more directly "historical" difficulties with subjectivism. First, we know that the prophets knew the distinction between subjective interpretation and divinely initiated inspirations; even the New Testament makes a distinction between the appearances and such inward illuminations as those of Peter and Stephen in Acts. Secondly, there is the dramatic change in the disciples, from despondent unbelievers to proclaimers of the cause of Jesus. Thirdly, there is the question of how to explain that a doctrine (the resurrection) that was peripheral for Pharisaism and even Jesus[83] moves to the center for the Jewish-Christian disciples. Finally, the very content in the notion of the resurrection was new, for as Pannenberg put it: "The primitive christian news about the eschatological resurrection of Jesus—with a temporal interval separating it from the universal resurrection of the dead—is, considered from the point of view of the history of religions, something new."[84]

On the other end of the spectrum is the "objectivist" view, which tends to literalize the resurrection narratives, denying the necessarily symbolic and imagistic language of the narratives. For it fails to explain why it was only the disciples who experienced the appearances, and if carried far enough, it would ultimately deny the "transhistorical" nature of the resurrection, reducing it to another simple revivification of a corpse. In the end, the fact that both these views have appeared in theological thinking indicates our hermeneutical principle that all interpretation of reality is a complex fusion of fact and interpretation. Without denying this fact-interpretation fusion, we might speculate that what the "appearances" are attempting to explain is a "heightening" or "transformation" of consciousness in the disciples themselves. There are historical reasons for why a culture, unaware of the distinction between subject and object to the extent that we are, and basing itself on a model of knowledge as "vision/sight" rather than understanding, would choose the language of "appearance" rather than "consciousness-heightening." Both kinds of language are a fusion of subjective-objective, but "appearance" language corresponds to the visual model of knowledge: what is "seen" is what "appears" or manifests itself. It is what archaic man "saw" that first gave him the conscious sense of learning, and it is this simple fact that promoted, until recent times, the dominance of the "visual" model. Thus, under their epistemological conditions, it was natural for the evangelists to choose the "appearance-language" while we might choose, under our own conditions, a language that more subtly describes the complex interweaving of both the objective and the subjective.[85]

In any case it was through the appearances—or what I am calling an experience of "consciousness-heightening"—that the disciples were brought to a new and deepened understanding of Jesus and his mission. This was the catalyst that caused them to attempt to explain what had occurred in Jesus in terms of "resurrection," or "exaltation," or "ascension," all language common to the Jewish heritage, but now given a new meaning in the light of Jesus. From this they inferred[86]—for they had not witnessed it—that Jesus had been raised from the dead, and this carried the further implication that Jesus' life, death and resurrection was not that of any ordinary individual but the revelation of God's being and will itself. As Lane helpfully put it:

> ... the inbreaking of the resurrection added a new and unexpected dimension to the significance of the life of Jesus. As such the resurrection of Jesus from the dead can only be understood as the explicit divine seal of approval, recognition, and confirmation of every thing Jesus had said and done. The ambiguity that surrounded the life of Jesus and the challenge of the cross is now gradually displaced.[87]

The Risen Jesus and the Confession of Jesus' Deity

Just why the inference that Jesus had been raised from the dead carried the further implication that Jesus' life, death and resurrection was the expression of God's very being is something that can only be understood against the background of Jewish thinking on the resurrection. But there can be no doubt that this is how the New Testament understands the matter, for this is why it projects Jesus' Messiahship and Lordship, and even, for John, his deity back into his earthly ministry. Perhaps Paul has this in mind when he opens his epistle to the Romans with, "concerning his Son, who was born of the seed of David according to the flesh, who was declared to be the Son of God with power, according to the spirit of holiness, by the resurrection of the dead." As Evans put it, the resurrection "is now seen to be the *fons et origo* of christian faith in the lordship of Jesus."[88]

It would take us too far afield to examine the history of the notion of resurrection.[89] There is no doubt that Christianity did not invent the notion, but that it is the result of a slow evolution in Persian, Greek and Jewish thinking. In the Jewish world of thought we can find these three strains of thought interwoven. What made the notion helpful in Jewish thought was the conviction that Yahweh was a God of life, of justice, and of fidelity to his promises on the one hand, and a growing sense among the prophets of the worth of the individual on the other (cf. Ez. 37; Is. 53). As O'Collins put it, resurrection belief was simply "a corollary of theism." It meant that "God would vindicate himself in the face of death and concomitant evils."[90]

We know, too, that in the late Jewish period there was great diversity of opinion on the resurrection. It is variously thought to occur only for righteous Israelites (1 Eno. 83–90), or for both the righteous and the unrighteous Israelites (1 Eno. 6–36), or for all men (2 Esd.). Coupled with this was a further diversity over the nature of the risen life, whether it would include a body, what kind of body, etc. The important element to note is that some apocalyptic expectation of the general "resurrection" of the dead was common in late Judaism. Such an event would be God's act at the end of history. As we have seen, the New Testament informs us that the Pharisees (Mk. 12.18), and apparently even Jesus (Mk. 12.25; cf. Mt. 8.11, 12; 24.30–31; 25.31–32), accepted some form of this belief. Paul, too, presupposes the belief, for he argues, "if there is no resurrection of the dead, then Christ has not been raised" (1 Cr. 15.13). But the "new" element, at least for the Christian disciples, was the resurrection of Jesus now. This must have meant to them that God was behind this Jesus and expressing his will in a final way now, inaugurating the apocalyptic end of time. As we have seen, this germinal insight triggered the process that eventually culminated in the confession of Jesus' deity.

Should we place such a stress upon the role of the resurrection-belief in our account of the genesis of the Christ-belief? Is it possible to maintain that alternate routes were traveled to the belief in Christ, and that the resurrection-belief was only one of the ways that mediated this genesis? Here we must bear in mind that there could be no such thing as a purely non-conceptually mediated experience of the Easter Christ, given the essentially linguistic and conceptual structure of human knowing. To know is to know through concepts, and our only question at this point is whether the death-resurrection conceptuality was the original and primary one eventually leading to the Christ-belief.

It must be said that in principle, purely theoretically, there is nothing against the possibility of other conceptual routes being traversed. Resurrection language was only one of the conceptual schemata available in Jesus' time. We have seen that exaltation terminology was also available and utilized. In principle what seems ultimately required is that Jesus lives in a transformed manner; that this is the ground of the transformation of consciousness of the apostolic Church; and that this apostolic generation was brought to the firm conviction of the inauguration of the kingdom in the man Jesus. But, beyond this question of principle we can ask the question of historical fact and inquire as to whether it is historically probable that some in the apostolic generation might have come to their Christ-belief independently of the resurrection-conceptuality. This question is not purely theoretical, for Helmut Koester appears to hold such a view, and partly in reliance upon him, also Edward Schillebeeckx.[91]

In response, we need first to distinguish between the resurrection kerygma and the more elaborate resurrection stories found in the four gospels. The latter bear the marks of theologizing, each from the point of view of the respective evangelists, while the former are much more primitive, probably from the earliest, pre-gospel liturgical and missionary tradition. Crucial here is the fact that this early, kerygmatic, credal tradition firmly proclaims the resurrection (Lk. 24.34; 1 Cr. 15.3–5), although sometimes without mentioning any appearances of the risen One (Rm. 1.3f, 10.9; Phil. 2.6–11; 1 Pt. 3.18–22, 4.6; Acts 2.23, 3.15, 5.31f). This surely argues for the historical priority of the resurrection-conceptuality. The absence of the appearances-tradition in some of the creeds may mean that this was only one of several attempts to explain the heightening of consciousness that brought the apostolic Church to its Christ-belief. It further strengthens my contention that we may translate these "appearances" into another idiom, as Paul also does, when he speaks of a "revelation" (Gal. 2.1–3) of the Lord and even of "seeing the Lord" (1 Cr. 9.1). Yet it is the merit of the appearances-tradition to have articulated the fact that knowledge that Jesus lives presupposes some transformation of the apostles' consciousnesses.[92]

Secondly, there are alternative ways of expressing the Easter event: Hebrews speaks of Jesus as the heavenly high priest (9.11–12); we have already noted the exaltation and ascension terminology; and Paul even speaks of Jesus as "living" (Rm. 14.9; 2 Cr. 13.4). Yet, as Raymond Brown puts it, ". . . it is not really clear that any of the 'alternative' language for Jesus' victory over death existed in Christianity independently of a belief in Jesus' resurrection from the dead."[93] Hebrews seems to know something like the death-resurrection tradition (13.20, 11.19); exaltation language may be a way of capturing the transformed, eschatological nature of the resurrection; and saying Jesus "lives" seems to be simply another way of saying "was raised" (compare 2 Cr. 13.4 with Acts. 2.23–24).

Thirdly, there is the problem of "Q," the early sayings source embedded in Matthew and Luke. What puzzles scholars is that this very early source nowhere mentions the kerygma of the death and resurrection of Jesus; it seems mainly composed of *didache* (teaching) rather than kerygma. But H. E. Tödt has argued that, if we search closely, Q seems to presuppose Jesus' death and resurrection. For Jesus' proclamation, which Q expresses, had been radically called in question by his death. The Church community of Q could only continue to hand down Jesus' eschatological proclamation if indeed Jesus had been vindicated by the resurrection. Thus, as Fuller puts it, ". . . side by side with the continuation of Jesus' eschatological proclamation Q also contains a christological kerygma—not the kerygma of the saving significance of the passion, to which the circles from which Q emanates had not yet arrived, but the kerygma of Jesus who in his earthly ministry spoke with the authority of the Son of Man vindicated in face of the rejection of men (Lk. 7.34; 9.58), and who will come again in order finally to vindicate the authority of his word (Lk. 11.30; 12.8f, 40; 17.24–30)."[94]

Finally, this brings us to the heart of the matter. Koester's theory that there are early creeds in the New Testament that know in their original form nothing of the death-resurrection conceptuality[95] presupposes that behind them there was some pivotal event bringing them about. If we take seriously the tradition of the disavowal of Jesus after the death, then some "event" must be the catalyst for the emergence of all the Christological creeds (this is what Tödt's theory proves for Q). That event I have termed the "transformation of consciousness" which has as its ground the living and transformed Jesus of Nazareth. The only question, then, is whether the conceptualization of this complex event was primordially that of the death-resurrection, at least in its kerygmatic form. Luke, in Acts, as we know explains Paul's experience of the risen Christ in terms of a "conversion" model (Acts 9), and Schillebeeckx argues that this may be the way the risen One was first experienced and conceptualized.[96] A conversion-conceptuality does not presuppose the death-resurrection schema, and it is something the disciples already knew from Jesus' own earthly acts of bestowing forgiveness. This would be sufficient to account for the credal strands that seem to know nothing of the death-resurrection, Schillebeeckx argues. Yet the problem still remains of just why the New Testament ultimately chose the death-resurrection schema as the final and normative one for articulating the Easter event. It clearly did not have to, for there were alternative schemata available. Partially we may surmise that the alternative schemata did not bring out as well the continuity between the earthly and resurrected Jesus—one who rises dies first, after all. It is clear that exaltation and ascension terminology lack any clear reference to the earthly (dead) Jesus. Yet this line of reasoning all seems rather logical and somewhat artificial. The problem is even more complex, I think, and a purely logical explanation does not quite work. For what was known to the Jewish world of Jesus' time was the resurrection of the dead in the last times, not the resurrection of an individual prior to the general resurrection. It is this surprising aspect that needs explaining and which cannot be accounted for on purely logical terms. This leads me, tentatively at least, to the conclusion that the resurrection schema was the original conceptualization that mediated the Easter experience to the disciples.

But why, we might ask, is the resurrection schema missing from Q and some other credal strands? We may argue that Q is not concerned with Jesus' events, but only with his sayings; it is, after all, a sayings source. As for the other creeds,[97] if we look closely, we will notice that they are all dominated by a rather exalted and celestial view of Jesus: (1) Jesus as the coming Lord of the future (1 Cr. 16.22; Rev. 22.20; 1 Cr. 15.51–52; Lk. 17.24); (2) Jesus as the divine man (Acts 2.22; 2 Cr. 3.1, 5.12, 4.5); (3) Jesus as Wisdom's Envoy and as Wisdom Itself (Lk. 11.49–51; Mt. 11.27; Phil. 2.6f; John's gospel perhaps?). Might we not argue that the death-resurrection schema did not lend itself to the concerns of these creeds, or that it was even suppressed, rather than that it was never known by them? In summary, then, I would say that historical probability inclines toward the priority of the death-resurrection conceptuality. At the very least, the New Testament maintains that this latter is the best of all available schemata.

Ultimately this reconstruction of the genesis of belief in Jesus carries us into the theology of history (Is a resurrection possible in view of modern man's understanding of history?) and into what I would call "Christian ontology" (How can "deity" be asserted of a man?). Since our next chapter will deal with the latter issue, I can content myself with only some preliminary comment on it and concentrate on the issue of the relation of a resurrection belief to our concept of history.

At the deepest level, Jesus' resurrection implies a quite specific theology of history. Theologians and philosophers have expressed it in various ways—history as an open-ended system (Rahner), as the transcendence of cyclicism (Eliade), as the emergence of genuine novelty (Process), as the dialectics of destiny and freedom (Niebuhr, Gilkey), as the battleground of hope (Moltmann), as the growing consciousness of a transcendent ground (Voegelin), but perhaps Jon Sobrino put it best:

> If reality is to be history rather than some eternal present understood in cosmological or existential terms, then the future must be viewed as something more than a possible 'plus' added to an incomplete present. It must be viewed as a promise. . . . [98]

Ultimately the resurrection of Jesus can only make sense if indeed history is promise. This cannot be proven, for it would require of us a knowledge of the total sweep of history. I am saying only that belief in Jesus' resurrection implies a promise-view of history. Such a view of history is an extrapolation, in terms of history, of what was at work in the one individual man Jesus. But the important question for us is not whether we can comprehend the total sweep of history but whether history itself does not merit trust in its promise-nature.

Karl Rahner made an important contribution here in his theological analysis of evolution.[99] Viewing evolution not only as a process of being becoming something "different"—the "rearrangement" of what is already present—but of being becoming "more"—leaps in being, in which the old surpasses itself—he maintained that this presupposed a transcendent ground as the condition of possibility of such "novelty" in evolution. In our own terms, we could say that the cosmic process reveals a "promise-character," because it reveals a genuine advance into novelty and a concomitant surpassing of chaos. Is what is true of the cosmos true of the humans who make up history? At the deepest level our new awareness of history only seems to confront us with our relativity, our conditionedness. But a historical consciousness not only means that we are aware of our conditioning but also that we are beings of hope who can enter into the historical, social process and alter it. Every advance in human self-making takes place against an at least implicit horizon of trust in the future, a belief that the future can be not just a "plus" but better. This, too, presupposes a transcendent ground of the future as promise. But are these observations too optimistic? Surely today the nineteenth-century cult of "progress" can no longer be accepted by a world that is aware of man's increasing ability to destroy, to inflict pain. But in addition to the history of evil and pain, there is a history of protest against them. And it may be true that the vast majority of men are not capable of the kind of hope-in-the-promise that makes genuine protest possible. But is not their "indifference" to pain, their "accommodation" to it, somehow the expression of a desire to survive and thus, itself, a form, however twisted and desperate, of hope in the promise? The mistake of nineteenth-century progressivism was not its belief in progress, but its belief that progress was simply a this-worldly, immanent process, itself created only by man. This set the conditions for the inflated egoism and cult of self-interest that ultimately led to the disasters—political and economical—of the twentieth century.[100] The promise-character of history means that history is not a self-fulfilling system, a closed system explicable only in terms of itself. God is part of the definition of history.

It is, then, in terms of such a view of history that Jesus' resurrection from the dead takes on meaning. Were history only a cosmic and nonhuman process of evolution, God as the transcendent ground would surely be sufficient to explain the advance of novelty over chaos, as the process thinkers put it. But history in the proper sense is a human process of hope, and Jesus' resurrection expresses in a properly human way that this hope is grounded in God's promises to man. In this sense, Moltmann can tell us that Jesus' resurrection "founds history that can and ought to be lived out, by pointing out the channel leading toward the future. . . ."[101] It seems to me that the dispute over whether Jesus' resurrection is to be considered a "historical fact" or "transhistorical reality" could be more properly adjudicated in terms of a promise-notion of history. It is not simply a case of the fact—as Niebuhr[102] thought—that historical facts are unique and unrepeatable, but that history itself is an open system, part of whose definition is openness to the God-of-promise. Only on the presupposition of a closed view of history need we presuppose that the resurrection is a simply "trans-historical event." On the open view of history, in which history is a movement toward a promise, history is itself transhistorical. The resurrection, if you will, is "historical" precisely because it points out the transhistorical futurity of history. Obviously this is only a sketch of the theology of history implied in the resurrection belief. A further issue, which we will treat later, is the nature of the risen life itself, and to what an extent we can even meaningfully speak of it.[103] But for the moment we are trying only to render explicit the underlying theology of history involved in our historical reconstruction of the resurrection, in accord with our hermeneutics.

Our account of the genesis of belief in Jesus' deity leads us to the view that the earliest disciples did not visibly "see" God in Jesus. Rather, under the impact of the resurrection, and facilitated by a gradual process of developing experience and understanding, the disciples theorized to the conclusion of Jesus' Lordship and deity. Kaufman helpfully put it this way: "The earliest disciples did not visibly see God in Jesus. . . . The doctrines of the incarnation and the deity of Christ are theories . . . intended to interpret the central fact of which the disciples (and the subsequent Church) were convinced, namely that here God—the ultimate limit of our existence and the ultimate reality with which we have to do—is encountered, not merely man."[104] The notion of the disciples actually "seeing" God would lead us to the problematic notion of God being just another object among the many empirical objects of the world, rather than the transcendent-immanent Father proclaimed by Jesus. It would also lead us to the view that the disciples a priori knew what God must be like, how this God must act; and from this a priori knowledge decided that this God was present in Jesus. Our view would maintain that the disciples only concluded to Jesus' deity historically, and this in such a way that their prior God-concepts were quite radically transvalued.

Let us try to give more precision to what we mean. We do not mean that the resurrection experience transformed a finite man—Jesus of Nazareth—into an infinite being. Nor do we mean that Jesus became a demigod, a kind of divine-human "mixture" in which neither the human nor the divine remains itself. [105] What we mean is that under the impact of the resurrection the disciples gradually came to an awareness of the "depth dimension" of Jesus' entire life; that is, that in and through his human life God was actively disclosing the divine being and will in a decisive and definitive way. Some exegetes would express this by saying that the implicit depth dimension of Jesus was gradually rendered explicit under the impact of the resurrection. In my own terms, I would say this is an example of the kind of development that moves from the undifferentiated (Jesus' life) by way of greater complexification (the resurrection experience) to a more differentiated understanding (Jesus' deity). The confession of Jesus' deity was surely not an instance of purely logical development on the part of the disciples, as if they could have simply "deduced" it from Jesus' pre-paschal ministry. This does not accord with what we know of that pre-paschal ministry, and most importantly it overlooks the decisive experience of the resurrection as a consciousness-heightening experience for the disciples. But if the doctrine of Jesus' deity was not a simple logical deduction from Jesus' pre-paschal ministry, neither was it a development simply "discontinuous" with the pre-Easter Jesus. This would force us to the view that Jesus' deity was simply "projection" on the part of the disciples, and not at all grounded in the reality of Jesus himself. This overlooks the fundamental distinction between the undifferentiated and differentiated. There is surely enough biblical evidence to warrant the conclusion that the undifferentiated "depth" dimension of Jesus was rendered more clearly differentiated through the resurrection, not created de novo through a projection of the disciples. We have seen how the resurrection narratives quite carefully point out that it is the Jesus whom the disciples have known who has been raised. The book of Revelation sums this up when it speaks of the transfigured "Lamb who was slain" (5.6). Further, we know that there is an implicit or undifferentiated Christology even present in the pre-paschal ministry of Jesus, something we should expect if indeed the resurrection fully discloses the depth dimension of Jesus. Thus, while Jesus proclaims God's kingdom, he knows that his own person is the agent of that kingdom (Lk. 11.20). This mediatorial function as the Father's agent causes him even to forgive sins (Mk. 2.1–12). While Jesus stands in the prophetic tradition as a believer in God's kingdom, yet there is an urgency in his message and a stress on that kingdom emerging now (Mk. 4.30f.; Mt. 11.6). He is even bold enough to speak with an authority that transcends the Torah (Mt. 5). Unlike the prophets who legitimated their message by appealing to Yahweh, Jesus relies upon his own word (Mt. 5.18; 6.2,5,16; 8.10). This enables him, unlike the rabbis, to issue a summons to discipleship of himself, even to the point of death (Mt. 8.19–22). Even in his prayer life Jesus consistently distinguishes between "My Father" and "your Father" (Mt. 11.27; Mk. 12.1–19; 13.32), thus indicating an unprecedented oneness with the Father. There is, of course, not likely going to be any consensus among exegetes about this "implicit" Christological element present in Jesus' ministry.[106] From our hermeneutical standpoint, we are dealing with what is only "implied" by the text, not clearly stated, and thus we are on a level more dependent upon the critics' reconstructive capacities. The evidence is simply ambiguous—undifferentiated—and the "weight" one gives it depends upon the role that the resurrection plays in one's reconstruction of the events in question.

But if we say that under the impact of the resurrection the disciples were able to bring to greater differentiation what was still ambiguous and undifferentiated in Jesus' ministry, this will then cast new light upon the kerygma. For example, the Palestinian kerygma tends to view Jesus as the agent of God's kingdom; the resurrection simply made it clear that this kingdom is indeed now entering history through Jesus. This differentiates, if you will, the implicit connection between Jesus and the kingdom-message in Jesus' ministry: Jesus' cause and his person cannot be separated. The Hellenistic-Jewish kerygma focuses around the title of *Kyrios* for Jesus; Jesus is seen to be actively interceding for humanity now. This kerygma differentiates the element of the *presentness* of the kingdom in Jesus' ministry. And finally, the Hellenistic-gentile kerygma perhaps takes the most daring step in the history of religions and views Jesus as God or at least as coming from God. This, of course, differentiates the fact that in Jesus' ministry it was indeed *God* and *God's* kingdom that was actively entering history through Jesus. Jesus brings about a new experience of God; he raises questions about God's own being itself. But finally there is also a kerygma of salvation too, as we shall see in our chapter on soteriology. Jesus brings salvation, that is what all the kerygmata want to say, and what the later soteriology of the New Testament will clearly say. This differentiates the fact that in Jesus' ministry God is acting in history as a God who is for humanity, oriented to humanity, overturning the conditions that make a human life incapable of full realization. This soteriology also differentiates the salvific element implicit in Jesus' death: it is an act of service, of agape, for humanity.

Notes

1. I have treated this from a complementary perspective in my *Christ and Consciousness,* ch. 4, "The Problem of Christ's Divinity in the Light of Christian Consciousness," pp. 85–98.

2. On the notion of the charismatic founder, cf. Aelred Cody, "The Foundation of the Church: Biblical Criticism for Ecumenical Discussion," THEOLOGICAL STUDIES 34 (1973), 3–18 and John Carroll Futrell, "Discovering the Founder's Charism," THE WAY, Supplement 14 (Autumn, 1971), 62–70.

3. Bornkamm, *op. cit.,* p. 25.

4. Most helpful: Robert A. Spivey and D. Moody Smith, Jr., *Anatomy of the New Testament: A Guide to Its Structure and Meaning* (New York: Macmillan, 1974), pp. 182–248; Pheme Perkins, *Reading the New Testament: An Introduction* (New York: Paulist, 1978); Floyd V. Filson, *The New Testament against its Environment* (London: SCM, 1963); Reginald H. Fuller, *The Foundations of New Testament Christology* (New York: Charles Scribner's, 1965); Norman Perrin, *Rediscovering the Teaching of Jesus* (New York: Harper and Row, 1967) and *A Modern Pilgrimage in New Testament Christology* (Philadelphia: Fortress, 1974); Bruce Vawter, *This Man Jesus: An Essay toward a New Testament Christology* (New York: Doubleday, 1973). Perhaps the two most complete summaries of Jesus-research currently available are John Reumann, *Jesus in the Church's Gospels: Modern Scholarship and the Earliest Sources* (Philadelphia: Fortress, 1968), very detailed; and Hans Conzelmann, *Jesus* (Philadelphia: Fortress, 1973), briefer. Now also see Joseph A. Fitzmyer's helpful summary, "Jesus the Lord," CHICAGO STUDIES 17 (1978), 75–104.

5. Gerhart Niemeyer, "Eric Voegelin's Philosophy and the Drama of Mankind," MODERN AGE 20 (1976), 32.

6. But see Ruether, *op. cit.,* pp. 55–57, for the strain of universalism in the Pharisees.

7. Jeremias, *The Prayers of Jesus,* pp. 11–65.

8. Kasper, *op. cit.,* pp. 74–78, also adds that the kingdom's futurity respects the hearer's freedom and ability to respond to Jesus' message. It flows in part, then, from the biblical notion of human freedom.

9. *Ibid.,* p. 92.

10. Jürgen Moltmann, *The Crucified God: the Cross of Christ as the Foundation and Criticism of Christian Theology* (New York: Harper and Row, 1974), pp. 112–159.

11. Ruether, *op. cit.,* p. 59.

12. *Origen's Commentary on the Gospel of Matthew,* XIV, 7 (*The Ante-Nicene Fathers* 10, edited by Allan Menzies [Grand Rapids, Michigan: Wm. B. Eerdmans, n.d.], p. 498).

13. See Fuller, *op. cit.,* pp. 102–141; Kasper, *op. cit.,* pp. 100–123; Norman Perrin, *The New Testament: An Introduction* (New York: Harcourt, Brace, Jovanovich, 1974), pp. 277–303; Edward Schillebeeckx, *Jesus: An Experiment in Christology* (New York: Seabury, 1979), *passim;* and Eduard Schweizer, *Jesus* (Richmond, Virginia: John Knox, 1971), esp. pp. 13–51.

14. Fuller, *ibid.,* p. 104.

15. Perrin, *The New Testament,* pp. 291–299.

16. Dominic Crossan, "Parable and Example in the Teaching of Jesus," NEW TESTAMENT STUDIES 18 (1971–1972), 295. Simply instructive rather than proclamatory parables: Mt. 13.44–46 (Hidden Treasure and Pearl); Lk. 14.28–32 (Tower Builder and King); Lk. 11.5–8 (Friend at Midnight); Lk. 18.1–8 (Unjust Judge).

17. Cf., on this, Perrin, *The New Testament,* pp. 296–299.

18. Fuller, *op. cit.,* p. 106.

19. Kasper, *op. cit.,* neatly summarizes the varied views on the kingdom, pp. 76–77. They range from liberal theology's view of the kingdom as a symbol of man's highest good, to Barth's view of it as God's absolute simultaneity with the present, to Bultmann's existentialist view. Each of these takes the future sayings somewhat seriously. Others deny their authenticity and argue only for the present sayings. The critical advance is to return to the biblical notion of an historical God who by acting in history opens it and pushes it to a new future. Rudolf Schnackenburg, *God's Rule and Kingdom* (Edinburgh: Nelson, 1963), suggests that "we shall have to abandon our empirical notions of time, which envisage time in our Western thinking as a continuously moving line, divisible into measurable sections ('spaces'). Biblical thought about salvation . . . asks what occurs in time and what 'fills' it, and enquires what action of God gives every time its character and significance" (p. 213). God's filling of time makes of time a promise and a future fulfillment. It is this prophetic experience of time as both God's promise (present) and fulfillment (future) that underlies the tension between present and future in Jesus' preaching of the kingdom (cf. pp. 127–129). Schnackenburg also holds that we should not think that Jesus was mistaken in his hope of the establishment of God's future kingdom—he rightly looked toward a fulfillment of history, of time, like the prophets. But we are entitled to maintain that he put no date on when the fulfillment would come. A sense of urgency there is in Jesus' message; a date of the end, that is rather doubtful. All the texts that indicate such a date (cf. Mt. 10.23; Mk. 9.1, 13.30) contradict Jesus' refusal to engage in such apocalyptic time calculations (Mt. 13.32 par.) and should be seen as post-Easter attempts to magnify the esoteric knowledge of Jesus (pp. 195–214). Norman Perrin, *Jesus and the Language of the Kingdom,* pp. 15–18, 197–199, has recently suggested that because of the mythical nature of the kingdom of God in Jesus' preaching, it is simply a mistake to ask literal questions of temporality. This is to change the myth into concept. Interestingly enough, he maintains that apocalyptic uses the kingdom notion as a concept, since it tries to describe carefully the reality and to date it. This may be a further reason for not ascribing time calculations to Jesus; in that sense I agree with Perrin. But I disagree in that I think we must attempt to translate the myth into concepts that we can understand, and this entails asking questions about temporality. The difficulty is in understanding the experience of temporality underlying the myth, and this is Schnackenburg's contribution. I would also tend to think that apocalyptic is also mythical rather than conceptual, but mythical in an uncritical and fanatical sense.

20. Cf. Neusner, *op. cit.*

21. Paul Winter, "Sadducees and Pharisees," in *Jesus in His Time,* ed. Hans Jürgen Schultz (Philadelphia: Fortress, 1971), p. 53.

22. Schillebeeckx, *op. cit.,* p. 231; cf. Bo Reicke, "Galilee and Judea," in Schultz, *ibid.,* pp. 28–35. Arriving at judgments about the Pharisees is enormously

complex, as a reading of Michael J. Cook, "Jesus and the Pharisees—The Problem as It Stands Today," JOURNAL OF ECUMENICAL STUDIES 15 (Supplement, 1978), 441–460, amply illustrates. My judgments about them in the text represent reasonable hypotheses in the light of my reading of such scholars as J. Neusner, R. Ruether, and particularly E. P. Sanders.

23. Fuller, *op. cit.,* p. 106.

24. Josef Blinzler, "Jesus and His Disciples," in Schultz, *op. cit.,* pp. 84–95.

25. See Schillebeeckx, *op. cit.,* pp. 213–218, and Willi Marxsen, "The Lord's Supper: Concepts and Developments," in Schultz, *ibid.,* pp. 106–114.

26. Marxsen, *ibid.,* p. 108.

27. *Ibid.,* p. 109.

28. Fuller, *op. cit.,* pp. 106–108, 125–131.

29. *Ibid.,* p. 107.

30. *Ibid.*

31. Kasper, *op. cit.,* p. 120.

32. See Fuller, *op. cit.,* pp. 108–131, and the earlier work by Ferdinand Hahn, *The Titles of Jesus in Christology* (London: Lutterworth, 1969).

33. See Albert Schweitzer, *op. cit.,* pp. 223–397, for the complete argument. Rudolf Pesch argues, in "Das Messiasbekenntnis des Petrus (Mk. 8.27–30). Neuverhandlung einer alten Frage," BIBLISCHE ZEITSCHRIFT 17 (1973), 178–195 and 18 (1974), 20–31, that Peter is basing himself not upon the political tradition of the Messiah, but upon that of the prophetic anointed one. See also Schillebeeckx, *op. cit.,* pp. 456–459, and 499–515, for the background on this nonpolitical messianic tradition. But the important element is that Jesus rebukes Peter and refuses to employ the title, even in this case. This tradition, however, may very well have made it easier for the post-Easter Church to apply the term to Jesus.

34. See esp. I. H. Marshall, "The Synoptic Son of Man Sayings in Recent Discussion," NEW TESTAMENT STUDIES 12 (1965–1966), 327–351, and "The Son of Man in Contemporary Debate," EVANGELICAL QUARTERLY 42 (1970), 67–87.

35. Fuller, *op. cit.,* pp. 119–125.

36. *Ibid.,* p. 42; cf. p. 36: "The present writer is now inclined to think that the poem in Dan. 7.13f is from an earlier source in which the term was used of an individual eschatological figure, that the writer of Dan. has combined it with the four earlier visions and added the interpretations vv. 15–18 and the poem of v. 27. But in doing so that writer does not intend to abandon the original individual understanding of the man-like figure. He is explaining it to be, like earthly kingship in Israel, the representative of the saints of the Most High. . . ." This figure understood as an individual reappears in Enoch and 4 Ezra.

37. *Ibid.,* p. 123.

38. Kasper, *op. cit.,* p. 69.

39. Schillebeeckx, *op. cit.,* p. 479. He notes that all the early Christological titles, or at least most of them, are associated with the eschatological prophet in the varied Jewish traditions of Jesus' time. This prophet title is then a kind of link leading to all the other titles. Yet, one might ask whether this is too logical, and we cannot be sure how widespread and commonly known was the Jewish literature upon which Schillebeeckx relies.

40. Fuller, *op. cit.,* p. 130; cf. pp. 125–131.

41. In the post-Easter tradition it is the Baptist who is Elijah *redivivus* (cf. Mk. 9.13).

42. Fuller, *op. cit.*, p. 127. For more background, see Schillebeeckx, *op. cit.*, pp. 441–472. For Elijah see Mal. 3.23–24 and Sir. 48.10–11.

43. *Ibid.*, p. 129.

44. For apocalyptic, see esp. David S. Russell, *The Method and Message of Apocalyptic* (Philadelphia: Westminster, 1964); Klaus Koch, *The Rediscovery of Apocalyptic* (Naperville, Ill.: Alec R. Allenson, 1972); and Paul D. Hanson, "Jewish Apocalyptic against Its Near-Eastern Environment," REVUE BIBLIQUE 78 (1971), 31–58, and "Old Testament Apocalyptic Re-examined," INTERPRETATION 25 (1971), 454–479. Kasper, *op. cit.*, p. 75, claims that apocalyptic "is not concerned with anticipatory reports of future events," but I am not altogether persuaded that we should necessarily think them that critical (this is more a product of our historical consciousness). See my *Christ and Consciousness,* pp. 28–44, on the pre-critical consciousness. A stimulating analysis of the hermeneutical issues involved is Karl Rahner, "The Hermeneutics of Eschatological Assertions," in *Theological Investigations* 4 (Baltimore: Helicon, 1966), pp. 323–346.
It is apparent that a "nationalistic" or "political" notion of the kingdom is missing in Jesus' preaching. The kingdom-notion was given a political twist in later Judaism—signifying the restoration of the Jewish polis—but this nowhere manifests itself as a part of Jesus' teachings. Cf. Schnackenburg, *op. cit.*, pp. 41–62, 95–104.

45. See Gordon D. Kaufman, *Relativism, Knowledge and Faith* (Chicago: University of Chicago, 1960), pp. 105–117, for an excellent discussion of this matter. Cf. Schillebeeckx also, *op. cit.*, pp. 583–594, especially for background on the Enlightenment.

46. See Raymond E. Brown, "Peter's Denials of Jesus," in his *The Gospel according to John XIII–XXI*, Anchor Bible Series #29A (Garden City, N.Y.: Doubleday, 1970), pp. 836–842, for an exegetical overview of this issue. The question of Mark's picture of the disciples is complex, and scholarship may be shifting from the view that Mark's view is mainly negative, although this does not alter the tradition of the disciples' incomprehension of Jesus. Cf. Jack Dean Kingsbury, "The Gospel of Mark in Current Research," RELIGIOUS STUDIES REVIEW 5 (1979), 101–107.

47. Kaufman, *Systematic Theology,* p. 179.

48. See Fuller, *op. cit.,* for the linear view and Robinson and Koester, *op. cit.,* for the simultaneous "trajectories" view. Cf. Larry W. Hurtado, " New Testament Christology: A Critique of Bousset's Influence," THEOLOGICAL STUDIES 40 (1979), 306–317, for an overview of current developments in the conception of the development of biblical Christologies. Most significant here is Martin Hengel's *Judaism and Hellenism,* 2 vols. (Philadelphia: Fortress, 1974), which argues that we cannot neatly separate Jewish from Hellenistic influences, and vice versa. A further important finding is that the title *Kyrios,* attributed by Wilhelm Bousset (see his *Kyrios Christos* [Nashville: Abingdon, 1970]) to Hellenism is now increasingly thought to be, as a divine title, attributed to Judaism. The breakthrough work here is Joseph F. Fitzmyer, "Der semitische Hintergrund des neutestamentlichen Kyriostitel," in G. Strecker, ed., *Jesus Christus in Historie und Geschichte* (Tübingen: Mohr, 1975), pp. 285–288. Another reason for reassessing the Jewish and Hellenistic in scholarship!

49. Gerald O'Collins, *The Resurrection of Jesus Christ* (Valley Forge, Pa.: Judson, 1973), p. 104.

50. The following analysis of the titles of Jesus is a good example of our first two hermeneutical operations; i.e., grasping what the text itself says and what it implies. The various titles (in the text) are used as clues for formulating hypotheses about what those titles imply of the growing understanding of Jesus.

51. Helpful here is David M. Stanley, *Boasting in the Lord: the Phenomenon of Prayer in Saint Paul* (New York: Paulist, 1973). Cf. also James D. G. Dunn, *Jesus and the Spirit. A Study of the Religious and Charismatic Experience of Jesus and the First Christians as Reflected in the New Testament* (Philadelphia: Westminster, 1975), pp. 199–342 ("The Religious Experience of Paul and of the Pauline Churches"). I am not maintaining that Paul was the first to grasp the *present* Lordship of the risen Jesus; Wilhelm Thüsing maintains that this was already grasped in the Palestinian Christology. Cf. his "Erhöhungsvorstellung und Parusieerwartung in der ältesten nachösterlichen Christologie," BIBLISCHE ZEITSCHRIFT 11 (1967), 95–108, 205–222; 12 (1968), 223–240.

52. Lane, *op. cit.,* p. 84.

53. Cf. D. E. H. Whiteley, *The Theology of St. Paul* (Philadelphia: Fortress, 1972), pp. 99–123.

54. Lane, *op. cit.,* p. 88.

55. *Ibid.;* cf. also Karl Rahner, "*Theos* in the New Testament," *Theological Investigations* 1 (Baltimore: Helicon, 1961), pp. 79–148.

56. See Raymond E. Brown, "Does the New Testament Call Jesus God?" in his *Jesus: God and Man* (Milwaukee: Bruce, 1967), p. 37.

57. See Fuller, *op. cit.,* pp. 243–259.

58. *Ibid.,* pp. 248–249.

59. Brown, *Jesus: God and Man,* pp. 1–38, lists as texts that "probably" name Jesus "God" the following: John 1.18; Titus 2.13; 1 John 5.20; Romans 9.5; 2 Peter 1.1. But the evidence is ambiguous. As even less probable, owing to textual variations and linguistic obscurities, are Galatians 2.20, Acts 20.28, 2 Thessalonians 1.12.

60. *Ibid.,* p. 33. It is to be understood that the development in Christological titles I have traced is only a summary that highlights the major breakthroughs. Many of the titles known by one Christological view are also known by the others, though reworked in the light of each view's presuppositions.

61. Herbert Stroup, *Founders of Living Religions* (Philadelphia: Westminster, 1974), p. 30.

62. Cf. Wagner, *op. cit., passim.*

63. Cf. Gustav Mensching, *Das Wunder im Glauben und Aberglauben der Völker* (Leiden: E. J. Brill, 1957), for an analysis of religion's tendency to lapse into superstition. A similar process in Christianity has been studied in Hippolyte Delehaye, *The Legends of the Saints: An Introduction to Hagiography* (Notre Dame: Univ. of Notre Dame, 1961).

64. Christmas Humphreys, *Buddhism* (Baltimore: Pelican, 1962), p. 51.

65. Cf. Ernst Troeltsch, *The Absoluteness of Christianity and the History of Religions* (Richmond, Virginia: John Knox, 1971), p. 147; cf. pp. 131–163.

66. Kasper, *op. cit.,* p. 175. Kasper relies on W. Maas, *Unveränderlichkeit Gottes. Zum Verhältnis von griechisch-philosophischer und christlicher Gotteslehre,* Paderborner Theologische Studien I (München, 1974). Cf. James P. Mackey, "The Faith of the Historical Jesus," HORIZONS 3 (1976), 155–174, for an illuminating inquiry into Jesus' deity, esp. p. 169: "The thesis has two parts. The first part has already been stated: every historical religion links its founder to its basic acknowl-

edgments about the ultimate reaches of reality (Siddhartha was Buddha or 'Enlightened One," Zoroaster was the prophet of Mazdah and his friend, and so on). The second part may be stated as follows: the manner and extent of this acknowledgment of the founder depends upon the kind of religion or the kind of faith which is in each case in question; and the faith of Jesus being what it was, the acknowledgment of Jesus in the Christian tradition could not stop short of drawing Jesus into the very center of the faith itself. That is to say, *Jesus* had to be acknowledged in the course of that central act of acknowledgment which in this particular faith is man's very (and only) contact with God." Mackey is saying, I take it, that a historical God is known only historically, *via* Jesus.

67. Cf. Adolph Harnack, *History of Dogma,* 7 vols. (New York: Dover, 1961), for the classic Hellenization theory.

68. Cf. Hans Schmidt, "Politics and Christology: The Historical Background," CONCILIUM 36 (1968), 72–84.

69. Cf. Filson, *op. cit.,* pp. 29–42. Attempts are made from time to time to note a Hellenistic *theos aner* influence in the New Testament. This would refer to the Hellenistic belief that certain charismatic human beings possess divine power, as found in Philostratus' *Life of Apollonius of Tyana* or Pseudo-Kallisthenes' *Life of Alexander.* Cf. Helmut Koester, "The Structure and Criteria of Early Christian Beliefs," in Robinson and Koester, *op. cit.,* pp. 216–219, who detects such a *theos aner* Christology among Paul's opponents in 2 Cr. The collections of Jesus' miracles in Mark and Luke may also be fashioned on this model. There seems no reason to question that this may well be a trend among some circles of Christians, although it should also be noted that Paul is very quick to correct such a view through his stress on his own tribulations as an imitation of the cross (2 Cr. 4.7f, 6.4f, 11.23f), and Mark corrects the miracles by placing stress on God and faith rather than power, and also through his stress on the sufferings of the Messiah. Luke perhaps carries the trend furthest, but still in a corrected fashion: it is faith that is crucial, not simply the prodigious. Kasper too, *op. cit.,* points out that this *theos aner* model was based on a biological descent from the gods, something clearly missing both in Judaism and the gospels: "For the strict monotheism of the Old Testament, the mythological, polytheistic and pantheistic background of such expressions made references to sons of God immediately suspect" (p. 109). Cf. also Michael Green, "Jesus in the New Testament," in his edited *The Truth of God Incarnate* (Grand Rapids, Michigan: Wm. B. Eerdmans, 1977), esp. pp. 36–42, against the recent attempt to reduce Christology to the *theos aner* model in *The Myth of God Incarnate,* ed. John Hick (Philadelphia: Westminster, 1977), esp. pp. 64–86, 87–121. This latter work seems particularly unsophisticated, both historically and theologically, in its handling of the Christological issues.

70. The epistemological priority of the resurrection is increasingly being taken more seriously. The works of Rahner, Pannenberg, Kasper, Moltmann, Sobrino and Kaufman all variously reflect this tendency.

71. Kaufman, *Systematic Theology,* p. 433, 431–432.

72. Helpful to me personally have been Édouard Pousset, "La resurrection," NOUVELLE REVUE THÉOLOGIQUE 91 (1969), 1009–1044, and "Croire en la resurrection," *ibid.,* 96 (1974), 147–166, 366–388; Gerald O'Collins, *op. cit.;* and C. F. Evans, *Resurrection and the New Testament* (London: SCM, 1970). Pousset's articles, from both a philosophical and historical viewpoint, are the most enlightening and subtle I have yet seen; they should be published in book form in English.

73. Some of the well-known discrepancies are as follows: (1) the difficulty in

reconciling the Galilean appearances with those in Jerusalem (Mt., except 28.9, Mk. 16.7, Jn. 21 vs. Lk., Acts, Mt. 28.9, Jn. 20, Mk's. appendix, 16.9f). Possibly those in Galilee were first, since the disciples very likely fled to Galilee after the crucifixion. (2) In John 19.39f Jesus' corpse is anointed immediately after the death, while in Luke 23.56, 24.1 and Mark 16.1, it is anointed only after the third day. (3) In Mark 16.1 three women visit the empty tomb, while in Matthew 28.1 only two come to visit. (4) The tomb is already open in Mark 16.4 and John 20.1, but in Matthew an angel must open it. (5) Mark's "young man in a white robe" (16.5) becomes two men in Luke 24.4. (6) Luke denies that any women saw Jesus at the tomb (24.22f), thus contradicting Matthew 28.9 and John 20.14f. (7) In John 20.19–23 the risen Christ confers the Spirit immediately after the resurrection, while in Luke 24.49 and Acts 1.5 the Spirit's conferral comes only after a considerable delay.

74. Resurrection language is earlier (1 Cr. 15 and Rm.), while exaltation language at the earliest appears in the post-Pauline Mark and Phil. 2.8f.

75. O'Collins, *op. cit.,* p. 51.

76. *Ibid.,* p. 52, a point noted by Thomas Aquinas: "Christus resurgens non rediit ad vitam communiter omnibus notam, sed ad vitam quandam immortalem et Deo conformem" (*Summ. theol.* 3, 55, 2); cf. Gerald O'Collins, "Thomas Aquinas and Christ's Resurrection," THEOLOGICAL STUDIES 31 (1970), 512–522. My translations and citations from Aquinas are from the following texts: *Summa Theologica,* 5 vols. (Madrid: Biblioteca de Autores Cristianos, 1941–1945); *Quaestiones Disputatae,* 3 vols. (Parisiis: P. Lethielleux, 1925); *Opera omnia,* edit. Leonina (Romae, 1882ff); *Opera omnia,* edit. Parmensis (Parmae, 1852–1873).

77. Kaufman, *Systematic Theology,* pp. 419–420, esp. n. 16.

78. O'Collins, *op. cit.,* p. 44; cf. Raymond E. Brown, *The Virginal Conception and Bodily Resurrection of Jesus* (New York: Paulist, 1973), pp. 113–125.

79. Mark (14.28, 16.7) and Matthew (28.10, 16–20) view the appearances as first occurring in Galilee, and this makes more sense than Luke's view that they were first in Jerusalem. We know that the disciples fled to Galilee after Jesus' death. We might speculate that Peter was the first resurrection witness, both because 1 Corinthians 15.5 explicitly says so and because of Peter's "primacy" throughout the gospels (Lk. 24.34, 22.32; Jn. 20.6, 21.15f; Mk. 8.29).

80. See X. Leon-Dufour, *Resurrection de Jésus et message pascal* (Paris: Seuil, 1971), pp. 126–130; and C. H. Dodd, "The Appearances of the Risen Christ: A Study in Form-Criticism of the Gospels," in his *More New Testament Studies* (Manchester: Manchester Univ., 1968), pp. 104–107.

81. Pousset, "La resurrection," 1021. He further suggests that the transitory nature of the appearances stems from the fact that they correspond to the disciples' transition from pre-paschal to paschal faith (1043).

82. See Willi Marxsen, *The Resurrection of Jesus of Nazareth* (London: SCM, 1970), p. 77, for the first view. He, of course, thinks that God was ultimately behind this inspiration, and so cannot be called a "humanist" on this matter. But the historical question is that of just how God was behind such an inspiration. For a radically subjectivist view see Hugh Jackson, "The Resurrection Belief of the Earliest Church: A Response to the Failure of Prophecy?" JOURNAL OF RELIGION 55 (1975), 415–425.

83. See O'Collins, *op. cit.,* pp. 106–107; and Evans, *op. cit.,* pp. 11–40, esp. pp. 39–40: "If the contentions advanced above are not wide of the mark, that is, if the doctrine of resurrection was not firmly fixed in Judaism, and if it is largely ab-

sent from the teaching of Jesus, then particular attention is focused on the actual resurrection of Jesus. It may be suggested that only this event, whatever it may have been, could have brought it about that there emerged in Christianity a precise, confident and articulate faith in which resurrection has moved from the circumference to the centre."

84. Pannenberg, *op. cit.*, p. 96; cf. O'Collins, *ibid.*, pp. 30–34.

85. Cf. Walter J. Ong, " 'I See What You Say': Sense Analogues for Intellect," in his *Interfaces of the Word: Studies in the Evolution of Consciousness and Culture* (Ithaca: Cornell Univ., 1977), pp. 121–144, for archaic man's preference for the visual model. Also helpful is Hans Jonas, "The Nobility of Sight: A Study in the Phenomenology of the Senses," in his *The Phenomenon of Life: Toward a Philosophical Biology* (New York: Harper and Row, 1966), pp. 135–156. James D. G. Dunn, *op. cit.*, p. 114, would seem to be indicating something similar to my own view: ". . . it was not the seeing itself nor the commissioning itself which was distinctive for Paul but the appearance as call, the encounter as commission. The commissioning did not come alongside, apart from the seeing. The appearance itself was the commissioning. The revelation was itself the gospel. . . . It was in the *Ineinander* (in-each-other-ness) of appearance and commission, of revelation and grace, that the distinctive and unsurpassable nature of the experience lay for Paul" (italics omitted).

86. The notion of the resurrection is an interpretation—a theory—employed by the New Testament authors to explain what occurred to Jesus. This is especially clear in the case of Paul (cf. 1 Cr.), who at times argues that Jesus has been raised because he knows beforehand that all will be raised. In other words, Paul falls back upon a prior belief to explain what has occurred to Jesus.

87. Lane, *op. cit.*, p. 71.

88. Evans, *op. cit.*, p. 148.

89. Cf. *ibid.*, pp. 1–40; O'Collins, *op. cit.*, pp. 101–116.

90. O'Collins, *op. cit.*, p. 104.

91. Helmut Koester, "The Structure and Criteria of Early Christian Beliefs," in Robinson and Koester, *op. cit.*, pp. 205–231, esp. pp. 223–229. Schillebeeckx, *op. cit.*, pp. 403–515.

92. With respect to the appearances, Raymond E. Brown, in *The Virginal Conception and Bodily Resurrection of Jesus* (New York: Paulist, 1973), p. 84, says: "While most scholars think that faith in Jesus' victory over death was first engendered by his appearance(s) to his followers, it is interesting that the shorter formulas . . . do not mention an appearance. Perhaps this is because they were formulated by those to whom the risen Jesus had appeared, men whose very activity as proclaimers of the risen Lord testified implicitly to such an appearance."

93. *Ibid.*, p. 75.

94. Reginald H. Fuller, *A Critical Introduction to the New Testament* (London: Duckworth, 1971), p. 74, relying upon H. E. Tödt, *The Son of Man in the Synoptic Tradition* (Philadelphia: Westminster, 1965).

95. See Robinson and Koester, *op. cit.*, pp. 211–223.

96. Schillebeeckx, *op. cit.*, pp. 360–397.

97. See note 95.

98. Jon Sobrino, *Christology at the Crossroads* (Maryknoll: Orbis, 1978), p. 251.

99. Karl Rahner, *Hominisation: the Evolutionary Origin of Man as a Theological Problem* (New York: Herder and Herder, 1965).

100. For a superb analysis of how a "closed" view of man—man understood solely in terms of himself apart from God—inevitably leads to narcissism and evil, see Hans Jonas, "The Abyss of the Will: Philosophical Meditation on the Seventh Chapter of Paul's Epistle to the Romans," in his *Philosophical Essays,* pp. 335–348.

101. Cited by Sobrino, *op. cit.,* p. 253.

102. R. R. Niebuhr, *Resurrection and Historical Reason: A Study of Theological Method* (New York: Scribner's, 1957).

103. Cf. our Chapters 6 through 9, on the "Christ-Experience," for various probings of the nature of the risen life itself.

104. Kaufman, *Systematic Theology,* p. 183.

105. Cf. Karl Rahner's important observation in his and Wilhelm Thüsing's *Christologie—systematisch und exegetisch* (Freiburg: Herder, 1972), pp. 55–56: "When the orthodox incarnational christology of descent says: this Jesus 'is' God, that remains true if it is rightly understood; as it stands, however, this statement could be understood in a monophysitic manner. For such statements as these, which are formulated and understood according to the norms of the *communicatio idiomatum,* nothing has been explicitly said about the fact that the 'is' as a copula is to be used and understood in a sense completely different from sentences in which the 'is' seems to us to have a similar or same meaning. For when we say: Peter is a man, this intends the real identification of the content of the subject and predicate. The meaning of the 'is' according to the usage of the christological *communicatio idiomatum* is precisely not based upon such a real identification, but upon a unique oneness of real differences always deeply a mystery, causing an unending abyss between it and other realities. For Jesus in and according to his humanity—which we say when we say 'Jesus,' 'is' not God, and God in and according to his divinity, 'is' not man in the sense of a real identification" (my transl.).

106. A point made by Raymond E. Brown, "Who Do Men Say that I Am?— A Survey of Modern Scholarship on Gospel Christology," in his *Biblical Reflections on Crises Facing the Church,* pp. 22, 36. Cf. C. F. D. Moule, *The Origin of Christology* (Cambridge: University, 1977), for the strongest expression of this view; cf. esp. pp. 2–3: ". . . the tendency which I am advocating as closer to the evidence, and which I call 'developmental,' is to explain all the various estimates of Jesus reflected in the New Testament as, in essence, only attempts to describe what was already there from the beginning. They are not successive additions of something new, but only the drawing out and articulating of what is there. They represent various stages in the development of perception, but they do not represent the accretion of any alien factors that were not inherent from the beginning. . . ." What I find missing in Moule is any careful attention to the role of the resurrection. Recently Rudolf Pesch, in his "Zür Enstehung des Glaubens an die Auferstehung Jesu," THEOLOGISCHE QUARTALSCHRIFT 153 (1973), 201–228, has argued that the origin of faith in Jesus lies *solely* in the earthly ministry. Paul's 1 Corinthians 15.3–5 is only an Old Testament septuagintal legitimation formula, and no proof about a resurrection experience can be derived from it. Further, he argues that the notion of the resurrection of an individual eschatological prophet was already available in Jesus' time, and could have sustained the disciples' faith and even been used by them after Jesus' death. Cf. on this Ulrich Wilckens, *Auferstehung: Das biblische Auferstehungs-zeugnis historisch untersucht und erklärt* (Gütersloh: Mohn, 1974), and Klaus Berger, *Die Auferstehung des Propheten und die Erhöhung des Menschensohnes: Traditionsgeschichtliche Untersuchungen zur Deutung des Geschickes*

Jesu in frühchristlichen Texten (Göttingen: Vandenhoeck und Ruprecht, 1976). But the crucial issue, it would seem, is not whether such traditions existed, but what caused the disciples to apply them to Jesus after his death. And even Pesch must admit that the confession of Jesus' deity is unprecedented and requires some unprecedented basis, as I have tried to show. Cf. John P. Galvin, "Resurrection as *Theologia Crucis Jesu:* the Foundational Christology of Rudolf Pesch," THEOLOGICAL STUDIES 38 (1977), 513–525.

The most recent attempt to account for the emergence of the kerygma without granting a catalytic role to the Easter experience is put forward by James P. Mackey, *Jesus the Man and the Myth* (New York: Paulist, 1979). While this is not the place to attempt a full analysis of this impressive book, some comments seem in order. Historically it seems to me that the radically new and concealed nature of Jesus' ministry and proclamation, as well as the tradition of the incomprehension of the disciples, is downplayed by Mackey, if not ignored. Thus he can fall back on the thesis that the "faith" of the historical Jesus somehow was "contagious" and "inspired" the disciples to believe in him. Further, and now somewhat more speculatively than simply historically, Mackey's interpretation of the "myth" of the resurrection—of the elements that make up this rather complex myth—seems somewhat narrow. The resurrection myth simply expresses the faith that the historical Jesus, particularly at this death, inspired in his disciples. It is the myth of the disciples' coming-to-faith, a faith not made possible or even deepened by anything other than the pre-Easter Jesus. If one asks where the myth derived from, Mackey would say that it was already available from Pharisaism. Yet this explanation does not adequately explain that Pharisaism looked toward the general resurrection at the end, not toward an individual resurrection before the end. Further, Mackey admits that there are other elements involved in the resurrection myth besides the element of the disciples' faith—viz., Jesus' appearances, his personal survival of death—but these play no formative role in the emergence of the kerygma, and in any case, because they "have no experiential counterparts" (p. 160) either to the disciples or to us, we cannot say anything about them anyway, other than that they might be "articles of faith" rather than items of historically probable knowledge (cf. p. 304, n. 23). (Given Mackey's radically historicist view of revelation, one wonders what an article of faith could be that has no experiential/historical correlate?). The main question I would ask at this point is whether Mackey has not too narrowly conceived the experiential correlates to the myth. If the "appearances" can accurately be described as a heightening of consciousness, it would seem that we have here an experiential correlate. But Mackey insists on interpreting these appearances in a naïvely objectivist manner, instead of in the imagistic and symbolic manner characteristic of myth. Were the "appearances" understood as mythic ways of expressing the really historical transformation of consciousness made possible by the risen Jesus, then they would not be "objective" proofs of anything, but only experiences of grace still calling for the free response of the disciples themselves. Such an experience of grace would be no more a coercive proof than Jesus' historical ministry, which Mackey falls back upon. This theory would also have the advantage of doing justice to more of the New Testament data, while Mackey's contagion theory is forced to ignore basically the important tradition of the appearances. Similarly for the personal existence of Jesus beyond death, one can question Mackey on whether this has no experiential correlate, as he claims. The promise-view of history that I will sketch in this chapter might be such a correlate, and in my Chapter 6 I explore further such correlates. The difficult issue in this area of eternal life is the experience of the self/person and whether it provides clues as to its fullest realization. As Rahner likes to claim, statements about individual eternal life are simply statements about what we know of the individual, but in the guise of fulfillment. Cf. Karl Rahner, "The Hermeneutics of Eschatological Assertions." Louis Dupré, in his *Transcendent Selfhood: the Rediscovery of the Inner Life* (New York: Seabury, 1976), has a more optimistic view of our ability to know of eternal life (cf. pp. 79–104).

IV

TOWARD A CHRISTIC GOD-CONCEPT: GOD AS *PATHOS* AND LORD

The Source of a Christological God-Concept

Our last chapter brought us to the view that, under the impact of the resurrection, the New Testament gradually came to the conviction that in and through the man Jesus God was manifesting the Divine Being and Will; and that decisively. On a most elementary level that means that for the Christian the entire life of Jesus—his birth, his ministry, his suffering and death, his resurrection-exaltation—is decisively disclosive of the Divine and thus the chief source of Christian God-knowledge. The Christian does not so much confess "Jesus is God," which would presuppose—without further qualification—that he simply knows who and what "God" is. The Christian confesses, "God is Jesus-like," meaning by the latter the entire existence of the man Jesus.

Historically it is instructive to note that, when an element of Jesus' life is singled out as disclosive of the Divine at the expense of the entirety of Jesus' life, the Christian God-concept becomes correspondingly truncated.[1] Thus, for example, an incarnation-centered Christology tends to concentrate the entirety of Christology in the birth of Jesus (view #1)—this was the tendency of the Logos Christology of the Alexandrian theologians of the great patristic period—Athanasius, Cyril of Alexandria, etc. It lies behind the common patristic axiom "God became man in order that man might become God," and it may also partly lie behind the prologue of John's gospel and the preexistence texts of the New Testament (cf. Phil. 2.6–15). But by ignoring the ministry, death and resurrection of Jesus as disclosive of God it quickly leads to a *deus ex machina* view of God—the god of "magic"—who can get along quite well without the Jesus of real history. Such a view presupposes an unhistorical view of the Divine, which, if it is not antihistorical is at least a-historical.

Another tendency is to stress the ministry of Jesus as solely disclosive of the Divine (view #2). I would say this was the great tendency of nine-teenth-century liberalism, which all too quickly wanted only a Jesus who reflected bourgeois enlightened attitudes. This same tendency shows up among more contemporary theologians and exegetes who concentrate the entirety of Christology into the words and deeds of the Jesus of the minis-try. This view, of course, fails to probe what the scandal of the cross may disclose about God, and the resurrection simply becomes a mythological manner of speaking of the message of Jesus. What is often not noted is that this implies that God is merely a good moral example, a supreme teacher perhaps, but not a being that actively enters into history to confront evil (the cross) and even to initiate a process of salvation (resurrection).

Yet another tendency is to concentrate the entirety of Christology into the cross (view #3). Perhaps this is the great tendency of periods of crises, when there seems to be little cause to believe in human progress and enlightenment. Yet there can be no doubt that the cross is an integral com-ponent of the Christian God-concept, for more than any other element of Jesus' life it accentuates the fact that the Christian God-concept is histori-cal. It means, as process theology tells us, that God is the "fellow sufferer who endures" (view #3) rather than simply a power over history (view #1) or a deist moral enlightener (view #2). In our own times the reappro-priation of this dimension of the Christian God-concept stems primarily from the theologians of liberation and emancipation,[2] who see in the cross of Jesus God's decisive "no" to all dehumanizing power structures in his-tory. As Sobrino put it, "In Jesus' cross . . . God's transcendence is refor-mulated in the categories of power, suffering, and love."[3]

There can be little doubt that historically this element of the cross of Jesus as a source of our God-knowledge has been the most difficult to keep in focus. Even in the gospels the sober realism of Jesus' cry of abandon-ment found in Mark—"My God, my God, why have you forsaken me?" (Mk. 15.37; cf. Ps. 22.2)—caused trouble for the other evangelists who sought to modify it through less scandalous expressions. Thus Luke re-places Mark's cry with the more serene, "Father, into your hands I com-mend my spirit" (23.46), making Jesus into a "confident martyr," as Sobrino put it.[4] John goes further and presents Jesus at the cross as God's Son who almost "regally" allows the executioners to put him to death. As Leo O'Donovan expressed it, "Kingship is the motif which . . . dominates the trial, and it is only John's gospel which, in an extremely precious pas-sage (18.33–38), presents Jesus as explaining his kingship."[5] It is only Paul who seems to keep the cross in focus (1 Cr. 1.23). We further see the loss of a cross-consciousness in the fact that the title "the suffering servant" as an appellation for Jesus, found in Acts (3.13, 26; 4.27, 30; 8.26) and 1 Pe-ter (2.22–24), is gradually replaced by the Christological titles "Lord" and "God" without further qualification. No doubt the later history of Chris-tian spirituality[6] has known its periods of devotion to the cross of Jesus—a kind of cross-mystique—but this was all too often an idealizing or trivializ-ing of the cross rather than a reappropriation of what the cross means for our concept of God. In part, as we shall see, the loss of the importance of the cross can be traced to the influence of Hellenistic conceptions of deity in Christianity. But I think we would be intellectualizing history were we to view Greek thought as the only operative factor here. The failure to take the cross seriously is probably more deeply linked with man's failure to take evil seriously, with our blindness and state of alienation. Here Käsemann's observation is pertinent: ". . . the cross . . . shows, in the perspective of salvation, that the true man is always the sinner, cannot at all help himself, is unable by his activity to overcome his infinite distance from God, and therefore remains part of a world lost, chaotic, given over to nothingness, awaiting the resurrection of the dead."[7]

Because the entire life of Jesus is the decisive source of our God-concept, we Christians must probe as deeply as possible what the cross implies about the reality of God. As we shall see later, it gives birth to a quite distinctive notion of divine transcendence as radical "immanence," to a notion of God as empathetic rather than apathetic, to a God as "tragically" involved in history rather than simply above history. In other words, the resurrection, by showing that God is "behind" Jesus' entire life, does not annul the cross but gives it enduring significance for our Christian understanding of God. Yet, were one to make the cross the sole source of our God-knowledge, history would lose its promise character and God's transcendence—and the elements of ecstasy, confidence and joy to which it gives rise (see Lk. 7.32)—would be jeopardized. God would be a world-immanent deity, himself one object among other objects struggling in the world, but no longer fully the transcendent deity preached by Jesus. In this light Paul is remarkable, for he always preserves a dialectical relationship between the crucified and the risen Jesus (see 1 Cr.).

Finally, Christology can be absorbed into the resurrection of Jesus (view #4). Instructively, Paul encountered this difficulty quite early, as his letters to the Corinthians illustrate.[8] Paul begins his first letter by praising the Corinthians, "richly endowed with every gift of speech and knowledge" (1 Cr. 1.5). But as we read on, a decided shift in tone occurs: "Brothers, the trouble was that I could not talk to you as spiritual men but only as men of flesh, as infants in Christ" (1 Cr. 3.1). And then, abruptly, he brings us to the central point: "I determined that while I was with you I would speak of nothing but Jesus Christ and him crucified" (1 Cr. 2.2). As Käsemann explains it, these Corinthians espoused a form of "Hellenistic enthusiasm." Thus the stress among them upon signs and wonders, esoteric knowledge, ecstatic utterances. Even the Eucharist was for them, primarily not a love and service feast, but simply an occasion for eschatological rejoicing and speaking in tongues. Their faith was concentrated solely in the resurrected and exalted Lord; hence, of the earthly Jesus they could say, "Jesus be cursed" (1 Cr. 12.3). What was occurring

was analogous to the mystery religions' preaching of the dying god restored to life, who brings along a new world in which his own people are to share. Strangely enough, therefore, the apostle had to take up a position . . . opposing [their] theology of resurrection.[9]

Hence Paul corrects the Corinthian's Christology by reminding them that it is the crucified one who has been raised (1 Cr. 15.3–4; cf. Phil. 2.9). This further indicates that their anthropology—their praxis—must be corrected; the sacraments are not simply moments for eschatological rejoicing, but events in which Jesus' death is proclaimed (1 Cr. 10.1–12). Paul is not denying the resurrection, but understanding it differently, in the light of the earthly and crucified Jesus. As Philippians 3.10 sees it, the result of knowing the power of the resurrection is that I "may share in his sufferings, becoming like him in his death."

Käsemann beautifully sums up the matter:

> . . . Paul contrasted his own theology of resurrection with that of the enthusiasts. His theology, too, is one of freedom; but it is that of people who are attached to Jesus, who are therefore distinguished by his cross, are called with him to suffer under the pious and the ungodly, under tyrants and institutions, are capable of brotherhood, and live on the strength of the first commandment. Its most important feature is that it is able to give freedom and to allow it to others. For it hands on what it has received, and thereby makes room for those who are caught in themselves and in their fears and sicknesses. Its business is to serve and help, and so it keeps alive the picture of Jesus. Thus far it remains directed towards earthly realities, instead of fleeing into heavenly realms. Jesus, too, came to those who needed him, and used his power so as to help them. This freedom is an anticipation of what things are to be like in the coming world and everlasting life.[10]

But it is not only the Corinthians' Christology that is in need of correction; their theodicy is, too. For when the resurrection becomes the whole of Christology, it becomes the sole source of our knowledge of God too. And then the Christian God-concept quickly erodes into solely a world-transcendent deity, an apathetic rather than an empathetic being. This kind of "god" quickly legitimates social passivity and indifference to the world, and perhaps that is why it is characteristic of all "enthusiastic" groups in Christian history. To quote Käsemann once again, "Unless the resurrected Jesus is confessed as the crucified Lord, the resurrection becomes only an ideogram for the glorification of the world, a term expressing a cosmological and anthropological ideology."[11] In a word, the resurrection highlights that God is a transcendent God of the promise; the earthly and crucified Jesus, that God's transcendence is not a-historical or apathetic, but one of involvement in human history.

In short, when we confess Jesus' deity we are saying that Jesus' entire existence discloses God to us. In the end, as we shall see, this leads us to a distinctively Christian God-concept, to a distinctive understanding of divine immanence and transcendence and their dialectical interrelationship.

Preliminary Observations on the God-Concept of Judaism and Hellenism

As we indicated in our last chapter, taking the step of confessing Jesus' deity was a more likely development for Judaism[12] than for Hellenism. The key insight from Judaism is that God and history, God and humanity, do not exist in a relation of competition or antipathy to one another. Israel's God is a historical God who remains faithful to his promises in history. As I indicated in my last chapter, this implies a quite distinctive metaphysics of being, in which being remains itself by giving itself away in love. Being is thought to be "ecstatic," going outside itself in surrender.[13] Israel's God, then, is not a self-enclosed Monad, but a Relational Being, and this is the necessary ontological presupposition for asserting that God could be the man Jesus, that God could be Jesus-like. It is now generally recognized that Greek thought, especially in its later Neo- and Middle-Platonic phases, tended to conceptualize the Divine as the "One," the self-sufficient Being, and therefore the Being free from the mutability, suffering and passion characterizing incomplete beings. The Old Testament God, however, was primarily a God-of-relationships, giving guidance and life in human history. Even the mysterious revelation of Yahweh's name (Ex. 3.14), while pointing to Yahweh's transcendence, indicates that that transcendence is not a world-absence, but a promise of involvement in Israel's misery and enslavement. For this reason the revelation of Yahweh's name does not "lift Moses" out of the world, but deepens his sense of mission to his people (Ex. 3.10). Further, the entire context of the revelation indicates that Yahweh reveals his name because this God wants his people to know that "I will be with you" (Ex. 3.12; 4.12, 15; 6.7). There is, of course, a profound sense of Yahweh's eternity and transcendence in the Old Testament, especially in the later prophets. But this is best understood as never-failing fidelity to the divine promises, rather than in a Greek static and uninvolving sense. Thus, for Hosea, Yahweh is "the Holy One in your midst" (Hos. 11.9), and Amos calls God "Immanuel" ("God-with-us"; Am. 5.14–15). Jeremiah emphasizes against the false prophets that God is "afar off," and not to be identified with their arbitrary messages, but he seems to have in mind too that there is no hiding place from this God (Jer. 21.23–32). Eric Voegelin[14] has said that in the exile Israel discovered God's transcendence; the exile was Israel's "exodus from itself," from its tendency to restrict Yahweh to itself. But the Old Testament also consistently depicts God as undergoing an "exodus from himself," as a God of relationship who hears affliction and gives guidance (Ex 3.7–8).

It is in this light, then, that we should understand Wilhelm Thüsing's observation on the relationship between the Christian confession of Jesus' deity and the Old Testament confession of monotheism:

> The Christ-belief is not a lessening, but a qualitatively new radicalizing of the Old Testament Yahweh-monotheism and its justly intense and emphatic confession, "Hear, O Israel, Yahweh, your God, is one." New Testament Christianity is in no way a "mystical religion" isolated from

the creative measure of fullness and breadth found in the Old Testament life of faith, but has rather been able to bring out the depth-dimension of this life of faith in a new way.[15]

Thüsing indicates that what ultimately stands in the way of appreciating how the Christ-belief radicalizes Jewish monotheism is an "all too individualistic concept of the God-relation," in which the "theological and sociological" presupposition for knowing God is overlooked; namely, history and our fellow brothers. I would want to add that the Divine reality itself is viewed too individualistically, as a self-enclosed monad, as a God without a world and without history. Such would be to overlook the biblical view of man as God's "image" (Gn. 1.26–27). The Christ-belief, then, is "not a surrender of the dynamic dialogical character of the Old Testament Covenant, but its maintenance, its 'setting in power' (Rm. 15.8)."[16] The Christ-belief, then, reveals more radically the dialogical character of God, and hence the characteristic Johannine "God is love" (1 Jn. 4.8, 16), through the man Jesus, the new "image" of God in history (Hb. 1.3).

This seems to be the inner tendency of Jewish monotheism itself. Already in Exodus the great revelation was Yahweh's desire to reveal the divine name, to be "dialogical," that is. The great Old Testament issue was not whether there was a God, but who was the "true God" and how was man to be receptive for this true God. It was assumed that God was dialogical and relational. The New Testament by indicating that one confesses Jesus as Lord through the Spirit (1 Cr. 12.3; Jn. 16.13) would seem to be indicating its desire to link up with this dialogical tradition of God, for in the Old Testament too God's dialogical revelation takes place through the Spirit (Joel 3.1f; Ez. 36.26f; Jer. 31.33f.). In this sense Thüsing remarks that the "promises of the Father through Jesus are not simply fulfilled or exhausted, but irreversibly placed in motion."[17] A new understanding of divine transcendence is opened through confessing Jesus' deity, in which God's being can no longer be perverted through viewing it as a lofty "paternalism"; it is truly dialogical. What decisively brings this out is the cross of Jesus, in which the love-character of God's dialogue comes through most intensively.

Seen in this light, then, Christology does not negate Judaism but radicalizes it. Without the Jewish God-concept, the deity of Jesus can only be misunderstood as a lapse from monotheism and a regression to some form of binitarianism or polytheism. But this brings us to the delicate question of the Jewish "no" to Jesus, to why historic Judaism did not sense in Christianity simply a more radical understanding of its own confession but rather its negation. It seems to me that this is a properly Christological question, for all the evidence indicates that we cannot simply write off the Jewish negation of Christology as a classic example of the prophetic "hardness of heart."

Part of the problem, I think, stems from what Voegelin has called the "cultural mortgages" imposed by historical conditioning. Here the main element is the shift in Jewish-Christian relations occurring between the pre-A.D. 70 and post-70 historical situation. The reader will note that, except for Paul, the greater bulk of the evangelical Christology, especially the crucial "deity" passages of John, was written after A.D. 70. The temple is destroyed, of course, after 70, and now in Roman eyes the Jewish people are tainted and suspect. Christians, we speculate, would want to appear favorable in Roman eyes, and this they could do by making clear their estrangement from Judaism. On the other hand, for Judaism the period is clearly one of crisis. With the destruction of the temple, the raison d'être of the Saducees, Zealots and Essenes is undercut and the Pharisaic party must now renew Jewish identity and provide Judaism with a theology of survival. It is helpful to note that Paul's letters are pre-70, and he gives no clear evidence of attributing Jesus' death to Judaism. In my opinion it is not Paul who espouses the anti-Semitism that does seem to characterize the other New Testament books and patristic Christianity. Except for the highly disputed text of 1 Thessalonians 2.14–16,[18] Paul is insistent that Judaism cannot be rejected (Rm. 11.1) on the grounds that "the gifts and the call of God are irrevocable" (Rm. 11.29; cf. Rm 11.26; 9.1). True, Paul wishes that the Jews were enlightened with respect to Jesus (Rm. 10. 2–3) and even preaches freedom from circumcision for gentiles, but his interest is to declare that with Christ we have moved into a new phase of God's revelation (Rm. 1.17; 3.21; 10.3), not that Judaism has been negated. Hence he maintains the holiness of the Law (Rm. 7.12) and the election of the Jews (Rm. 11.28), something we would expect if Christology is a radicalization of monotheism. Yet, apart from Paul, the evidence is clear that "the foundations of anti-Judaic thought were laid in the New Testament,"[19] and this must surely have had its effects both upon the Jewish "reception" of Christ and the Christian understanding of him. I think we are at the point now when we must clearly admit at least a strain of anti-Semitism in Matthew, for example, when he tells us that while the gentiles will sit at the Messianic Banquet, the sons of the kingdom will be cast out into outer darkness (Mt. 8.11f; Lk. 13.25). But what is a "strain" in the synoptics becomes, as Ruether tells us, a systematic and philosophized anti-Judaism in Hebrews and John. "John," says Ruether, "moves the 'crime of the Jews' very close to what will become the charge of 'deicide,' i.e., that the 'Jews,' in killing Jesus, commit the religious crime of rejection and murder, not merely of God's prophet, but God's revealed self-expression."[20]

In any case, the shift after 70 certainly affected the Jewish "reception" of Jesus. Just as it enabled Christians to distance themselves from the Jewish understanding of monotheism and to rethink it in the light of the resurrection, so this time caused the Pharisees to further accentuate their understanding of monotheism so as to sustain Jewish identity in a period of crisis. Here Ruether's observation is pertinent that in Jewish eyes the Christian movement was seen as but another example of Jewish messianism, of "the lively expectation of a historical redemption which had kept

Palestinian Jewry at a fever pitch for three centuries, instead of sober attention to the path of salvation which God had commanded through his Torah."[21]

But is there a properly theological reason for the Jewish "no" to Jesus, a motive that stems not simply from cultural misunderstanding but from theological principle itself? Here, I think, theologians cannot ignore Ruether's view that Christology, at least as understood from the New Testament to Chalcedon, is inherently anti-Semitic. In her important *Faith and Fratricide,* her argument is basically twofold. First, she maintains that Christians both historicized and spiritualized the eschatological promises of the prophets and Jesus. The historicization tendency stems from the delay of Jesus' return; this caused a loss of the sense of the future expectation of Jesus and a focusing on the Church, to the exclusion of Judaism, and thus a tendency to absolutize and finalize Jesus. The spiritualization tendency, stemming mainly from Hellenism, can be seen in John, who interprets the promises of the messianic era in terms of inward, unhistorically observable transformations. Secondly, she maintains that coupled with this is the anti-Judaic tendency of the Christians to solidify their position by explaining the Jewish nonacceptance of Jesus as a result of what the prophets called the Jewish blindness, reprobation and infidelity. The prophetic negative critique of Israel is projected wholly onto Judaism by the Christians, and thus Christianity lost any negative critical principle for itself. This is what Ruether calls "the left-hand of Christology," and it eventually legitimated the patristic *Adversus Judaeos* tradition.[22]

Although still not fully published, Ruether's *Messiah of Israel and the Cosmic Christ: a Study of the Development of Christology in Judaism and Early Christianity*[23] carries her argument further. She proposes that Jesus' Messiahship was originally much more Jewish than the scriptures imply; namely that it was "political, revolutionary, and recognizable within history."[24] This element has been suppressed by the spiritualizing and deeschatologizing (historicizing) tendencies mentioned above. And under the influence of Hellenism (gentile and Jewish), Christianity eventually effected a unique synthesis between the Hellenistic, cosmological Archetypal Man and the Jewish eschatological Messiah, by projecting both onto Jesus and by deeschatologizing the latter.

I personally am very grateful to Ruether for exposing the anti-Semitic elements in the New Testament so forcefully and for forcing me to rethink the issue of Christology and monotheism. Here I do not want to dispute this sad anti-Semitism, but only to probe whether the Christological confession of Jesus' deity is inherently anti-Semitic. First, it can be said that even in the New Testament there are Christologies that show no signs of anti-Semitism. As noted, it is not at all clear that Paul is anti-Semitic, and his Christology is a very "high" one. Further, Ruether makes her strongest case on the view that the need to explain the crucifixion led the evangelists to a simultaneous exalting of Jesus and reprobation of the Jews. Besides the fact that her stress on the crucifixion as generating Christology ignores the role of the resurrection, we know that there are Christologies in the New Testament in which the death of Jesus plays no significant role, as, for example, the wisdom Christology of Colossians 1.15–20. This is enough to indicate that not every Christology is essentially linked with a negative, anti-Judaic element.

But what of the historicizing and spiritualizing tendencies that Ruether so strongly stresses? Would this necessarily lead to an anti-Semitic Christology? Her view is that the delay of the second coming caused the first, and Hellenism caused the latter, while both necessarily reinforced the negation of Judaism. But is it proper to say that the delay of the parousia originated Christianity's claims for Jesus, or that it served as one catalyst for a rethinking of Jesus' decisive place in Christianity? Here we come to Ruether's tendency to ignore the resurrection. For without the resurrection the delay of the parousia would have led to the invalidation of Jesus, not his exaltation. The primary reality for Paul is the resurrection, not the delay of the parousia. Under the pressure of the latter, he rethinks the implications of the resurrection; he does not create it *de novo*. And as we have seen, this does not land him in an anti-Semitic stance. Further, there is a quite definite historicizing tendency in Christology, insofar as Jesus is viewed not simply as an object of "future" hope but as a risen Lord active now in history. But again, this belief was not simply a creation of the Church caused by the delay of the parousia, but a deeper insight into just how historically involved God wants to be. While this could lead to a collapse of the sense of the future—an unreal sense of finality—we have seen how Paul deals precisely with such a problem among the Corinthian Hellenists by reminding them that the cross has not been negated by Jesus' resurrection but raised to the level of the very revelation of God's being. Ruether ignores Paul's profound theology of the cross and how it negates any simplistic finalizing of Jesus. Personally, Ruether's stress on the historicization tendency as leading to anti-Judaism appears quite weak to me. It is precisely the stress on the historical that characterizes Judaism and which led it to a rejection of confounded Messianisms: "Judaism, in all of its forms and manifestations, has always maintained a concept of redemption as an event which takes place publicly, on the stage of history and within the community."[25] And it is precisely this historical and very Jewish view of redemption that enabled Christianity ultimately to see in the man Jesus God's very revelation.

The spiritualizing tendency, which Ruether links with Hellenism, cannot be disputed. Not only the gospels and Jesus, but the Pharisees themselves "interiorized" religion. But the interior is not played off against the exterior, especially in John, whom Ruether considers the most spiritualized of all the gospels. But Ruether's point is that under the influence of Hellenism this spiritualizing was exaggerated, thus enabling Christianity to lose sight of the yet incomplete nature of redemption by viewing it as a private, invisible happening. Thus the ability to project Hellenistic "Archetypal Man" myths onto Christ. But she has not come to terms with the profound way in which Hellenism was Christianized, a process beginning even in the scriptures. This is an uncritical acceptance of the Hellenization of dogma thesis, and fails to come to terms with the Christian "mutation" of Greek metaphysics and religion, something partly made possible by Jewish principles themselves.

My point is that the Jewish "no" to Jesus does not stem from an inherently anti-Semitic Christology. The fact is that, in principle, Judaism and Christianity are not irreconcilable. Against Scholem, for example, who thinks that Christian use of the Old Testament interprets it against its very grain, my reflections lead me to agree with Von Rad:

> The question should be put the other way round: how was it possible for the Old Testament traditions, and all the narrative, prayers, and predictions, to be taken over by the New Testament? This could not have happened if the Old Testament writings had not themselves contained pointers to Christ and been hermeneutically adapted to such a merger.[26]

The confession of Jesus' deity is only understandable on the Jewish view of God. There is, however, a Jewish "no" to Christ and it does not stem from Jewish stubborness. But it is instructive that this "no" stems from the post-70 situation, and thus from Voegelin's "cultural mortgages." (The fact is that after 70, Judaism and Christianity followed different historical paths, and this different history is what ultimately separates the two, for history creates a different sort of person. It is history, and not an inherently anti-Semitic Christology, which is the issue.) The future of Jewish-Christian relations does not lie in trivializing Jesus and thus rendering him of no interest to Judaism, but in bringing out the "Halakic" meaning of Jesus; that is, in exploring how the God of history really manifested his historicality—his dialogical reality—in Jesus.[27]

While Hebrew reflection on God led Judaism to a view of God as involved in history, Greek and Hellenistic reflection tended to focus on the problem of order in society and thus on "God" as the ground of this order. It is, I think, primarily the differences in experience that generated different foci on the Divine. The Hebrew people, from their earliest foundations in Abraham through the exile, were a "moving" people. God was experienced as not only "behind" them but "ahead" of them, as not only the ground of their "order" but as involved with them, as the impetus to "disorder," to movement, to novelty, to the suffering of the exile. This is why we can say that the confession of God in the man Jesus was an easier development for Judaism than for Hellenism. For the classical Greek philosophers, however, it is the experience of political disorder in Athenian society that leads them to search for order and a ground of order. This search for order is even true of the pre-Socratics, who view the key function of the Divine as the ground of what is normal and regular in the cosmos and in experience. This insight can even be found in the pre-philosophic Olympian deities, which are always "immanental . . . integral to the normal order of events."[28]

The consequences for the Greek God-concept are many, but here I would only single out two. First, the notion of divine transcendence. The classical Greek philosophers do know an experience of divine transcendence, namely, the transcendent search for an order beyond the Homeric gods, the Socratic search within the depths of the soul, and even the search of the Orphic mysteries for the Divine. Perhaps, as Voegelin has indicated, this experience of transcendence is clearest in Plato and Aristotle, who underwent a leap in being, an opening of their souls to the Divine: "Both Plato's eroticism of the search (*Zetesis*) and Aristotle's intellectually more aggressive *aporein* recognize in 'man the questioner' the man moved by God to ask the questions that will lead him toward the cause of being."[29] But Voegelin distinguishes between the "noetic differentiation" that occurred among the Greeks and the "pneumatic differentiation" of the Judaeo-Christian traditions: "In Israel it assumed the form of historical existence of a people under God; in Hellas it assumed the form of personal existence of individual human beings under God."[30] This difference in tone in the experience of transcendence explains why the Greeks and the later Hellenists focused on the Divine as the source of unity, justice, and the good, since these were the problems most apparent to the individual philosopher in Athenian society. God as "the ground of order" is their key intuition. What Carmody says of Plato is not an unfair generalization of classical Greek thought in general:

> The core of Plato's knowledge of God . . . is his own experience of Spirit. . . . By an ascesis to maximize its freedom, the Platonic soul can advance in contemplation of the Ideas. The prime idea, that of the Good, is therefore conceived as the foremost objective of the divinization process. Man becomes like God by fanning the spark of the divine in himself—by developing the capacity of his nous to contemplate the good. His dim conception of the divinity is extrapolated from his own spiritual qualities, as transcendence opens them out. This makes divinity spiritual, ideal, good, and immortal.[31]

Experientially Voegelin has adequately shown that this is genuine transcendence that we find in the Greeks, for they are conscious of the pull of the Divine from beyond, of a tension filled in-betweenness: "Plato was just as conscious of the revelatory component in the truth of his *logos* as the prophets of Israel or the authors of the New Testament writings."[32] It is not the fact of transcendence but the different quality of its experience that differentiates Hellas from Israel. For the latter, it is the experience of history, with its flux and change, that chiefly qualifies the experience. For Hellas, flux and change—that is disorder—is precisely what the Greek deity did not stand for. We know that the Greeks did not ignore the problem of disorder, of the irrational. But we also know that they did not integrate it into their reflection on the Divine. It remained "necessity" (*ananke*), fate (*moira*), and of it Plato said: "Even God is said not to be able to fight against necessity."[33]

Secondly, we turn to the problem of divine apathy. *Apatheia,* as a doctrine clearly formulated, appears only in the post-Aristotelian schools of the Epicureans, Skeptics, and Stoics. For them happiness is *ataraxia,* a state of mental calm, issuing from *apatheia* (absence of passion) and *autarkeia* (self-sufficiency). Zeno saw passion (*pathos*) as "a movement in the soul contrary to reason and to the soul's very nature."[34] While Zeno did not deny the existence of passion but only denigrated it, Chrysippus even denied its existence in the man of reason. This kind of thinking, I propose, can be traced back to the Greek experience of divine transcendence. Remember that that transcendence was discovered through the search of the *nous* to maximize the forces of order in society. Passion, which stood on the side of disorder, could not be an authentic aspect of transcendence. Passion also involves the ability to suffer, to undergo change, and this, too, must be excluded from the experience of the Divine. Hence Plato defines the Good as that which "differs in nature from everything else in that the being who possesses it always and in all respects has the most perfect sufficiency and is never in need of any other thing."[35] Aristotle carries this further, viewing God as fully self-sufficient: "since he is in need of nothing, God cannot have need of friends, nor will he have any."[36] Aristotle's God is a "final" cause, not an "efficient" one: this God moves others purely through attraction, but is himself completely unmoved and indifferent.

These reflections on the Greek God-concept are important because they enable us to see how difficult it was for the early Church to come to an adequate understanding of the biblical confession of Jesus' deity in a primarily Hellenistic world. The Greek notions of divine transcendence and *apatheia* had been solidified and systematized as doctrines in the schools of Middle and Neo-Platonism by the time the post-biblical Church began its reflection on Jesus. This difficulty first manifests itself in the second and third-century controversies of "Monarchianism" and "Modalism," which were essentially attempts to think through the relation of Jesus' divinity to Jewish monotheism. The former thought of the divine in Jesus as the impersonal power (*dynamis*) of the Father (Theodotus of Byzantium, Paul of Samosata); for the latter, the divine in Jesus was a particular "epiphany" (*modus*) of the Father (Noetus, Praxeas, Sabellius). In either case, what lies behind this speculation is primarily the Hellenistic God-concept as a self-sufficient entity. God can only be the self-sufficient Father, not Jesus.

But it is the case of the third-century Arius that most dramatically illustrates the Hellenization of Christology. Arius's denial of the divinity of Jesus is a well-known chapter in the history of Christology. What is worth underscoring here is that the Arian denial of Jesus' divinity did not stem from any pre-modern brand of secularism but rather from a very Hellenized conception of the deity.[37] Arius's God was "the only unbegotten, the only eternal, the only one without beginning, the only true, the only one who has immortality, the only wise, the only good, the only potentate."[38] Under the pressure of the developing theology of the Trinity, Arius makes room for a "Triad," but only the "Monad" is eternal. Pelikan calls this an "uncompromising view of divine transcendence";[39] we can see behind it the apathetic deity of Hellenism. Though allowing a special place to Jesus' *Logos* as "before time" but not eternal, his fear of involving God in mutability and corporeality could not allow him to take the step of affirming Jesus' deity. Pelikan puts it helpfully: "Such a total transcendence was necessary not only for the sake of the utter oneness of God, but also because of the fragility of creatures, which 'could not endure to be made by the absolute hand of the Unoriginate.' "[40] I think Grillmeier[41] makes an important observation when he says that all these heresies are basically "archaic." This means that they fail to recognize that the God-concept has been radicalized through Jesus. They have failed to perceive the development that has occurred in God-thinking through Jesus.

In general the Fathers affirmed Jesus' divinity, and this from the very earliest period (cf. 2 Clem. 1.1–2), but this was for more soteriological than theoretical motives. It was Arius's role to raise the issue in a more purely theoretical way, and the issue was met finally by the Council of Nicaea (325). In taking the step, through the help especially of Athanasius, of affirming that the Divine in Jesus was "only-begotten" and *"homoousios,"* they were really preserving the more Jewish God-concept, although we cannot be certain that they understood the matter in this way. Athanasius probably had more soteriological motives in mind, especially the Eastern view that the *Logos* had become man so that men might become God. And the later confusion after Nicaea[42] tends to confirm that the Fathers did not explicitly grasp that the biblical God-concept was the deeper issue. One suspects that we are only aware of this because of our greater sensitivity to history and God's role within it. Especially difficult for the Fathers was the issue of *apatheia* in the Divine: how could an incarnate God suffer and die? Yet, although perhaps the depth of the suffering of the cross does not fully come out, the Fathers sought not to negate the Divine *Pathos:* "The timeless . . . impalpable, beyond suffering, who for our sake was subject to suffering" (Ignatius of Antioch).[43] However, a particularly important contribution toward a reappropriation of the Hebraic dialogical character of the God-concept stems from the great Cappadocians (Basil, Gregory Nazianzus, Gregory of Nyssa), whose insight was appropriated by the Church at the first Council of Constantinople (381). Their reflections take place in the context of Trinitarian speculation and the issue of the Spirit's divinity, which as we will see, are all issues implied in the confession of Jesus' deity. What they suggest is a distinction between *ousia*—the one divine nature—and *hypostasis,* a term that they quite originally understood to mean the concrete manner in which that divine nature is realized. Here we seem to have a break, away from Greek abstract thinking in terms of "nature," to a more Judaeo-Christian kind of thinking in personalistic, almost historical categories.[44]

The Danger of Confessing Jesus' Divinity

Already in the New Testament, as we have seen, the new exalted status accorded Jesus became a "problem." We have seen how Paul had to correct the exaggerated resurrection Christology of the Corinthian Hellenists, and by implication their God-concept. They did not view the cross of Jesus as a continual source of their Christological-and-God-thinking. Christ was being turned into another "apathetic" Hellenistic deity, rather than the revelation of the God who appeared in the entire life of Jesus, especially the Jesus of the passion and death. Mark's gospel engages in a strategy similar to Paul's determination to know only Christ and him crucified (1 Cr. 2.2). His is the gospel that stresses the passion most acutely, despite his belief in the risen Jesus. Evidently the situation of persecution under which he wrote enabled Mark to recover the cross as a constant source of his theological thinking. Similarly I know that it is customary to read the letter to the Hebrews as an early attempt to understand Jesus in Jewish priestly terms as the new and final high priest. But it is also possible to view it as a critique against any attempt to identify Jesus with any merely "cultic" deity, deities that were common in the highly syncretized world of the first century. Such cultic deities fostered the notion that God could only be mediated by priests and sacrifices, that God was only to be found in a sacred space and time. Hebrews is telling us that a quite different conception of God has emerged in Jesus, which makes it inappropriate to liken him to a cultic deity. The key point I am trying to make is that the entire life of Jesus is the source of our God-knowledge. This means that we do not simply know beforehand who or what God is. We cannot assume that Jesus is another Hellenistic and cultic deity. Only his entire life can tell us. Yet, as religious history tells us, the tendency is great to fashion Jesus over according to our prior God-concepts.

A scholar who has carefully pondered the "deformations" to which Christianity is subject is Eric Voegelin.[45] Before proceeding with our more systematic observations on a Christological God-concept, a dialogue with Voegelin will help us avoid distortions in the Christian God-doctrine, distortions that admittedly history illustrates all too readily. For the most part, Voegelin has been engaged in the elaboration of a general philosophy of history in his *Order and History,* and so his tendency is to stress the broad thread of continuity throughout the great breakthroughs in history. Thus he will pay special attention to the continuity between the "noetic" differentiation that occurred among the Greek philosophers and the "pneumatic" differentiation stemming from the prophets and Jesus. Underlying both he discerns a common noetic core, an awareness that existence is experienced as an "in-betweenness" (*metaxy*), a movement of transcendence in which "the Beyond of the *metaxy* reaches into the *metaxy* in a participatory event." Existence, that is, is "experienced as part of a reality which extends beyond the In-Between."[46] This gives rise to the experience of existence as a system of pulls and counter-pulls, as an experience of life offering us a direction that can either be pursued or avoided: "There is direction in existence; and as we follow it or not, life can be death, and death life eternal" (cf. Rm. 8.13).[47] The awareness of the transcendent "Beyond" does not, then, eliminate our human responsibility: the self becomes a force that "must decide the struggle of the pulls through cooperation with the sacred pull of reason (*Logos*) and judgment (*logismos*)."[48] The awareness of God in Jesus does not eliminate the experience of living in the "in-between": it rather confirms that the "Beyond of the *metaxy*" is participating in our *metaxy*. Thus Voegelin reminds us that what was primarily going forward in Jesus was man's growing awareness of the Divine, not just items of information about a man called Jesus.

> The divine Sonship is not revealed through an information tendered by Jesus, but through a man's response to the full presence in Jesus of the same unknown God by whose presence he is inchoatively moved in his own existence. The Saving Tale can be differentiated beyond classic philosophy, as it has historically happened through Christ and the Gospel, but there is no alternative to the symbolization of the In-Between of existence and its divine Beyond by mythical imagination.[49]

But Voegelin is most helpful in his description of the distinctive features of the Christian God-concept. For while there is a common noetic core between Hellas and Jesus, Voegelin carefully maintains that the "differences between prophecy, classic philosophy, and the Gospel must be sought in the degrees of differentiation of existential truth."[50] He even goes so far as to maintain that the full comprehension of man's relation to the Divine Beyond takes place through the life and death of Jesus. While classical philosophy marks an advance over mythic and cosmological thinking, in which the Divine is viewed purely immanently and intracosmically, it did not completely break from cosmological thinking, as the case of Plato illustrates. With Jesus and Christianity, however, we have a more differentiated understanding of the Divine than that found even among the philosophers. Voegelin concentrates on the Incarnation belief as the key indication that Christianity became aware, not only of God's transcendence like the philosophers, but of that God's response to mankind, of the Divine initiative in human history. Thus the gospel symbolism of a God who "becomes man to gain his life by suffering death."[51] In our terms we could say that Christianity became decisively aware, through Jesus, of God as a relational Being, involving and opening the Divine Reality to human history. Accompanying this, at least in the case of Paul, is a deeper penetration of history's meaning. To be sure, both Plato and Paul experience and know history as a directional movement, illuminated by the noetic and pneumatic differentiations which make that directionality apparent. But Paul's awareness of the resurrection goes beyond Plato's awareness of a "Before and After." Voegelin maintains that "the classic meaning *in* history can be opposed by Paul with a meaning *of* history, because he knows the end of the story in the transfiguration that begins with the Resurrection."[52] I think it important to appropriate Voegelin's insight that there is a greater comprehension of history in Paul than in Hellas, and this because of the resurrection, but I would qualify it somewhat. Paul apparently became aware of history as promise through the resurrection, not of some items of information about the end. He never loses his sense of history as still open: "When, finally, all has been subjected to the Son, he will then subject himself to the One who made all things subject to him, so that God may be all in all" (1 Cr. 15.28). I think this insight of Paul's is directly linked with his stress on Jesus' cross as not annulled by the resurrection but raised to a revelation of God's own being. Most basically the cross tells us that God is within history, involved in its painful struggle. In Voegelin's terms, the Pauline meaning of history is that there is meaning in history. Voegelin does not seem to be aware of Paul's struggle with the Corinthian Hellenists and their "false" view of the resurrection according to Paul.

Voegelin is especially sensitive to the deformations to which Christianity is subject; perhaps that is why he tends to view the Corinthian Hellenists' view of the resurrection as the central one. In any case, here we come to what motivated this dialogue with Voegelin: the danger of confessing Jesus' divinity. Voegelin's basic thesis, which I want to appropriate, is that Christianity is especially prone to the danger of doctrinalization. That is, Christianity tends to be seen as items of information detached from the experiences that generated it in the first place. We can apply this insight to Jesus' divinity, although here we go beyond Voegelin. Once the step is taken of confessing Jesus' divinity, there is the danger that this "divinity" will be detached from the concrete experience and life which qualifies it: Jesus of Nazareth. For the New Testament we come to learn who "God" is through Jesus. That is why the gospels were written and why they project their awareness of Jesus' divinity into his earthly existence. But there are inner Christian tendencies to detach "divinity" from Jesus' earthly existence, to treat his divinity as another piece of information like our common notions of "deity," and then the radicality of the Christian God-concept is lost. This was the Hellenistic Corinthians' tendency: to think of Jesus as another Hellenistic deity, like those of the mystery religions. One surmises that this same tendency lies behind all the great Christological disputes of the fourth and fifth centuries. And insofar as these tendencies are still operative today, we too run the same danger of distorting the Christian God-concept.

What are the "deforming tendencies" to which Christianity is particularly prone, and that cause it to detach its own understanding of Christ from the experiences and questions which generated its Christ-belief in the first place? One such, as Voegelin understands it, is that Christianity is particularly prone to deprecate earlier insights into the truth of existence. We can note this in Paul's tendency to denigrate philosophical wisdom (cf. Rm. 1.26–32), and in his ambivalence toward the Jewish Law (cf. Rm. 9– 11). As Voegelin puts it, possibly without sufficient nuances:

> Paul is a quite impatient man. He wants the divine reality of the primary experience of the cosmos right away differentiated as the world-tran-scendent divinity that has become incarnate in Christ; he considers it in-excusable that mankind should have passed through a phase in history when the immortal God was represented by images of mortal men. . . . Moreover, in his Jewish disgust with pagan idols he makes the historical phenomenon of the cosmological myth responsible for cases of dissolute life he can observe in his environment and considers further adherence to them, with consequent moral dissolution, God's punishment for hav-ing indulged in idolatry in the first place (Romans 1:26–32)."[53]

It is, of course, characteristic of every new movement that it tends to exag-gerate the novelty of its own insights and to denigrate the insights of older movements. But, Voegelin notes, this tendency is especially acute in the case of Christianity, born as it is by the experience of Israel's eschatologi-cal hopes being realized in Jesus. Voegelin speaks here of Christianity's "lack of noetic controls," its tendency thus to derail into an enthusiastic, esoteric movement. Our classic example of this is that of the Corinthian Hellenists, already essayed. What Voegelin enables us to grasp, however, is that this derailment is an inner tendency of Christianity itself, and thus it-self a constant temptation for us today. When it occurs, the doctrine of Christ's divinity, instead of expressing the Divine involvement in human history, becomes a means through which the Christian denies history and seeks to escape from it.

A further, terribly important derailment that Voegelin has done much to recover is the gnostic one.[54] Gnosticism is a terribly complex phenom-enon, with origins that clearly predate Christianity. Perhaps the best way to characterize it is as a broad movement of personal and social alienation occurring in the first millennium, traceable to the intense political and spiritual disorder of that period. This experience of alienation is the key to its mythic imagery, its principal tenets, and its ethics. As Jonas has shown, its imagery revolves around the themes of man as an "alien" in the world; worldly existence as a struggle between "light and darkness," "life and death"; man's psychological mood as one of "dispersal," "sinking," "forlornness," "dread," "homesickness," "numbness," "intoxication"; the experience of salvation as a call outside the world. Particularly important is its inversion of the traditional allegorical meaning of the great myths as an expression of "protest" to worldly wisdom: The "serpent," not Eve, brings gnosis; Cain, not Abel, is the great gnostic; Prometheus, not Zeus, the one who points the saving way. As Jonas put it:

> Instead of taking over the value-system of the traditional myth, it proves the deeper 'knowledge' by reversing the roles of good and evil, sublime

and base, blest and accursed, found in the original. It tries, not to demonstrate agreement, but to shock by blatantly subverting the meaning of
the most firmly established, and preferably also the most revered, elements of tradition.[55]

Its use of myth, despite the overlay of rationalization in the systems of Ba-
silides and Valentinus, is not accidental. It brings out the primarily affective, nonrational, and dramatic tone of this tendency.

Gnosticism's principal tenet, radical dualism, is also traceable to its
protesting alienation. "God" is absolutely transmundane, not only separate from but alien to the cosmos. The relation that governs God and the
cosmos is not just indifference but active antagonism. Here we have a psychic state of alienation projected into a metaphysical system. Similarly
with its ethics, which moved in two directions. The ascetic tendency gives
expression to the denigration of the corporeal and the cosmos; the liber-
tine, to the "worthlessness" of the cosmos. But both are antinomian, actively antagonistic to the cosmos, seeking its ruin. One hasn't penetrated
gnosticism deeply enough if he misses this tone of antagonism and protest.

What Voegelin has explored is Christianity's ability to derail into
gnosticism.[56] Voegelin does not claim that Christianity is gnostic; his focus
is on a tendency toward gnosis: "Considering the history of gnosticism,
with the great bulk of its manifestations belonging to, or deriving from, the
Christian orbit, I am inclined to recognize in the epiphany of Christ the
great catalyst that made eschatological consciousness an historical force,
both in forming and deforming humanity."[57] I am not convinced that theologians have pondered carefully enough the possible affinities between
Christianity and the gnostic spirit. Quite clearly gnosticism's God is not
the historically involved God that lies behind the confession of Jesus' divinity and which alone can make sense of that divinity. The Church ultimately recognized this when it officially condemned the gnostic heresy.
Yet, Voegelin warns us of an inner Christian tendency towards the gnostic
derailment,[58] and one would do well to pursue this clue from one of our
time's most insightful analyzers of historical movements. Could it be, as
Voegelin intimates, that the experience of novelty in Christ, and the consequent lack of noetic controls, tends to denigrate the old order of human existence? Certainly one can speak of a tendency toward a Christian
"dualism," in which the revelation occurring in Christ is separated from
the rest of human history. God is contracted into the Christ and his followers, and the world is set apart as the plane of the simply worldly and
nondivine. It is but a small step from this kind of dualism to world-devalu-
ation and possibly alienation from the world. As Voegelin put it, the new
revelation of God in Jesus can become so intense that this God's "relations
to the reality of which it is the center are neglected or interrupted."[59]

Now I am not maintaining that the confession of Jesus' divinity inherently implies the derailments of which Voegelin speaks. But history shows
that this doctrine can quickly legitimate these tendencies and feed them.

Surprisingly, Christianity's strength—the sense of novelty in Jesus—can quickly become its liability.

Probing the God-Concept in the Light of Jesus

1. *Preliminary Philosophical Observations:* I would like to close this chapter by offering some observations toward the reformulation of the God-concept in the light of Jesus. It is clear that if the Christian conviction is that God is known through the existence of Jesus of Nazareth, then Jesus becomes part of the definition of God. Our very understanding of Being itself, of the Ultimate in reality, must be comprehended in the light of Jesus. This obviously involves enormous epistemological and metaphysical questions, the most important being how can man know God at all? Some take the stand that if God is a radically transcendent Being, then the Divine cannot be known at all. Man is a finite being in a finite world, and simply cannot lift himself out of history to a transcendent perspective. To be sure, man knows at times an experience of self-transcendence, in hope, in protest, in love, play and humor, but this is an immanent form of transcendence, not the absolute transcendence of the world we usually associate with the Divine. On this view, then, God is a being extrinsic to the world and history, and we can easily see how it generates its opposite: the denial of God. For if God is so radically extrinsic to us, then not only can we not know the Divine, such knowledge would be irrelevant to our earthly existence. The polemics of the Enlightenment against God were clearly a protest against an extrinsic God who turned man's attention away from the world and a necessary historical catalyst for a reappropriation of a more "mature" vision of the Divine. The difficulty with these forms of "theism" and "atheism" is that they tacitly presuppose that God is a self-enclosed Monad and not a relational Being. In part, what seems needed is a distinction between the fullness of the Divine Reality—God *in se*—and God insofar-as-that-God-relates-to-us—God *pro nobis.* While we cannot know the former, perhaps we can know the latter, and unless one wants to make a radical separation between being and action, then we can trust that the *Deus pro nobis* does link us with the *Deus in se.* This is clearly not a "proof" for God's existence, at least as that term is conventionally understood. What we are rather trying to do is to develop an epistemological and metaphysical alternative to "theism" (in the above sense) and "atheism." The metaphysical alternative is to entertain the notion that Being may itself be relational, which certainly does not contradict our own experience of being-in-relationships. The epistemological alternative is to recognize that one can come to know Being (God) only through entering into relationships. The self-enclosed individual is precisely the one who cannot discover the relational dimension of reality itself. My difficulty with the notion of a "proof" for God stems from the fact that it presupposes some abstract position from which we can lay hold of God. But if God (Being)-

as-Relational can only be encountered through surrendering ourselves in relationships, then no such abstract locus can be had.

This can be put in other terms. Voegelin speaks of the noetic and pneumatic discoveries of Hellas and Israel as that of "man's in-between-ness" (*metaxy*). I cannot resist citing him once again: "Existence has the structure of the In-Between, of the Platonic *metaxy*, and if anything is constant in the history of mankind it is the language of tension between life and death, immortality and mortality, perfection and imperfection, time and timelessness, between order and disorder, truth and untruth, sense and senselessness of existence; between *amor Dei* and *amor sui, l'âme ouverte* and *l'âme close;* between the virtues of openness toward the ground of being such as faith, hope, and love and the vices of infolding closure such as hybris and revolt; between the moods of joy and despair; and between alienation in its double meaning of alienation from the world and alienation from God."[60] In-betweenness, of course, presupposes that the very structure of Being is itself relational. Another way to speak of this is to imagine that Being has the structure of Love. Love, as we earlier indicated, implies a metaphysics of Being-as-ecstatic. Being remains itself precisely by losing itself in the other. Being is not destroyed by its out-going; it is what enables Being to be. Nor is this an over-romanticized notion of Being. for love involves not only surrender, but agony and suffering as well. Now I would suggest that the above is the proper epistemological and metaphysical horizon for understanding a Christological God-concept. For confessing that God is to be known through the man Jesus is simply another way of saying that the ultimate in reality is itself a relationship-in-love, that Being outgoes itself in the human and in history.[61]

Further, when we maintain that Jesus is the source of our God-concept, we do not intend to say that he is the only source. I believe it is one of Voegelin's most important contributions to theology to have explored the experience of transcendence both among the Greeks, and in his *The Ecumenic Age,* among the Oriental religions. This forestalls us from contracting all of our God-knowledge into Jesus. Were Jesus our only source, this would ultimately negate our suggestion that the very structure of Being is relational. We would be shrinking Being to only one of its relations—Jesus—and devaluing all its other relations. It is only if Being itself is relational that Jesus can reveal "Being" to us. We do not enhance Jesus by devaluing other aspects of reality—by making him the great metaphysical exception, as it were. Rather, the Christian case for the decisiveness of Jesus as a source of our God-knowledge can only be maintained if the relational structure of all reality reaches its concentrated expression in him.

But how is one to know if the very structure of Being has reached its most concentrated expression in Jesus? Here we simply must admit the ambiguity in our own experience of the structure of Being. As Voegelin maintains, we are an "in-betweenness," experiencing a pull outside ourselves and yet a counterpull back to ourselves, a movement toward altruism and one toward egocentricity, one toward joy, another toward despair.

We simply cannot deduce a priori what is the ultimate structure of the real from our own ambiguous experience. We indeed experience Being as Relational, but we cannot know a priori if "the play of the pulls . . . is luminous with truth"[62] as Voegelin would put it; or, if the relationality of Being is truly that of love. Concretely this can only be known historically; which is to say, in our somewhat clumsy terms, that if Being is relational, it itself must tell us what its ultimate nature is by relating to us historically. This requires that we take the relational nature of reality very seriously; that is, that we be ec-static, open to the possibility of a relationship of love. We must be attuned to what Voegelin has called the "maximal experiential differentiation" in history:

> This consequence can be formulated as the principle that a theory of human existence in society must operate within the medium of experiences which have differentiated historically. There is a strict correlation between the theory of human existence and the historical differentiation of experiences in which this existence has gained its self-understanding. Neither is the theorist permitted to disregard any part of this experience for one reason or another; nor can he take his position at an Archimedean point outside the substance of history. Theory is bound by history in the sense of the differentiating experiences.[63]

But if Jesus is such a "maximal differentiation"—and that can only be known through attunement to his history, which this book attempts— what is his relation to the other "differentiations" of Being throughout human history? Here I would like to suggest that a God-concept derived from Jesus can (1) confirm, (2) enrich or radicalize, (3) protest against, and (4) heal other experiences and conceptions of the structure of reality. Such a God-concept would confirm other moments of differentiation in history in which man became conscious of God as ecstatic and loving Being. The commonality between Jesus and, say, Buddha, Mohammed and Plato would indicate that something is going forward in history which can be called the outgoing, gratuitous aspect of God's reality. A Christic God-concept could also enrich/radicalize by intensifying and highlighting what was only vaguely felt or only ambiguously known of God. We saw, for example, how the confession of Jesus' divinity intensifed the dialogical/relational dimension of the Jewish God-concept and removed any tendency to view the Divine in an authoritarian and paternalistic manner. Further, a Christic God-concept would protest against any view of God that negates the essentially relational and dialogic aspect of the Divine. The Greek tendency toward thinking of the Divine as a self-enclosed and apathetic deity, the tendency to think of God as sheer "power" and "force," impersonalistic views of the deity, atheism–all would find their protest in the figure of Jesus. But it is not enough to protest. A Christic God-concept should foster the kind of dialogue that truly heals other experiences and understandings of reality. While there are many forms of healing—therapeutic

techniques, psychoanalysis, etc.—our view would emphasize that no profound and ultimate healing can occur until one's deepest orientation to reality—his deepest self-understanding—is set right. Every other healing is
only partial, not radical, that is, not reaching to the roots of the person and
society.[64] This is how a Christic God-concept can make its contribution.

2. *The Theological Recovery of a Christic God-Concept:* There is now
a growing recognition that the Christian God-concept has too uncritically
been influenced both by late Greek notions of the Divine as self-enclosed
and apathetic and by more contemporary Western notions of power and
self-interest as the ultimate values of life. This recognition has especially
taken place among Christologians, for it is especially the reality of Jesus
that most intensively forces us to recover the essentially dialogic/relational
dimension of the Divine. A first step, then, for our Christic reformulation
of the God-concept is simply a recovery of our tradition, of the horizon in
which such a God-concept makes sense. I have already partially attempted
this above, and now, in a more concentrated form, I will try to indicate the
essential stages involved in this recovery.

First, such a recovery demands a renewed appreciation of the distinc-
tiveness of the Jewish God-concept. While there is no one Jewish God-concept, when we consider the matter historically and not abstractly we can
safely say that the prophetic, apocalyptic, sapiential, and more agnostic
God-traditions of the Hebrew scriptures have been taken over and reworked in the light of the primarily historical and relational view of God
stemming from Jewish origins in Abraham and Moses. This is why the
writings of the Hebrew scriptures constitute a "canon"—the various views
found there have been absorbed into Hebrew history and must be understood against the background of that history of relating to God. In this
sense, then, I would give priority to the historicality of the Jewish God-
concept, and with Moltmann, I would call attention to Abraham Heschel's
articulation of God as *Pathos* as an appropriate understanding of Judaism's God.[65]

Heschel does not pretend to analyze God *in se.* Rather he has power-
fully attempted to probe the prophetic experience of God, the *Deus pro nobis,* and in so doing he proposes the category of *"pathos"* as a kind of
summary of the prophets' God-concept and experience. As Heschel says,

> The essential meaning of pathos is therefore not to be seen in its psycho-
> logical denotation as standing for a state of the soul, but in its theologi-
> cal connotation, signifying God as involved in history. He is engaged to
> Israel—and has a stake in its destiny.[66]

Heschel does not intend to compromise the prophets' awareness of the divine transcendence, but to stress that it is a covenantal transcendence, a
"transcendent relatedness, a divine claim and demand":[67] "Behold, to the
Lord your God belong heaven and the heaven of heavens, the earth with
all that is in it; yet the Lord set his heart in love upon your fathers and

chose their descendants after them, you above all peoples, as at this day" (Dt. 10.14–15). For the prophets, the Divine was not encountered as *Numen* but as *Pathos,* supremely ethical rather than mysteriously irrational. God was mysterious, but this mystery disclosed ethical meaning: "Clouds and thick darkness are round about him, righteousness and justice are the foundation of his Throne" (Ps. 97.2). Through the Divine *Pathos* the gulf between God and human society is bridged, and any legalism in the relations between God and man is transcended, for *pathos* means there is room for the unique, for new dimensions in history. As Heschel sums it up:

> The prophets never identify God's pathos with His essence, because for them the *pathos* is not something absolute, but a form of relation. Indeed, prophecy would be impossible were the divine pathos in its particular structure a necessary attribute of God. If the structure of the pathos were immutable and remained unchanged even after the people had "turned," prophecy would lose its function, which is precisely so to influence man as to bring about a change in the divine pathos of rejection and affliction.[68]

We can thus see why the prophets never developed an apathetic and unrelational view of God, such as occurred among the later Greeks. I would only refer the reader back to our earlier section to refreshen the sense of the contrast between the hellenic apathetic and the prophetic pathetic God. Heschel further brings out the depth of what he means by *pathos* in his analysis of Hosea. There he indicates that Hosea discovered "a dramatic tension in God"[69] between his anger and his compassion. This especially comes out in Heschel's interpretation of Hosea's marriage to a prostitute (Hos. 2–3). While Buber, for example, sees this as a symbol of Israel's betrayal of God, Heschel sees it as God's own pedagogy, God's way of educating "Hosea himself in the understanding of divine sensibility."[70]

Quite clearly Heschel has developed a God-concept in conscious opposition to the immobile and unemotional deity of Hellenism and much of the Christian tradition. His ontology centers on Being-as-Involvement, which never separates Being from its action and movement. He brings this point home by saying that biblical man does not concentrate on being (what is) but on "the surprise of being"[71] (what can be through the Divine *pathos*). Nor does Heschel intend *pathos* as merely an anthropomorphism, a metaphorical manner of speaking. *Pathos* is not a personification onto God of the prophets' own attributes, but something the prophets discovered, often against their own will. "It is an oversimplification to assume that the prophets, who were so deeply aware of the grandeur and transcendence of the Creator of heaven and earth as well as of the failure and frailty of human nature, should have sought to invest God with human qualities."[72] *Pathos* neither humanizes nor anesthetizes God, but brings out his authentic concern. Heschel's most startling illustration of this is in his taking seriously the "wrath of God" (Jer. 10.10). For many, this aspect of the Hebrew scriptures wrongly leads them to view the Old Testament precisely as "old" and "displaced" by the New Testament revelation of God as love. Heschel feels that this attitude results from a psychological view of wrath, rather than from a theology of *Pathos*. It presupposes the immobile God and not God-as-Involvement. The latter helps us to see the divine wrath as God's refusal to be neutral to evil. "Its meaning is . . . instrumental: to bring about repentance; its purpose and consummation is its own disappearance."[73] Thus, the Divine anger is always temporary (Micah 7.18–20; Is. 26.20, 54.7–8, 57.16–19; Jer. 3.5,12).

While an apathetic God generates an apathetic humanity the God of *Pathos* creates *homo sympathetikos*. Heschel sums up his analysis of the prophetic consciousness in this way: "An analysis of prophetic utterances shows that the fundamental experience of the prophet is a fellowship with the feelings of God, a sympathy with the divine pathos, a communion with the divine consciousness which comes about through the prophets' reflection of, or participation in, the divine pathos."[74] He devotes a large part of his analysis to differentiating the prophetic *sympatheia* from Hellenism's ecstasy and modern psychology's psychosis. The prophet knows no loss of consciousness, no lack of concern for the world, no sense of fusion with the Divine. "It is true that the prophet is overwhelmed by the divine word that comes to him; but it is the consciousness of being overwhelmed, the consciousness of receptivity, and the ability to respond to the word that are outstanding features of his experience."[75] There is no merging with God, but an intensification of God's difference from the prophet: "Woe is me! For I am undone; for I am a man of unclean lips, and I dwell in the midst of a people of unclean lips; for my eyes have seen the King, the Lord of hosts" (Is. 6.5; cf. Jer. 18.6; Hos. 11.9; Ps. 144.4; Ex. 3.6; Gn. 18.27). Rather than a loss of consciousness, the prophets know an intensified sense of vocation and mission (Am. 8.4–6). Their concern is not for the esoteric mysteries, as in Hellenism, but for the marketplace. As Heschel sums it up:

> What makes possible the prophetic act within his consciousness is . . . a transcendent act, an ecstasy of God.
> What stands out as essential, unique, and decisive is the prophetic participation, his affecting and witnessing the thinking of the Lord.
> . . . the sphere in which prophetic anthropotropism finds expression is history; the emotions with which it is charged are sympathy for God, sympathy for man: the course of its piety runs from God to man. The point of departure is the divine pathos, the end is the sphere of man.[76]

Secondly, I would suggest that the reappropriation of the above is the essential horizon for understanding the Christian confession of Jesus' divinity. When we confess that in and through the life of Jesus God was decisively revealed, we mean that in and through Jesus' life of *sympatheia* the Divine was encountered as decisively *Pathos*. With Thüsing I would say that the Christ-belief radicalizes this by bringing out its deeper implications and by removing ambiguities in the God-concept. The Christ-belief is the "setting in power" of the Pathetic God (Rm. 15.8).

The Jewish consciousness of God as *Pathos,* of Being-as-Involvement, was of course discovered and mediated through the Covenant. This is still true even for the prophets, who hearken back to the Covenant as the basis for illuminating their experience and mission (Jer. 7, 5.1–6; Hos. 6.8–10; Mic. 2.1–2, 8–9, etc.). The Christian consciousness of God-as-Involvement is mediated through the entire existence of Jesus (Acts 4.12; Jn. 1.18; Mt. 11.27). And thus it is to Jesus' existence that we must look for the possible radicalization and setting in power of this new God-concept. To the extent that our own modern existence seems alien to Jesus, we can create an openness to what was going forward in Jesus by concentrating on our own moments of *sympatheia,* and asking what they imply about the ultimate structure of reality. I would suggest, then, that we look to the cross and resurrection for God's "final" revelation of his Being through Jesus. One can say that the cross and resurrection concentrate and sum up what Jesus was about, what he was trying to tell us about God.

How, then, does Jesus' cross and resurrection radicalize the Jewish God of *Pathos* and Involvement, removing its possible ambiguity and setting it in power (Rm. 15.8)? It is clear that Jesus' cross raises questions about God. We have already seen how Jesus' radical intimacy with God placed him in opposition to Judaism and merited for him the title of "blasphemer" (Mk. 14.63–64), a charge partially responsible for Jesus' cross. Despite the fact that the anti-Semitic tendency of the New Testament probably exaggerates Jesus' opposition to Judaism, we can be certain that the scriptures preserve an authentic reminiscence in stressing the opposition from Judaism. The charge of "blasphemy" indicates that Judaism disagrees with Jesus' God-concept. At the very least, if our supposition is true that Jesus stands in direct continuity with the prophetic God of *Pathos,* then there must have been ambiguity in the Jewish mind about that God. What I would postulate is that the implications flowing from the prophetic consciousness of God were not yet clear in Judaism. The diatribes between Jesus and the Pharisees as described in the gospels may or may not be true (cf. Mk. 2.23–28; Mt. 15.14; Lk 11.46). I am inclined to think they are exaggerated by an anti-Semitic tendency.[77] What is more important, it seems to me, is that the Jewish God-concept was linked to the Covenant, and thus to the Jewish people and its institutions. While there are tendencies in the later prophets to articulate a divine universalism, still Jewish history shows that this remained ambiguous. The Pharisees did effect a universalism of a certain kind after Jamnah,[78] but this was still tied to acceptance of Jewish institutions. What is very clear in Jesus, however, is the universality of the God of *Pathos,* an ability to believe that he transcends the temple, the cult, and class distinctions (cf. Jn. 18.36). In part then, Jesus frees the God-concept from the cultural mortgages of the covenant. In other words, we can say that the cross reveals how universal the dialogical God of Judaism is, how ec-static, as Heschel put it. John simply says "God is Love" (Jn. 4.8,16).

Here let me be as precise as possible. I am not saying that Judaism was or is a religion of works-righteousness, with a lack of consciousness of God's grace, and that Jesus went to the cross because his message and life transcended such legalism. I can find no evidence that Judaism ever lost its consciousness of God's covenant as his gift of grace. The rabbinic and apocalyptic literature of late Judaism all presupposes this and never denies it. Works were commanded, yes; but they were considered a response to grace, not its cause. Nor am I saying that Judaism had lost a sense of God's gracious presence in its life, as is sometimes argued, and that Jesus went to his death because he "restored" a consciousness of that presence. For example, it is sometimes argued that under the twin influences of the exiles and Hellenism that late Judaism came to view God as distant and remote, his only contacts with men being through angelic intermediaries. The apocalyptic literature, with its stress on intermediaries, is usually adduced as evidence for this. Yet the entire Rabbinic and apocalyptic tradition was clearly based on the attempt to cultivate the presence of God in a thorough and methodical way (there is not even any reason to doubt that the Pharisees, the predecessors of the Rabbis, differed in this). The notion of the kingdom of God, it is true, was "transcendentalized" by the prophets and even more by apocalyptic, thus seeming to remove God to a distance. But this must be balanced by the sense of God's presence even now, a "sense" that runs through all the Jewish literature, so far as I can tell. I think we should say that God's kingdom and presence was thought to be both present and future for Judaism. What I would maintain is only that the implications flowing from the Jewish consciousness of God were still ambiguous, mainly because Judaism linked access to God to the covenant. In the case of Jesus, however, the note of universal access to God comes through clearly, for Jesus summons all, just and sinners (Mt. 8.11f; Lk. 13.28f). It is Jesus' claim to speak for God in this way, I think, that brings him into opposition to Judaism.

But as we earlier saw, Jesus was executed by crucifixion (the Roman penalty for political crimes) and not by stoning (the Jewish penalty for blasphemy). Thus, Jesus' cross reveals that Jesus was in opposition to the Roman world too. We have already seen that Jesus could not simply be identified as a Zealot in Roman eyes. Nor can we say that Jesus was executed for purely political reasons, for this projects our separation of religion and politics into Jesus' period. I postulated earlier that the Romans sensed in Jesus something even more dangerous than the Zealots. Namely, his life called into question their entire conception of power and domination and the religious world view which legitimated that power. Voegelin helpfully calls this the tendency toward "pragmatic conquest" and gigantomachia,[79] and this tendency was itself made possible and legitimated by a religious world view in which the emperor and the imperial order reflected the sacred structure of the cosmos. In such a cosmological mind set the

Divine was associated with the "power" and "force"[80] of the cosmos. The classic Greek philosophers do initiate a break from such cosmological thinking, but the later Greek and Roman tendency toward a self-interested and apathetic view of the Divine illustrates that the old divine-as-power conception was not transcended. Thus, the cross reveals that Jesus was in opposition to a power-conception of the deity. A quite different conception of Divine transcendence as *Pathos* is what is revealed on the cross.

Now it is possible to say that in the cross God is revealed as ec-static, or truly relational, and that unambiguously and radically. But this could not be known without the resurrection; without that the cross would not have revealed Divine *Pathos,* but only human tragedy. At the very least, then, Jesus' resurrection "confirmed" that God was to be encountered in Jesus' life and its concentrated climax of the cross. But the question we must ask is whether Jesus' resurrection only "confirms" the cross or whether it itself reveals God in a way peculiar to it? As the exegete C. F. Evans asked it, "Was the resurrection creative, or was it simply probative?"[81] It certainly was probative. So much is undisputed, for this is why the gospels can "read" Jesus' Messiahship and Divinity back into his earthly life. Yet the New Testament also seems to indicate that the resurrection was creative, that it has its own story to tell about God. We can see this in a number of New Testament indications. We should note that the appearances of Jesus always go in hand with the awareness of a new mission. The famous Lucan narrative of Emmaus ends with the disciples who have experienced the risen Jesus returning to Jerusalem to tell what they have seen and heard (Lk. 24). Luke further develops this in Acts, where witnessing to the resurrection is by way of the apostolate (Aa. 1.8, 2.32, 3.15, 5.32, 10.40). Matthew describes a universal commissioning by Jesus (28.18–20). Even though these texts have been elaborated in the light of Easter, still we can surmise that they record a new awareness of vocation and mission made possible by the resurrection, a new experience of "being empowered" by God. Paul will further speak of the "body of Christ" and Christ's continuing presence in the Church. He is telling us that the resurrection makes possible a new experience of community and of the identity that comes from such a community. Matthew puts this in his own terms by stressing baptism as the entrance into this new community and the great commandment of love as its ethics. Most remarkable is the outbreak in the New Testament of Spirit-language,[82] which is universally present there. The fact that in many texts this Spirit is not distinguished from Christ preserves for us the precious connection between the resurrection event and this new experience. This language, I would surmise, can be explained by the fact that through the resurrection a new awareness of God became possible among the brethren. God is now affectively felt as an "empowering presence" thwarting the forces that would make the new experience of mission and community impossible. As Paul put it, "You did not receive a spirit of slavery leading you back into fear, but a spirit of adoption through which we cry out 'Abba!' (that is, 'Father'). The Spirit himself gives witness with our spirit that we are children of God" (Rm. 8.15–16).[83]

If we were to try to generalize these indications into terms consistent with our analysis, we would propose that the resurrection reveals God as revitalizing history in a new way. God is now experienced and known as history's sovereign Lord, making possible a new human identity, a new experience of community, a new ability through the Spirit to thwart the forces of oppression, a new sense of vocation. As we earlier put it, history's promise character is now decisively manifested. To use Heschel's terms, the Divine *Pathos* is initiating a history of *Sympatheia*.

In summary, then, a new awareness of divine transcendence opens up through Jesus.[84] God is revealed as *"Pathos* and Lord." What does this mean? Divine transcendence and Divine immanence, Divine sovereignty and Divine *Pathos,* are not a simple dichotomy. The Divine transcendence is relational and ec-static, involving itself in the world and the world's processes by way of *pathos* and not by way of crippling power and giganto-machia. It is another way of saying that the Divine is Love. The two terms—*"Pathos"* and "Lord"—are essentially linked to each other. Neither can be absorbed into the other, but each establishes a relation of creative "tension" in which each interpenetrates the other. Without *pathos,* sovereignty becomes mere power; without sovereignty, *pathos* becomes tragedy. The relation is a dialectical one, but not in the Hegelian sense in which thesis and antithesis resolve themselves into a synthesis. Here the dialectic is only temporary. But the dialectics between *Pathos* and Lord is a permanent one. This, I believe, is why Paul not only speaks of "Jesus Christ" (Lord) but also of him as "crucified" (*Pathos*), and both always in the same breath: "I determined that while I was with you I would speak of nothing but Jesus Christ and him crucified" (1 Cr. 2.2).

It seems to me not unimportant that confessing God as *"Pathos* and Lord" entails accepting the simultaneous "femininity" and "masculinity" of the Divine.[85] That this has been lost to our consciousness, as the debates over whether God can be said to be feminine and whether women should be admitted to the priestly ministry show, only illustrates to what an extent we have severed the Divine *Pathos* from the Divine sovereignty. There can be little historical doubt that the loss of the feminine dimension is tied to cultural factors. The symbol of the feminine, the *magna mater,* stems of course, from nature. Like nature, it evoked the experience of totality (womb), harmony, vital replenishment, and happiness, on the one hand, and nature's flux, change and unpredictability on the other. The masculine, however, evokes man's mastery over flux and change, and thus a sense of mastery and timelessness. Scholars debate just when the feminine was supplanted by the masculine, but one can surmise that both the shift from an agrarian society (nature-oriented society) to an urban society (master-oriented society), and the shift from mythical to rational thinking in Greece forwarded the process.

In any case, the image of the "Divine *Pathos*" should again reawaken the feminine divine principle. It is the Divine *Pathos* that vitally replenishes us by its *ec-stasis* with us: "O Jerusalem! Jerusalem! How often have I longed to gather your children as a hen gathers her brood under her wings" (Mt. 23.37), said Jesus. And this replenishment finds its remarkable symbolization in John's gospel, when from the side of the crucified one "blood and water flowed out" (Jn. 19.34), But the maternal, like nature, is unpredictable, precisely because it is involved with flux and change. So, too, it is the Divine *Pathos* of the cross that involves God in the unpredictability of human history. Dame Julian of Norwich had recovered the Divine *Pathos* when she said "our heavenly Mother Jesus may never suffer us who are his children to perish, for he is almighty, all wisdom and all love, and so is none but he, blessed may he be."[86]

But God manifests herself through Jesus not only as *Pathos* (Mother) but also as Lord (Father). The Divine is androgynous, and this means again that "*Pathos*" and "Lord," maternity and paternity, can never be separated, but exist again in that creative, interpenetrating tension that we can call the "divine dialectic." Just as the sovereignty severed from *Pathos* becomes sheer power and dominance, so the same holds for the severance of paternity from maternity; *Pathos* without sovereignty would become mere emotionalism and sentimentality.

A further important consequence of the confession of the "pathetic sovereignty" is the recognition of two different, but still dialectically related, postures to which it gives rise; namely, Christian worldly protest and involvement on the one hand, and Christian mystical ecstasy on the other. The posture of worldly involvement, even to the point of martyrdom and death, traces itself ultimately to the *Pathos* of the cross. It is there that the Divine involved itself in man's historical struggle against evil and oppressive social forces. God, if you will, did not manifest herself as either above oppression or neutral to it, but as against it. The early Church preserved this intuition when it viewed the monastic flight into the desert as a movement to do battle against the evil one, Satan.

It is, however, primarily the theology stemming from Latin America and critical social thought that is enabling us to reappropriate this element of the Divine hostility to evil and oppression revealed on the cross. Unlike the earlier monastic struggle with evil in the desert, this theology stresses not only the struggle against personal evil, but that against public and socialized forces of oppression. Jesus' death, as Moltmann told us, was not a private death like heart failure, but a public one, inflicted by public powers of oppression. Deep pondering of the cross leads South American Christologian Jon Sobrino to propose "suffering as a mode of being for God." The cross shatters all our prior conceptions of God, Sobrino maintains; it is even against them: "God appears on the cross *sub specie contrarii.*" For Sobrino, the cross means there is no access to God from what is positive in existence, "whether nature, history or human subjectivity." The cross forces us to reformulate the whole problem of God. God is to be recognized through what seems to be quite the opposite of divine: i.e., suffering. God on the cross explains nothing; he criticizes every proffered explanation.

Thus, we recognize God, not in what seems natural to us, but in what is alien to us and against us: the oppressed. "Merely by being there, the oppressed call into question those who approach, challenging their 'being human'; and this radical questioning of what it means to be a human being serves as the historical mediation of our questioning of what 'being God' means."[87]

I have no doubt that there is a terribly important intuition here. In fact, the works of Moltmann and Sobrino are among the few books I've read in recent years that have not only terribly challenged me to my depths, but deepened whatever spirituality is within me. It is particularly another critical theologian, Gregory Baum,[88] who has challenged my prior inattentiveness to the cross and forced me to ponder it more deeply. Yet, even recognizing all of this, I still have reservations about the theological conclusions Moltmann, and particularly Sobrino, draw from the cross. Let me try to express more carefully what I mean.

First, we should pay careful attention to the South American situation as a theologian like Sobrino experiences it. There the difficulty is primarily a modern form of "feudalism," maintained primarily by the armies (which are aristocratic and quite unlike, say, the American army), and legitimated by a form of religion that clearly resembles medieval Christendom. In this kind of milieu, we have a clear opposition between the propertied aristocracy and the largely propertyless masses. No resolution of this problem can ensue until there is a clear redistribution of property concomitant with a heightening of self-respect on the part of the "masses." Thus, this situation clearly calls for radical change; it is quite literally a situation of "contraries" confronting one another: the propertied and the landless. Any relevant posture on the part of the Church must include a recognition of this contrariety and try to make sense of it theologically. Hence, the "return to the cross" and the posture of protest.

If we turn to the United States now, there we find that the key difficulty is not precisely feudalism (although we have our "aristocratic classes," these do not mainly stem from inherited land) but industrialism and technology. Now these latter have tended to relativize the importance of land and to elevate the role of products and their manufacture as the key to the American level of life. But with technology comes a mentality whose "underside" we are now only beginning to recognize. In my *Christ and Consciousness* I tried to indicate that technology implies an epistemology of analysis and dissection, of mastery and control, and when not balanced by other factors, at the extreme an epistemology of exploitation. In American society we even find ourselves applying this epistemology to ourselves, and it can lead to a crippling self-dissection and doubt, to a desire for self-mastery and mastery over others, and at the extreme, to human exploitation. Thus, we find ourselves in American society searching for what I would call a more "contemplative" or "mystical" life-style, which breaks through the endless cycle of self-focusing, self-aggrandizement, and agitated activism, perpetuated by our society. It is not passivity that is the goal, but the relativization of the self and its desires and activism. The agitated "desire for more" needs relativizing by a trust and confidence in the sovereignty of God. When this is lost, man absolutizes the finite while only the Divine can bring that "consolation" that alone brings peace. Could it be that an excessive focusing on the cross would only breed more agitation and self-doubt, not less?

My purpose is to illustrate that faith in the pathetic Lord can generate two spiritualities, each needing the tension that comes from the other. But what I would query is whether someone like Sobrino preserves the dialectical tension between the Divine *Pathos* and the Divine sovereignty, between the cross and resurrection? It is not true that the resurrection only elevates the cross to the level of a divine mystery, as Sobrino likes to say. The resurrection has its own story to tell about God, about the Divine sovereignty, about the ability to break through evil and oppression, about this world—its nature, its history and human subjectivity—as being God's even if this remains unrecognized. There is no "Divine dialectics" if the resurrection only confirms the cross. It is precisely because this dialectic exists that under particular historical experiences one finds oneself torn between protest and peace, evil and good, sorrow and joy. While the cross denies us the ability to anesthatize the resurrection, the resurrection denies us the ability to tragicalize the cross by elevating sorrow, protest and negation to the level of absolutes. In other words, the élan of protest and the contemplative élan of joy are both legitimate dimensions of the Christian faith. It seems to me that mystics like John of the Cross and Teresa of Avila know this. Their "dark night" was not a mere prelude to mystical ecstasy, but a continual moment of it. But neither was the dark night the only word that God had for the mystics. There is also the sanjuanist celebration of the world in the *Living Flame of Love*. It is not a matter of "balance" but of "tension."

Secondly, the critical social theory that undergirds the reflections of thinkers like Moltmann and Sobrino probably has a lot to do with their concentration on the cross. Critical hermeneutics is a hermeneutics of critique and suspicion. This leads its practitioners to concentrate on the underlying alienating structures in human life and to develop constructive alternatives to them. I have no doubt that implicit in this hermeneutics is an "emancipatory élan" and a concomitant trust in a transcendent reality that can truly turn human history into a history of promise. But this élan remains only implicit. The critical stance of suspicion remains always the governing factor, lest one derail into a false utopia and hope. Hence Sobrino's statements that the cross negates all positivity, that God can be found only in the negative and protest, etc. My difficulty is that the only implicit emancipatory élan and confidence in the Divine transcendence never functions as a conscious epistemological principle in this system. Hence, perforce, critique becomes the "absolute," if not intentionally, at least in practice. Thus, the radical seriousness of all protest movements and the lack of a sense of joy and even humor. Yet this is profoundly unbiblical, for besides the element of trust and joy found even in Jesus, protest is always presented in the scriptures as a protest for something better, not just simply protest without further qualification. What I am trying to indicate is that belief in the "pathetic Lord" elevates not only the cross (protest and negativity) but also the resurrection (confidence and positivity) to conscious epistemological principles. In a word, worldly involvement and contemplative ecstasy are legitimate consequences of Christian faith.

A Further Difficulty

Clearly this new awareness of divine transcendence and immanence opened up in Jesus calls into question our inherited view of the Divine as "immutable" and "uninvolved" in human history without further qualification. A theological pioneer in this matter, Karl Rahner, put it this way: "With respect to the immutability and atemporality of God Christian theology should keep in mind the dogma of the true Incarnation and temporalization of the *Logos* and not make her task easier than it is."[89] In another place, Rahner shows some sympathy with a form of "panentheism" as perhaps a promising route to pursue:

> This form of pantheism does not simply identify the world with God in monistic fashion (God, the 'All') but sees the 'All' of the world within God as an interior modification and manifestation of God, although God is not absorbed into the world. This doctrine of the immanence of the world in God is false and heretical only if it denies creation and the distinction of the world from God (and not only of God from the world) . . . ; otherwise it is a demand that ontology undertake thinking out much more profoundly and much more accurately the relation which exists between absolute and finite being (that is, the reciprocal conditioning of unity and difference as they grow in the same proportion).[90]

There are, of course, many reasons why contemporary philosophers and theologians need to rethink the relation between absolute and finite being: the problem of our awareness of historical change and God's involvement in it; the need to rethink God's relation to the problem of evil; the compatibility between Divine Providence and human freedom; and finally, the reappropriation of the biblical and Christological God-concept as relational and historical. Our focus is on the latter, and in our opinion, this takes priority, insofar as we consider Jesus to be the decisive disclosure of God's being. Inasmuch as our reflections lead us to agree with others working in this area, this would indicate that we are achieving a greater consistency in our God-concept and that we are perhaps on the right track.

In my opinion, three possibilities present themselves on this matter.[91] First, we have what is traditionally called the "theistic" option,[92] which views God's "immutability" and the world's "mutability" as contraries. The use of the word "immutability" need not occupy our focus; I think entirely too much is made of it. The biblical term "fidelity" (Ps. 102.26–28; Is. 90.2; Jn. 1.17) perhaps expresses the meaning better, but we must recognize what the Divine fidelity implies. As J. Galot put it:

> That this fidelity is vividly underlined in the expressions of the continuity of the Divine action [in the scriptures] is undeniable. But it also seems that this fidelity is founded upon a continuity in being. The promise made to Moses "I will be with you" is based upon the revelation of the Divine name, "I Am" (Ex. 3. 12–14). The existential meaning of "I Am," based upon the assurance of an indefectible presence, does not invalidate its metaphysical meaning. When the psalmist prays to God, "O You who are steadfast," he is thinking of a perseverance in being, as opposed to the condition of the earth and the skies which exhausts itself and perishes" (Ps. 102.26–28).[93]

What should rather occupy our focus is the relation that is thought to exist between the divine, immutable fidelity and historical, human mutability. It is one of contraries. Thus, the principle operative here is that of noncontradiction: "something cannot be this and not-this at the same time." The second possibility is traditionally called pantheism, and as is well known, this view collapses the contrariety between the Divine, immutable fidelity and historical, human mutability by identifying one with the other. What is not always noticed is that this view follows the principle of noncontradiction also. Because something cannot be this and not-this at the same time, there must be no "not-this," is its form of reasoning. An interesting question to pursue is to what an extent the theistic view generates the pantheistic one. In any case, on the theistic view, God must be thought of as extrinsic to worldly mutability. If this is so, pantheism reasons, then that "God" has no relevance to this world and could not even be known. Hence pantheism's move to a wholly intrinsicist "God." What seems to underlie both the theistic and pantheist options, at least in their classic meaning as presented above, is a static, solipsistic and thus unrelational notion of the Divine Reality. The Divine immutability is understood nonhistorically and nonrelationally, rather than as a dialectical reality in constant historical relation to human history, as the more biblical notion of the divine immutable fidelity seems to be understood. The key aspect of the Divine fidelity seems to be its implication that God is outgoing, involving, in relationship with man, and so one cannot speak of a contrariety between the Divine, immutable fidelity and man's historical mutability. The biblical view forces us to entertain here, rather, a relationship of compatibility.

But a third possibility presents itself, which has traditionally been called panentheism, but which I would prefer to call theopathy, to distinguish it clearly from the various other forms of panentheism.[94] Here the Divine, immutable fidelity and historical, human mutability are not thought of as contraries, but as reciprocal relations. The principle operating here is not the logical one of noncontradiction, but the dialectical one of universal correlativity, as the Hegelians put it. Although it was Hegel who recovered this principle in our own times, the notion is profoundly biblical and found throughout the writings of the Christian mystics. And it is not without import that Hegel in part discovered it through his pondering of the incarnation. In any case, this principle of "universal correlativity" would assert that "everything is itself precisely by being related to something else. . . . it brings about a higher union between the very general idea of something being itself (affirmed by the principle of identity) and the very general idea of something being not-itself (denied by the principle of noncontradiction) under the guise of the idea of something being itself as related to what is not-itself."[95]

The key insight is that being-is-relational, which is tacitly denied by theism and pantheism. We can confirm being's relationality from our own experience, for we know ourselves as both an "I" (unique) and yet as "related to others." The relationship is dialectical, for it is precisely through relating to others that we become ever more unique and rich. Correlativity and uniqueness are not contraries but compatibles. Similarly, Christian mystical experience tells us that it is precisely the experience of self as excluding others that must finally be transcended through communion with the Absolute and creation. In other words, the principle of noncontradiction must be transcended through the principle of universal correlativity. In the highest state of mystical contemplation, as we find it described in John of the Cross and Teresa of Avila, what we have is distinction not through the exclusion of others but through the affirmation of others in love.[96] This notion of the self as relational is found in Paul: "The life I live now is not my own; Christ is living in me." Yet this relationship with Christ does not destroy Paul's uniqueness, but heightens it: "I still live my human life, but it is a life of faith in the Son of God, who loved me and gave himself for me" (Gal. 2.20). Elsewhere Paul will say: "The Spirit gives witness with our spirit that we are children of God" (Rm. 8.16).

I would suggest that to ponder God in the light of Christ forces us to enter into this kind of dialectical imagination. The revelation of God in Christ forces us to recognize that God is a Being of involvement and relationship to mankind, that God is the Divine *Pathos* in other words. This must mean that God's immutable fidelity and man's historical mutability are not contraries but compatibles. God is immutably faithful precisely through involving herself in human history, by extending the Divine *Pathos* "outwards" into the domain of history. God's Being, in other words, might be usefully imagined as the supreme—the divine—instance of universal correlativity, in which the Divine Being is itself precisely while being related to what is "not-itself." Just as for us, on our plane, remaining unique precisely while relating to others holds true, so, for God, on the divine plane, remaining uniquely and immutably faithful precisely while involving herself with us holds true. If this were the case, then in the case of God we would have a correlativity not based on need, as in many of our relationships; nor based on imperfection; but based solely, as Heschel might say, on the "ecstasy of God." God's involvement in our mutability—the "Divine Temporality"—would be sheer grace and love, sheer *Pathos,* in other words.

Does this make sense of the Divine *Pathos,* the Divine involvement in the processes of the world manifested on the cross? Here we have, of course, the most dramatic form of our theopathy,[97] of the divine ec-stasis in human mutability and suffering. Here it might rightly be asked whether we have not "trivialized" the depths of the suffering that God undergoes on the cross. Is it enough to maintain that God's correlativity is never based on need when Jesus on the cross seems to approach despair, if the Marcan version of the passion is correct? Here I would maintain only that we have not entered into our dialectical mode of thinking if the cross leads us to think that God somehow ceases to be God through the agony of the cross. The scriptures are aware of this and thus describe the cross as a "divine condescension," a "Divine Self-Emptying," a true *"kenosis"* (Phil. 2.5–9). Perhaps on the level of our own experience we might ask ourselves who truly experiences pain, suffering, and evil the more—the one whose life is most characterized by love, or the one only moderately or even indifferently attuned to love? This is a lesson that the mystics have yet to teach us. The Teresian "I die because I do not die" is a classic expression of the simultaneity of love and pain, fullness and emptiness, grace and *kenosis*—of an anthropathy somehow grounded in and pointing to theopathy.

In other words, God is revealed in Jesus as both *Pathos* (correlativity) and Lord (supremely unique). To surrender either of the two aspects is ultimately to surrender the dialectical mode of thought demanded by theopathy. Of course this view entails profound implications for a host of other issues that go beyond the scope of this book. For example, God can be viewed as both master of history (Lord) and yet granting history a true openness and future (*Pathos*); as not overcome by evil and oppression (Lord) and yet struggling with evil from the inside and not impassible (*Pathos*); as the Creator and Redeemer of mankind (Lord) and yet not destroying our genuine freedom (*Pathos*).[98] But what is crucial is to recognize the dialectical relationship of compatibility and not opposition between the Divine Immutability and human mutability.

Minimally, I think this would entail the following consequences. (1) God remains God. That is, God is sovereign Lord, creator and sustainer of all. In this sense, the Divine is truly unique and quite radically transcendent. (2) God is universally correlative, or supremely "immanent" as the tradition would say. The divine mode of being is not by way of opposition to or dominance over other beings, including beings enmeshed in history and temporality, but by way of affirmation through love. As Gilkey has helpfully seen, this entails a form of "self-limitation" on the part of God:

> The limitation on God's sovereignty in history is achieved . . . not through the notion of the finitude of God as one factor in the process balanced by other factors. Nor is God "in the grip" of a process which transcends and so makes him possible, since as the power alike of being, of freedom and of possibility, he is the ground of process. The limitation on God's sovereignty is understood as the self-limitation of God in creating and preserving a finitude characterized by freedom and so by self-actualization.[99]

Actually it is not so much self-limitation—as if God had to hold back his sovereignty—as it is the fact that *kenosis/Pathos* is the mode of the Divine Being. (3) As supremely correlative, not only does God influence the world with its humanity, but it influences him. The relationship is reciprocal, and thus God really is involved in human temporality and human suffering. But as the creature participates in this process in a creaturely way, so the Divine participates within it in a divine way, and thus not from need, not from imperfection, but from *kenosis* and love (*Pathos*). That this could be thought to diminish the divine participation in process and suffering anesthetizes the depth of Love, and projects our limited experience of process and love onto God herself.[100]

A Christological God-Concept and Trinitarianism

I would like to conclude this chapter by offering some reflections on the implications of our view for Trinitarian theology. Briefly we can see how our view implies Trinitarianism, if we keep in mind the following points. First, while God is revealed as *Pathos* and Lord in Jesus of Nazareth, no claim is being made that this revelation exhausts the full reality and mystery of God. The revelation of the Divine *Pathos* and Sovereignty tells us what God is for us, but necessarily cannot fully disclose what God is in the fullness of her own reality. God, in the traditional terms, is "Father," the transcendent and strictly mysterious ground of all that is. A Christological God-concept is then not a new form of Jesus-ology that shrinks the Divine Reality into Jesus (cf. 1 Cr. 15.28). Secondly, the disclosure of the Divine Reality in Jesus as *Pathos* and Lord tells us not only what God is for us but that God is for us, that the Divine Reality is relational and not a self-enclosed, apathetic deity. In classical terms, this means that God is "Son," that God is really a self-communicating Being. Thirdly, the Divine Relationality, the Sovereign *Pathos,* is disclosed in Jesus as revitalizing history by initiating a history of *sympatheia*. God is not only relational but relationalizing. In classical terms, this means that God is Spirit, the companion and sustainer of all that is. The Divine *Pathos,* as it were, means that God is oriented "outwards," not solipsistic, and thus able to penetrate history and involve herself within it. The Trinity is actually the condition of the possibility of a Christological God-concept.[101]

Historically it is helpful to note, as Gordon Kaufman[102] has illustrated, that all forms of monotheism/unitarianism actually imply Trinitarianism and require it for the completion of their thinking. This fact is not just a piece of historical curiosity, but illustrates that Trinitarianism gives expression to real experiences of the Divine Reality. For example, if we take a monotheism of the Father, this view either implies that God is relational (Son) and relationalizing (Spirit), or it regresses to a form of Deism and *apatheia*. Unitarianisms of the Son have appeared in Christian history classically in the case of Marcion and more recently in contemporary movements that imitate Jesus but think it possible to dispense with Father and Spirit. But either this Son is truly the really transcendent (Father) and the sovereign sustainer and renewer of history (Spirit) or he is not "God." Unitarianisms of the Spirit have appeared in Montanism classically, and more recently in spiritualist movements that shrink the God-experience to personal "religious" and inward experience. But either this spiritual experience (Spirit) is authentically that of the transcendent God (Father) whose nature is *Pathos* and Sovereignty (Son) or it is idolatry.

Ultimately, overcoming an apathetic view of the Divine and entering into a relational view of God as Sovereign *Pathos* is what lies behind Trinitarian speculation and makes it so precious for Christianity. Thus, Trinitarianism is not an idle piece of ecclesiological speculation but an expression of how God is in relation to us, our world, and our history.

Notes

1. See O'Collins, *op. cit.*, pp. 125–131, whose thoughts have inspired this section.

2. See especially Moltmann and Sobrino, *op. cit.* According to Moltmann, pp. 45–65, 207–214, whereas patristic and medieval theology saw in the cross an example to be imitated by the Christian, whether through committed eschatological suffering, through martyrdom, or through monastic imitation of the martyrs, it was Luther who recovered the cross as an element revealing something about both the incarnation and about God. Moltmann points especially to Luther's Heidelberg disputation of 26 April 1518, thesis 20: "So it is not enough and no use for anyone to know God in his glory and his majesty if at the same time he does not know him in the lowliness and shame of his cross. . . . Thus true theology and true knowledge of God lie in Christ the crucified one" (cited on p. 211). I am not convinced, however, that Luther radically negates knowledge of God from other sources, as Moltmann thinks. There is a balance and dialectic between the cross and other sources of God-knowledge missing in Moltmann's interpretation. Luther says it is only "not enough" to use other sources and ignore the cross; he is attacking a "rationalistic" scholasticism.

3. Sobrino, *ibid.*, p. 219. Also helpful here is Martin Hengel, *Crucifixion: In the Ancient World and the Folly of the Message of the Cross* (Philadelphia: Fortress, 1977); Nadejda Gorodetzky, *The Humiliated Christ in Modern Russian Thought*

(New York: AMS, 1973/1938); and John Saward, "The Fool for Christ's Sake in Monasticism, East and West," in M. Basil Pennington, ed., *One Yet Two: Monastic Tradition East and West* (Kalamazoo, Michigan: Cistercian, 1976), pp. 48–80.

4. *Ibid.*, p. 185.

5. Leo J. O'Donovan, "Approaches to the Passion," WORSHIP 48 (1974), 139.

6. Cf. Irénée Noye *et al.*, *Jesus in Christian Devotion and Contemplation* (St. Meinrad, Indiana: Abbey, 1974).

7. Ernst Käsemann, "The Pauline Theology of the Cross," INTERPRETA-TION 24 (1970), 159.

8. Essential reading here is Ernst Käsemann, "For and Against a Theology of Resurrection: I and II Corinthians," in his *Jesus Means Freedom* (Philadelphia: Fortress, 1970), pp. 59–84.

9. *Ibid.*, p. 66.

10. *Ibid.*, pp. 80–81.

11. Käsemann, "The Pauline Theology of the Cross," *art. cit.*, 175.

12. Quite helpful is Denis Baly, *God and History in the Old Testament: the Encounter with the Absolutely Other in Ancient Israel* (New York: Harper and Row, 1976).

13. Cf. Lane, *op. cit.*, p. 118: "God cannot be encountered 'over' or 'above,' 'beyond' or 'beneath' one's encounter with reality. Man's experience of God does not normally take place on a vertical or a one-to-one basis. Rather man can experience God only in and through the finite medium of the world in which he lives. Conversely, God communicates himself to man in and through the finite medium of created reality. . . . Ultimately of course the truth of this theological principle rests upon the foundations of cognitional theory and epistemology. All knowledge and understanding including knowledge and understanding of God, is derived from man's experience of the world in which he lives."

14. Voegelin, *Order and History* 1, p. 491.

15. Rahner and Thüsing, *op. cit.*, p. 228 (my transl.). See this entire section, "Neuheit und Kontinuität im Verhältnis der christologischen Theo-logie des N T zur Yahwe-Theologie des A T," pp. 227–233, upon which I rely here.

16. *Ibid.* (my transl.). Thus, Jesus is not viewed as a deity independent of God the Father. His "I am" acts not simply on his own, but by the Father's will (cf. Jn. 8.28).

17. *Ibid.*, p. 230 (my transl.).

18. Scholars maintain that this passage is likely a later interpolation, for in the undisputed letters of Paul the Jews are never accused of Jesus' death. In 1 Corinthians 2.8, Paul only accuses "the rulers of this age." Cf. Thomas A. Idinopulos and Roy Bowen Ward, "Is Christology Inherently Anti-Semitic? A Critical Review of Rosemary Ruether's *Faith and Fratricide*," JOURNAL OF THE AMERICAN ACADEMY OF RELIGION 45 (1977), 199: "It is difficult to see how Paul is any more anti-Judaic than other Jewish sectarians such as those at Qumran, who like Paul, believed that God was doing a new thing in the history of salvation. Unlike the Qumran sectarians who expected the destruction of 'mainstream' Jews (whom the sectarians considered apostate), Paul hoped for/expected the salvation of all Israel (Rm. 11.26)."

19. Ruether, *op. cit.*, p. 226.

20. *Ibid.*, p. 114; cf. Jn. 8.43–47. Ruether's thesis is that anti-Semitism is the "left hand" of Christology, yet there are gospel Christologies that show no trace of the anti-Judaic. Cf. Idinopulos and Ward, *art. cit.*, 196–197.

21. *Ibid.,* p. 61.

22. *Ibid.,* pp. 64–182.

23. The conclusion has been published: "An Invitation to Jewish-Christian Dialogue: In What Sense Can We Say that Jesus Was 'the Christ'?" THE ECUMEN-IST 10 (1972), 17–24.

24. Michael B. McGarry, *Christology after Auschwitz* (New York: Paulist, 1977), p. 88.

25. Gershom Scholem, *The Messianic Idea in Judaism and Other Essays on Jewish Spirituality* (New York: Schocken, 1971), p. 1.

26. As cited by W. D. Davies, *The Gospel and the Land* (Berkeley: University of California, 1974), p. 399, n. 24.

27. Ruether sounds profoundly un-Jewish when she suggests in her *Faith and Fratricide,* p. 256, that Easter should be seen "not as superseding and fulfilling the Exodus, but as reduplicating it." This lands us in a cyclic and unhistorical view of God, more Hellenistic than Jewish. Davies's proposal would seem more fruitful, *ibid.,* p. 403: "The other possibility . . . is that which would interpret Christianity, not in kerygmatic, but in Halakic terms. . . . would it be possible to conceive of Christianity adequately, not primarily as a way of belief, a creed, but rather as a way of life, as *agape?* It is certain that if Christianity finds the essence of its life in creeds such as those of Nicaea and Chalcedon, there can be no ultimate *rapprochement* with Judaism. On the other hand, could not a halakically oriented Christianity be at home with Judaism, or, at least, remain as a merely schismatic aspect of it?"

28. Wolfhart Pannenberg, "The Appropriation of the Philosophical Concept of God as a Dogmatic Problem of Early Christian Theology," in his *Basic Questions in Theology* 2 (Philadelphia: Fortress, 1971), p. 124. Standard for this question are W. K. C. Guthrie, *The Greeks and their Gods* (Boston: Beacon, 1955); Gilbert Murray, *Five Stages of Greek Religion* (New York: Doubleday, 1955); Werner Jaeger, *The Theology of the Early Greek Philosophers* (Oxford: Clarendon, 1947).

29. Eric Voegelin, "The Gospel and Culture," in Donald G. Miller and Dikran Y. Hadidian, eds., *Jesus and Man's Hope* 2 (Pittsburgh Theological Seminary, 1971), p. 62. Here we will find a rather helpful summary of *Order and History* 2-3. It is of course clear that Plato has not fully articulated this experience. Cf. John Carmody, "Plato's Religious Horizon," PHILOSOPHY TODAY 15 (1971), 52–68, esp. 60–61: "The question of the *gods* in Plato seems logically insoluble. I see it as an area where he did not push for full consistency. Perhaps the principal force here is then cultural. The long history of divinities among the Greeks, and the practical advantages to piety in the pantheon, were heavy social stays on philosophical purification. So, Plato shows definite complexity in his regard for the gods. On the one hand, he is highly critical of their unedifying presentation by Homer. On the other hand, he is conservative toward the traditional deities and legislates devotion to them. . . . The symbols of popular religion are important, for without them there is no pedagogy in divinity for the polis."

30. Voegelin, *Order and History* 2, p. 169. In his first three volumes of *Order and History* Voegelin generally used the terms "Reason" and "Revelation," whereas in volume 4, *The Ecumenic Age,* he shifts to those of "noetic" and "pneumatic differentiation."

31. Carmody, *art. cit.,* 59.

32. Voegelin, "The Gospel and Culture," *op. cit.,* p. 75. Cf. "Reason: the Classic Experience," SOUTHERN REVIEW 10 (1974), 252: "With their discovery of

man as the *zoon noun echon,* the classic philosophers discovered man to be more than a *theotos,* a mortal: He is an unfinished being, moving from the imperfection of death in this life to the perfection of life in death."

33. Plato, *Laws,* 741a. The translations of the classical authors are those of Heschel, *op. cit., passim.*

34. Cf. Abraham J. Heschel, *The Prophets,* p. 33, citing J. Arnim, ed., *Stoicorum Veterum Fragmenta* (Leipzig, 1903–4), pp. 205–206. We are mainly in Heschel's debt for exposing the divine *apatheia* of Hellenistic thought as contrasted with the divine *pathos* of prophetic thought. Cf. also E. R. Dodds, *The Greeks and the Irrational* (Boston: Beacon, 1957), pp. 5f, 38f, 185f.

35. *Philebus,* 60c. Plato is rather complex on this issue. In *ibid.,* 21d, 60e, 63e, he seems to oppose *apatheia:* "I want to know whether anyone of us would consent to live, having wisdom and mind and knowledge and memory of all things but having no sense of pleasure and pain and wholly unaffected by these and the like feelings?" And in the *Timaeus,* as is well known, he invents the demiurge to account for the way in which the Divine enters into our world of *Pathos,* as if indicating that *Pathos* and the Divine must somehow be interrelated.

36. *Eudemian Ethics,* VII, 1244b.

37. See Jaroslav Pelikan, *The Christian Tradition 1, The Emergence of the Catholic Tradition (100-600)* (Chicago: University of Chicago, 1971), pp. 193–210. Essential reading here would be Aloys Grillmeier, *Christ in Christian Tradition 1, From the Apostolic Age to Chalcedon (451)* (Atlanta: John Knox, 1975).

38. Pelikan's translation, *ibid.,* p. 194, of *Ep. Alex. 2.*

39. *Ibid.*

40. *Ibid.,* p. 195, citing *ap. Ath. Ar.* 2.24.

41. Cf. Grillmeier, *op. cit.,* pp. 37–53, where he applies the term to early Jewish-influenced Christologies, but the term is also apt to the subject in question, and Grillmeier's own explanation of the matter reinforces this view.

42. For the controversy over the term *homoousios* and the alternatives proposed, cf. Pelikan, *op. cit.,* pp. 207–210.

43. Letter to Polycarp, III, 2 (Lightfoot, II, p. 343). Generally, however, it was Jesus' humanity that was thought to have suffered; suffering was not an issue for "God" properly (cf. Origen, *De Principiis,* IV, and Augustine, *Sermo* 183, IV, 5).

44. See Basil, *Ep.,* 38.1 and Gregory of Nyssa, *Tres dii.* Helpful on the general background of the Cappadocians is B. Otis, "Cappadocian Thought as a Coherent System," DUMBARTON OAKS PAPERS 12 (1958), 95–124.

45. Helpful here are Webb, *art. cit.;* and Bruce Douglass, "The Gospel and Political Order: Eric Voegelin on the Political Role of Christianity," JOURNAL OF POLITICS 38 (1976), 25–45, and "A Diminished Gospel: A Critique of Voegelin's Interpretation of Christianity," in Stephen A. McKnight, ed., *Eric Voegelin's Search for Order in History* (Baton Rouge: Louisiana State University, 1978), pp. 139–154.

46. Voegelin, "The Gospel and Culture," *op. cit.,* p. 91, p. 76.

47. *Ibid.,* p. 67.

48. *Ibid.,* p. 73.

49. *Ibid.,* p. 91, p. 76.

50. *Ibid.,* p. 75. On p. 60 Voegelin maintains that it is this common noetic core which enabled Christianity and Hellenism to interrelate, thus allowing Christianity to become a worldwide movement instead of remaining "an obscure sect" that probably would have "disappeared from history." Elsewhere he speaks of

Christianity as the "fulfillment" and "confirmation" of Hellas (*The New Science of Politics* [Chicago: University of Chicago, 1952], p. 78).

51. *Ibid.,* p. 76. In *The New Science of Politics,* p. 78, he puts it this way: "The experience of mutuality in the relation with God, of the *amicitia* in the Tho-mistic sense, of the grace which imposes a supernatural form on the nature of man, is the specific difference of Christian truth."

52. Voegelin, "The Pauline Vision of the Resurrected," *Order and History* 4, p. 258.

53. In "The Gospel and Culture," *op. cit.,* p. 77; on pp. 81–82 he sums up the assets and liabilities of Christianity: (1) it is richer (than Hellas) by its univer-salism, poorer by its neglect of noetic control; (2) broader by its appeal to the inar-ticulate humanity of common man but more restricted by its bias against the articulate wise; (3) more imposing by its tone of divine authority but imbalanced by its apocalyptic frenzy; (4) more compact by absorbing much of mythical imagina-tion, but more differentiated through "the intensely articulate experience of loving-divine action." It is clear that I am using Voegelin as a "catalyst" for my own re-flections on the issue of Jesus' divinity.

54. His most careful treatment is in *Science, Politics and Gnosticism* (Chica-go: Henry Regnery, 1968), esp. pp. 85–88.

55. Hans Jonas, *The Gnostic Religion: the Message of the Alien God and the Beginnings of Christianity,* p. 92; for the gnostic imagery, pp. 48–99. Also helpful here is Hans Jonas, "The Gnostic Syndrome: Typology of Its Thought, Imagina-tion, Mood," in his *Philosophical Essays,* pp. 263–276.

56. For a helpful overview of Gnostic research see R. McL. Wilson, *Gnosis and the New Testament* (Philadelphia: Fortress, 1968).

57. Voegelin, *Order and History* 4, p. 20.

58. Voegelin, "The Gospel and Culture," p. 95, where he refers to the apoca-lyptic image of the field marshal in the book of Revelation. An alternative interpre-tation is found in Elisabeth Schuessler Fiorenza, *The Apocalypse,* Herald Biblical Booklets (Chicago: Franciscan Herald, 1976).

59. *Ibid.,* p. 99. In *The New Science of Politics,* p. 122, he adds that Christian faith demands a life of tension and uncertainty that few can tolerate; hence the common regression into apocalypticism.

60. Eric Voegelin, "Equivalences of Experience and Symbolization in Histo-ry," p. 7, as cited by John H. Hallowell, "Existence in Tension: Man in Search of His Humanity," in McKnight, *op. cit.,* pp. 121–122.

61. Particularly helpful for working through the ecstatic or "love-character" of Being is Frederick D. Wilhelmsen, *The Metaphysics of Love* (New York: Sheed and Ward, 1962), esp. the chapter "Being as Ecstasy in Contemporary Spanish Philosophy," pp. 53–95, and Robert O. Johann, *The Meaning of Love: An Essay to-wards a Metaphysics of Intersubjectivity* (Westminster, Md.: Newman, 1955). These works are significant insofar as they have penetrated to the loving character of Be-ing itself. Also helpful are Josef Pieper, *About Love* (Chicago: Franciscan Herald, 1974) and Daniel Day Williams, *The Spirit and the Forms of Love* (New York: Harper and Row, 1968), although Williams's work to my mind does not bring out the radicality of Being's ecstasy because of its process-influenced metaphysics. I find it also terribly significant that Hegel ended up with a love-notion of Being, pri-marily because he insisted on reflecting on the philosophical significance of the in-carnation. Cf. James Yerkes, *The Christology of Hegel,* American Academy of Religion Dissertation Series 23 (Missoula, MT: Scholars Press, 1978). Hans Urs von Balthasar should be particularly noted as someone who has tried consistently

to develop a theology based on the nature of God-as-Agape. Cf. his *Love Alone* (New York: Herder and Herder, 1969), which sets out his basic methodology, found more fully in his *Herrlichkeit: Eine theologische Ästhetik,* 3 vols. (Einsiedeln: Johannesverlag, 1961–1969) and *Theodramatik* (Einsiedeln: Johannesverlag, 1973). Cf. the helpful analysis of Von Balthasar in *Communio* 2 (1975) No. 3 ("The Achievement of Hans Urs von Balthasar").

62. Voegelin, "The Gospel and Culture," p. 71.

63. Voegelin, *The New Science of Politics,* p. 79. Voegelin has not fully articulated criteria for what constitutes such a maximal experiential differentiation, but his view of consciousness would indicate that the degree to which Being becomes luminous is the key. See his *Anamnesis* (Notre Dame: University of Notre Dame, 1978), esp. pp. 14–35, 147–174, 183–213. Tentatively I am following Kohlberg, as we have seen, in employing the criteria of evaluative discrimination and evaluative integration.

64. Cf. Bernard J. Tyrrell, *Christotherapy: Healing through Enlightenment* (New York: Seabury, 1975).

65. Moltmann, *op. cit.,* pp. 267–278, and Heschel, *op. cit.,* pp. 1–11, 27–58, 87–103, 206–253, 263–272. There is a tendency in both to attempt to prove Judaism's and Christianity's uniqueness by devaluing other traditions. I think this is a mistake, for it makes of the "unique," not what is richer and more encompassing, but what is "odd," the "spectacular." Voegelin's attempt to probe the underlying experiences of traditions (esp. those of Hellas) and his refusal to focus on derailments strikes me as more promising. Cf. Maurice Friedman, "Abraham Heschel among Contemporary Philosophers: From Divine Pathos to Prophetic Action," PHILOSOPHY TODAY 18 (1974), 293–305.

66. Heschel, *op. cit.,* p. 6.

67. *Ibid.,* p. 7.

68. *Ibid.,* p. 11.

69. *Ibid.,* Volume 1, p. 46.

70. *Ibid.,* p. 56.

71. *Ibid.,* Volume 2, p. 43.

72. *Ibid.,* p. 49.

73. *Ibid.,* p. 66.

74. *Ibid.,* Volume 1, p. 26. Plato comes close to this in his notion of "participation," which is why I think it a mistake to exaggerate the differences between Israel and Hellas, as Heschel tends to do.

75. *Ibid.,* Volume 2, p. 132.

76. *Ibid.,* pp. 213, 214, 222.

77. Cf. Neusner, *op. cit.*

78. Ruether, *Faith and Fratricide,* pp. 55–57. Cf. E. P. Sanders, *Paul and Palestinian Judaism* (see note 19, Chapter 5), esp. pp. 419–428, for the evidence confirming the view of Judaism set forth here. He excludes only the book of IV Ezra. On the question of the theme of universal access to God in Jesus' message, see Schnackenburg, *op. cit.,* pp. 95–104, esp. pp. 99–100: "On account of its purely religious character, the gospel of God's reign preached by Jesus is directed to all mankind. This remains true in spite of his consciousness that he was sent to 'the lost sheep of the house of Israel' (Matt. 10:6; cf. 15:24). But this indisputable statement sets no limit to his universal salvific will. It indicates the way ordained by God in which salvation is to be brought to them, namely through the ancient people chosen by God to whom Jesus was sent. . . . Jesus summons them all, the just and sinners . . . even despised groups like publicans and prostitutes. The notion of a 'holy

remnant' that he is to gather together from Israel is foreign to his mind." Schnack-enburg, I think, brings out more clearly the note of universality in Jesus' life and message than does Joachim Jeremias, who says: Jesus "envisaged the participation of the Gentiles in a different way, not in the form of the Christian mission, but as the inrush of the Gentiles in the eschatological hours, now so imminent (Matt. 8.11f.)" [*The Parables of Jesus* (London: SCM, 1972), pp. 64–65; cf. his *Jesus' Promise to the Nations* (London: SCM, 1958)]. Finally, I still think it is possible and necessary to maintain that Jesus breaks through the prophetic and apocalyptic notions of the kingdom of God, despite the fact that God's kingdom and presence is felt to be both present and future in the prophets and apocalyptic. What is a *hope* for the prophets and apocalyptic—God's good gifts—is becoming an actuality in Jesus. God, if you will, was felt to be present *in hope and trust* in the prophetic and apocalyptic literature which stresses the kingdom of God notion.

79. Voegelin, *Order and History* 4, pp. 212, 215.

80. Cf. G. van der Leeuw, *Religion in Essence and Manifestation,* 2 volumes (New York: Harper Torchbooks, 1963).

81. Evans, *op. cit.,* p. 147; cf. pp. 147–169, for "creative" aspects of the resurrection.

82. Helpful here is George T. Montague, *The Holy Spirit: Growth of a Biblical Tradition* (New York: Paulist, 1976).

83. Evans, *op. cit.,* pp. 159–160: "The second line of Paul's thought on resurrection is the opposite of formal, and is thoroughly empirical and experiential. This is not so much in relation to himself and to his own private experience. As Marxsen observes, when speaking of his own conversion Paul does not refer specially to having seen Jesus as the Risen One, and conversely, when speaking of the resurrection he does not refer to his own conversion experience. The connection is rather with the Chrisian life as such as being life in the Spirit. For Paul, the hallmark of Christian experience is that it is existence in the Spirit of those who have received the Spirit, i.e. the effective power and presence of God.

"This life of Spirit has three particular characteristics: . . . 'newness' (cf. Rm. 7.6, 'to serve in the newness of Spirit'); . . . life . . . (Rm. 7.6f, 2 Cr. 3.6f, Rm. 8.6–11, Gal. 3.21); the Spirit is called a 'first installment' . . . and 'first-fruit'. . . . ''

84. Particularly helpful for thinking through this complex issue are the works of Heribert Mühlen, *Die abendländische Seinsfrage als der Tod Gottes und der Aufgang einer neuen Gotteserfahrung* (Paderborn: Ferdinand Schöningh, 1968) and *Die Veränderlichkeit Gottes als Horizont einer zukünftigen Christologie: Auf dem Wege zu einer Kreuzestheologie in Auseinandersetzung mit der altkirchlichen Christologie* (Münster: Aschendorff, 1969). Cf. the latter, p. 34: ". . . sind Kreuz und Auferstehung nur zwei Momente eines und desselben Geschehens, nämlich der Zeitwerdung der göttlichen Liebe in ihrer wirhaften Existenzweise."

85. Helpful here are "Woman: New Dimensions," THEOLOGICAL STUDIES 36 (1975), no. 4; Manfred Hoffmann, "Transcendence and Mystery in History," IDOC 71 (1975), 46–59; Rosemary Radford Ruether, "From Misogynism to Liberation," 106–118.

86. Julian of Norwich, *Showings* (New York: Paulist, 1978), p. 301. Helpful on the role of the feminine in Judaeo-Christianity are J. Edgar Bruns, *God as Woman, Woman as God* (New York: Paulist, 1973), and his "Old Testament History and the Development of a Sexual Ethics," in William Dunphy, ed., *The New Morality* (New York: Herder and Herder, 1967), pp. 55–81. Perhaps few lived out the androgynous nature of Christianity as well as Teresa of Avila: cf. Ernest Larkin, "Saint Teresa of Avila and Women's Liberation," SISTERS 45 (1974), 562–568.

87. Sobrino, *op. cit.,* pp. 217, 199, 221, 222–223.

88. See his excellent *Religion and Alienation: A Theological Reading of Sociology* (New York: Paulist, 1975). Here we come upon the complex question of critical social theory, as formulated by such thinkers as Habermas, Adorno and Horkheimer, and further applied to theology by Metz, Moltmann, and Sobrino. Cf. Martin Jay, *The Dialectical Imagination: A History of the Frankfurt School and the Institute of Social Research, 1923–1950* (Boston: Little, Brown and Company, 1973), for the relevant bibliography. Primarily this movement wants to continue the liberating tendencies of the first phase of the Enlightenment (the philosophies of Hume, Kant, etc.) through the critical use of reason, but views that first phase as too naïve, insufficiently aware of how reason is grounded in society with its dehumanizing tendencies (Marx) and in man's own alienation complexes (Freud). It is not just "reason," but the "critical reason" of the Enlightenment's second phase in Marx and Freud that is the tool of liberation. Further, the critical use of reason leads, not to meaning and contemplation through new philosophical and speculative systems (Enlightenment I) but to a liberating praxis and social renovation (Enlightenment II). Hence this movement's "suspicion" of metaphysics. Habermas, for example, bases his program on the insight that with the advent of critical reason man can now control and make history rationally. To do this in a manner freed from possible alienation, one must not accept a "norm" of what man should be but critically analyze social relationships again and again to discern to what an extent liberation has not been achieved. The refusal to engage in metaphysics of the systematic kind means that one will be motivated by a concern for praxis and not simply speculation. Yet, Habermas carefully distinguishes critical theory from critical praxis. To absorb theory into praxis is to fall into political fanaticism and lose one's critical reason. Cf. Jürgen Habermas, *Knowledge and Human Interests* (Boston: Beacon, 1971).

There is, of course, a "norm" for critical theory—namely, the at least implicit concern for human emancipation—but it seems to be a wholly heuristic, one might almost say hesitantly, a wholly negative norm. Edward Schillebeeckx put it this way: "... the critical theory is not based exclusively on scientific analysis. It depends in the first place on a fundamental ethical option in favor of emancipation and freedom" (*The Understanding of Faith: Interpretation and Criticism* [New York: Seabury, 1974], p. 125). But Schillebeeckx may go too far when he says "there is ... a tendency to make negativity itself into a new fetish and to intensify 'no' until it becomes an absolute, and this in turn favours the growth of a new form of alienation" (*ibid.,* p. 127). I would say that critical theory's goal is positive but its method is negative. But this positive goal remains unclarified and unidentified (remember the refusal to engage in systematic metaphysics). In this sense Schillebeeckx is right to see here a tendency toward negativism. Yet it seems to me that the refusal to articulate this goal of emancipation in any clear or systematic manner enables the critical theorist to lapse into ideology. For we all operate from at least implicit presuppositions, and the refusal to articulate them is to become their victim. It is not enough to say that critical theory has articulated its presuppositions in the form of a "care for emancipation." For there is no pure, a-historical care, but only the concrete care of the individual influenced by society, religion, value systems, etc. Ultimately, I think, an emancipatory goal, if it is not to become the legitimation of a particular social program, requires a norm transcendent to society, sufficient to sustain one's critical consciousness and a conviction of meaning and courage. This would inevitably mean that critical theory, too, cannot get along without metaphysics and theology.

89. Karl Rahner, *Schriften zür Theologie* 9 (Einsiedeln: Benziger, 1970), p. 321 (my transl.).

90. Karl Rahner and Herbert Vorgrimler, *Theological Dictionary* (New York: Herder and Herder, 1965), pp. 333–334.

91. I have been greatly helped by Joseph Donceel, "Second Thoughts on the Nature of God," THOUGHT 45 (1971), 346–370, and Michel Gervais, "Incarnation et Immuabilité Divine," REVUE DES SCIENCES RÉLIGIEUSES 50 (1976), 215–243.

92. Classical theism, to my mind, should not be identified with the position of Thomas Aquinas, for Aquinas has critiqued, in the light of scripture, both Aristotle and Plato. Cf. Per Erik Persson, *Sacra Doctrina: Reason and Revelation in Aquinas* (Philadelphia: Fortress, 1970), esp. pp. 93–158. There is in Aquinas, I think, an ecstatic, love-oriented notion of Being and God struggling to expression, despite the Greek categories. It is not apathy, but pure liberality, that Thomas ascribes to God: "It might even be said that the biblical concept of God's dealings with creation and salvation as a free gift requires" Thomas's "more profound metaphysical interpretation in order to be expressed with clarity within the scope of Thomas's thought. Only a God who as *ipsum esse* is absolutely transcendent and independent of the world can give in pure *liberalitas*, since by his giving he does not gain any benefit for himself, and the absolute dependence of the creature conveys the truth that all things come from God" (Persson, *ibid.*, p. 140). Cf. John H. Wright, "Divine Knowledge and Human Freedom: the God Who Dialogues," THEOLOGICAL STUDIES 38 (1977), 450–477, and Metz, *op. cit.*, for rather subtle interpretations of Aquinas.

93. Gervais, *art. cit.*, 232, citing J. Galot, *Vers une nouvelle christologie* (Paris: Duculot-Lethielleux, 1971), p. 79 (my transl.).

94. The panentheisms of Whitehead and Hartshorne obviously come to mind. While I continue to learn much from them and their commentators, I can express my hesitancies here rather briefly: (1) they lack a theory or doctrine of creation, presupposing "process" as a given, and this causes one to question just how total their systems are; (2) God would seem to be one element among other elements in the universe, albeit a supreme element, but not the transcendent creator and sustainer of *all* that the scriptures speak of; (3) in God's dealings with actualities (on the process view) it is only the "aim" that God supplies, and again God seems just one element among many in the universe; (4) finally, there is ambiguity as to whether God's "primordial nature" is real or simply hypothetical. For the nuances and differences of Whitehead and Hartshorne, see *Two Process Philosophers: Hartshorne's Encounter with Whitehead,* American Academy of Religion Studies in Religion 5 (Missoula, MT: Scholars Press, 1973). For general accounts, see Ivor Leclerc, *Whitehead's Metaphysics* (Bloomington: Indiana University, 1958), esp. pp. 189–208; John Carmody, "A Note on the God-World Relation in Whitehead's *Process and Reality,*" PHILOSOPHY TODAY 15 (1971), 302–312: Robert C. Neville, "Neoclassical Metaphysics and Christianity: A Critical Study of Ogden's *Reality of God,*" INTERNATIONAL PHILOSOPHICAL QUARTERLY 9 (1969), 605–624.

95. Donceel, *art. cit.,* 366–367, citing Franz Gregoire, *Études hégéliennes* (Louvain: Béatrice Mawvelaerts, 1958), p. 124. Cf. Emil L. Fackenheim, *The Religious Dimension in Hegel's Thought* (Boston: Beacon, 1967): ". . . Hegel's life-long endeavor was to find the Absolute not beyond but present *in* the world . . ." (p. 79); and "Hegel rejects from the outset all ultimate dualisms, such as between Reason and the actual world" (p. 80). Cf. now Hans Küng, *Menschwerdung Gottes: Eine Einführung in Hegels theologisches Denken als Prolegomena zu einer künftigen Christologie* (Freiburg: Herder, 1970), and especially Yerkes, *op. cit.,* for creative

applications of Hegel to Christology. It seems to me that the hesychast theology of Gregory Palamas is based on dialectical thinking insofar as it maintains that God's own *un*created energies participate in human life; here is a fertile and largely untapped source for theopathic thinking. Cf. John Meyendorff, *A Study of Gregory Palamas* (London: Faith, 1964), esp. pp. 202–227; EASTERN CHURCHES REVIEW 9 (1977), nos. 1–2; and Christos Yannaras, "The Distinction Between Essence and Energies and Its Importance for Theology," ST. VLADIMIR'S THEOLOGICAL QUARTERLY 19 (1975), 232–245.

96. Cf. Louis Dupré, "The Mystical Experience of the Self and Its Philosophical Significance," INTERNATIONAL PHILOSOPHICAL QUARTERLY 14 (1974), 495–511, and his more complete treatment, "The Mystical Vision," in his *The Other Dimension: A Search for the Meaning of Religious Attitudes* (Garden City, N.Y.: Doubleday, 1972), pp. 484–545. Also see W. Norris Clarke and Beatrice Burkel, "The Self in Eastern and Western Thought," in John J. Heaney, ed., *Psyche and Spirit: Readings in Psychology and Religion* (New York: Paulist, 1973), pp. 163–173, esp. p. 169: "We suggest as an hypothesis for philosophical exploration that it is possible also to have distinction not merely through determination and exclusion of the other but through affirmation of the other in love. This would be a purely positive plurality through pure affirmation, without implying any determination, limits, barriers, or exclusion between the lover-affirmer and the loved-affirmed, at least within the field of consciousness, if the mutual response were total on both sides." It appears to me that Aquinas's notion of the person as capable of becoming "all" approaches this (cf. *De Veritate,* 2,2).

97. We are, of course, not advocating a new form of the older theopaschite error. Cf. Moltmann, *op. cit.,* pp. 229–230, who helpfully indicates: (1) Nicaea, against Arius, rightly said that God is not changeable, but "the conclusion should not be drawn from this that God is unchangeable in every respect, for this negative definition merely says that God is under no constraint from that which is not of God" (p. 229). (2) "The mainstream church maintained against the Syrian monophysites that it was impossible for God to suffer. God cannot suffer like creatures who are exposed to illness, pain and death. But must God therefore be thought of as being incapable of suffering in any respect? This conclusion is not convincing either. Granted, the theology of the early church knew of only one alternative to suffering and that was being incapable of suffering (*apatheia*), not-suffering. But there are other forms of suffering between unwilling suffering as a result of an alien cause and being essentially unable to suffer, namely active suffering, the suffering of love, in which one voluntarily opens himself to the possibility of being affected by another. There is unwilling suffering, there is accepted suffering and there is the suffering of love. Were God incapable of suffering in any respect, and therefore in an absolute sense, then he would also be incapable of love. If love is the acceptance of the other without regard to one's own well-being, then it contains within itself the possibility of sharing in suffering and freedom to suffer as a result of the otherness of the other. Incapability of suffering in this sense would contradict the fundamental Christian assertion that God is love, which in principle broke the spell of the Aristotelian doctrine of God. The one who is capable of love is also capable of suffering, for he also opens himself to the suffering which is involved in love, and yet remains superior to it by virtue of his love. The justifiable denial that God is capable of suffering because of a deficiency in his being may not lead to a denial that he is incapable of suffering out of the fullness of his being, i.e. his love" (pp. 229–230). Cf. also the helpful comments on *kenosis* in Ch. Duquoc, *Christologie: essai dogmatique* (Paris: Cerf, 1972), Vol. 1, *L'homme Jésus,* pp. 171–186.

98. It would appear to me, at this stage of my reflections on process thought, that Whitehead, and Hartshorne even more strongly, still move within the ambit of the principle of noncontradiction in their reflections on the God-world relationship, rather than within the ambit of the dialectical principle of correlativity. Cf. Robert C. Neville, "The Impossibility of Whitehead's God in Christian Theology," PRO-CEEDINGS OF THE AMERICAN CATHOLIC PHILOSOPHICAL ASSOCIATION 44 (1970), 130–140, esp. 132–133: "Human independence or ontological freedom from God is the virtue most often appealed to in the Whiteheadian conception of God. . . . The point is: because God is not identified with creativity as such, having only his own specification of it (other finite individuals having their own specifications of it), men have their own independent being, underived from God, however interdependent God and the world are in other respects. And because being in this case means a specific act of creativity, harmonizing a given multiplicity into the individual's own concrete self, the independent being is independent self-determination, or freedom. Whitehead notes God's influence on other actual occasions with the doctrine that God contributes in the initial phase of concrescence a value orienting the subjective aim of the occasion; in later phases the occasion can modify the subjective aim according to self-determined emphasis. Allowing all this for a moment, I want to point out this kind of freedom is a mixed blessing.

"Whitehead must acknowledge God to be an external limit on human freedom, just as other external things are limits to our freedom. All objective things limit freedom in that they are given as initial data required to be harmonized in the prehending occasion's concrescence. God's datum is so important as to determine the initial state of the subjective aim. Whereas finite occasions do determine themselves, still God is like a mammoth Jewish mother, structuring all possibilities and continually insisting on values of her own arbitrary choice. In the long run there is a metaphysical guarantee, considering creatures' immortality in God's life, that no one can damn himself, and the possibility of self-damnation seems to me a touchstone of freedom, beyond the therapy of chicken soup.

"The Whiteheadian answer is that the limitations contributed to an occasion by the world and by God are not negative, in any sense limiting freedom, but rather are positive values; limitation is essential to value. I accept that limitation is essential to value, but emphasize that freedom for Whiteheadians is supposed to be an occasion's own creativity in determining his own final limitation within the range of possibilities inherent in the initial data. That is, an occasion chooses what limitation or value he will become, given the alternate possibilities for harmonizing the initial data. Insofar as God determines the value through the subjective aim in the initial data, the alternatives for the occasion's own choice are diminished. Even if there is always a residue of self-determined emphasis left to the occasion, the function of God is still to force-feed a man's intentions just as other men do.

"The way to get around this objection is to say God's contribution of possibilities and values is somehow identical with the occasion's process of self-determination. But this would require the denial of the ontological independence of God and finite occasions.

"From the standpoint of religious and ethical experience I submit both human self-determination and divine determination of men are felt in the same acts."

Aquinas, I think, is much more within the ambit of our dialectical, correlative manner of thinking in his notion of the relationship between primary and secondary causality. God does not give an impulse to the world from outside the world, but grounds by his presence within the world the universal play of cause and effect (*Summ. cont. gent.*, 2, 21; 3, 67f). Further: "To diminish the perfection of the creature would be to diminish the perfection of God's causality" (*ibid.*, 3, 69); "The one and the same effect is produced by the subordinate cause and by God, directly by both, though in a different way" (*ibid.*, 3, 70); "And just as he does not prevent the activities of natural causes being natural by moving them, so too when moving the voluntary causes he does not make their activity non-voluntary but rather brings it about in them" (*Summ. theol.*, 1, 83, 1, 3). Even if Aquinas spoke of the relations between God and the creature as "secundum rationem tantum," it must not be forgotten that for him the foundation of these relations was real: "potestas coercendi subditos est in Deo realiter" (*De pot.*, 7, 11, 3). According to Gervais, *art. cit.*, 241–242, Aquinas insists on the rational character of God-creature relations because their relation is not one of the same order (mutual in that sense), but rather one of a transcendent Being transcending creation and the created being.

99. Gilkey, *op. cit.*, p. 307. This term is in part inadequate; it should not imply that God must "coerce" himself to be *pathos,* relationship. We are dealing with a *kenosis,* a Being who is ecstatic love.

100. Does God only experience change or actually change in herself? This, I think, must rest upon an insight into what change itself is. Change, I propose, comes from the random possibility for actualization present in nature and the sheer possibility for actualization stemming from human freedom. But as sovereign Lord, God does not change in herself but only in the creature who undergoes change. Rather than saying God changes, I would say that the divine self-limitation creates the very possibility of change/possibility. With Karl Rahner, we can transpose Augustine: "assumendo tempus, creat tempus." For a philosophical exploration of a view that approaches this, see Robert C. Neville, *God the Creator: On the Transcendence and Presence of God* (Chicago: University of Chicago, 1968), *passim.* His program can be gleaned from p. 1: "God is the creator of the world and . . . all his various connections with the world ultimately refer to creation. In particular, that God creates the world means that he is both transcendent of it and immanent within it. Surprisingly, making the notion of creation central allows for much stronger claims both of transcendence and immanence than are possible for approaches that concentrate on one or the other. For instance, the immanence lauded by the view that God is a finite individual interacting with other elements in the world does not show God to be as close to the heart of everything finite as does the view that all things exist as termini of God's creative act. Nor is the transcendence alleged in the claim that God is wholly spiritual as august and mysterious as the transcendence required of one who creates everything determinate, *including his own character as creator of the world. "* The italicized words represent a key intuition that may go far in reconciling temporality with God.

101. Few have put this better than Raimundo Panikkar, *The Trinity and the Religious Experience of Man* (New York: Orbis, 1973), p. 68: "Now what we would venture to suggest—with the Gospel in hand and at heart—is the Father, *Source,* the Son, *Being, the Thou;* and the Spirit, *Return to Being* (or Ocean of Being), the *we. "* He refers to Eph. 4.6: "God above all, through all and in all." Kasper, *op. cit.,* pp. 249–268, has penetrated through to the Trinitarian underpinnings of Christology. Because of his notion of the Spirit, some refer to his Christology as a "Spirit Christology"; for example, on p. 250: "The Spirit is, as it were, the theological transcendental condition of the very possibility of a free self-communication of God in history." Thus, according to the scriptures, the incarnation takes place "in the Spirit": Jesus is conceived by the Spirit (Lk. 1.35); baptized in the Spirit (Mk. 1.10); acts through the Spirit's power (Mk. 1.12); the Spirit is present at the cross (Hb. 9.14); the resurrection is an event in the Spirit (Rm. 1.4, 8.11; 1 Cr.

15.45). This same Spirit also universalizes the work of Christ in history (Jn. 16.7, 20.22; Rm. 8.18–30). The danger of a Spirit-Christology is that it might underplay the uniqueness of Jesus, reducing him to only a charismatic, Spirit-inspired figure. Hence the need for a stress on the resurrection as the event revealing Christ's uniqueness, and the need for a stress on the Son within the Trinitarian Family. Cf. Philip J. Rosato, "Spirit Christology: Ambiguity and Promise," THEOLOGICAL STUDIES 38 (1977), 423–449.

102. Kaufman, *Systematic Theology,* pp. 243–252.

V

THE CHRISTIC SELF: CHRISTIAN
REFLECTION ON THE SELF OF JESUS

Two Typologies: the Isolated Self and the Relational Self

To illustrate what I would call a "Christic notion of the self," it will be helpful to typify in general terms two notions of the "self." The one, "isolated selfhood," increasingly is a phenomenon of modern times; the other, "relational selfhood," characterizes the biblical and early Christian experience of the self. Not only will this typology enable us to understand why disputes about Christ's "person" have arisen, it will also clarify and deepen our own self-understanding. The "isolated self" type stems from a view which would maintain that life's goal is the enhancement and actualization of a well-developed "ego." Just what the "ego" is need not detain us at this moment. It is at least a cipher for the following experiences: (1) that we know ourselves as different from others and thus as "unique" in some sense; (2) that we experience self-responsibility for our actions; and (3) that despite change, we know a basic thread of continuity in our lives, enabling us to fashion some kind of identity for ourselves.

But our ego-development comes at a great price. It is normally a late development for the child, emerging only after she has basically mastered both the forces from within the unconscious and those from without—societal forces—which threaten to overwhelm one. Anthropologists speculate that ego-emergence was a late development for the human species too, coming only after the attainment of mastery over the tendency to regress to pre-ego phases of development. On this view, then, the "ego" symbolizes the human ability to adapt to multiple influences and yet to preserve a basic identity while so adapting.

By itself, this notion of the ego and the kind of person it fosters is deeply individualistic and manipulative. Self-development is an individualistic project of controlling the forces that confront one. The specific historical origins of this "isolated self" are somewhat shrouded in mystery, but I am inclined to trace it to the emergence of reason in classical Greece.[1] If Voegelin is correct, our "relational self" would characterize Plato and Aristotle,[2] yet the later Greeks exalt reason as the organ of control over nature and man. The ability to reason critically, after all, is that which enhances our independence from the views of others (and thus our own experience of individuality) and our capacity for mastery over ourselves and others.

However that may be, few would dispute that there are forces in modern society which foster our isolated self.[3] Mainly we would point to a style of awareness at least partly characteristic of our Western technological culture. Adrian van Kaam puts it this way:

> Our culture sets great store by utility, efficiency, and success. It fosters aggressive analytical reflection which helps build science, technique, and efficient organization. Because we are so efficiency minded, we even examine ourselves in an aggressive analytical way when we engage in introspection.[4]

Technology, of course, is based upon an epistemology of analysis and control of nature. It can enhance man's experience of mastery and manipulation, and if this experience is exalted to the level of the goal promising man the "good life," then this same technological epistemology is applied to the person himself. Introspective methods of analysis and dissection of the person's psyche then tend to breed a kind of self-preoccupation and narcissism locking the individual up within himself. This is perhaps confirmed by the fact that the great diseases and "killers" of our times are no longer diseases stemming from the external environment—virus-related diseases. Man's analytic prowess has increasingly brought this under control. What rather is on the increase is anxiety- and meaning-related diseases—mental disorders, addictions of all kinds, ulcers, heart trouble, etc. Precisely what we would expect from self-preoccupation and narcissism.

We can note the application of this dissective mentality in the fields of psychoanalysis and critical social thought. Psychoanalysis is only possible because analysis is applied to the realm of the psyche. Through it, as Erich Fromm has pointed out, the concept of "truth" has received a new dimension:

> In pre-analytic thinking a person could be considered to speak the truth if he believed in what he was saying. Psychoanalysis has shown that subjective conviction is by no means a sufficient criterion of sincerity. A person can believe that he acts out of a sense of justice and yet be motivated by cruelty. He can believe that he is motivated by love and yet be driven by a craving for masochistic dependence. A person can believe that duty is his guide though his main motivation is vanity.[5]

While this discovery can lead to greater self-knowledge and responsibility, in the hands of our isolated self it all too often reenforces the inability to trust one's own inner motivations, thus further leading him to a brooding self-preoccupation. And a similar tendency can be found in the social sciences, for there too, the application of the analytic epistemology has given social reality a new dimension. Through the social critiques of Marx and especially the new critical school, the "social" is no longer what it appears to be on the surface. It becomes ambiguous and is seen to embody alienating and dehumanizing structures and "values." Technology has its underside in the depersonalization of the worker; capitalism breeds the subservience of man to profits and products; a high standard of living nurtures egocentricity, competitiveness, and aggression.[6] As with self-analysis, so with social-analysis—in the hands of the isolated self the social fabric, too, can no longer be trusted. One is forced back upon herself, and the vicious circle of self-preoccupation is further enhanced.

Besides technology, the realities of pluralism and the information "explosion" should also be noted as factors reenforcing our isolated self. Karl Rahner speaks of a qualitatively new experience of pluralism today.[7] To be sure, prior ages knew plurality, in customs and even viewpoints, but in the West this was accompanied by an all-embracing world view held in common. Thus, there were Protestants and Catholics, but both agreed on God's reality and gift of salvation. Today's pluralism is more radical, for it is the world views that have divided. The communications media and our new global experience have heightened our awareness of competing value systems and ways of life. Allied with all this is the specialization of the sciences and the information explosion it has spawned. It is no longer possible for any one person to control all available information. One must turn to and depend upon "experts." Further, this trend will probably only increase in the future. Surprisingly, the more the information uncovered, the more ignorant each individually becomes.

Both pluralism and the information explosion could foster a more complete kind of person. Diversity can lead to greater depth, less naïve simplicity, and even more creativity. Yet, it can also foster greater ambiguity, doubt in one's inherited value system, and a sense of incapacity in the face of life's complexity. John Dunne speaks of the loss of what the ancients called wisdom: "It has been said that we have forgotten being, that we have turned from the pursuit of wisdom to the pursuit of science, that our age far surpasses previous ages in science, in the knowledge of particular beings, but shows no corresponding advance in wisdom."[8] What Dunne means by wisdom is the capacity to evaluate and thus integrate the knowledge of "particular beings" to which we are increasingly exposed. Thomas Aquinas called this the capacity to order: "It is the wise man who orders, for the ordering of things is possible only with a knowledge of things in their mutual interrelations as well as in reference to something above and beyond them—their end."[9] One can only speculate that the underside of pluralism and extensive information is the self-doubt that furthers the locking of the person up within herself, that furthers individualism, solipsism, isolationism.

Adrian van Kaam, through his extensive clinical experience, has noted that with the isolated self goes what he terms "introspection":

> Introspective reflection tends to the analytical and aggressive.... It purposely loses sight of the totality and goes at its object aggressively.... Introspective reflection makes our own self and its urgency for instant self-realization central, embroiling us in a futile battle against time and against real or imagined competitors for success and survival.... Isolated self-actualization becomes the measure of all things.[10]

When introspectionism begins to dominate the personality, Van Kaam alerts us to four principal effects following in its wake. First, as the isolated self tends to focus upon himself, there ensues a gradual experience of being overwhelmed by the various limitations of his own personality. "I have come to the conclusion," says Van Kaam, "that the person who sees himself in isolation must necessarily see himself as a depressing collection of countless limitations ... in appearance, health, background, knowledge, temperament, virtue, intelligence, emotional range and intensity, chances and opportunities."[11] Because self-development is a completely individualistic project, all is felt to depend upon this individual. There is room only for seriousness, for tautness; and the discovery of one's limitations only intensifies rather than lessens this tautness. With self-focusing, secondly, goes a tendency to dwell upon and overrate one's childhood history. "Introspection implies retrospection within his closed off inner world."[12] As one searches for the causes of his limitations, he is further solidified in his past. The sense of the future, of possibility, recedes. Thirdly, all of this simply further enforces a crippling self-doubt that only gives one further reasons for excusing his lack of self-control. He can always appeal to one of the many limitations he has unearthed. In the most extreme cases, finally, the isolated self gradually severs contact with reality and prefers the dwelling place of his own richer fantasy life. "This fantasy world of the introspectionist is often marked by illusionary projects and make-believe accomplishments."[13]

Clearly our portrait of the isolated self is an idealized type, not necessarily corresponding with full exactitude to any one person in society. As a "type" it enables us to lay hold of tendencies in society, and to speculate as to the furthest consequences of these tendencies, once they break free of other counterbalancing factors. For the most part I have relied upon the observations of psychoanalysts, whose work with patients often reveals our society's "underside."[14] Thus I prefer to speak only of a *tendency* in the direction of our isolated self. The isolated self is, as it were, the underside of other, more positive factors. I agree with Andrew Greeley that we should not create a new myth of the modern alienated man. As he has well observed, a complex and tightly knit industrialized society doesn't lead only in the direction of isolationism; it can open up new opportunities, both for intimacy and for more informal relationships. It can increase the depth of knowledge and sophistication of individuals, and thus make relationships more interesting. It can lengthen the life cycle, and thus promote greater time for reflection on the "ultimates" in life. And further, we should beware of exaggerating the supposed differences between modern, technologized man and peoples of preindustrialized cultures. A number of traditional cultures have entered into industrialization while preserving and building upon the traditions and values of preindustrialized culture. This is perhaps true of many of the ethnic communities in the United States—the Polish, the Mexicans, the Germans, the Basques, etc. I am particularly sensitive to the phenomenon of the Basques, coming from a Basque family as I do. Basque studies are an excellent confirmation of Greeley's view that "contemporary man is not much different from his ancestors but has acquired some new skills, perspectives, and experiences, as well as a much longer life expectancy and greater social and geographical mobility. . . . "[15] Yet, as Greeley must admit, we also should not create a new myth of the fully integrated modern person. Society still has its underside, perhaps more expressively disclosed in the alienated intellectuals and the larger numbers of people suffering from mental and the new physical disorders. Intellectuals are often revealers of what is only latent in the rest of society. Further, ethnic communities, among whom older traditions are strong, are not a fully reliable guide to the tendencies in an industrialized society. One would also want to study groups among whom industrialization has been most intense since the 1800's, groups without strong ethnic traditions. And finally, we must deal with the reality of evil and oppression in society—the phenomenon of wars on a world scale, of human subservience to profit, of anti-feminism, of totalitarianism, of genocide—and ask what factors tend to foster these sorts of things. In this light, we are surely justified in speaking of at least a *tendency* toward our isolated self.

If we turn now to the biblical and early Christian experience, we find a quite different experience of the self. I prefer to name this the "relational self," for on this view one becomes a self, not through preserving one's independence vis-à-vis others, as with the isolated self, but precisely through relating to others, by pouring oneself out to the other. A number of contemporary philosophers have recovered this notion of the relational self, most notably G. W. Hegel: "In friendship and love I renounce my abstract personality and thereby obtain a concrete personality. The authentic reality of the person, then, consists in submerging oneself ontologically in the other."[16] Teilhard de Chardin would say that in the realm of the personal, union does not annihilate but differentiates each. Obviously there are cases where union becomes absorption, merging, and the loss of the self. But if we study the prophets, Jesus, and many of the great Christian mystics, what we find is that in the process of pouring themselves out to others, their "self" is heightened and enriched, not lost. One can see such a notion of the self underlying art, romance, intellectual discovery, social reform, and the religious adventure. In each case the person pours herself into the "other"—the desire for beauty, the surrender demanded by eros, the attractive pull of the truth, the utopian desire for social reform, the fascination of the religious Mystery—and finds herself in a newly enriched way. The consciousness of being a self—the strength of our first ideal type—is not lost; it is only widened to include the necessary contribution of the "other" to our self-constitution.

The classic paradigm for the relational self in the Hebrew scriptures is, of course, the covenant. Through his surrender to God, Moses gains a new awareness of himself and a new sense of mission to the Hebrew people. Most remarkable is the new awareness of the self found in the prophets. We must remember that this was in function of their relationship with God. As Eichrodt expressed it, "Most remarkable . . . are the new form and forceful concentration of the relation with God, which had hitherto simply been described as the fear of God, and is now expressed in words like faith, love, thankfulness, and knowledge of God, which are filled with spiritual tension." Eichrodt sums up his analysis of the prophetic experience of God by saying that "the man to whom God's demand comes is recognized as a person, an I, who cannot be represented or replaced by any other."[17] Eric Voegelin has particularly noted the strong sense of the self in Jeremiah's autobiographical pieces (Jer. 12, 15, 20), in which his relationship with God made of him the great critic of Israelite society: "In Jeremiah the human personality had broken the compactness of collective existence and recognized itself as the authoritative source of order in society."[18] As we find Jeremiah himself putting it, "When I found your words, I devoured them; they became my joy and the happiness of my heart, because I bore your name, O Lord, God of hosts" (Jer. 15.16). Here we should recall Heschel's analysis of the prophet as *homo sympathetikos.* His relation with God led, not to a merging with, but a sense of his difference from God. Rather than a loss of selfhood and psychic incapacity, the prophet senses a call to enter into society to renew it in the name of God.

These observations on the self as relational can be extended into the New Testament. The Johannine notion of "indwelling" points to our experience of selfhood in which union differentiates: "Abide in me, and I in you" (Jn. 15.4). There is a union, a pouring of self into relationship: "that they may be completely one" (Jn. 17.21–23), and yet no loss but a heightening of the self: "In that day you will know that I am in my Father, and you in me, and I in you" (Jn. 14.20). But what of Paul? Actually, far from being the isolated self that many commentators have pictured him, I consider his experience the clearest example of our relational self. Paul knows the experience of union, of pouring himself into Christ: "The life I live now is not my own. Christ is living in me" (Gal. 2.20). But this leads to greater self-differentiation: "I still live my human life, but it is a life of faith in the Son of God . . ." (Gal. 2.20). Perhaps Paul's classic formulation of our relational self is the following:

You did not receive a spirit of slavery leading you back into fear, but a spirit of adoption through which we cry out 'Abba!' (that is, 'Father').

The Spirit himself gives witness with our spirit that we are children of God" (Rm. 8.15–16).

Over a decade ago Krister Stendahl produced a remarkable study of Paul that confirms the notion of selfhood in Paul which I have been describing.[19] Stendahl's main aim is to combat the tendency to view Paul as the great Christian introspectionist, as perhaps Augustine, Luther, and Bultmann had a tendency to do. On such a view, a Pauline statement such as that found in Romans 7.19—"I do not do the good I want, but the evil I do not want to do is what I do"—is given an existentialist interpretation as if Paul were filled with self-doubt, brooding over and trapped in his isolated self. Yet, Stendahl tells us, if we look at the Pauline corpus as a whole, we find "that Paul was equipped with what in our eyes must be called a rather 'robust' conscience."[20] In Philippians 3 Paul indicates that before his conversion he did not brood over the Law; his attitude had been "flawless" with respect to it (Phil. 3.6). Even after his conversion he does not turn to brooding over his former anti-Christian activities: he forgets what is behind him (Phil. 3.13). Paul's references in Romans (2.17–3.20) to the "impossibility" of fulfilling the Law have nothing to do with an existential sense of personal incapacity. In Romans Paul is simply trying to say that the way of the Law has been surpassed by the way of grace opening up through Christ. Even his awareness of sin (Rm. 1–3) is always embraced within a prior awareness of God's grace and the confidence stemming from it: ". . . his grace toward me was not in vain; on the contrary, I worked harder than any of them—though it was not I, but the grace of God which is with me" (1 Cr. 15.10; cf. Rm. 3.21–8.39).

Stendahl's interpretation of the famous Romans passage (Rm. 7) cited earlier is especially striking: " . . . little attention has been drawn to the fact that Paul here is involved in an argument about the Law; he is not primarily concerned about man's or his own cloven ego or predicament."[21] The diatribe style of 7.7–12 shows that Paul is concerned with the Law and whether it can be said to be the cause of sin. In 7.13–25 he makes the elementary distinction between the Law as such and sin, in order to rescue the Law as one of God's gifts. "The possibility of a distinction between the good Law and the bad Sin is based on the rather trivial observation that every man knows that there is a difference between what he ought to do and what he does."[22] And not to be missed is the fact that Paul never identifies the "I" with evil or sin: ". . . it is not I who do it, but the sin which dwells in me." Once the issue of the Law had waned, and the West had grown more introspective, it became possible to read a kind of introspectionism in Paul, but only by overlooking his statements on the goodness of the ego and the will (Rm. 7.18). "We should not," says Stendahl, "read a trembling and introspective conscience into a text which is so anxious to put the blame on Sin, and that in such a way that not only the Law but the will and mind of man are declared good and are found to be on the side of God."[23]

Paul, then, stands in the tradition of the relational self. We can surmise that his relationship with God through Christ strengthened and intensified both his experience of selfhood and his sense of mission to the gentiles. Such lies behind the confidence and joy he expresses throughout his letters, but especially in Romans 8.38–39. The Pauline self is, as it were, co-constituted by a transcendent Divine Self (Rm. 8.15–16), freeing him from introspectionism and leading him in the direction of a radical alterity.

Let us now try to give more precision to our relational self. If we ponder the classic experiences of the self implied in the covenantal relation, in the prophetic consciousness, in the Johannine and Pauline writings, we find a vertical and a horizontal dimension to the self. Vertically we can speak of the self's relation to God. This is the all-encompassing relation, which both grounds the self's experience of individuality (the self is addressed as a "thou") and summons it to a mission, a vocation, a sense of destiny. Horizontally, we can speak of the self's relation to self, to other humans, and to nature and history.[24] Here we have in mind several factors. The "self" becomes through its relations, positive or negative, with its own past, its own body, its friends and enemies, its society, and even its natural habitat. On this view the "person" *is* relationality. In Kasper's very helpful words,

> Personal being is essentially mediation. Because he is a person, a human being is placed on both horizontal and vertical planes; he is the being in the centre. Yet this centre is not inherently static, but one that is dynamically drawn out beyond itself. In this movement man never comes to rest. He is open to everything, fitted for society yet constantly thrown back on himself, orientated towards the infinite mystery of God, yet mercilessly bound down into his finitude and the banality of his everyday concerns.[25]

Such is why *persona* comes from both *per* and *sonare,* "to sound through." One becomes a self/person through allowing both the vertical and horizontal dimensions to sound through one. If we push our reflections further and ask what is the ontological condition of the possibility of such a relational self, we must posit that Being Itself is relational. In other words, the relational God of Judaeo-Christianity, the Sovereign *Pathos,* grounds a relational universe. Because God is Love—remaining herself yet pouring herself into others—the universe, too, is such a dynamism of love. Or, as Heschel might put it, theopathy grounds a universe of sym-pathy. On these terms, the horizontal and vertical dimensions of the human person develop in direct, not inverse, proportion to one another.[26]

As the isolated self experiences life as an individualistic project of self-making, the relational self experiences it as a profoundly social project grounded in the Divine Mystery. The relational self experiences itself not as isolated from but as united with an ultimate source of meaning. It experiences wholeness and integration, for this experience of selfhood "integrates our lives contextually, that is, it helps us live in the context of the whole of reality, of which we are a part, and with its divine all-pervading source."[27]

Jesus in the Light of the Relational Self

Here I would like to do no more than simply indicate that our notion of the relational self is the proper horizon for understanding the "self" of Jesus. This is not, of course, a biography of Jesus or even a psychologizing of him. We are consciously aware that we are going beyond the New Testament texts and probing what is only "implied." But only a sheerly positivistic view of history would deny that all historical reconstruction is ultimately based on the imaginative and reconstructive capacities of the interpreter. Insofar as our interpretation is able to unify the data and point out relationships that have not been grasped before, it can be seen as an attempt toward a more comprehensive understanding of Jesus. The historico-critical restriction on writing a biography of Jesus is needed insofar as it warns us against eisegesis. The nineteenth-century lives were not inadequate because they sought to *interpret* Jesus. Unless one is a positivist, all history involves interpretation; there is simply no other way to comprehend the "data." It was the *kind* of interpretation the nineteenth-century questers engaged in that was off target. Now, briefly expressed, my governing hypothesis will be that we find the relational self realized in Jesus in a most radical way, which leads me to posit what I would call "the Christic self." After probing this, we will go on to examine the implications the Christian community has drawn from its experience of this Christic self.

Here, first, I would single out Jesus' experience of prayer as indicating the radicality of the coincidence of the vertical and horizontal dimensions in his life. Prayer, after all, is not simply one element among many in an individual's life—unless it has degenerated to a mechanistic level—but a manifestation of the depth and central orientation of the person.[28] Although the biblical texts have been written in the light of the Easter faith, we can be reasonably certain that in those instances when the texts stress Jesus' radical orientation to the Father, rather than Jesus himself, that they maintain an original reminiscence. It is perhaps John's gospel that reflects most strongly the post-Easter deepened view of Jesus' prayer life.

First we should note how Jesus' prayer manifests the radicality of his vertical relation with the Divine Mystery, the Father. In this sense it simply concentrates the general New Testament theme that Jesus lived entirely from the Father, something expressed under the general notion of Jesus' obedience (Mk. 14.36; Lk. 2.49; Phil. 2.8; Rm. 5.19; Hb. 5.7-9; Jn. 5.19, 5.30). Here, I think, we should view "obedience" in its etymological sense of "listening to" and "openness to" that possible revelation of the Father. In this sense of openness to the Father, Jesus' prayer shows that such was the all-encompassing dynamism behind his entire life. Certainly, like all pious Jews, he practiced prayer in the Jewish mode. We find him blessing food (Mt. 14.19, 15.36, 26.26) and attending the Sabbath service (Lk. 4.16). Undoubtedly he practiced the custom of the *Tephilla* (cf. Dn. 6.11), that of praying at the three fixed hours of the day. This was still a common Christian custom for the earliest disciples (Aa. 3.1, 10.3, 30; *Didache* 8.3), and Jeremias's study leads him to observe "that no day in the life of Jesus passed without the three times of prayer: the morning prayer at sunrise, the afternoon prayer at the time when the afternoon sacrifice was offered in the Temple, the evening prayer at night before going to sleep."[29]

But the texts enable us to go further and observe what is most characteristic of Jesus' prayer. For he is not satisfied with the fixed tradition of prayer. According to the synoptics, Jesus' entire life is embraced in an atmosphere of prayer; that is, in a posture of openness to the Father. Jesus' public ministry begins and ends with prayer (Lk. 3.21, 23.46). When he chooses the twelve (Lk. 6.12f), in teaching (Lk. 11.1), before curing (Mk. 9.29), and while trying to strengthen his disciples (Lk. 22.32), he prays. Particularly at critical moments, as at the Garden of Olives, does he pray (Mt. 11.25; Lk. 10.21; Mk. 14.35–36). Further, he prays in the Aramaic vernacular (Mk. 14.36, 15.34), removing prayer from the sacral liturgical sphere where only Hebrew was spoken, expressing its everyday quality. In Jeremias's words, Jesus places prayer "right in the midst of everyday life."[30] Finally, his relationality to the Father in prayer is grounded upon the relational God of *pathos,* as the uncommon address "Abba" reveals. This Aramaic colloquialism, taken from the child's language of intimacy, reveals the depth of Jesus' relationship with his Father.

But Jesus' prayer life manifests the radicality of the horizontal dimension in his life. Thus, he teaches his disciples to pray (Lk. 11.1f). This does not mean that they had not learned to pray previously. It rather reveals that Jesus is other-centered, that he wants to give them a new orientation in life, a new self-identity as the community that addresses the relational God as "Abba" too. It is perhaps Jesus' critique of prayer that reveals the depth of the horizontal pole, however. He condemns those alienating forms of prayer that tear down the possibility of real community and foster personal blindness and what the prophets called "hardness of heart." It is important to emphasize that this critique of prayer was not accidental to who Jesus was. It manifests to what an extent he actually poured himself out to others. Thus he criticizes prayer that fosters self-deception (Lk. 18.11), prayer that turns men away from commitment to the world and humanity (Mt. 7.21), prayer that legitimates the oppression of others (Mk. 12.38–40).

Secondly, we find the *coincidentia oppositorum* of the vertical and horizontal poles in Jesus' experience and preaching of God's kingdom. If Jesus' prayer reveals his relational self in its most intimate and concentrated form, his commitment to the kingdom expresses this in its more public and manifest form. The vertical pole reveals itself in the fact that Jesus preached, and poured himself into, *God's* kingdom. The "kingdom" notion, as we well know, is a complex eschatological reality signifying the ultimate reality or *telos* for human history. Since Albert Schweitzer broke away from the nineteenth-century liberal view of the kingdom as merely a symbol for the yearnings of the average bourgeois citizen, we have recovered its eschatological nature. This means that the kingdom is first and foremost God's gift and grace, and a justice, peace, and love that only he can grant. Once we grasp this, and the extent to which Jesus was committed to it (Mk. 13.33; Lk. 12.32; Mt. 6.10; Mk. 4.26, 29), then the dispute about whether the kingdom is temporal or existential, future or present, collapses.[31] For Jesus' God-centeredness means that God can be counted on both now and in the future.

The horizontal dimension in Jesus' experience of the kingdom evidences itself in the fact that Jesus preaches God's *kingdom*. Jon Sobrino has brought this out well:

> . . . Jesus did not talk simply about "God" but about "the kingdom of God."
> Jesus adopts as his own the Old Testament conception of God, which contrasts with that of Greek thought. The Old Testament view is that God acts in history in a specific way, and that his action cannot be separated or isolated from his basic reality. . . . "God exists" means that God "acts" or "reigns." The "reign" of God is part of his very reality.[32]

And thus, again, relating to God grows proportionately with relating to mankind. In Jesus, the vertical and horizontal are never separated. He strives, then, *to act* for men and women, to establish true sisterhood and brotherhood (Lk. 2.9; cf. Is. 65.17), to thwart the forces that make this fellowship impossible, and he calls for reform and repentance (Mk. 1.15). What we find here is a peculiar synthesis of what has been called the apocalyptic and the prophetic notions of the kingdom found in the Hebrew scriptures. For the former, the kingdom was an eschatological (final) reality God alone would bring. For the apocalypticist it was never entirely clear whether this futurism and God-centeredness represented a kind of denigration of the world and historical responsibility. The prophets, on the other hand, stressed the kingdom as a critical norm for bettering society in the present. Both elements—the more vertical stress of the apocalypticists and the horizontal stress of the prophets—find their coincidence in Jesus.

Mark's gospel brings our coincidence out rather clearly. The famous apocalyptic discourse of Mark 13, while containing apocalyptic elements (13.7–8, 14–20, 24–27), balances these by a stress upon the prophetic interest in critiquing and reforming society now. Thus apocalyptic stress on the future is mollified: rather than useless speculation and absorption in the future (13.5–7, 24–27, 33–37), the believer should recognize that testimony to Jesus is called for now (13.9–10). This is the time for the beginning of suffering (13.8), and the gospel must first be preached to all (13.10). Undoubtedly this passage reflects Mark's own theological concerns. Yet it helpfully illustrates, although in a "later" way, the peculiar manner in which Jesus combined both a deep concern for this present world and an openness to the future, transworldly reign of God.

It is also not without importance that Jesus' peculiar combination of the vertical (apocalyptic) and horizontal (prophetic) enables his proclamation of the kingdom to avoid both the pitfalls of fanaticism and despair in his ministry. Fanaticism inevitably comes when one identifies God's kingdom with a particular realization of it within history. This was perhaps the Zealots' tendency. Here the finite and temporal realization is raised to the level of an absolute. Despair follows when one realizes that no finite realization can exhaust the kingdom of the Lord. It always remains ahead of us, God's gift. Jesus, on the other hand, preaches a kingdom that indeed must take a finite form in history (the horizontal-prophetic dimension), yet he never simply identifies this with the fullness of the divine kingdom (the apocalyptic-vertical dimension).

Once we note the coincidence of the horizontal and vertical in Jesus' life we can understand why Jesus' love command takes the double form that it has and becomes the central element in his own preaching. There is, of course, doubt whether Jesus was entirely original in his coupling of the love command to God and to neighbor (cf. Dt. 6.5; Lev. 19.18), since we can find this in other contemporary Jewish writings.[33] But what stands out as unique to him was that he made the love command "central within the context of his proclamation about the coming rule of God"; it is "given a central, determinative role as the principle for *interpreting* . . . the moral requirements of the whole law."[34] This centralization of the double love command expresses, I think, how intensely Jesus' entire life was thoroughly relational: he was what he was because he poured himself out both to God and to man (the neighbor).

Thirdly, in this brief survey of the relational features of Jesus' self, we can note that we should expect our coincidence of opposites in the biblical testimonies concerning Jesus' death and resurrection. Although the resurrection will again be the subject of our next chapter, it will be helpful at this point to indicate its relevance to Jesus' relational selfhood. To be sure, Jesus' death most dramatically climaxes his entire life of pouring himself out, both to God and to mankind. It seems to me exaggerated to say that Jesus experienced his death as one of abandonment by the Father. Though undoubtedly he experiences fear at the prospect of his impending death, his overwhelming attitude is one of confidence and trust in his Father (Mk. 14.36). It should not be overlooked that it is Mark's gospel that both least mollifies Jesus' death struggle (Mk. 14.34, 36; 15.34, 37) and yet emphasizes how that death is Jesus' final act of surrender (obedience) to the Father. Mark carefully uses the passive *paradidomi* (to be handed over) throughout the passion narratives as a way of indicating that Jesus' death is a surrender unto and into God (13.9, 11, 12; 14.10; 15.1, 10, 15). Mark then seems to want to present Jesus' death as the climax of his vertical relation to God, the climax of his emptying himself out into the Father. But also for Mark Jesus' death is an emptying out for others (Mk. 15.31). The Barabbas episode (15.6–15) illustrates this rather well, for Barabbas goes free through Jesus' death.[35] As such it is paradigmatic for the later Christian notion that Jesus' death was an intense act of love for mankind, an act in which men would now be empowered to be free, like Barabbas. Finally, I would also indicate that the resurrection can be usefully examined from this perspective of the relational self. Please recall that we have said that we are both a relating unto God and unto man, simultaneously. Surrender unto God always brings with it a greater openness to mankind. Although we will probe this more fully in our next chapter, we can say that the scriptures note this twofold dimension in Jesus' resurrection. It is both an "exaltation" (our vertical pole) and a new mode of presence among mankind (our horizontal pole; cf., viz., Mt. 28.20), a new way of being with us.

Let me close this brief survey of Jesus' relational selfhood by indicating what I think can only be called its "radical" nature. This is as much true of Jesus' relationship to God as it is of his relationship with us. It is not true, of course, that Jesus is totally new in the way in which he brings to realization our relational self. In a later section on Jesus' possible "uniqueness" we will indicate that this is important, because it means there is a point of contact between Jesus and other men. Voegelin's interpretation of Plato and Aristotle has persuaded me that we find the relational self expressed in them: they know themselves to be living in the *metaxy*, in the "in-between," in the center of the vertical and horizontal poles of being human. The covenantal experience, too, especially as it was known to the prophets, was essentially a greater realization of our relational selfhood.

Yet it must be said that there is a newness in the way in which Jesus realizes his life of relationships. His God-relationship can only be described as unconditionally intimate and intense in its quality, as his unique use of the expression "Abba" indicates. He "knows" God as one whose own love is unconditional in its extent—he allows the rain to fall on the just *and* the unjust (Mk. 5.45)—and in this sense Jesus' relation with God transcends the limits of the covenantal experience. This God-experience is undoubtedly the source of his own experience of inner authority and freedom (cf. Mt. 25.31–46).[36] Similarly the quality of his horizontal relations manifests the same unconditional character. His proclamation of love of the enemy (cf. the good Samaritan), his association with sinners (Mk. 2.5), his attempt to free the ruling class from its ideology (Mk. 7.15)—all manifest the new quality of his relationship with mankind. As Pesch put it,

> His free demonstrations of solidarity did not set up new battle lines, but infiltrated beyond all lines. Jesus remained free in relation to everyone, and wanted to make everyone free for everyone else.[37]

Particularly symbolic of this new horizontality is Jesus' relationship with women.[38] This is simply a further confirmation of the androgynous nature of selfhood seen as relationship. For one becomes a self (independent, masculine pole) not through the exclusion but through the affirmation of others (dependent, feminine pole). The fact that Jesus' relations with women are so extraordinary, given the repression of women in Jewish culture, simply highlights Jesus' own inner reconciliation with his own femininity. In any case, as Rosemary Ruether has reconstructed the evidence, Jesus' life demonstrates a remarkable openness to the feminine.

For example, some of Jesus' closest associates were women, and these remained faithful to the end, unlike his male disciples. Luke 8.1–3 tells us that Joanna and Susanna went with him on journeys "in a way that must have seemed highly unconventional in traditional society."[39] He holds up women's faithfulness as the model of the kingdom (Lk. 21.1–4, 7.36–50), and even describes himself as a "mother hen" worrying over Jerusalem (Mt. 23.37; Lk. 13.34). But he goes further and openly violates the patriarchal taboos on women. He actually heals a woman with a flow of blood, allowing her to touch him (Mk. 5.25–34; Mt. 9.20–22; Lk. 8.43–48). Such a woman was regarded as unclean, and breaking this taboo may be the reason she is described as so terrified. Jesus also breaks other taboos: he speaks with an outcast Samaritan woman (Jn. 4.27), when in law it is permitted to speak only with one's wife. His reformulation of the divorce teaching (Mt. 19.3–9) elevates woman to a coequal status with man. And most remarkably, he models the Christian life after the feminine image of "service" (Mt. 20.25–28, 23.8–11), not after the male image of power and subordination. Ruether, I think, has most perceptively summed the matter up in this way:

> . . . although Jesus held up the image of service to overthrow a ruling-class concept of hierarchical power for men, he does not use this image of service to reinforce the image of women as servants. On the contrary, the one person whom he rebukes for being "much occupied with serving" is a woman, Martha. In traditional Judaism the place of women was in the kitchen. Men alone were called to study the Torah with the rabbi. By vindicating Mary's right to join the circle of disciples and students of the Teacher, Jesus overthrows the traditional concept of women's place as upheld by Martha. "Mary has chosen the better part which shall not be taken from her" (Lk. 10.38–42). The principles of christian community are founded upon a role transformation between men and women, rulers and ruled.[40]

The "Christic Self": Christian Reflection on the Self of Jesus

The doctrine of the ecumenical Council of Chalcedon on the unity of the divine and human in Jesus, the crystallization of centuries of dogmatic speculation and even dispute, attempted to clarify the remarkable manner in which the two poles of Jesus' existence—the divine and the human, the vertical and the horizontal—coalesce in his person. This was already a development that had its beginnings in the New Testament. Here it is important to remember that the New Testament simply assumes as a fact that Jesus was utterly human, something nicely summed up for us in the Lucan statement: "And as Jesus continued to grow in body and mind, he grew also in the love of God and of those who knew him" (2.52). We know, for example, that Jesus could be sarcastic (Mt. 23), that he knew anger (Mk. 11.15f), that he experienced human anxiety (Mk. 14.32f), that he was tempted (Mt. 4.1–11), even that he was perhaps ignorant and possibly mistaken about the question of the timing of the kingdom's arrival (Mk. 5.30–33).[41] But what is already a biblical datum and here the focus of our interest is the unique and new unity of the divine *and* human in Jesus.

This is a development that occurs, of course, after the Easter event. The basic pattern is the reading of Jesus' divine status back into his earthly, human ministry. He is viewed simultaneously as both God and man (John), *Kyrios* and servant (Paul), Messiah and rabbi (synoptics). To express this in terms of our analysis, the New Testament asserts in Jesus a unique unity of the vertical and horizontal poles in his existence. Paul's formulation can serve as the symbol for this faith intuition: "His state was divine, yet he did not cling to his equality with God but emptied himself to assume the condition of a slave, and became as men are; and being as all men are, he was humbler yet, even to accepting death, death on a cross" (Phil. 2.6–8). In various ways the New Testament makes it clear that this divine-human unity is unique and unexpected in history. On the one hand, it uses the motif of the "rupture" or "leap" in human history to bring this point home. Matthew's genealogy is instructive in this regard (1.17–25). Historically we can enumerate a number of motives for the formulation of genealogies: to establish tribal identity, to undergird status, etc.[42] What is extraordinary is the theological use Matthew makes of Jesus' genealogy. He traces Jesus' descent through five women (Tamar, Rahab and Ruth, Uriah's wife and Mary), while descent was normally traced solely through the male. This suggests that a rupture is occurring in history through Jesus, a reversal of transformation of God's relation with mankind. This rupture-motif is further brought out by the *kind* of women we find here: Tamar and Rahab acted as harlots (Gn. 38; Joshua 2, 6); Ruth seduced Boaz one night during a grain festival (Ruth 3); and Uriah's wife was guilty of adultery with David (2 Sm. 11–12). The virgin birth, while a way of highlighting Jesus' divine status—he is conceived by the Holy Spirit—also suggests this rupture-motif, for a "virgin" birth is a departure from the regular course of human history. History is taking a new turn in Jesus,[43] God is relating to humanity in a new way. Similarly Paul uses the contrast between the Old Adam and the New Adam to develop his own understanding of the rupture inaugurated in history (Col. 3.9–10; 1 Cr. 15.45).[44]

On the other hand, we have the motif of fulfillment in the biblical descriptions of Jesus. The most common manner of expressing this is the citation of passages from the Hebrew scriptures, thus indicating that God's relation with mankind comes to a new climax and fulfillment in Jesus.

This is particularly evident in John's gospel: "There are at least twenty-five quotations from the Old Testament in John; six are quoted in such a way as to make clear that a claim of fullfillment is being made, and fourteen begin with a formula such as 'Scripture is fulfilled,' 'Scripture says,' 'the word was fulfilled,' 'it is written,' 'Isaiah says' " (cf. Jn. 12.15, 40; 13.18; 15.25; 19.28; 19.36, 37; 1.51; 10.16; 6.45, 31).[45] Paul, however, has perhaps most forcefully proclaimed the fulfillment-motif: "in the fullness of time" God sent forth his only Son (Gal. 4.4).

With a number of contemporary theologians,[46] I think that this new *coincidentia* of the divine and human in Jesus can best be approached in the light of the notion of the relational self sketched above. If to be "person"/"self" is essentially to be an openness, a relation, to both God and man, then the New Testament is implying that in Jesus we find the "person" realized in the most complete sense. The two dimensions co-constituting the human person—the vertical and all-embracing openness to God and the horizontal openness to humanity—find in Jesus their most intense realization: he is both God and man. This last statement only expresses with more clarity and decisiveness the relational selfhood we have found exhibited throughout Jesus' life. Jesus is *persona:* the Divine and human "sound through" *(per-sonare)* him in the most complete way. That such a divine-human unity could be possible at all must ultimately presuppose that God is not an impenetrable and unparticipable Being but the relational Being pointed to in our notion of the Divine *Pathos.*[47] Throughout the rest of this section, then, I will employ the terms "the Christic self" to give expression to this new and unique divine-human unity realized in Jesus.

Such an understanding of Jesus' self or person builds, of course, upon centuries of Christological reflection and struggle, as well as upon more contemporary developments in the comprehension of the human person. Although the divine-human unity we have sketched above is clearly asserted in the scriptures, the issue of just how to understand the relation of the divine and human in Jesus was not explicitly raised until the Christological disputes of the patristic period. These disputes, I think, are increasingly well known,[48] and so we can be content with a sketch of the highpoints of this development. First, one gains the impression, from a study of these disputes, that the relational notion of the "self" sketched above was struggling to emerge. This is certainly the case with Chalcedon (451) whose basic intent was to steer a middle course between Monophysitism and Nestorianism, both of which were thought to compromise the divine-human unity in Jesus, either by contracting all in the Divine *Logos* (Monophysitism) or by ontologically separating the divine and the human (Nestorianism).[49]

The crucial passage from Chalcedon should be cited: "We confess one and the same Christ . . . in two natures without confusion, without change, without division, without separation, the difference of the natures having been in no wise taken away by reason of the union but rather the properties of each being preserved and both concurring into one person and one *hypostasis*" (*DS* 302). Here we have on the one hand a reaffirmation of Nicaea: Jesus is consubstantial *(homoousios)* with the Father in Godhood. On the other, the new contribution necessitated by the Monophysitism-Nestorianism dispute: by its distinction between "natures" and "person" *(hypostasis)* it preserves the unity in duality and duality in unity that we find in Jesus. Here precisely we have our principle that union differentiates rather than annihilates the person. The divine-human unity in Jesus is just such a union in differentiation. Such a development in Christian thought, I think, could only have been possible on the basis of the Judaeo-Christian God of *Pathos* and the corresponding Christian experience of the self as relational. Understood in this light, Chalcedon can be considered a profound use and yet transmutation of Hellenic thought, with its tendency to view the Divine as a self-enclosed Monad.

I would particularly single out two aspects of Chalcedon's contribution. First, it takes up and corrects the earlier contributions stemming from the Alexandrine and Antiochene theological traditions. The Alexandrines, particularly under Cyril's leadership, sought to preserve the *unity* of the divine-human Jesus through their model of the *Logos-sarx*. But this model does not grant sufficient significance to Jesus' humanity, which is more than mere "flesh" *(sarx)*, possessing also a human intellect and will. This was the danger of this model that the Church had already corrected in its condemnation of Apollinaris. Thus the Antiochenes sought to express this correction through their model of the *Logos-anthropos*. Here *anthropos* encompasses not simply the "flesh" but the entirety of Jesus' humanity, at least in principle. The difficulty here is then the *unity* of the divine and human in Jesus. Chalcedon, under the pressure of the extremist factions of both the Alexandrines and Antiochenes clearly intended to accept with Alexandria the stress on the unique *unity* of the God-man and with Antioch the stress on the notion that this unique unity does not annihilate the differences of the divine and human but rather preserves them. Hence the crucial phrase, "the difference of the natures having been in no wise taken away by reason of the union. . . . "

Chalcedon's use of the term *hypostasis,* from which our more modern "the hypostatic union" derives, is the second contribution deserving mention. The key element to note here is that this term was borrowed from the Trinitarian speculations of the Cappadocians, where it carried the connotations of "relationship" as between Father, Son, and Spirit. As such, *hypostasis* was already a term expressing our relational concept of the person. "Person" was not the isolated ego or self-enclosed Monad, but dynamic ecstasis, mutuality, relationality, through which we have union in differentiation. As such, the term was especially apt for expressing the union in differentiation of the divine-human reality of Jesus.

There were, of course, shortcomings at Chalcedon, and the Church, precisely to preserve the truth of the Council, was compelled to go beyond it. Chalcedon, for example, seemed to contract into an abstract formula about the inner constitution of Jesus the whole concrete and dynamic life of relationships characteristic of Jesus in the scriptures. The use, further, of the term "nature" runs the danger of depersonalizing Jesus' humanity and of not clarifying the key differences between the ways in which the divine and human each contributes to the singular unity in Jesus. For example, one might think that the divine and human "natures" co-exist in a relationship of equality, while in actuality the divine is the transcendent ground and condition of the human. Finally, as many are pointing out today, Chalcedon omits any reference to the redemptive significance of the singular unity in duality that is Jesus. Of what salvific import is its rather complex and subtle definition?

The next great turning point was taken by the second Council of Constantinople (553), which continued the Alexandrine focus on the hegemony of the *Logos* in the unique unity of Jesus. This Council clarified that the one *hypostasis* was that of the *Logos* which assumed the human nature of Jesus. Despite the fact that this leaves unclarified the full reality and autonomy of Jesus' humanity, it does indicate that ultimately the reality of Jesus is based upon the Divine Itself as the condition of its possibility. But this Council even does more. By speaking of the *Logos* as assuming Jesus' humanity, it is presupposing our relational notion of God as *ec-static,* outgoing. This, I think, is the real import of Constantinople's contribution. Implied in this doctrine of *enhypostasis* is a quite dynamic and relational notion of "person" whereby unity does not lead to a merging but a differentiation of the divine and human. As Kasper expresses it, "This doctrine of *enhypostasis* developed by Leontius, of the 'in-existence' of the human nature in the divine *hypostasis,* must therefore be seen in its dialectical character, whereby unity and distinction increase in direct, not inverse proportion."[50] The third Council of Constantinople (680–681) clarified this unity in distinction by indicating the full reality of Jesus' humanity: he indeed has a human will and human manner of acting, though this is dependent upon the Divine Will. Finally, then, the unity in difference had come to full dogmatic clarity.

The climax of Christological development was perhaps reached by Richard of St. Victor in the twelfth century. His Trinitarian speculation led him quite consciously to our relational notion of "person": *"Naturae intellectualis incommunicabilis existentia."*[51] One is a "self" (*incommunicabilis*) precisely through going *out,* through relating *to* the other (*ex-istentia*). It is, I think, along these lines that the most fruitful approach to Jesus' personhood travels. The Christic self (*incommunicabilis*) is constituted precisely through its relationship (*ex-istentia*) to the divine and human. It is a union through differentiation.

A second, major observation on this complex history is that it was necessary to wait until the more modern interest in the person and subjectivity before our relational notion of the self could be decisively clarified. Here, it seems to me, there are two developments that are really significant and which point in the direction of our relational concept of the person. On the one hand, we have modern man's more differentiated awareness of himself, since the Enlightenment, as a free, self-positing being. While this can lead, and has led, in the direction of the autonomous and isolated ego, it was also a necessary insight into the full reality of the human personality. This means that "personhood" is no mere abstract reality, but a dynamic becoming and real self-actualizing. Any view of Jesus' person, then, would have to grant him this real autonomy of personality if it were to do justice to his complete humanity. The second and more recent development is the growing awareness that the human person is a being in- and with-the-world, in- and with-others. This comes to expression particularly in Hegel on the philosophical level, although it is a truth especially brought to light by contemporary psychology and sociology.[52] Not only, in other words, is the person autonomous and self-positing, but these very capacities are in part made possible and heightened through our existence in and relation to the world and other human persons. Autonomy and dependence, difference and unity, co-constitute one another. These two developments have enabled us to recapture on a more conscious level what was the lived experience of personhood for the Judaeo-Christian tradition: one becomes an "I" (the Enlightenment emphasis on autonomy) precisely through relationships (the post-Enlightenment insight into human interdependence). The crucial contribution of the Judaeo-Christian tradition, of course, is to widen this new understanding of the person by including God within its horizon. The "I" is not only a lived relationship on the horizontal level, but this is embraced and supported by a lived relationship to the Divine on the vertical level.

In summary, then, by way of this long historical detour, we arrive at the notion of "person" most apt for expressing the unique reality of Jesus. Personhood is seen to embrace two dimensions. On the one hand, we have the experience of being an "I," a unique identity. On the other, we have the experience of becoming this "I" through our relationships to others, to the world, and ultimately to God. As Teilhard de Chardin so well understood, in the realm of the personal, union differentiates rather than annihilates. In the most intense manner, the Christian tradition affirms that Jesus' person, both divine and human, is a unique instance of such a union in differentiation.

Some Further Probings

1. Jesus' sinlessness and human growth: In the light of our relational notion of the self probed above, it is now possible to explore two further New Testament traditions concerning Jesus. Tradition, in its later, more developed sections, asserts the sinlessness of Jesus (Jn. 8.46, 14.30; 2 Cr. 5.21; Hb. 4.15, 7.26; 1 Pt. 2.22; 1 Jn. 3.5). It is instructive that Hebrews both asserts this sinlessness and yet rather strongly and dramatically highlights the real humanity of Jesus:

> It was essential that he should . . . become completely like his brothers
> so that he could be a compassionate and trustworthy high priest of

God's religion, able to atone for human sins. That is, because he has himself been through temptation he is able to help others who are tempted (Hb. 2.17–18; cf. 4.15, 5.8).

Sin must here be seen in the biblical perspective as a rupture in the covenantal relationship with God. Because in Jesus the God-relationship has achieved its most complete human realization, such a rupture as sin presupposes does not occur. Yet, and this too is scripture's witness, such sinlessness in no way detracts from Jesus' authentic humanity. We might note that scripture nowhere maintains that Jesus *could* not sin; only that he did not. I think we can make sense of this startling sinlessness in Jesus and yet his real humanity if we remember our key insight regarding the relational self: the more intense the vertical relationship with God, the more actualized is the horizontal, human pole of our existence. Sinlessness, in other words, does not signal an incapacity for authentic human growth; it is human growth at its height.

The issue of Jesus' human growth (cf. Lk. 2.52) is a particular difficulty for Roman Catholics, given the decrees of the Holy Office on this matter against the Modernists at the turn of the century. One gains the impression that the more recent decree on the "Historical Truth of the Gospels"[53] has substantially modified the earlier Roman position, calling for a new theoretical framework for the question. For this more recent decree speaks of Jesus adapting himself to the cultural framework of his times, a statement that seems to imply an openness to Jesus' essential historicity and growth. Contemporary theologians, as Raymond Brown indicates, would prefer a stronger phrasing of the matter: "Most Catholic scholars would speak more openly of Jesus' own limited knowledge rather than of his accommodating himself to the limited knowledge of his times."[54] On the deepest level, I think, the Roman position was an outgrowth of the Scholastic dependence upon an unrelational notion of the self—the self as defined by Boethius, as we have seen. On such a view, the person is understood individualistically as complete in itself and only "accidentally" modified by relationships with others. Here, too, we can notice the echo of later Hellenism, with its view of the self as an enclosed and isolated being. Following such a view would inevitably mean that were Jesus to be the complete "person," he would have to be a fully finished reality, "perfect" in himself, lacking nothing. Hence, then, the claims for his fullness of knowledge, of wisdom, and even of the beatific vision of eternity.

On the relational view of the self we are here positing, the "perfection" of the person stems precisely from the depth of openness to both God and to mankind. This view is also quite dynamic and historical, realizing that relationships can occur only in and through time. Once relationships, on both the vertical and horizontal planes, are seen as constitutive of the person, one must make room for a real, not accidental, personal growth on all the levels of the "self." One can, with Karl Rahner,[55] speak of a *positive nescience* which stems both from the always greater reality of the Divine and from the further growth in human relationships that is always possible on the historical level. Rahner still thinks it is possible to speak of a "vision of God" enjoyed by Jesus throughout his life, although he distinguishes this from the fullness of the "beatific vision," and considers this vision of God to be an implicit, pre-conscious God-awareness subject to growth and clarity on the conceptual level. Our position would, of course, quickly agree with this view of Rahner's, since we have maintained that our God-relationship is the all-embracing and supporting relation in human existence. Yet I think our position would perhaps more clearly note that the relationship to God characteristic of Jesus is not merely consciously and conceptually clarified, but also subject to growth on the ontic level itself. That is, it is not just Jesus' human knowledge that grows in greater clarity; it is his humanity itself. Yet, having said all of this, it would seem that it is possible to combine at least the *concerns* of the Roman position with our own. The former, I think, wishes to highlight the singularity of Jesus' person: In Jesus we are forced to recognize a unique realization of the person. Our position would put this in broader historical and relational terms, stressing that this unique "person" realized and actualized himself historically, socially, and dynamically.

2. *The Christic self as androgynous:* We have earlier indicated the feminine dimension in the Divine *Pathos;* the image of *Pathos* might perhaps reawaken that dimension. Since it is this sovereign and holy *Pathos* which ultimately grounds a relational universe and is the final foundation of humanity's relational nature, we should expect this femininity to manifest itself in the person of Christ, the supreme manifestation of relationality. One of the difficulties with a view of Jesus' person that overlooks his relational nature is that it is excessively "masculine." A view of his person as complete and enclosed within itself has room neither for receptivity and mutuality on the one hand, nor for the change and unpredictability characteristic of human relationships on the other. Our view, on the other hand, would indicate that the marvel of the Christic self is androgynous: an autonomy and selfhood ("masculinity") precisely through the unpredictability of mutuality ("femininity"). Ultimately I would posit that this androgynous dimension of the Christic self accounts for the remarkable way in which Jesus related to the women of his own time. Because he was fully reconciled to his own femininity, he could be reconciled to the feminine within his society.

I am aware that linking the feminine to the receptive pole of the person again runs the danger of a male hegemony and legitimation of masculine autonomy and power. It is an easy tendency to bifurcate the masculine and feminine, hypostatizing the masculine in the male and the feminine in the female. Such a bifurcation means that masculine autonomy becomes oppressive domination and feminine mutuality becomes a sentimental dependency. By speaking, however, of the androgynous reality of the *one* person Jesus, I hope that such a bifurcation can be overcome. In the case of Jesus we have a new model of the human person in which mutuality and reciprocity are actualized precisely through the same process in which autonomy and uniqueness are brought into being. In the citation which follows from Rosemary Ruether, I think an intuition similar to our own is struggling to emerge, despite its apparently contradictory tone:

> The liberation of women, as well as men, from sexist hierarchicalism cannot happen as long as this symbolism of masculinity and femininity remains. This symbolism must ever rob women of human integrity, while men, even in their passivity, are given a sado-masochistic model of human relations. The entire psychodynamics of relationships must be entirely transformed, so that activity is not identified with domination, split from a receptivity as dependency. We must envision a new model of reciprocity in which we actualize ourselves by the same processes that we support the autonomy and actualization of others. This demands not only a transvaluation in psychic imagery, but a revolution in power relations.... The symbol for this is not an "androgyny" that still preserves sexist dualism, but that whole personhood in which women can be both I and Thou.[56]

Hopefully our Christic androgyny does not fall under the censure of Ruether. For we have sought to show throughout that the Christic self is precisely both I and Thou, an identity in union.

3. The "unique" Christic self: Some time ago a controversy broke out in American Catholic theology on the question of Jesus' uniqueness.[57] The issue is an important one, for it forces us to probe not only what the tradition means by Jesus' uniqueness, but also its importance and relevance to mankind at large. This question is not an entirely new one. One of the intentions of Chalcedon in terming the "union" of the divine and human in Jesus "hypostatic" was to indicate that in him we encounter, not simply God's "moral" union with man through the divine creativity or even through grace, but a quite unique, ontic union between God and man. The issue, it seems to me, is one of how to do justice to this uniqueness in Christ, which the tradition indeed affirms, and yet not denigrate God's relation with every human person, which the tradition also affirms. I should add that my own treatment of the Christic self raises this issue in the most acute way, for I have claimed that the more general Judaeo-Christian experience of the self as co-constituted by God is the proper horizon for coming to understand the more specific instance of the Christic self.

As we might expect, several alternatives present themselves. One is to argue for an absolute distinction between Jesus and other human beings. But what could such a position really mean? If thought through, it would compromise Chalcedon itself, which proclaims Jesus' full humanity: "consubstantial with us in his humanity." Furthermore, it would raise an important soteriological question: if Jesus is absolutely unique among men, how then could men and women ever come to understand him? All understanding between humans presupposes that they share something in common which renders mutual comprehension possible. What would be the purpose of a revelation that no one could possibly understand? To speak of "revelation" here would simply make no sense at all; revelation presupposes comprehension. Yet another alternative moves us to the other extreme, that which posits no profound difference, at least in principle, between Jesus and other human beings. We might hypothesize that perhaps these two positions are interrelated. If one so singularizes Jesus that he becomes absolutely distinct from other human beings, then one begins to wonder whether this utterly unique Jesus can possibly have any relevance to mankind at all. Thus, perhaps the first position breeds the second. As with the first position, let us then probe some of the consequences that flow from this one. First, I think we could say that it contradicts our own experience of selfhood. Karl Rahner, who views the incarnation as the unique fulfillment of human openness to the Unlimited God, put it this way:

> ... this potency does not have to be realized in every man. For the fact of our creaturehood and our sinfulness and our radically perilous situation reveal in the light of the Word of God that this potency has not been actualized in us.[58]

Our own experience of communion with God is vague and fragile. We know ourselves as self-transcending, as an unrestricted desiring, as a quest for union with the Unconditional in life, but not as the fulfillment of all of this. What our experience seems to tell us is not that we ourselves constitute the marvel of the hypostatic union but that we stand in need of it as the answer to our longings. Further, from a soteriological standpoint, if God's relationship with Jesus were no different in principle from that which other humans enjoy, then the reality of Jesus could in no way "clarify" and "answer" our yearning for the transcendent.[59]

I would, then, argue for a mediating position that attempts to do justice to Jesus' difference from and yet sameness with the rest of humanity. I think we can throw some, possibly fragile light on this issue by probing somewhat more carefully just what we mean by claiming Jesus' uniqueness. The notion of uniqueness involves a sameness and difference that is often overlooked. On the isolated ego model, essayed earlier, uniqueness tends to be thought of in terms of independence and exclusivity. The goal of human development is thought to be an individualistic project in which the self masters both the internal, psychic forces and external, environmental factors confronting one. Independence is valued as the characteristic of the well-adapted and developed person. But with independence comes exclusivity, for on this view it is a sign of weakness to be dependent upon others. One suspects that it is this model of the self, of the person, already a tendency in Hellenistic thinking, that has dominated our perception of Jesus and perhaps even legitimated the imperialistic claims of Christianity. Jesus is unique, so this thought pattern opines, because he is most independent, most different, most self-reliant, most exclusive of others. However, on the relational model of the self, uniqueness and inclusiveness are correlates. To be unique does not mean to exclude others, but rather to be deeply in tune with others, related to them, "dependent" upon them. To so deeply learn from and be co-constituted by others that one simply stands out as one who more intensively manifests what is potentially true of all. As one grows into one's relationships with others, one becomes more of a self, more unique, more an "I." In this thought pattern, then, we can begin to see that in affirming Jesus' uniqueness, we are claiming that he brings to expression in his Christic self what is less intensively true of others. The uniqueness of the Christic self is constituted, not by its exclusion of others, but by its inclusion of them.

It is along these lines, it seems to me, that we can avoid the pitfalls of the first two options above and yet make sense out of and continue to affirm the unique Christic self. Unlike option one, Jesus is not so different from the rest of us that we lack a "point of contact" with him whereby he can truly illuminate our existence. Unlike option two, Jesus is not so similar to us that his Christic self tells us nothing that we could not discover without him. In other words, a relational notion of the self transcends the old issue of whether Jesus is utterly different or simply a different instance of what the rest of us are. He is a sameness *and* difference. What, then, does this Christic self reveal? Nothing less than the mystery of God and man. On the one hand, the Christic self lights up what it is to be human: he shows us that being human is a living relationship unto God and unto man. Now we can see why Paul speaks of Jesus as the "first born of all creation" (Col. 1.15), "the head" (Eph. 1.22), who "unites all things in heaven and all things on earth" (Eph. 1.10). For Irenaeus, as is well known, Jesus "recapitulates" mankind, bringing it to its completion. On the other hand, the Christic self lights up the mystery of God. Through the Christic self we now have a mode of access to God. The Christic self reveals what kind of God we are indeed searching for, a God of Sovereign *Pathos,* and not a self-enclosed divine Monad. The person of Jesus "focuses" for us the more vague presence of God in every person. This is why Paul speaks of the mystery that has been hidden for many ages and is now revealed in Jesus (Eph. 1.9; 3.9); Jesus is God's "secret plan" (Col. 1.27; 2.2).

Notes

1. Cf. my *Christ and Consciousness,* pp. 57–61. This typology has been inspired by Han Fortmann, "The Dangerous Ego," in his *Discovery of the East* (Notre Dame, Ind.: Fides, 1971), pp. 83–91.
2. Voegelin, *Order and History,* 1, p. 3; 4, pp. 74, 271, 330.
3. Cf. my *Christ and Consciousness,* pp. 175–182.
4. Adrian van Kaam, *In Search of Spiritual Identity* (Denville, N.J.: Dimension, 1975), p. 175.

5. Erich Fromm, *Psychoanalysis and Religion* (New Haven: Yale University, 1963), p. 77.

6. Cf. Robert L. Heilbroner, *Business Civilization in Decline* (New York: W. W. Norton, 1976), p. 113: "The tendency of a business civilization to substitute impersonal pecuniary values for personal nonpecuniary ones" and p. 114: "A business civilization regards work as a means to an end, not as an end to itself. The end is profit, income, consumption, economic growth, or whatever, but the act of labor itself is regarded as nothing more than an unfortunate necessity to which we must submit to obtain this end."

7. Cf. my "Rahner's Theology of Pluralism," THE ECUMENIST 11 (1973), 17–22, for further analysis and bibliography.

8. John Dunne, *The Way of All the Earth, p. 95.*

9. *Summ. cont. gent.,* 2, 24. Cf. Kieran Conley, *A Theology of Wisdom: A Study in St. Thomas* (Dubuque: Priory, 1963), pp. 83–84, for translation and commentary.

10. Van Kaam, *op. cit.,* pp. 174, 182.

11. *Ibid.,* p. 185.

12. *Ibid.,* p. 186.

13. *Ibid.,* p. 191.

14. See Erich Neumann, *The Origins and History of Consciousness* (Princeton: Princeton University, 1954), pp. 381–384, "The Schism of the Systems; Culture in Crisis."

15. Andrew M. Greeley, "Sociology and Theology: Some Methodological Questions," PROCEEDINGS OF THE CATHOLIC THEOLOGICAL SOCIETY OF AMERICA 32 (1977), 53. For the phenomenon of the Basques, see William A. Douglass and Jon Bilbao, *Amerikanuak: Basques in the New World* (Reno, Nevada: Univ. of Nevada, 1975).

16. G. W. Hegel, *Lectures on the Philosophy of Religion, Together with a Work on the Proofs of the Existence of God* 3 (London: Kegan Paul, Trench, Trubner and Co., 1895), pp. 24–25.

17. Walther Eichrodt, *Man in the Old Testament* (London: SCM, 1966), pp. 21, 23.

18. Voegelin, *Order and History* 1, p. 485. Cf. my *Christ and Consciousness,* pp. 19–57, for the historical route Israel had to travel before it became conscious of this new relational experience of selfhood. Personally I think the accusation that Voegelin excessively individualizes the prophetic experience of the self to be unfounded, inattentive to the return to society that Voegelin is careful to explore in his volume one of *Order and History.* The accusation is that of Bernhard W. Anderson, "Politics and the Transcendent: Voegelin's Philosophical and Theological Exposition of the Old Testament in the Context of the Ancient Near East," in McKnight, *op. cit.,* pp. 62–100.

19. Krister Stendahl, "The Apostle Paul and the Introspective Conscience of the West," HARVARD THEOLOGICAL REVIEW 56 (1963), 199–215. Interestingly, E. P. Sanders refers to Paul's view as a "participationist eschatology," following and clarifying Albert Schweitzer's *The Mysticism of Paul the Apostle* (London: Macmillan, 1955). Cf. E. P. Sanders, *Paul and Palestinian Judaism: A Comparison of Patterns of Religion* (Philadelphia: Fortress, 1977), p. 549; cf. pp. 447–474.

20. *Ibid.,* 200.

21. *Ibid.,* 211.

22. *Ibid.,* 212.

23. *Ibid.,* 213–214.

24. The notion of the vertical and horizontal has been adapted from Kasper, *op. cit.,* p. 246: ". . . a person only exists in threefold relation: to himself, to the world around, to his fellowmen. . . . These relations on the horizontal plane . . . are so to speak crossed and supported by the all-embracing relation of man to God. . . . This applies both to the uniqueness and to the unbounded openness of the person. The uniqueness of each person demands absolute acceptance; this is why the person is sacred and of inviolable dignity. . . . In unbounded openness, the person points beyond everything limited into the infinite mystery of God. The uniqueness and openness both require a ground, consequently the person is not only a reference to, but also a participation in God's nature."

25. *Ibid.*

26. Karl Rahner has, of course, classically formulated this in our times.

27. Van Kaam, *op. cit.,* p. 176. He speaks of the relational self engaging, not in introspectionism, but in "transcendent self-presence." "It is called transcendent because it enables us to transcend, that is, to go beyond, the practical and sentimental meanings things may have for us in terms of our own private needs, ambitions, drives and expectations. Transcendent self-presence pushes us beyond the limited here-and-now meanings of our own particular problems, childhood traumas, sensitivities, faults, and projects" (p. 176). It is our "totalizing tendency": ". . . an aspiration for all that is, for participation in a beyond that generates and encompasses us." When it is refused, it "returns as a totalizing tendency that has lost its true object. We feel impelled to totalize frantically all kinds of little beyonds that we have made absolute, such as status, money, honor, success, and popularity. We do not know how to overcome these fixations on earthly concerns that wear us out, for we have lost our openness to the original source of all totalizing tendencies: the refused tending toward the absolute and the subsequent aspiration for the eternal" (pp. 111–112).

28. See the classic, Friedrich Heiler, *Prayer: A Study in the History and Psychology of Religion* (London: Oxford, 1932). Cf. also Jeremias, *The Prayers of Jesus,* and Sobrino, *op. cit.,* pp. 146–178. Jesus was certainly a mystic, if by this we mean an intense experience of our relational self. The traditional mystical phenomena are missing (levitations, etc.), possibly because Jesus' oneness with the Father was such an integrated dimension of his person (cf. Mk. 1.35, 6.46; Lk. 6.12). These phenomena seem to arise from a bodily-psychic reaction to profound oneness with God, a reaction caused by the slow and painful process of integration. I hope to return to the question of mysticism in a forthcoming study of Christ and mysticism. I am inclined at this point to say that the heart of Christian experience and of mysticism is our relational self, but that our relationality admits of degrees and greater/lesser intensification. Perhaps the summit of such relationality is what is known as mysticism in Christianity. Cf. also James D. G. Dunn, *op. cit.,* pp. 11–92, for a rather extensive treatment of Jesus' religious experience. He somewhat qualifies Jeremias's views (pp. 23–26), but to my mind not convincingly.

29. Jeremias, *ibid.,* p. 75; see pp. 72–75 for the historical details.

30. *Ibid.,* p. 76.

31. See Sobrino's helful summary, *op. cit.,* pp. 61–67.

32. *Ibid.,* pp. 41, 44–45.

33. Cf. Victor Paul Furnish, *The Love Command in the New Testament* (Nashville: Abingdon, 1972), pp. 59–69.

34. *Ibid.,* pp. 195, 64–65.

35. Spivey and Smith, *op. cit.,* pp. 235–236.

36. Cf. Rudolf Pesch, "Jesus, a Free Man," CONCILIUM 3 (1974), 66: "His

free God, who is not bound by the Law, not frozen into the role of a judge, gives him an 'autonomous' consciousness which harmonizes with the strivings of the unconscious for autonomy. For Jesus, the dualism of autonomy and external authority is broken because the source of authority, freedom, itself preserves autonomy."
37. *Ibid.,* 61.

38. See Rosemary Radford Ruether, *New Woman New Earth: Sexist Ideologies and Human Liberation* (New York: Seabury, 1975), pp. 63–85.

39. *Ibid.,* p. 64.

40. *Ibid.,* p. 66.

41. Cf. Raymond E. Brown, "How Much Did Jesus Know?," in his *Jesus: God and Man,* pp. 39–102. Cf. Cyril of Alexandria's comment, cited by Brown, p. 102: "We have admired his [Jesus'] goodness in that for love of us he has not refused to descend to such a low position as to bear all that belongs to our nature, included in which is ignorance" (*PG* 75, 369).

42. Raymond E. Brown, *The Birth of the Messiah* (Garden City, N.Y.: Doubleday, 1977), pp. 57–95.

43. Cf. Karl Rahner, "Virginitas in Partu," in his *Theological Investigations* 4 (Baltimore: Helicon, 1966), pp. 143–162. For the historical question, see Brown, *ibid.,* pp. 517–533.

44. Whiteley, *op. cit.,* pp. 112–114, esp. 113: "In *Galatians* the main stress is laid upon solidarity, while in *Colossians* this is secondary, and the chief emphasis falls upon the contrast between the old and the new."

45. Howard Clark Kee, *Jesus in History: An Approach to the Study of the Gospels* (New York: Harcourt, Brace and World, 1970), pp. 217–218.

46. Especially in the case of Karl Rahner and Walter Kasper; this is in keeping with the Thomistic tradition.

47. Thus, the Hellenization of doctrine theory is inadequate here, as we have sought to show.

48. Basic here are Grillmeier, *op. cit.;* R. V. Sellers, *Two Ancient Christologies* (London: SPCK, 1954) and *The Council of Chalcedon* (London: SPCK, 1961); P. Smulders, *The Fathers on Christology* (De Pere, Wisconsin: St. Norbert Abbey, 1968); John Meyendorff, *Christ in Eastern Christian Thought* (Washington, D.C.: Corpus, 1969), esp. on the Neo-Chalcedonians; and Ignacio Ortiz de Urbina, "Das Symbol von Chalkedon: Sein Text, sein Werden, seine dogmatische Bedeutung," in Aloys Grillmeier and Heinrich Bacht, eds., *Das Konzil von Chalkedon: Geschichte und Gegenwart* (Würzburg: Echter, 1951), I, pp. 389–418.

49. At least this is how Monophysitism and Nestorianism have been classically understood; their intentions, however, may very well have been orthodox. For Monophysitism, see Meyendorff, *ibid.,* pp. 17–31; for Nestorianism, see Grillmeier, *ibid.,* pp. 559–568.

50. Kasper, *op. cit.,* p. 242. One will notice that the tradition investigated Jesus' relation with the *Logos* rather than with the Father. The problem with this is that it gives the impression that Jesus' self-constitution is a private inner affair, between himself as human and his own divine *Logos.* As is evident from my own treatment, I have explored Jesus' relationality with the Father, which is the more biblical approach. It is his relation with the Father that grounds his oneness with the *Logos.*

51. Richard of St. Victor, *De Trinitate,* IV, 22, 24 (*PL* 196, 945–947). Cf., for an overview of Richard, Ewert Cousins, "A Theology of Interpersonal Relations," THOUGHT 45 (1970), 56–82. The Scholastic development and contribution here is terribly complex. Certainly the intent of all the Christological theories was to pre-

serve the unique unity in duality of Jesus. The *Habitus* theory, by which the *Logos* simply assumes a human body and soul, was condemned in 1177 (*DS* 750) since it seemed to undercut Jesus' humanity by giving it a purely passive role. The *Assumptus* theory, condemned by Aquinas, wanted to hold that the *Logos* assumes not just a human nature but a complete human being. Aquinas felt that this compromised Second Constantinople's view of the *enhypostasia* in the *Logos,* and thus he continues within this line of thought. Later Scholastics of the Scotist school proposed a moderate *Assumptus-Homo* theory, which both preserved the *Logos* as the one subject in Christ and yet made room for a full humanity. Despite the intent of all these theories, one gains the impression that the underlying difficulty was the notion of "person" or *hypostasis.* Aquinas and the majority of the Scholastics followed Boethius's celebrated definition: *"persona est naturae rationalis individua substantia."* Here "person" is viewed substantialistically and individualistically, rather than in the dynamic, relational terms of the Victorines, Leontius of Byzantium, and the Eastern Christian tradition. Maximus the Confessor preserved the Eastern relational concept: "For there is evidently a union of things insofar as their physical distinction is preserved" (*Opuscula theologica et polemica,* 8[*PG* 91, 97A]). Cf., on this, Lars Thunberg, *Microcosm and Mediator: the Theological Anthropology of Maximus the Confessor* (Lund: C. W. K. Gleerup, 1965), pp. 140–152, 454–459.

The later Scholastics, while working within the restrictive Boethian view of "person," were clearly struggling to transcend it by pointing out that Jesus' humanity could lack nothing by way of authentic human personhood. Bañez stressed that Jesus' humanity loses nothing by subsisting in the *Logos;* in fact, his human personality would be less complete if it subsisted in a human "person." Bañez interprets "person" as a *modus subsistendi,* and on this view Jesus' humanity subsists in the Divine Person/*modus subsistendi.* The Scotists carried this further by viewing human personality in purely negative terms as "non-dependence." Hence, for them, nothing positive is lacking by saying that Jesus' "person" is purely that of the *Logos.* Suarez, finally, attempts a mediation between the Bañezian and Scotistic views. Human personality is not merely a negative reality but a positive one, the *human* manner of existing. This is replaced in Jesus by the divine manner of existing which results in a created mode of union of the two natures. Thus, against Bañez, Suarez wants to say that nothing is lacking to Jesus' humanity; and against the Scotists, that the mode of union is a positive, not simply negative, reality. Cf., for a helpful summary of the Scholastic development, Kasper, *op. cit.,* pp. 238–243; P. Josepho A. De Aldama *et al., Sacrae Theologiae Summa* 3 (Matriti: Biblioteca de Autores Cristianos, 1953), pp. 11–242.

Somewhat apart from these Scholastic theories is Duns Scotus, who bases his view of the incarnation on a discussion of the notion of "person." For Scotus, one becomes a person either through dedication to God or through closure, a life of independence from God. In Jesus the dedication to the *Logos* actualized his person (Cf. Heribert Mühlen, *Sein und Person nach Duns Scotus,* 1954, pp. 95f, as cited by Pannenberg, *op. cit.,* p. 296). Our view would follow Pannenberg, *ibid.:* "This solution retains a shadow of disjunction Christology only because it understands the dedication to God not as the dedication of Jesus to the Father, but in the pattern of the two-natures doctrine as dedication of Jesus' human will to the divine will of the Logos. This was done instead of recognizing Jesus' dedication to the Father as the basis for his identity with the Son or the Logos." The views of the Reformation tradition are rather complex: cf. Pannenberg, *ibid.,* pp. 298–323. Luther, of course, accepts Chalcedon's doctrine of the one person in Jesus, and thus teaches a real *communicatio idiomatum,* without going beyond this. Zwingli only considers the *communicatio* to be figurative, and thus Jesus cannot really be present in the Lord's supper, as he is only figuratively oned with the *Logos.* Calvin and Melanchthon appear to have repeated Luther's view. Martin Chemnitz's view laid the basis for the Formula of Concord: ". . . the attributes cannot simply be disconnected from their natures so that they could transfer to another nature, but that nevertheless a real perichoresis of natures in the sense of the figure of fire and iron takes place" (Pannenberg, *ibid.,* p. 300). As we can see, these views are struggling toward a relational notion of the person without yet going beyond Chalcedon, with its attempt to mediate between Monophysitism and Nestorianism. Karl Barth repeats the *enhypostasia* of Jesus in the *Logos* view, without going further, while Paul Althaus speaks only of the "paradoxical" character of Jesus' divine-human unity. Perhaps the most interesting development was that of a kenotic theology, beginning in the seventeenth century. Following Philippians 2.7, this notion of self-emptying by God had played a role in Origen, Athanasius, Gregory of Nyssa, Cyril of Alexandria, Augustine, etc., where it referred to God's assumption of a human nature in Jesus. In other words, for the Fathers the focus was on Jesus, not on God as such. God's *kenosis* helped explain Jesus' human nature, but it was not thought to say anything further about the reality of God herself. According to Pannenberg, this same patristic viewpoint of the *kenosis* prevailed in the seventeenth and eighteenth-century kenoticists. It was the nineteenth-century kenoticists who took the step of saying that God empties himself (Sartori, Thomasius, etc.). The difficulty here was that these theologians were still thinking of God in Hellenistic terms as unchangeable, independent, etc., and thus a self-limitation on God's part was needed. In my view, *kenosis* does not mean that God must restrain himself, but that he is ec-static and relational in himself. Cf. the very helpful work by Geddes MacGregor, *He Who Lets Us Be: A Theology of Love* (New York: Seabury, 1975), esp. pp. 59–110, on kenoticism. I might end by saying that had Thomas Aquinas pursued both his relational notion of "person" that he touched on in his treatise on the Trinity (cf. *Summ. theol.* 1, 29, 4: "Relatio autem in divinis non est sicut accidens inhaerens subiecto, sed est ipsa divina essentia. . . . ;" "*persona* significat relationem in recto, et essentiam in ibliquo. . . . ") and his notion of the human person as "open to all" or "able to become all" (cf. *De Veritate* 2, 2), then he might have differentiated the relational notion of the human person and of God. These are hints that I have received from my study of Aquinas which I hope I am properly pursuing.

52. Both trends can be noted in Christology. The interest in subjectivity and thus the desire to grant Jesus a fully autonomous humanity manifested itself particularly in Catholic Christology's reflection on Jesus' human consciousness. After Deodat's resumption of the *Homo-assumptus* theory in the 1930's, in which he asserted a duality of love between the *Logos* and the man Jesus, the papal encyclical *Sempiternus Rex* (commemorating Chalcedon's 1500th anniversary) declared that in Christ we have only one ontological subject, although this does not necessarily rule out an independent although obedient human consciousness in Jesus. This, then, began a lively discussion among Catholic Christologians, with sides being taken not unlike those of the Antiochene and Alexandrine views in the patristic period. The strict Thomists argued for only the Divine "I" in Jesus, ontically and psychologically (the echo of the Alexandrines). The Scotists (echo of Antioch), especially through P. Galtier, argued that consciousness belongs to nature, not to person, and thus can be attributed to Jesus the man, although united with the *Logos* ontically and psychologically. More recently, M. de La Taille and Karl Rahner helpfully argued that unity with the *Logos* means the fullest realization of Jesus'

humanity. Cf. M. de La Taille, *The Hypostatic Union and Created Actuation by Uncreated Act* (Indiana: West Baden College, 1952), following a line inspired by Aquinas's subtle notion of the relationship between primary and secondary causality (see our note 98, Chapter 4). Rahner's classic formulation of this: "The incarnation of God is therefore the unique, *supreme*, case of the total actualization of human reality, which consists of the fact that man *is* in so far as he gives up himself" (*Theological Investigations* 4, p. 110). Cf. on all this Aldama, *ibid.*

The move from interest in subjectivity to a more concrete, relational approach to Jesus was initiated by Piet Schoonenberg. His earlier work argued for an *enhypostasia* of the *Logos* in the humanity. Later he modified this and claimed that one can speak both of an *enhypostasia* in the *Logos* and in the man. Perhaps we can say that Schoonenberg is still within the Boethian view of "person," although struggling to transcend it. Cf. Kasper, *op. cit.*, pp. 243–245; Piet Schoonenberg, *The Christ: A Study of the God-Man Relationship in the Whole of Creation and in Jesus Christ* (New York: Herder and Herder, 1971), esp. pp. 75–91 and "Process or History in God?," THEOLOGY DIGEST 23 (1975), 38–44.

53. See especially *Mystici corporis* (1943; *CT* 495): "But the knowledge and love of our divine Redeemer . . . are more than any human intellect or heart can hope to grasp. For hardly was he conceived in the womb of the Mother of God, when he began to enjoy the beatific vision; and in that vision all the members of this mystical body were continually and unceasingly present and he embraced them with his redeeming love" (cf. *CT* 479, 481, 486, 487, 488). But cf. also the 1964 decree of the Biblical Commission, "The Historical Truth of the Gospels," which reads: "Jesus followed the modes of reasoning and of exposition which were in vogue at the time. He accommodated himself to the mentality of his listeners. . . . " as cited by Brown, *Biblical Reflections on Crises Facing the Church,* p. 113.

54. Brown, *ibid.,* p. 112.

55. Karl Rahner, "Dogmatic Reflections on the Knowledge and Self-Consciousness of Jesus," in his *Theological Investigations* 5 (Baltimore: Helicon, 1966), pp. 193–215.

56. Ruether, *New Woman New Earth,* pp. 57–58.

57. Cf. Seely Beggiani, "A Case for Logocentric Theology," THEOLOGICAL STUDIES 32 (1971), 371–406 and John F. Haught, "What Is Logocentric Theology?," *ibid.,* 33 (1972), 120–132.

58. Karl Rahner, *Spiritual Exercises* (New York: Herder and Herder, 1965), pp. 102–103.

59. Cf. the interesting comments in Roch Kereszty, "Reflections on the Foundations of Christology," COMMUNIO 1 (1974), 392–393: "I see at least two reasons which make the historical uniqueness of the Incarnation intelligible. The Incarnation, if it is to accomplish its purpose as God's definitive self-revelation, must reveal the Son as he is within the Trinity. But there is only one Son within the Trinity. Therefore, more incarnations of the same Son would rather conceal than reveal his personal oneness.

"The other reason is based on a premise these theologians all accept as true: the growing unity of mankind demands a growing convergence of all religions. I submit, however, that the once-for-all fact of the Incarnation initiates a movement toward a more radical unity of mankind than the assumed plurality of Incarnations. . . . this one physico-spiritual focus of the concrete person of Christ seems to be more in harmony with man's physico-spiritual nature than postulating many incarnations (to varying degrees in various individuals) of the supra-historical Logos. The latter would establish only a spiritual unity based on the unity of the Logos." Cf. also Victor White, "Incarnations and the Incarnation," DOMINICAN STUDIES 7 (1954), 1–21. I might add that the uniqueness of the incarnation seems in keeping, not only with the physico-spiritual/personal nature of the human person, but also with the historical and "pathetic" nature of the Divine essayed throughout these pages.

PART THREE

THE CHRIST-EXPERIENCE

VI

EXPLORING THE CHRIST-EXPERIENCE I: FOUNDATIONS[1]

One of the key motifs of the New Testament, although variously expressed, is that of the continuing presence and salvific influence of the risen Lord. One of the earlier ways in which this comes to expression is through the tradition of the resurrection "appearances." However these are further explained, they at least imply the risen Jesus' presence among his disciples. But this experience of Jesus' presence has not yet been reflected upon in these appearance narratives. Those narratives rather seem to be preserving various discontinuous experiences known to have occurred in the pre-gospel tradition. As the New Testament comes to be written, we can notice a tendency to systematize and universalize this earlier experience of Christ's presence, just as we noted a tendency toward a more developed Christology. In Paul we have what some have called his "Christ-mysticism"[2] (Gal. 4.6, 2.20; Eph. 1.23; Col. 3.3), and it is remarkable that Paul rarely alludes to the pre-Easter Jesus. His Jesus is the risen Lord, active now in the universe. Matthew seems to employ the wisdom tradition (cf. 2 Bar. 3.29–4.4) to describe Jesus as "Emmanuel, God with us" (Mt. 11.18f; 11.28–30; 23.34–36, 37–39), and this "Emmanuel" is universalized, like holy Wisdom (Mt. 28.20). Even Luke, which some scholars claim has a very undeveloped Christology, tending to refer to the Spirit rather than the risen Jesus, attributes an active salvific influence to the "name" of Jesus (Aa. 3.6; 8.6–8, 12; 9.34; 19.17). As we would expect, John perhaps carries this trend furthest. John transforms the "Son of Man" image found in Daniel 7 (cf. Mk. 14.62)—where it refers to a future figure bringing judgment—by having this figure bring judgment now through Christ (Jn. 5.23–30; 12.31, 44–50). As Pheme Perkins puts it:

> For John, then, Jesus is the Son of Man in full glory. Christians are not waiting for some glorious return. Not surprisingly then, he can speak of believers as those who have seen Jesus' glory (1.14; 2.11).[3]

John furthers enforces this presence of the Son of Man through his "I Am" sayings: Jesus ("I Am") is bread of life (6.35, 41, 48, 51); life (8.12); gate (10.7, 9); good shepherd (10.11, 14); resurrection and life (11.25); way, truth and life (14.6); the vine (15.1, 5).[4]

Because of the singular importance of the resurrection as the catalytic event fostering this deepened experience of and reflection upon Jesus' presence, it would be well to dwell upon it here somewhat more carefully. Although scholars variously emphasize the resurrection as either a past, future, or present reality, there is no doubt that at least one facet of the resurrection experience is its *present* efficacy in the world of humanity. Through it, the Christian experiences Christ's efficacious presence *now*. I am inclined, further, to agree with Peter Hodgson that epistemological priority should be given to the resurrection's *present* efficacy:

> In my view, the present *is* the epistemological and ontological fulcrum of the resurrection event as a whole, as may be demonstrated by the New Testament appearance traditions, but it would be a mistake to try to reduce the resurrection *just* to the experience of and participation in the present lordship of Jesus. For that lordship has a past basis and contains a promise for the future as well.[5]

We can appeal both to fundamental epistemological considerations and to the biblical evidence itself for our priority of the present in the resurrection event. From the epistemological viewpoint, it is because the resurrection makes possible a present experience of the Lord that the disciples are both able to infer that Jesus has indeed been raised from the dead (past) and that he has opened up a new future for them. Interpretations that overlook the resurrection's present efficacy by overstressing either its pastness or futurity do not enable us to comprehend how the disciples *became aware* of this pastness or futurity. This could have happened only if the resurrection were an event modifying their consciousness *now, in the present.*

Further, the resurrection appearances and the language in which they are clothed all imply Jesus' active presence now in the disciples' midst. Although Luke's Emmaus narrative (Lk. 24.13–35) is a stylized account reflecting his own theological concerns, still it agrees with the other appearance narratives in pointing out how the risen Jesus funds a new experience of community and gives the disciples a new sense of mission. The vocabulary of the resurrection, too, is peculiarly apt for expressing the presence of the Lord, rather than his absence. The two terms commonly used for the resurrection—ἐγείρειν and ἀνιστάναι—were quite frequently employed in the Septuagint in the sense of a present activity within the world. Ἐγείρειν does carry the notion of "being awakened from sleep" in the apocalyptic tradition, and this may be one of its meanings in the New Testament, although this must be balanced against the fact that the New Testament has given the term a new meaning by indicating that the resurrection is not the revivification of a corpse. Much more consistent with New Testament usage is the Septuagint meaning of 'ἐγείρειν as either (1) to raise up a figure in history (Judges 2.16, 18; 3.9, 15; 1 Kgs. 11.14, 23; cf. Aa. 13.22; Mt. 3.9; Lk. 1.69) or (2) to be stirred to action (Jer. 6.22; Is. 19.2; cf. Mt. 11.11; Lk. 7.16; Jn. 7.52). 'Aνιστάναι (verb) and ἀνάστάσις (noun) also generally connote "to install" someone in a function (Hb. 7.11, 15), to "rise" to action (Lk. 10.25), to commence acting (Gn. 21.32), and to "raise up" or "send" a figure in history (Dt. 18.15, 18; Jer. 23.4; Aa. 3.22).[6] This brief semantic study particularly corresponds to Paul's notion of the risen Jesus as the *Kyrios*/Lord, the one actively sharing now in the Father's reign over the world (Rm. 1.4–5; 4.24; 10.9; 1 Cr. 15.24–25; 2 Cr. 4.14). Note especially Romans 10.9: ". . . if you confess with your lips that Jesus is Lord and believe in your heart that God raised him from the dead, you will be saved."

It is evident that the New Testament does not distinguish whether Jesus is present because he is God or because he is risen. Historically we might surmise that the more original experience and understanding is that of Paul. That is, Jesus is present because he has been raised up and exalted as *Kyrios*. As the later New Testament begins to develop a more elaborate Christology, this active presence of the risen Jesus is variously linked to his status as Emmanuel (Matthew), as the one upon whom the Spirit has been poured (Luke), or as the glorious and exalted Son of Man (John) and divine *Logos* (John). In time I will be suggesting that these two explanations of Christ's presence are really two dimensions of the selfsame mystery, and really should not be separated.

What is the importance of this doctrine of Christ's continuing presence? The New Testament has no theorized view of the matter, but simply unassumedly links Christ's presence with all of the "gifts" traditionally expected from God: Jesus as risen brings a new identity and a new experience of mission (Lk. 24.13–35), he brings life in the Spirit (Gal. 3.2; 4.29–5.25; 1 Cr. 15.1–20), newness (Rm. 7.6), the first fruits of eternal glory (Rm. 8.21f; 2 Cr. 3.17f; 5.55f), and in the more elaborated sections of the New Testament, he alone is the way to the Father (Jn. 15.4) and through no other name can salvation be given (Aa. 3.17–24). The great Greek fathers would later generalize this through the notion of humanity's divinization through Christ.

As we have indicated, the later sections of the New Testament trace this "presence" of the Christ to the divine status he enjoys. In time, the Johannine *Logos* Christology would inspire the fathers to develop a universal *Logos* Christology fashioned in the categories of Middle Platonism. For example,[7] Clement of Alexandria initiates this style of thinking, because of his openness to the Platonistic philosophies of his day. The *Logos*, for him, becomes man (Jesus) so that man may learn how to become God. He further initiates the notion of *theopoiein:* this *Logos* in Jesus actually "divinizes" mankind. Despite Origen's complicated and questionable *Logos*-doctrine, there is no doubt that he intends to further and even to systematize what Clement had begun. He goes beyond Clement by indicating that the *Logos*—God's presence with mankind—is to be found, not only in the historical Jesus, but also in scripture and in the Church's continuing life. Athanasius views Jesus as the perfect icon/*Logos* of God. This *Logos* deifies man by restoring man and conforming man ever more exactly to the divine image/*logos* according to which (*kat' eikona*) he has been made. Gregory Nazianzus has perhaps most distinctively captured the notion that through the *Logos* God has personalized humanity's relationship to the Divine: "My Christ is my constant companion," as he likes to repeat. With this the main lines of the *Logos* speculation are complete. Later Greek fathers, especially Cyril, would systematize these insights into a complex, philosophical *Logos*-theory.

This mode of explanation, then, is "from above," from the side of God or the *Logos,* and is rightly attempting to indicate that Christ's universal presence is an aspect of the Divine Mystery. Why is this? Again, I think we are brought back to the specific Judaeo-Christian experience of God as relational *(Pathos)* and dialogical. Christ is the way, if you will, in which God remains a dialogical partner with mankind. This kind of thinking is impossible on the later Hellenistic view, in which the Divine is envisaged as the self-enclosed, a-worldly Monad. Karl Rahner made an important contribution here when he indicated that our great danger today in our desacralized world is precisely to think of God as "without the world," utterly transcendent, without the divine dialogue with humanity. Despite our best intentions our supposedly sophisticated, transcendental view of God would evaporate into the apathetic deity of Hellenism rather than being the revelation of the Sovereign *Pathos.* Christ, then, the Greek fathers are telling us, is the way in which the Divine remains *pathos* toward the world. Let us listen to Rahner:

> We may speak about the *impersonal* Absolute without the non-absolute flesh of the Son, but the *personal* Absolute can be truly *found* only in him, in whom dwells the fullness of the Godhead in the earthly vessel of his humanity. Without him every absolute of which we speak or which we imagine we attain by mystical flight is in the last analysis merely the never attained, objective correlative of that empty and hollow . . . infinity which we are ourselves. . . . This, however, can be found only where Jesus of Nazareth is, this finite concrete being, this contingent being, who remains in all eternity.[8]

This reflection causes Rahner, then, to view Jesus as part of the very definition of God for all eternity. In our terms, Jesus is God's relationality toward humanity: "Jesus, the Man, not merely *was* at one time of decisive importance for our salvation, i.e. for the real finding of the absolute God, by his historical and now past acts of the cross, etc., but—as the one who became man and has remained a creature—he is *now* and for all eternity the *permanent openness* of our finite being to the living God of infinite, eternal life; he is, therefore, even in his humanity the created reality for us which stands in the act of our religion in such a way that, without this act towards his humanity and through it (implicitly or explicitly), the basic religious act towards God could never reach its goal."[9]

It is worth noting that, although thinking of God in these dialogical terms seems to be the ultimate presupposition underlying the tradition's stress on Christ's universal presence and mediatorship, this God-concept becomes explicit in the letter to the Hebrews. This letter is all the more remarkable since it is expressed in the idiom of Middle Platonism, and yet it ultimately critiques the latter's nondialogical God-concept. As we know, Hebrews uses the allegorical and typological exegesis of the Old Testament common among Alexandrine Jews. This involved many of the philosophical categories of Middle Platonism, as the case of Philo well illustrates. Thus, Hebrews, employing its Platonism, will contrast the unchangeable and perfect world of the divine with the changing, perishable world of the senses and of temporality. Philo had used this contrast too, but for him it indicated the spiritual progress of the soul from the level of a crassly material understanding of the Hebrew scriptures to a more penetrating, spiritual comprehension. Hebrews, however, will employ this contrast by identifying Judaism itself with the imperfect and perishable, and Christ and Christianity with the spiritual and perfect (Hb. 12.18–29). Hebrews even goes so far as to describe the final goal of Christian life in the Hellenistic category of "rest" (Hb. 4.3f), as distinct from the unrestful wandering of the Jews (Hb. 3.6–4.13). Besides the evident anti-Semitic strain, we seem to be a long distance from the specifically Christian view of God as *Pathos* and as related to human history.

But notice that Hebrews dispenses with Middle Platonism when it attempts to describe the work of Christ. Instead of being a Platonic intermediary between the Divine and humanity, shielding the Divine from worldly contamination, Jesus the Son becomes our direct link with God (Hb. 1.1–4). Further, he is this link, this mediator, not because he has transcended temporality, but because he has entered it, enduring its sufferings and temptations (Hb. 5.7–10). Even as the "eternal high priest," Jesus has not abandoned the world of temptation, but he remains a sympathetic and merciful high priest (2.16–18; 4.14–5.3). As Pheme Perkins expresses it: "You could say that Hebrews views the perfection of Jesus as exemplified in his feeling *(Pathos)* for his brothers who remain in the realm of weakness, temptations, sin and pilgrimage."[10] Here we have the specifically Christian God-concept breaking through, which forces the author of Hebrews to abandon, or at least transvalue, the great themes of Middle Platonism. I have spent this time on Hebrews because it appears to me to be paradigmatic of the way in which the reality of Christ caused Christianity to break through to a notion of the Divine as *Pathos* and dialogical, avoiding, thus, the Hellenistic tendency toward *apatheia*.

We can even go further. If the mediatorship of Christ means that God remains dialogical—a "Thou"—in the presence of humanity, it also means that mankind remains a "thou" in the presence of God. Because God is a

"Thou" for us through Christ, the paradigmatic form of religious experience in the Judaeo-Christian tradition is not an extinction of the self and a merging with God, but rather a heightening of the self, a union through differentiation. Abraham Heschel had already noted this difference between the loss of consciousness fostered by the Hellenistic religions and the heightening of it in prophetic religion.[11] We can employ a similar comparative analysis between the Hellenistic religions and Paul, the apostle in whom the Christ-mysticism is most intense. What we will find is that Paul's Christ-experience and relationship heightens his self-awareness rather than lessens it.

Religions can view the religious experience as an extinction of the self for at least two reasons. In the archaic religions, where the deity is conceived in sensuous terms, the paradigmatic religious experience is that of a Dionysiac frenzy, a sort of sensuous letting go. In the more spiritualized Hellenistic religions, where the deity is conceived as a-worldly, invisible, and utterly spiritual, the religious experience becomes one of a Neo-Platonic trance in which one is lifted from the world with its mundane concerns. My thesis will be that the Judaeo-Christian experience of God as mediated in Christ rather heightens one's self and world concern, one's self and world consciousness; one's experience, that is, of being a "thou."

Heschel explores a number of differences[12] between the prophetic consciousness and that of the religions fostering a loss of consciousness. We can follow his lead in our own analysis of the Pauline Christ-experience. We can speak, first, of a lack of frenzy in the prophetic God-experience and in the Pauline Christ-mysticism. Frenzy was typical of the archaic religious experience, and Israel particularly encountered the problem in its dealings with the religions of Syria and Canaan (cf. 1 Kgs. 18.26–29). Here we have a linking with the deity through a kind of sensuous "letting go" experience. The basic notion is that while the divine is inaccessible to man in his normal state of consciousness, it becomes available through a state of delirium and intoxication. "The less there is of man, the more there is of God; the less there is of the mind, the more there is of the divine," says Heschel.[13] For the prophets this not only depersonalizes God; it depersonalizes the individual: "These also reel through wine, and stagger through strong drink; the priest and the prophet . . . they are confused because of wine, they stagger because of strong drink; they reel in vision, they totter in judgment" (Is. 28.7). We have already seen how Paul encountered a Hellenized form of such religious enthusiasm and frenzy at Corinth (cf. 1 Cr. 4). Apparently the Corinthians interpreted the Christ-experience much as a form of Dionysiac ecstasy/frenzy. What is important is that Paul's Christ-mysticism leads him to correct this enthusiasm. Paul recalls the theme of the crucified Christ to bring home the point that the Christ-belief leads to the suffering and commitment characteristic of the earthly Jesus. Paul further relativizes the Spirit's gifts (1 Cr. 12–14) by indicating that they are to be ruled by love (1 Cr. 13) and ordered to the

Church's common welfare (1 Cr. 12.7). In the end, what is operative here in Paul is the view that the redeeming grace of God through Christ frees the believer to produce the fruit of the Spirit in her life: love, joy, peace, long-suffering, kindness, goodness, faithfulness, meekness, self-control (Gal. 5.22f; cf. 5.1, 13, 16, 25). What Filson says of the Christian experience of the Spirit also applies to the Pauline Christ-mysticism: "Characteristic of the New Testament gift of the Spirit is the fact that it enriches but does not replace the human experience and ability."[14]

Secondly, the notion of merging with God is absent from Paul's Christ-mysticism. Merging implies a form of self-dissolution and absorption in the absolute, and was a common religious goal among the archaic and Hellenistic mystery religions. Even for the more sophisticated "mystical" philosophers, absorption in the One (Plotinus) meant removal from the terrestrial and ephemeral. What we encounter in the prophets, however, is an intense awareness of God's grandeur and supreme difference from the prophet, even during the very act of prophetic revelation from Yahweh (Gn. 18.27; Ex. 33.20; Hos. 11.9; Is. 31.3). At times it may appear that the New Testament parallels the theme of merging with the deity in its use of the indwelling *Logos* doctrine, which, in Paul's case, may have been borrowed from the Stoics (cf. Col. 1.13–23; Hb. 1.1–4; 1 Cr. 8.6; Jn. 1). But the parallel is only partial. For example, in the scriptures the "divine spark" is never identified with the soul, as with the Stoics. Further, the Son or *Logos* always remains "personal," and is identified with the human individual Jesus (Jn. 1.14). Paul does report one experience which seems to lift him "into the third heavens," but even here "it was 'he' who was caught up, and he 'heard' things there (2 Cor. 12.4); there was no complete absorption even in this unique experience."[15] When Paul tells us that "Christ lives in me" (Gal. 2.20), he immediately adds that "I still live my human life, but it is a life of faith in the Son of God, who loved me and gave himself for me." Thus, rather than merging, what we find in Paul is a union in differentiation resulting from this Christ-mysticism.

Thirdly, as with the prophets, Paul's Christ-mysticism does not lead to a deprecation of consciousness. We can easily grasp that the chracteristics of frenzy and of merging with the gods can lead to a devaluation of the human self and human society. The paradigmatic religious experience, then, will take an esoteric form, removed from the common affairs of humanity, and will even be sought for its own sake, apart from any further relevance to the needs of the human community. It is quite clear that we meet an experience quite different among the prophets:

> There is no collapse of consciousness, no oblivion of the world's foolishness. The prophet's will does not faint; his mind does not become a mist. Prophecy is consciousness and remembrance of the scandals of priests, of the callousness of the rich, of the corruption of the judges. The intensity and violence of the prophet's emotions do not cause his intelligence to subside.[16]

Now we have already seen how Paul's Christ-mysticism heightened his own self-awareness. Instructive here is his own account of his conversion (Gal. 1.11–16). While he tells us that "God . . . chose to reveal his Son in me," this is immediately linked, like the prophets, with a new sense of vocation and mission: "So that I might preach the Good News about him to the pagans." Paul's Christ-experience has rather intensified his confidence in the face of every evil: "For I am certain of this: neither death nor life, no angel, no prince, nothing that exists, nothing still to come, not any power, or height or depth, nor any created thing, can ever come between us and the love of God made visible in Christ Jesus our Lord" (Rm. 8.38–39).

This leads us to our final note: Paul's Christ-experience leads him to the market place, like the prophets before him. It is not absorption in the worldless absolute, but heightened worldly concern that characterizes Paul. This is the case even if it may be true that he expected Christ's return rather immediately. In the case of the prophets the return to the market place takes the form of a critique of society's injustices (cf. Amos 4.4–6). In the case of Paul, it primarily takes the form of his absorbing commitment to the gentile mission, although throughout his letters he manifests a concern with all facets of the Christian life, from slavery to worship. Crucial here for comprehending Paul is his Corinthian Christology, in which his Christ-mysticism is one of the crucified and risen Jesus, and thus a Christ that leads always to the cross and the worldly involvement implied in that cross.

In the end, what underlies the heightened consciousness of the self as a thou-within-the-world is the experience and understanding of God. When God is viewed as above the world and indifferent to humanity, the religious goal becomes one of leaving the world, a form of world indifference. For the Judaeo-Christian tradition, God is intensely concerned with the world and history; the Divine is "dialogical," as we have said. For the New Testament, and for Paul especially, the experience of God as dialogical is heightened through Jesus Christ. Heschel puts it this way: "We may, therefore, suggest the following contrast: The Neo-platonists knew of a tradition of ecstasy; the prophets knew of a tradition of theophany."[17] In the case of Paul, we have a tradition of "Christophany." Thus, we can approach the question of Christ's universal presence and mediatorship from the point of view of the Judaeo-Christian experience and concept of God. This is the ultimate foundation of Christ's mediatorial presence. The tradition, however, also links Christ's mediatorial presence with the resurrection. Pursuing this further line of thought affords us a deepened clarification of the doctrine of Christ's mediation, this time, "from below" as it were.

Paul's *Kyrios* Christology is the classic New Testament example of a theology of Christ's risen presence. As risen and exalted, Christ shares in his Father's covenantal governance of the cosmos. Although the patristic theologians, as we have seen, normally explore Christ's mediatorship from the angle of their *Logos* speculation, occasionally they will link it to the resurrection. For example, Gregory of Nyssa: "Just as, in the instance of this body of ours, the operation of one of the organs of sense is felt at once by the whole system, as one with that member, so the resurrection principle of this Member, as though the whole of mankind were a single living being, passes through the entire race, being imparted from the member to the whole by virtue of the continuity and oneness of the nature."[18] Maximus the Confessor occasionally explores this line of thought too: ". . . he who penetrates yet further and finds himself initiated into the mystery of the Resurrection, apprehends the end for which God created all things from the beginning." And further: ". . . Christ, too, is all in all . . . as a center upon which all lines converge. . . ."[19]

We have already indicated that the resurrection language and appearances seem suggestive of Christ's presence. It is now time to explore the intuition somewhat more fully. Let me say that an exploration of Christ's mediatorship from the perspective of the resurrection is a necessary complement to the above *Logos* speculation. In some ways it is even a corrective. For the *Logos* approach is "from above," from the divine level, and taken by itself, it does not clarify from the human, this-worldly side the mediatorial role of Christ. It is this latter focus that will be illuminated for us through the resurrection. One of the aspects of the biblical presentation of the risen Lord most suggestive in this regard, which can introduce us to this issue, is the fact that Jesus' resurrection is never identified with the resuscitation of a corpse. No gospel actually describes the resurrection, as John, for example, describes Lazarus's revivification (Jn. 11.1–44). The risen Lord is, in fact, unrecognizable (cf. Lk. 24.16), while the resuscitated Lazarus is easily recognized. The resurrection accounts are rather trying to indicate that Jesus has undergone a decisive change in his existence. For example, the "third-day" motif (cf. Hos. 6.1; Gn. 22.4; 42.18; Ex. 19.11, 16), the traditional day of Yahweh's theophany and deliverance in salvation history, appears in the resurrection narratives (cf. 1 Cr. 15.4), thus suggesting another decisive event in God's salvation history. Thomas Aquinas was of the opinion that Jesus' resurrection was, then, not a return back to life as we know it, but the entry into a qualitatively new mode of being: "The risen Christ did not return to life as it is commonly known by all of us, but entered into a life somehow immortal and conformable with God."[20] The exaltation Christology as found, for example, in Philippians 2.5–9 (cf. 1 Tm. 3.16) would seem to confirm Aquinas's view. It brings home the fact that "the Resurrection was no return to earthly life and transcended any mere resuscitation of a corpse."[21]

The decisive change that Jesus has undergone, I would suggest, is that Jesus now as risen participates in the Father's universal presence within the world. He has entered into the Father's "glory" (Jn. 2.11; 13.32; 17.1, 5). The biblical texts themselves further suggest this by indicating that Jesus' death is not a destructive experience, but a culminating one, bringing his life to its completion (cf. John's notion of "the hour": 17.7). Such a view requires, of course, that we attempt to understand death not simply as a destructive reality but rather as an expansive one, made such through a final surrender of ourselves to God. From the perspective of the Christian notion of the self analyzed earlier, this makes good sense. For we understood the human person/self as a living relationship both to God and to humanity-in-the-world. Death, on this view, could be seen as the final earthly moment of openness and relationality to the Divine and to mankind. The final, earthly moment, that is, of becoming a "person." While this would apply to every person, in the case of the Christic self we are dealing with a "person" in which complete and total openness to God and to mankind is realized. We could suggest, then, that Jesus' death and resurrection is a "universalizing" experience, rendering Jesus radically open to God and humanity. Far from being absent from the world, Jesus now participates in his Father's universal presence within it: "If I be lifted up from the earth, I will draw all things to myself" (Jn. 12.32).

What I am suggesting, then, is that as risen the Christic self remains a universal presence with and among mankind. Through the universalized presence of the Christic self God remains a dialogical Partner with mankind for all eternity. As such, the risen, Christic self does not replace our normal human relationships with one another, nor are others mere "means" to a supposedly better relationship with the risen Lord. Rather is the risen Christic self a universal, co-present partner implicit in all of our relationships, mediating the Divine *Pathos:* "Where two or three are gathered together in my name, there am I" (Mt. 18.20).

William Johnston made an important contribution here by suggesting that we view the resurrection as "a movement away from absorption towards universality, away from self-centeredness towards cosmification."[22] "Absorption" might be taken to refer to our isolated self, clinging to herself and her own fears; caught, that is, in self-centeredness. The movement toward universality and cosmification would characterize our relational self: that is, becoming a self precisely through surrender unto others and unto the Divine. This is but another manner of speaking of the mystery of love, which is precisely to become a self by "losing" oneself in the other. The resurrection, then, is simply love's completion. If love universalizes, by enabling us to transcend clinging self-centeredness, then the resurrection is simply love's universalization. On these terms, the risen Christic self could be understood as a co-present principle of universalizing love. Here is how Johnston expresses his intuition:

> The Church fathers loved to quote the words of Jesus: "It is to your advantage that I go away" (John 16:7); and they would comment that by his departure and the ensuing separation Jesus was liberating the disciples from excess absorption, leading them on to the cosmic dimension of his risen existence. They might well have added that in all friendship separation plays an important role in leading friends away from absorption to an even greater universality.[23]

Helpfully, Johnston notes how Paul's letters manifest "a growing intimacy with Christ, together with a growing thrust towards cosmification, reaching a climax in the later epistles where Paul enjoys the closest union with a risen Jesus who is coextensive with the universe."[24] This Pauline friendship with Christ, he suggests, is a model and archetype of all human friendships. Christ is present within all our friendships, cosmifying and universalizing them. We can perhaps explain this only in the Teilhardian manner as a union which differentiates: "to such an extent that the more a person becomes Christ the more he becomes himself. . . . That is why friendship with the other never excludes friendship with Christ, as friendship with Christ cannot exclude the other."[25]

Once we understand the risen Christic self in these terms, it becomes a matter of high theological importance that the scriptures emphasize the relationship between *women* and the resurrection. Apart from more properly historical questions, the key reality is that the scriptures recognize that "To know this mystery we need to know it in a feminine way."[26] On our terms this makes excellent sense, for if the resurrection is the mystery of universalizing love—a love beyond self-centered clinging—only a self of feminine other-centeredness could really be attuned to this mystery.

Here I will simply follow O'Collins's insightful analysis of the role of the feminine in the resurrection event. It deserves careful pondering, especially in the light of the androgynous elements we have uncovered throughout our entire analysis of Christology. O'Collins focuses on the gospels of John and Mark, finding a highly developed feminine symbolism in them. In John, for example, the feminine "encloses" the Easter mystery. Jesus, in the farewell discourse, is described as comparing his death and resurrection to the experience of childbirth:

> You will weep and lament, but the world will rejoice; you will be sorrowful, but your sorrow will turn into joy. When a woman is in travail she has sorrow, because her hour has come; but when she is delivered of the child, she no longer remembers the anguish, for joy that a child is born into the world. So you have sorrow now, but I will see you again and your hearts will rejoice, and no one will take your joy from you (Jn. 16.20–22).

This symbolism is further developed by Mary's presence at the cross (Jn. 19.25–27) and by the Magdalen's witnessing at the empty tomb (Jn. 20). Here we might compare both the cross and the tomb to the fruitful womb that holds the child and later delivers it to new life. The figure of birth pangs is a common one in the Hebrew scriptures for God's saving intervention in history and for the divine giving of new life (Is. 26.17f, 66.7–14). Paul uses it too, when he tries to describe his own apostolic mission: "My little children, with whom I am again in travail until Christ be formed in you . . ." (Gal. 4.19). The feminine note seems to want to indicate that Jesus' death, the anguish of birth, is the prelude to new life. Like birth, we are dealing here with an experience of love, a movement from self-centeredness to other-centeredness. Mark's gospel adds to John's by underscoring how the male disciples fail to understand the Easter mystery. Every time Jesus attempts to explain his approaching death and resurrection, they cannot deal with it (Mk. 8, 9, 10). Their focus is on self-centered clinging and personal greatness (Mk. 9.33f). It is the women who remain faithful throughout Jesus' agony (Mk. 14.3–9, 15.40f, 16.6) and who witness to the marvel of the resurrection.

This view of the risen Christic self, while highly tentative and speculative, conforms both to our notion of the Christic self as relationality and to our dialogical notion of God. The doctrine of Christ's mediatorial presence, then, simply forces us to grapple with the deeper implications of what we have already discovered in our probing of the Christ. This view also makes sense of the traditional Christian stress on the resurrection as that not simply of the soul, but of the flesh (in the biblical sense), that is, of the whole person. While the immortality of the soul fosters an image of the risen state as one of the isolated individual, the image of the flesh's resurrection brings out the social, more relational dimensions of the risen existence. For "flesh" is precisely that through which we are inserted into the world and in relationship to others.

Clearly some may have enormous intellectual difficulties with our view. For example, the doctrine of Christ's universal presence may seem to some an elaborate doctrine of what really transcends our own experience and thus of something about which we can know nothing in any case. But is that really the case? Although we certainly lack the requisite experience to know *what* such a universal presence might be, we do not necessarily lack the experience for trusting *that* it is. For this doctine is simply a further extrapolation from our belief in and the experience of God as "dialogical" and from our own experience of ourselves as a lived relation to God and to humanity.[27] Others, however, might object that our explanation is too vague and elusive, not empirically verifiable.[28] Presumably, however, the same argument could be made against God. The point, it seems to me, is that just as God is not one object among many in the world observable to the empirical senses, neither is God's dialogical presence one such object. Were this the case, Christ would be "localized" and thus not truly universal. But if Christ's presence is not empirically verifiable, this does not necessarily mean that it is not "real." Wherever God's Divine *Pathos* is creating authentic love, there is the mystery of Christ. This, by the way, casts some light on what we might mean by Christ's "presence." Surely this is not a purely "physical" presence; someone could be physically present and still not personally present through love. Yet Christ's "presence" is precisely that of God's cosmic, universal love. Similarly, Christ's presence is not a purely "psychological" phenomenon; this again would be to reduce Christ to a projection of our own psychic states rather than to view Christ as God's *Pathos* meeting mankind. The presence of Christ is simply the Divine *Pathos,* the divine cosmic and universal love.

Finally, and possibly most difficultly, some will have problems with our view because it seems to presuppose a naïve notion of personal identity and continuity on the part of Christ. Our view seems to reside in a "substantialist" view of the person, in which the self is viewed as basically self-contained and absolute, on the deepest level perduring for all time. Only on these grounds can we posit a perduring presence of the Christic self. The obvious difficulty with substantialism, of course, is that it is a-historical and does not come to terms with the profound way in which human persons undergo change throughout time. There is simply not a human "substance" perduring throughout time; every aspect of the human being is temporal and thus in process. Furthermore we know that what gives us our "sense" of personal identity is precisely our temporal relationships to other human beings and to the world around us. When these aspects of temporality are removed at death, would it not be more wise to admit that even this "sense" of personal identity ceases?

On our view, however, personal identity and continuity does not stem from a private, inner "substance" accidentally modified through time and eternity, but from a dynamic and continuous lived relation unto others and unto God. It is not an a-temporal substance that grants us our identity, but precisely our lived relationships. I think Hans Jonas, who has reflected on this issue quite deeply, made the point well:

> Only those entities are individuals whose being is their own doing . . . : entities, in other words, that are delivered up to their being for their being, so that their being is committed to them, and they are committed to keeping up this being by ever renewed acts of it. Entities, therefore, which in their being are exposed to the alternative of not-being as potentially imminent, and achieve being in answer to this constant imminence; entities, therefore, that are temporal in their innermost nature, that have being only by ever-becoming, with each moment posing a new issue in their history; whose identity over time is thus, not the inert one of a permanent substratum, but the self-created one of continuous performance; entities, finally, whose difference from the other, from the rest of things, is not adventitious and indifferent to them, but a dynamic attribute of their being, in that the tension of this difference is the very medium of each one's maintaining itself in its selfhood by standing off the other and communing with it at the same time.[29]

Further, this self-constitution through relationships is ultimately grounded in a relational God, a God with and for the world and others, and this is what gives us the hope that the self can perdure beyond death. Thus, again, we are brought back to our notions of the self-as-relational and God-as-relational as the final foundations of our view. All else seems an extrapolation from these two *fundamenta*.

Notes

1. The title of this chapter has been influenced by Robert L. Schmitt's excellent "The Christ-Experience and Relationship Fostered in the Spiritual Exercises

of St. Ignatius of Loyola," STUDIES IN THE SPIRITUALITY OF JESUITS 6 (1974), no. 5.

2. Paul has a quite developed theory of incorporation into Christ, which of course developed as Paul pondered the resurrection experience. Cf. David Stanley's *Christ's Resurrection in Pauline Soteriology* (Rome: Analecta Biblica 13, 1961), which traces a development in (1) timing, (2) beneficiaries, and (3) causality in Paul's exploration of the resurrection. For example, in 1 Thes. 4.13–18 (c. A.D. 50) Paul thinks of the resurrection as only future (eschatological), the beneficiaries are only Christians, and leaves unexplored how the causality will operate, except to say that it will occur "through Jesus." In 2 Cr. 5.15 (c. A.D. 55/56) the resurrection is seen as exercising a present influence and the beneficiaries are universalized, but the causality remains unexplored. Finally in Romans (c. A.D. 57) the resurrection is both present and future (6.4–5); the beneficiaries are clarified: all baptized Christians (6.4f), Israel (11.15), all creation (8.19f); the causality is finally seen to be the death and resurrection (4.24f). Also important for Paul's Christ-mysticism are his technical prepositional phrases in reference to Christ: *dia, eis, syn, en*. All carry the meaning of Christ's active presence in human life. Particularly note Joseph A. Fitzmeyer, *Pauline Theology: A Brief Sketch* (Englewood Cliffs, N.J.: Prentice-Hall, 1967), pp. 67–73, esp. pp. 69–70: ". . . the most common use of the phrase *en Christo* is to express the close union of Christ and the Christian, an inclusion or incorporation that connotes a symbiosis of the two. 'If any man is in Christ, he is a new creature' (2 Cor. 5:17). This vital union can also be expressed as 'Christ in me' (Gal. 2:20; 2 Cor. 13:5; Rom. 8:10; Col. 1:27; Eph. 3:17). The result is that one belongs to Christ (2 Cor. 10:7) or is 'of Christ'—a 'mystical genitive' that often expresses the same idea (cf. Phlm. 1 and Eph. 4:1; 3:1; or Rom. 16:16 and 1 Thes. 1:1). The phrase should not be limited to a spatial dimension, for it often connotes a dynamic influence of Christ on the Christian who is incorporated into him. There are also at times ecclesial (Eph. 1:10; Gal. 1:22) and even eschatological dimensions to the phrase (Eph. 2:6). The Christian so incorporated is actually a member of the body of Christ; he is part of the Whole Christ."

W. D. Davies views this Pauline teaching on incorporation into Jesus as the axis of Pauline thought, contrary to contemporary Protestant thought, which stresses the doctrine of justification by faith: "It is a simplification and even a falsification of the complexity of Paul's thought to pin down Justification by Faith as its quintessence . . . the centre of that thought is to be found . . . in his awareness that with the coming of Christ the Age to Come had become present fact, the proof of which was the advent of the Spirit: it lies in those conceptions of standing under the judgment and mercy of a New Torah, Christ, of dying and rising with that same Christ, of undergoing a New Exodus in Him and of so being incorporated into a New Israel, the community of the Spirit" (*Paul and Rabbinic Judaism: Some Rabbinic Elements in Pauline Theology* [New York: Harper Torchbooks, 1967], pp. 222–223). E. P. Sanders, *op. cit.*, pp. 434–442, agrees. This might also be a valid inference from Krister Stendahl, *Paul among Jews and Gentiles* (Philadelphia: Fortresss, 1976); Stendahl's special contribution is in dislodging the doctrine of justification by faith from the central position in Pauline thought. Even Ernst Käsemann, while still highlighting the centrality of justification by faith, has emphasized the importance of the theme of incorporation into Christ: in Paul's letters "Christ emerges as the Cosmocrator, who in our bodies takes possession of the present world as its Lord and in his own body inaugurates the new world" ("The

Pauline Doctrine of the Lord's Supper," in his *Essays on New Testament Themes,* p. 135). The resurrection experience is of course the key catalyst behind Paul's thinking: the shift of the aeons has occurred in Jesus. Whiteley, *op. cit.,* p. 155, sees the biblical notion of solidarity as enabling Paul to so stress our incorporation into Christ. Also helpful: Robert C. Tannehill, *Dying and Rising with Christ: A Study in Pauline Theology* (Berlin: Töpelmann, 1967) and James D. G. Dunn, *op. cit.,* pp. 301–342 (on Paul's Christocentrism).

3. Perkins, *op. cit.,* p. 249.

4. *Ibid.,* on these gospel Christologies: p. 211: "Matthew's Christology is not based on Moses typology but on a Wisdom typology"; p. 267 (Luke); pp. 249–250 (John).

5. Hodgson, *op. cit.,* p. 223. Hodgson has a tendency to follow Marxsen too uncritically. Cf. my Chapter 3 on the subjectivist view of the resurrection. This stress upon the resurrection as implying the present efficacy and presence of Jesus has been denied by Ulrich Wilckens, *Resurrection: Biblical Testimony to the Resurrection: An Historical Examination and Explanation* (Atlanta: John Knox, 1978), p. 122: "The appearances were not handed down in tradition as disclosures of ever new encounters with the risen Christ, but as unique acts conferring legitimation of their authority to the first basic witnesses. After them there is no promise of an *encounter* with the risen Christ till the end of time." Quite frankly I think such a view contradicts the great amount of evidence I am endeavoring to supply in this chapter, particularly that concerning Paul's Christ-mysticism. It seems more prudent to say that the appearance traditions are rather relatively undifferentiated attempts to explain Christ's presence and have not fully thought out the implications involved. On the other hand, it does seem valid to maintain that there is a difference between Christ's presence as pointed to in the appearances and his later presence within history. Paul, for example, differentiates his later experiences of Christ from his resurrection appearance (compare 2 Cr. 12.1f with 1 Cr. 15.8). John's gospel draws a distinction between those who have seen and believed, and those who have not seen and have believed (Jn. 20.29). Here I would suggest that what makes the appearances different from Christ's later presence within history is their character as founding the Church and inaugurating the Christian mission, which was surely unique and not shared by later generations. The transformation of consciousness symbolized by the appearances inevitably meant founding the Church and beginning the mission for the first generation; for us the Lord's presence can only mean continuing what was begun by our Church founders. Further, I would say that the presence of the Lord for future generations does not simply depend upon the witness of the first generation that received the appearances; however, the *explicit awareness* of the Lord's presence does so depend. For good accounts of the Church-founding and mission-inaugurating character of the appearances, see Reginald H. Fuller, *The Formation of the Resurrection Narratives* (New York: Macmillan, 1971), and Norman Perrin, *The Resurrection according to Matthew, Mark, and Luke* (Philadelphia: Fortress, 1977).

6. Cf. *ibid.,* pp. 244–252, upon whose analysis I rely. Cf. also Evans, *op. cit.,* pp. 22–27, esp. p. 26.

7. George A. Maloney, *The Cosmic Christ: From Paul to Teilhard* (New York: Sheed and Ward, 1968), pp. 113–181. For the technical philosophical nuances stemming from Middle Platonism, see Pelikan, *op. cit.,* p. 145.

8. Karl Rahner, "The Eternal Significance of the Humanity of Jesus for Our

Relationship with God," in his *Theological Investigations* 3 (Baltimore: Helicon, 1967), pp. 35–46, 43–44 (this citation). This is the one article to which Rahner most often refers, interestingly enough.

9. *Ibid.*, p. 44.

10. Perkins, *op. cit.*, p. 282.

11. Heschel, *op. cit.*, Vol. 2, pp. 104–146, upon whom I rely.

12. *Ibid.*, pp. 133–145.

13. *Ibid.*, p. 135.

14. Filson, *op. cit.*, p. 78; cf. pp. 71–81.

15. *Ibid.*, p. 93. For Whiteley, *op. cit.*, p. 39, this experience indicates that "It is beyond question that for St. Paul the human being is more than his physical body."

16. Heschel, *op. cit.*, Vol. 2, p. 139.

17. *Ibid.*, p. 145. There is, of course, a genuine form of Christian mysticism, but it lacks the element of world-denial typical of some other forms of mysticism.

18. *De Oratione Catech. Magna,* 26, p. 489, as cited by Maloney, *op. cit.*, pp. 154–155.

19. *Capita Theologica et Oeconomica, PG* XC, 1108A–B, and *Mystagogica, PG* XCI, 665–668, as cited by Maloney, *op. cit.*, pp. 276, 279.

20. *Summ. theol.*, 3, 55, 2. Cf. O'Collins, "Thomas Aquinas and Christ's Resurrection," *art. cit.*, 521–522 (my transl.).

21. O'Collins, *The Resurrection of Jesus Christ*, p. 52. Cf. his helpful *What Are They Saying about the Resurrection?* (New York: Paulist, 1978), pp. 63–67. As we have seen, the New Testament variously describes what has occurred to Jesus after his death as a "resurrection" and as an "exaltation." The exaltation-notion is coupled with that of the resurrection in order to differentiate what has occurred to Jesus from, say, an exaltation like Elijah's (Mk. 9.44f, 15.34f). The exaltation-motif seems to connote an event of transformation, while that of the resurrection carries a redemptive connotation (Rm. 4.25).

22. Johnston, *Silent Music: the Science of Meditation* (New York: Harper and Row, 1974), pp. 160–161. Also very suggestive for thinking through the implications of Jesus' risen presence is G. Martelet, *L'au-delà retrouvé: Christologie des fins dernières* (Paris: Desclee, 1975), esp. pp. 159–162. Karl Rahner has the fascinating notion that Jesus' resurrection "created 'heaven' " and this makes sense if he is as risen the ground of a cosmic love. Cf. "Resurrection. D. Theology," in *Sacramentum Mundi* 5 (New York: Herder and Herder, 1970), p. 333. Here it is of course apparent that while I fully recognize that the risen life can and should be expressed in the symbolism of myth, I am more optimistic than some in our ability to meaningfully speak about this life which is risen. The difficulty, as I said earlier, is not that the resurrection is expressed in the pictorial symbolism of myth, but in adequately penetrating through to the experiential correlate giving rise to the myth. William Johnston's especial contribution is in enabling us to imagine such correlates. The risen life itself is not of course available to us, but surely our orientation toward and movement toward it is, and this real experience supplies the basis from which an extrapolation about eternal life can be made. Or, to come at it in another way, belief in eternal life is a corollary of belief in God and his covenant with us. Such belief is an extrapolation from our present experience of belief, of God's covenant with us. Here it is of course evident that the resurrection myth of late Judaism and Christianity is quite different from the dying-rising myths of archaic religions. The latter myths are not yet aware of the possibility of an existence transcending earthly existence, for they are not yet aware of a God who transcends

nature/earth. For these myths, the dying and rising of the "stars" and "seasons" suggests the dying and rising of humanity regularly and cyclically *upon this earth.* Cf. for the data on resurrection myths in the archaic religions Pierre Grelot, "The Resurrection of Jesus: Its Biblical and Jewish Background," in P. de Surgy, ed., *The Resurrection and Modern Biblical Thought* (New York: Corpus, 1970), pp. 1–29, esp. pp. 2–6, 7, 13–16 (on the Iranian and Jewish views).

23. *Ibid.,* p. 163.

24. *Ibid.*

25. *Ibid.,* p. 164.

26. O'Collins, *What Are They Saying About the Resurrection?,* pp. 95–102; this citation, p. 98. O'Collins argues for a form of androgyny: ". . . I realize that 'feminine' and 'masculine' are principles of being human. Even if a woman in her capacity to bear children and in other ways expresses for us the 'feminine,' we should identify neither feminine with female nor masculine with male" (p. 98).

27. See Eric Voegelin, "Immortality: Experience and Symbol," HARVARD THEOLOGICAL REVIEW 60 (1967), 235–279, for the experiential ground of such an extrapolation.

28. John H. Hick, *Death and Eternal Life* (New York: Harper and Row, 1976), pp. 228–235, for what is, I think, an unfounded critique of Karl Rahner's *On the Theology of Death* (New York: Herder and Herder, 1965), whose position resembles my own.

29. Hans Jonas, "Biological Foundations of Individuality," in his *Philosophical Essays,* pp. 185–204; this citation, p. 187.

VII

Exploring the Christ-Experience II: Reflections on Soteriology

It is now appropriate to extrapolate further from this Christ-experience and relationship and to explore, with the Christian and theological tradition, what it implies for humanity as a whole. This is traditionally know as "soteriology," or the study of Jesus Christ as the universal Savior of humanity at large. One will notice that we are pursuing this question of the Christ-experience in a manner that moves from the particular and specific to the more general and universal. Thus we are moving from the Pauline Christ-experience to the larger question of how Christ saves mankind at large. Our reason for this is to help the reader to grasp that the Christ-experience speaks to facets of our own lived experience. Only in this way can the Christ-experience be protected from the charge of idle speculation.

The reader will also notice that our book did not begin with a probing of our own Christ-experience, but rather with a concentrated study of Jesus Christ himself. We did not begin, that is, with soteriology but with Christology. By grounding soteriology in Christology we avoid the danger of reducing soteriology to our own limited experience, with its legitimate but usually narrow concerns and interests. As we have seen, this was one of the limitations of the nineteenth-century liberal quest for the historical Jesus, for it projected its own image of the liberal bourgeois intellectual, with his desire for autonomy, back on to Jesus and his message of salvation.

To begin, then, soteriology is an imaginative extrapolation from the Christ-experience and relationship. A theory, in other words, that attempts to probe the furthest implications of the Christ-experience for humanity as a whole. While it may seem shocking to describe the doctrine of salvation as a "theory," it is certainly evident that it is not a matter of brute empirical observation or even personal experience. To bring this point home, let us listen to Paul on the matter. Paul, for example, tells us that "When all things are subjected to him, then the Son himself will also

212

be subjected to him who put all things under him, that God may be everything to everyone" (1 Cr. 15.28). It is from just such a biblical intuition that soteriology is constructed, for notice that it "generalizes" the importance of Christ, claiming his saving works for all mankind. Yet this Pauline intuition is clearly not something that Paul could know from his own experience. Who could experience all of "mankind" or really know from experience its future course? Paul is clearly generalizing from the Christ-experience that he and others of the apostolic generation knew, probing its furthest ramifications. This same movement toward universalizing the import of the Christ-experience characterizes the New Testament as a whole: 2 Cr. 5.19; 1 Cr. 15.22–25; Mk. 10.45; Eph. 1.7; 1 Pt. 1.18–19; Hb. 2.14–15. What is the ground for such universalistic claims, if it is not simply a matter of one's personal experience? Gordon Kaufman put this well when he said "memory" constitutes the ground:

> Remembrance of what God has done in the past gives rise to hopes for what he yet shall do. . . . Just as Old Testament experience and faith grew out of reflection on memories of the exodus and covenant when God's mighty arm delivered his people from bondage to Egypt, so here God's great gift of himself and his forgiveness in Christ is the sufficient ground for confidence about what is really happening in present and future.[1]

Kaufman sees this appeal to memory in Paul: "He who did not spare his own Son but gave him up for us all, will he not also give us all things with him?" (Rm. 8.32). In our terms, the ground of soteriology is the Christ; the former extrapolates the significance of Christ onto humanity at large.

Because soteriology is and must be a "theory," the proper question to ask is not whether it should be a theory, but what kind of theory best seems to probe the implications of the Christ for humanity at large. As we have indicated earlier in grappling with Christology, the characteristics of a more adequate theory are (1) its ability coherently to integrate all the data pertaining to a particular question, and (2) its ability to cast new light on old questions and thus to reveal what remained unknown heretofore.

With Aulén,[2] we can fruitfully explore the biblical "type" or notion of soteriology, which he termed the "classic theory." There is clearly, of course, no one soteriological theory in the scriptures. The Christ-experience was still too new, its implications only inchoatively experienced and intuited, for us to expect anything like a systematized theory of the matter. What we seem to encounter rather are a cluster of images and symbols: Christ's gift of salvation is described either negatively, as a being set free from sin, principalities and powers, the law and death, in which case "redemption" (*apolutrosis*) is used (Rm. 3.24; 1 Cr. 1.30; Eph. 1.7; Col. 1.14; Hb. 9.15). Or positively, as a union, peace, reconciliation, or at-one-ment between God and men, in which case the Greek *katallge* (Rm. 5.10, 11.15; 2 Cr. 5.18; Col. 1.20) is used. Alternative symbols also appear: Christ is a "ransom" (Mk. 10.45; 1 Tm. 2.6); he brings "salvation" (Mt. 1.21; Jn. 3.17; 1 Tm. 1.15; 2 Tm. 2.10; Hb. 5.9); he is a "sacrifice" (Eph. 5.2; 1 Cr. 5.7; Hb. 9.25), or an "expiation" (Rm. 3.25), who sheds his "redemptive blood for the many" (Mt. 26.28; Rm. 5.9; Hb. 9.12, 14; Rev. 5.9).

What enables us to speak of a biblical "type" of soteriology, however, is the fact that underlying the cluster of biblical images are two fundamental affirmations about the Christ. On the one hand (1) Christ breaks and overcomes the power of evil and sin in the world (Col. 1.13; Rm. 8.39) and, on the other (2) a new experience of freedom and at-one-ment with God and humanity now becomes possible (Gal. 5.1, 13; Jn. 10.10; 2 Cr. 5.17). Biblically expressed, Christ brings both redemption from (*apolutrosis*) evil and sin and at-one-ment (*katallge*) with God and humanity. Thus, the realities of evil and sin are taken seriously, and through Christ God is seen to be overcoming those realities and inaugurating a new history of freedom. If we attempt imaginatively to penetrate below the level of these symbols and intuitions to their funding experience, we would propose that the scriptural authors are universalizing their own Christ-experience and relationship. For example, Paul "knows" a new experience of at-one-ment with God through Christ. As we have seen, he experiences his self as actually co-constituted through Christ: "The life I live now is not my own; Christ is living in me. I still live my human life, but it is a life of faith in the Son of God, who loved me and gave himself for me" (Gal. 2.20). This new experience of at-one-ment with God through Christ has "relativized" the power of evil and sin in his own life: "Who will separate us from the love of Christ? Trial, or distress, or persecution, or hunger, or nakedness, or danger, or the sword? . . . For I am certain that neither death nor life, neither angels nor principalities, neither the present nor the future, nor powers, neither height nor depth nor any other creature, will be able to separate us from the love of God that comes to us in Christ Jesus, our Lord" (Rm. 8.35–39). As I put this in another place, "Because the Judaeo-Christian defines himself in terms of a transcendent source of personal identity, he is potentially able to relativize all things finite."[3]

Let us pursue this fundamental Pauline and New Testament experience further. First we note that Paul uses the cosmic and mythological imagery of God in battle with the cosmic powers of evil and sin in order to describe the realities from which we are redeemed through Christ. God has now broken the dominance of evil powers: "He has delivered us from the dominion of darkness and transferred us to the kingdom of his beloved Son" (Col. 1.13). Christ has actually engaged Satan in cosmic conflict: "The children of a family share the same flesh and blood; and so he too shared ours, so that through death he might break the power of him who had death at his command, that is, the devil; and might liberate those who, through fear of death, had all their lifetime been in servitude" (Hb. 2.14–15; cf. 1 Cr. 15.25–28; 1 Pt. 1.18–19; Eph. 1.17; Mk. 10.45; Phil. 2.8–11). As Kaufman says, "This was a meaningful way to understand both the present disorder, terror, and bondage—for what is more chaotic than a bloody battlefield?—and the means through which it was at last being transformed into the kingdom in which God would be fully sovereign."[4] Yet it is apparent that if modern man is to understand God's act of salvation, some reinterpretation of this cosmic symbolism is called for. For we simply no longer experience the world's evil and sin in these hypostatized terms.

A further difficulty: this cosmic imagery of Christ the Conqueror is expressed in the nonhistorical terms of a battle already won (Col. 1.13) or soon to be concluded (1 Thes. 4.16). Yet it is apparent to us that the realities of evil and sin have magnified, rather than lessened, in human history. What was once a meaningful imagery to others runs the danger of obscuring just how it is that Christ brings redemption to us in our time with our enormous experience of evil and sin.[5]

But the key insight, in any case, is that man is described as in bondage to evil powers, in the grip of forces from which he cannot extricate himself. Here, of course, we directly confront the biblical imagery of evil and sin as somehow the result of cosmic, demonic powers. So far as I can see, we can approach this imagery from two points of view. From that of our contemporary historical and scientific consciousness, we can speculate that belief in demonic powers—universally held among archaic and universal religions—is the result of a prescientific mentality. For the prescientific, there was no clearly differentiated ability to distinguish subject from object, external reality from one's own spontaneous, affective response to that reality. Thus, as Charles Davis helpfully put it, "Belief in demons was not, therefore, a belief grounded upon a gathering and careful weighing of data and a testing of hypotheses: it was simply an imaginative, spontaneous expression of the personal impact of various occurrences."[6] With Davis, I, too, would maintain that to return to a simple prescientific belief in such demonic powers would be a mistake. For our modern historical and scientific consciousness at least in some respects represents an advance over the archaic mentality and provides a more coherent understanding of the universe. As Davis put it, "Few of us would prefer a witch doctor to a physician in ordinary illnesses."[7]

A second approach, however, would be to recognize that belief in demons was, in some respects, a simply less differentiated and symbolic expression of real human experiences. The scientific consciousness becomes scientism when it simply rejects the demonic out of hand, without attempting to penetrate the level of experience which gave rise to such a belief. From this point of view, we can speculate that belief in demons expresses man's experience of being in the grip of seemingly hostile and evil features within the world. Within the Christian ambit, unlike other religions, this experience was symbolically expressed in the figure of Satan, who becomes a figure of almost pure evil, actively seeking to control men's destinies.

The Christian stress upon Satan, rather than simply upon demons, is a perplexing question to scholars. There seems no clear parallel to it in the non-Christian traditions, which seem content with demons rather than with one Satanic leader. This belief is even a latecomer to the Judaeo-Christian tradition, too. The prophets attack the evil in man's heart and have a tendency to treat the demons as false gods. The apocalyptic literature, perhaps reflecting the influence of Persian dualism, reasserts demonology, and the Satan of the New Testament is a late development of apocalyptic.

Why this Christian stress upon Satan? Davis suggests that it "is a symbol that sin or evil is taken with ultimate or eternal seriousness."[8] Evil is no minor force, but truly demonic, threatening man's very salvation. Alan Watts suggests that this is a result of the Judaeo-Christian view of God as absolutely good. Evil then becomes the absolute antithesis of God, very evil itself.[9] No doubt this can and has led the Christian to repress the evil side of life, since it is so utterly horrible and opposed to God. One might explain an intense fascination for the demonic as a repressed fear of the unintegrated evil in one's own life. Yet I do not think that one can write off the Devil, à la Watts, as simply the result of Judaeo-Christianity's belief in a purely good God. For the Judaeo-Christian God, as we have argued, is a God of *Pathos,* actively entering into man's historical struggle with evil and sin, directly confronting it, rather than repressing it. Watts' view of God conforms more to the late Hellenistic view rather than the Judaeo-Christian conception. Yet we can recognize the grain of truth in Watts' view. Believing in a God that is apathetic, as we have said, uninvolved in man's historical struggle with evil, could foster a repression of the evil in one's life, stemming from an intense fear of this evil.

An alternative interpretation of Satan, and one that brings us to the heart of the matter, has been provided by scholars like Trevor Ling and Paul Ricoeur. Ling suggests that Satan expresses "the spirit of unredeemed man's collective life, that which dominates the individual, and stifles his growth in truly personal life; a spirit, moreover, which is characterized by a constant effort towards self-deification."[10] Ricoeur offers a similar interpretation of the serpent in the Adamic myth:

> . . . the serpent represents the following situation: in the historical experience of man, every individual finds evil already there: nobody begins it absolutely. If Adam is not the first man, in the naively temporal sense of the word, but the typical man, he can symbolize both the experience of the "beginning" of humanity with each individual and the experience of the "succession" of men. Evil is part of the interhuman relationship, like language, tools, institutions; it is transmitted; it is tradition, and not only something that happens. There is thus an anteriority of evil to itself, as if evil were that which always precedes itself, that which each man finds and continues while beginning it, but beginning it in his turn. That is why, in the Garden of Eden, the serpent is already there; he is the other side of that which begins.[11]

The point is that evil cannot exhaustively be explained in personal, individual terms. The collective, unified symbol of "Satan" gives expression to the collective situation of evil and sin in which men find themselves. In part, as Davis says, without the symbol of Satan "or the cumulative social tradition of evil . . . men will ignore social evils for which they do not consider themselves personally responsible."[12] But there is more. It would be a mistake, I think, simply to identify "Satan" with the cumulative effects of men's personal sins. One does not need the symbol "Satan" for that; the image of "sinful mankind" will do. As Davis intimates, citing Ricoeur, "The serpent (Devil) is more than the excess of human sin over the sins of human individuals; the serpent is the Adversary, 'the pole of a counterparticipation,' namely, a source of 'iniquity beyond man.' "[13] Evil is more than the result of man's guilt, even man's collective guilt, as the case of Job illustrated.[14] I believe here we come to the heart of the biblical symbol of "Satan." That is, it expresses the fact that beyond the personal sources of sin and alienation, beyond even the social and collective sources of alienation stemming from man's cumulative guilt, there is a deeper source of sin and alienation, too, that actively confronts man and which man can never fully overcome, either personally or socially. Schillebeeckx has elaborated on this:

> There is, for example, that human suffering which cannot be resolved by social or political measures. Man can still be broken by isolation even in the best social structures, since these cannot automatically make man and society good and mature. Nature can be humanized to a very great degree, but it will always remain alien to man (death is an example of this). Finally, man's finite nature may make him trust in God or it may lead to isolation and anxiety. Within human history, then . . . there is no single identifiable subject which can bring about man's total salvation or a state of real "wholeness" in him.[15]

In other words, "Satan" gives expression to this deepest level of sin and alienation which transcends man and even humanity. It is possible to conceive of man ameliorating the evil that stems from his own and other's collective guilt. Indeed there is a thread of progress in this respect, insofar as psychological and sociological techniques of therapy do seem to improve men's lot. But beyond all of this lies "Satan," the ultimate threat of alienation and sin, and which man on his own cannot thwart.[16] A helpful example of this is provided by modern medical developments. In an age when modern science has practically overcome diseases carried by viruses, we recognize an increase in such nonvirus related diseases as ulcers, cancers, addictions of all kinds, and heart disease. It is not enough simply to say that the modern stresses of our technological society are at the root of these new diseases. What is at their root is man's deepest level of alienation, the lack of meaning and love in his existence, which no amount of bettering the social fabric will necessarily bring about. It is this deepest level of the peril of alienation, which rebounds on all other levels of human life, which I think the biblical symbol of Satan magnificently brings to expression. It is in this sense, then, that the biblical soteriology takes evil very seriously. By stating that Christ does battle with Satan, scripture is maintaining that "those alienations which cannot be removed by scientific and technical means used by man"[17] are decisively overcome in Jesus.

This interpretation of the symbol of Satan, while it fully recognizes that many New Testament passages employing the Satan-symbol can be understood as referring to the evils of society (cf. especially the temptation narratives, which seem to equate Satan with the destructive use of social power [Mt. 4.1–11, Lk. 4.1–13]), also does justice to those passages which seem to view Satan/the Satanic as actually having society in its grip. Here Satan is not to be simply identified with social evils; Satan actually transcends society (cf. Eph. 6.12; Jn. 12.31; 1 Jn. 5.19; Col. 2.15; 1 Cr. 15.24; Rm. 7.11, 13–20). What is this Satanic threat that cannot simply be identified with man's collective, societal evil? That, therefore, cannot simply be overcome by an amelioration of man's social structures? That holds every society in its grip, no matter how "good"? It is, I propose, precisely that kind of alienation which man, either by himself or through social projects, cannot overcome by himself. According to the New Testament soteriology, it is with this that Christ does battle.

Paul's (and the New Testament's) second fundamental experience is that it is through Christ that God is overcoming man's bondage to evil and sin; to, as we have said, that deepest level of alienation and sin which no amelioration of the individual's and society's situation can necessarily change. As we have said, this is not simply a matter of empirical observation. While we can discern a thread of progress in human history, there also seems to be an increasing history of evil and sin. This was certainly true for Paul, for he describes himself as living "between the times"—between, that is, the event of Christ and the final completion of Christ's work at the end of time. We have already noted the various obstacles to salvation Paul encountered (cf. Rm. 8.35–39); he even graphically maintains that "all creation groans and is in agony even until now" and that "we ourselves . . . groan inwardly . . . (Rm. 8.22–23). The ground of Paul's confidence, then, is not a mystical insight into the future course of all humanity, for this is not a part of his experience. The ground, rather, is his experience of Christ. It is this experience which gives him hope for the future: "In hope we were saved" (Rm. 8.24).

What is it about Paul's Christ-experience that grounds such a hope? Paul, as we have said, knows a new experience of God through Christ. In the Christ God shows himself to be the Divine *Pathos,* a God with and for the world. This Divine *Pathos* reveals that the ultimate structure of the universe is not apathy, with the consequent alienation and sin which this would bring in its wake, but a *Pathos* which is ultimately victorious. The actual structure of history is shown to be Divine *Pathos* rather than *apatheia,* and thus a meaningful process embraced by and grounded in the divine care. This view of soteriology, then, does not anchor its hopes for salvation in the possible progress of Western civilization (Liberal soteriology), nor in an atonement simply transacted some two thousand years ago and somehow relevant to us now (Anselm), nor in an example of love which somehow inspires us today (Abelard), but in God. Because God is a God with and for the world, actually involved in the world through sovereign *pathos,* we can trust that alienation can indeed be overcome.

Paul further explores just how the Divine *Pathos* actually enters human history to transform it into a meaningful process that overcomes human alienation. He refers us to the risen Christ as his explanation.

For example, in an important study written some twenty-five years ago, Bruce Vawter came to the conclusion that for Saint Paul it is the risen Christ who "stands directly in a causal relation to the forgiveness of sins, to the salvation of mankind."[18] Dwelling particularly on Paul's First Corinthians 15.13–17, Vawter maintained that Paul's argument is that without the resurrection our faith "would not be merely 'vain' (*kene*), as in v. 14, i.e., lacking a real object, but also that it would be 'false' (*mataia*), i.e., without avail or effect."[19] As Paul put it, "If however Christ has not risen, false is your faith, you are still in your sins" (1 Cr. 15.17). Or again, "Now not for his (Abraham's) sake only was it written that 'It was credited to him,' but for the sake of us also, to whom it will be credited if we believe in him who has raised Jesus our Lord from the dead, who was delivered up for our sins, and rose again for our justification" (Rm. 4.23–25). This Pauline causal linkage between the risen Christ and our salvation also finds its non-Pauline echo. Mark, for example, who views Jesus as the suffering son of man who saves mankind, always links that suffering with the resurrection (cf. Mk. 9.30). "Luke, who designed his two-volume work as a study of the redemption effected through the first Advocate, Jesus Christ, and the other Advocate, the Holy Spirit acting in the church, has made the glorification of Christ the connecting link between the two phases of this basically same truth: it is with the Ascension that he ends his Gospel, and it is with the Ascension that he begins the Acts," says Vawter.[20]

The Greek fathers preserved this causal view of the resurrection, and Augustine too, at least in one instance, but in general the Latin fathers tended to weaken the resurrection's efficacy, viewing it simply as a divine confirmation of Jesus' life and death.[21] Perhaps the nonmetaphysical Western tendency had something to do with this, but in any case Aquinas, perhaps in reflecting upon the Greek fathers, recaptured the causal role of the resurrection in effecting redemption: "In justification two things happen at once: namely, the remission of fault and the newness of life through grace. If we are speaking of efficient causality, both the passion and the resurrection of Christ are a cause of justification."[22] In more recent times, the Reformation polemics have tended to obscure the causal efficacy of the risen Christ in effecting redemption. On the one hand, the Protestant reaction against the Catholic notion of "meriting grace" caused Catholic authors to stress Christ's passion as the event in which he "merited" grace for us, thus again reducing the resurrection to the role of merely "confirming"

Christ's life and death. Protestantism, on the other hand, with its doctrine of redemption through imputation by God, was not in a position to reassess the redemptive role of the resurrection either.

Let us recall, for a moment, our explanation of the risen Christ. This, we have tried to indicate, is not some esoteric doctrine imported into Christianity simply from Greek or Stoic speculation about a cosmic *"Logos."* It is rather a consequence of the Christian belief in God as relational and dialogical, as actually involving herself in history. The risen Christ is the way in which God remains a dialogical partner with mankind in history. We should not misunderstand this. For example, the cosmic and universal Christ does not replace our neighbor, as if our neighbor were not worthwhile in herself, but only insofar as Christ is "within her." Nor is our neighbor a mere means to a supposedly better relationship with the cosmic and risen Christ. Rather, the risen and universal Christ is a reality of universalization in the midst of history, persuasively drawing mankind away from self-absorption and narcissism toward the dimensions of his more cosmic and universal—that is, "risen"—love. It is as a universal, co-present partner implicit in all of our relationships that the Christ mediates—or, better, "is"—the Divine *Pathos.* William Johnston put this very well:

> The same is true of all the resurrection appearances of Christ: he is suddenly present as another in the midst of friends. Then their attention, no longer absorbed in one another, is drawn towards "only Christ." They are still united, closely united, but the pull of the divine centre is now so strong that it annihilates all tendency to absorption in one another, drawing their gaze towards itself.[23]

Through the risen Christ, then, the Divine *Pathos* makes possible—actually grounds—a new experience of history, a new possibility of human existence and community, and in this sense saves mankind from that deepest source of alienated existence. For we must finally ask what it is that impedes the possibility of authentic community and solidarity in history. I am aware that some would want to stress the priority of the transformation of social structures as the principal means through which an authentic human solidarity can be achieved. But my probing of the New Testament symbol of "Satan" has led me to believe that the deepest source of alienation transcends even humanity's social structures, and is rooted in the threat of meaninglessness and lovelessness, the anxiety caused by death, and by man's own finite nature as a finitude which can lead to isolation and anxiety rather than to trust in the Infinite. Thinking of salvation primarily in terms of the reform of social structures does not seem to penetrate deeply enough the full depth of Christian thinking about salvation. It overlooks the fact that the deepest problem is not the social structure but the threatened and alienated freedom of man. As Langdon Gilkey put it, ". . . as the history of democracy shows, greater self-determination does not guarantee greater freedom from sin. . . . present oppressors are precisely those who have in the past been liberated."[24] Interestingly enough, to think primarily in terms of reformed social structures only further obfuscates for man his own personal guilt and failure and consequent need for ultimate meaning and love. Historical experience has also taught us that it seems to foster fanaticism—a desperate and obsessive "clinging" to a particular social program, a form of idolization and fixation—or despair—because of the inevitable failure of all social programs. From my viewpoint, the deepest problem is clinging, fixation, self-absorption—all forms of an anxious but derailed search for ultimate meaning and love. And it is freedom from such self-absorption that the risen Christ can bring. His universal, "cosmic" love draws us outside ourselves towards his risen love, and frees us, therefore, for solidarity and community. In this sense, God through the risen Christ provides the necessary ontological ground for authentic community.[25]

We might close by indicating several additional implications of this view. First, a somewhat puzzling issue is the fact that the tradition is not completely clear on whether it is Christ's death or his resurrection that saves mankind. We can find support for both points of view, since it appears that the scriptures do not clearly differentiate Christ's death from his resurrection (cf. viz., Rm. 8.32, 5.6; Gal. 11.4; 1 Cr. 15.3).[26] Were the resurrection merely the vindication—the "divine approbation"—of Christ's death, the issue could easily be resolved in favor of the death, but we have already seen that such a view makes no sense of the biblical tradition and would, in any case, dissolve the importance of Christ's risen presence among mankind. Perhaps the most helpful proposal to this issue was provided by David Stanley in the context of a commentary on John's revelation: ". . . I saw a Lamb standing, a Lamb that had been slain" (Rev. 5.6). Stanley comments:

> . . . the message of this grandiose vision is that Jesus Christ, become Master of history through His earthly life, death, and resurrection, is what He now is in virtue of His past existence upon earth. If he depicts the Lord Jesus as eternally adorned with the stigmata of His sacred passion, the seer has thereby called our attention to this significant theological truth by selecting the one most striking event in Jesus' mortal life: His passion and death. What our author clearly implies, however, is that all the mysteries of Jesus' earthly history, from the cradle to the grave, have been mysteriously endowed in His glorified humanity with a totally new and enduring actuality. The saving mysteries . . . retain in Him, as He now exists, a perennial, dynamic reality which remains ever contemporary with the ongoing process of history.[27]

What Stanley is suggesting is that it is a mistake to play off Jesus' life, death, and resurrection against one another. Strictly speaking, it is really the "person" of Jesus who saves mankind. The resurrection, in other words, does not annul Jesus' life and death; it rather renders them "universally" effective in history.

A final question needing some comment is the "personal appropriation" of the redemption offered us through Christ. The traditional distinction between "objective" and "subjective" redemption, while highlighting Christ's role as the objective ground of redemption, does not appear to me to be entirely satisfactory. For on these terms, redemption appears as something extrinsic to history and to man, rather than as the ground that makes history meaningful in the first place. We are already within the redemptive process. And yet, does not this latter formulation seem to render redemption something that only God does through Christ—but what about human freedom and human response? I think a proper response to this must ultimately rest upon the insight that the risen Christ mediates the Divine *Pathos* to mankind. Because God is a God of *Pathos,* this means that redemption is neither a form of divine coercion—which saves man without regard to human freedom—nor simply a form of divine persuasion, as process theology would maintain—this would make God simply dependent upon man's free response. Rather is redemption, I think, a divine suffering-with and involvement in man's history. It is the Divine Love meeting human narcissism, universalizing it, breaking it out of self-clinging and moving it toward the cosmic love of the risen Christ. This Divine "Love," if you will, differs from a kind of divine "coercion," for it is capable of transforming man, yet without doing violence to him. It differs from a simple "persuasion," for the Divine Love is more than that—it can actually change us, even against our "will," yet without violating our genuine humanity.

Notes

1. Kaufman, *Systematic Theology,* p. 400. Kaufman, whose outline of the issues involved in this area has greatly helped me, has written one of the best studies on this question I have come across.

2. Gustaf Aulén, *Christus Victor: An Historical Study of the Three Main Types of the Idea of the Atonement* (London: SPCK, 1931/1970).

3. Thompson, *Christ and Consciousness,* p. 124.

4. Kaufman, *Systematic Theology,* p. 394.

5. I am passing over the patristic contribution to soteriology, since the subject was never really a matter of strict controversy for the fathers, and such explanations as are given are sporadic and fragmentary. Joseph F. Mitros, "Patristic Views of Christ's Salvific Work," THOUGHT 42 (1967), 415–447, has helpfully isolated six types of patristic soteriological thinking. Each develops a facet of the biblical view, under the influence of Hellenistic categories. For more complete analyses, see L. Richard, *The Mystery of the Redemption* (Baltimore: Helicon, 1965); H. E. W. Turner, *The Patristic Doctrine of Redemption* (London: Mowbray, 1952); and J. Rivière, *The Doctrine of the Atonement: A Historical Essay* (St. Louis, MO: Herder, 1909).

The cosmic imagery of Christ in battle with Satan led some of the fathers to the notorious ransom theory (Origen, Gregory of Nyssa, Ambrose, and Augustine), by which Christ was held to have paid a ransom to Satan. Very likely the idea derived both from the biblical imagery and from the current practice of manumission. Just as a slave was liberated through the payment of a ransom to his owner, so mankind was redeemed through Christ's payment of the ransom of his blood to Satan. Origen elaborated this through the notion that God deceived Satan by leading him to think that he had defeated Jesus upon his death, when in fact the resurrection was the real victory. "The Evil One had been deceived and led to suppose that he was capable of mastering the soul and did not see that to hold him involved a trial of greater strength than he could successfully undertake" (*In Matt.*, 16, 8, as cited by Mitros, *ibid.*, 424). Gregory of Nyssa carried this furthest, actually maintaining that Satan had a strict right over sinners. A just God would respect Satan's rights, not conquering him by force but rather by engaging him in a contest/bargain. God, as it were, caught Satan by the bait of Jesus' humanity on the hook of his divinity. "The Deity was hidden under the veil of our nature, that, as is done by greedy fish, the hook of the Deity might be gulped down along with the bait of the flesh and thus life being introduced into the house of death and light shining in the darkness, that which is contradictory to light and life might vanish away: for it is not in the nature of darkness to remain where light is present or of death to exist where life is present" (*Orat. Cat.*, 17–23, as cited by Mitros, *ibid.*, 425).

It was partly this cosmic imagery that led Anselm in the eleventh century to revise this ransom theory, for it seemed to call into question God's sovereignty over the cosmos (*Why God Became Man*, I, VI and VII, in Eugene R. Fairweather, ed., *A Scholastic Miscellany* [New York: Macmillan, 1970], pp. 106–110). In Kaufman's terms, *Systematic Theology*, pp. 395–396, n. 5: "The problem, as Anselm formulated it, was essentially that of the stained and strained relationship between lowly man and the Lord of the universe (rather than God in mortal conflict with the powers of evil). What analogy could be more fitting for this new formulation than the relationship between Lord and serf as found in the contemporary social structure? Lowly man has violated God's holy will—a mere serf has defied the Lord of the universe—and this creates an intolerable situation. God must assert his righteous lordship over the cosmos through punishing, even destroying, the evildoer. However, God is merciful and wishes to forgive man, reestablishing community with him. How, now, can God's righteousness and proper honor be maintained, on the one side, while man is forgiven and restored to fellowship with God, on the other? Obviously, the problem is completely beyond solution from the human side. God is the infinite and absolute being, and this means that even the slightest peccadillo is of immeasurable weight: here of course the feudal conception that the measure of guilt increases in proportion with the status of the one whose honor is violated is clearly at work. It is, then, impossible for man ever to make reparation for his disobedience to God, for it is necessary that such a reparation be infinite. Here, then, is the answer to the question why God became man: though perfectly innocent of any sin, by offering himself up for sacrifice on the cross, the God-man Jesus was able to offer an infinite reparation, at once satisfying God's honor and making it possible for God, for Jesus' sake, to remit to other men as reward what Jesus had won and wished to bestow upon them."

As Fairweather, *ibid.*, pp. 54–58, has indicated, Anselm does stress the divine humility and mercy (read: *Pathos*), at least in intention, thus overcoming a sheer legalistic view of redemption as well as the notion that an angry God somehow needs to be placated. Yet, guilt and sin seem to be "things" able to be simply transferred, in accordance with the feudal penitential view; God's love and her divine sovereignty are not, at least apparently, in harmony; guilt alone seems to be the cause of the incarnation; Jesus' death and resurrection are in no way treated as effecting redemption; and, finally, reparation seems the result of a mere divine *Fiat*. The key question for us today is that of just how the Christ event of two thousand years ago can be thought to mediate redemption realistically to us now, but this question is left untreated by Anselm.

Aquinas corrected Anselm by treating his arguments as "suitable" rather than as "proofs" for how God should act with mankind (*Summ. theol.*, 3, 1, 2), thus safeguarding God's freedom. I think the key element behind Anselm is that God cannot save man without man's own cooperation. The medieval notion of solidarity between Christ and other men forms the background to Anselmian speculation. Thus, in the end, redemption is not a matter of mere divine *Fiat*, but something that operates through human solidarity, but it is this element of solidarity that is not clearly expressed or thought through. Cf. the helpful study of J. Patout Burns, "The Concept of Satisfaction in Medieval Redemption Theory," THEOLOGICAL STUDIES 36 (1975), 285–304.

6. Charles Davis, *Body as Spirit* (New York: Seabury, 1976), p. 110.

7. *Ibid.*

8. *Ibid, p. 114.*

9. Alan W. Watts, *The Two Hands of God: The Myths of Polarity* (New York: Braziller, 1963). Other religions did not differentiate evil from the absolute, but were rather somewhat dualistic, at least in this sense.

10. Trevor Ling, *The Significance of Satan: New Testament Demonology and Its Contemporary Relevance* (London: SPCK, 1961), p. 83.

11. Paul Ricoeur, *The Symbolism of Evil* (Boston: Beacon, 1969), pp. 257–258.

12. Davis, *op. cit.,* p. 120.

13. *Ibid.,* p. 121.

14. Ricoeur, *op. cit.,* makes it clear that the Adamic myth does not reduce evil to man's personal fault purely and simply, nor even to man's collective or social fault: ". . . evil must enter into the world by a sort of catastrophe in the created" (p. 240). And further: "The figure of Job bears witness to the irreducibility of the evil of scandal to the evil of fault, at least on the scale of human experience; the theory of retribution, which was the first naive expression of the moral vision of the world, does not account for all the unhappiness of the world" (p. 314).

15. Edward Schillebeeckx, "The 'God of Jesus' and the 'Jesus of God,' " CONCILIUM 93 (1974), 113. I am not sure as to whether Ling, Davis, or even Kaufman has penetrated to this level of the demonic/evil.

16. In a sense, I think, Watts is correct that "Satan" is a corollary of theism. One can penetrate through to the real horror of evil only when one recognizes its obverse. Whether the interpretation of the demonic advanced here is in accord with Catholic doctrine rests upon a careful hermeneutics of the statements of the Fourth Lateran Council (*D* 428; cf. *D* 237, 427). It would appear that this Council intends only to combat a form of dualism; it only assumes the existence of angels and demons.

17. Schillebeeckx, *art. cit.,* 114. From this point of view one can perhaps recognize more adequately the limitations of Abelard's soteriology (The other eleventh-century alternative to Anselm). Abelard views the key problem as that of "lovelessness" in human existence. This lovelessness is overcome "through a unique act of grace manifest to us" that "we have been justified by the blood of

Christ and reconciled to God," an act which "frees us from slavery to sin . . . [and] wins for us the true liberty of sons of God," by evoking from us a "deeper affection . . . so that we do all things out of love rather than fear—love to him who has shown us such grace that no greater can be found" (*Exposition of the Epistle to the Romans,* Second Book, commentary on Rom. 3:19–26, transl. from *Library of Christian Classics,* X [Philadelphia: Westminster, 1956], pp. 283–284). Abelard seems to opt for the view that simply seeing God's love in Christ will transform men's hearts: ". . . if they . . . see the glory prepared for them by God's mercy, at that moment, along with discernment, the love of God is born in them" (*ibid.,* p. 287). What is not clearly expressed here is the fact that the problem of evil and sin is so profound (Satanic) that a mere change of men's hearts is insufficient. God must be actively involved throughout the process of redemption. Kaufman's observation is pertinent here, *Systematic Theology,* p. 399, n. 8: "If this humanistic tendency is carried to an extreme, God as a genuinely active agent may drop out of the picture entirely, the unbreakable bondage to sin and self may be forgotten, and the Gospel interpreted largely as an exhortation to follow Jesus' moral example of self-sacrifice. Certainly this was not Abailard's intention, but developments along this line occurred in the liberal protestantism which found his view preferable to either the classic or the Anselmic view." The liberal view has come to be identified with the nineteenth-century progressivist tendency (1) to fail to recognize the enormity of evil and (2) to identify redemption with a man-made utopianism or belief in progress.

18. Bruce Vawter, "Resurrection and Redemption," CATHOLIC BIBLICAL QUARTERLY 15 (1953), 13.

19. *Ibid.,* 12. This is the usual meaning for *mataia* in the New Testament: Jm. 1.26; 1 Cr. 3.20; 1 Pt. 1.18; Aa. 14.14.

20. *Ibid.,* 22.

21. Cf. David M. Stanley, "Ad historiam exegeseos Rom 4, 25," VERBUM DOMINI 29 (1951), 257f. Augustine's one text: *Serm.,* 236 (*PL* 38, 1120).

22. *Summ. theol.,* 3, 56, 4. Cf. Nicholas Crotty, "The Redemptive Role of Christ's Resurrection," THE THOMIST 25 (1962), 54–106, for a thorough genetic study of Aquinas's position.

23. Johnston, *op. cit.,* p. 161.

24. Gilkey, *op. cit.,* p. 237; cf. pp. 236–238.

25. Kasper has based his own reinterpretation of redemption on the notion of human solidarity, claiming that such solidarity requires a ground (viz., the Christ) to sustain it; cf. *op. cit.,* pp. 221–225.

26. See O'Collins, *The Resurrection of Jesus Christ,* pp. 117–122.

27. David M. Stanley, "Contemplation of the Gospels, Ignatius Loyola, and the Contemporary Christian," THEOLOGICAL STUDIES 29 (1968), 429–430.

VIII

EXPLORING THE CHRIST-EXPERIENCE III: A STUDY OF BÉRULLE'S CHRISTIC SPIRITUALITY

Introductory

This study of the Christological spirituality of Pierre Cardinal de Bérulle, the "founder" of the seventeenth-century French school of spirituality, requires an introduction. There are, of course, many worthy candidates from the Christian tradition for inclusion in a book such as this. Particularly outstanding for Christology would be any of the great Greek fathers, Symeon the New Theologian, Gregory Palamas on the Eastern side; Bonaventure, Thomas Aquinas, Francis of Assisi, Ignatius Loyola, and the Spanish mystics Teresa of Avila and John of the Cross from the Western side. But few writers have achieved the remarkable synthesis of Christology that we find in Bérulle's *Discours de l'estat et des grandeurs de Jésus.* Further, Bérulle has quite consciously attempted to integrate the insights of systematic Christology with the needs of Christian spirituality, and so we find in him a balanced interest in Christ and the Christ-experience, the two major themes of our work.

What gives Bérulle a particular contemporaneity is the fact that he stands at that turning point in Western history when our "isolated self," essayed earlier, begins to emerge. Man, in the seventeenth century, owing to the new awareness of reason as a self-liberating instrument and its fruitful application to technology, was beginning to understand the good life as an individualistic project of self-realization. As we will see Van Kaam put it further on in this study, man was gaining "a heightened fascination with his own world, and his ego at the center of it," which "led him to concentrate excessively on what happened in his isolated interiority." What Eric Voegelin has called the symbols of open existence—God, man, the divine

origin of the cosmos, and the divine *Logos* permeating its order—were losing their vitality and being replaced by the symbols of a self-saving ego and
an immanently closed world. Bérulle's own "Copernican Revolution"—as
he called it—was a quite conscious attempt to present a Christian alternative to this closure of the self. In essence, through the exemplarist categories of Neo-Platonism, Bérulle denies that man is a being locked up in
himself because God is not a self-enclosed, isolated Being. In Bérulle we
find a systematic exploration of the Relational God of Christianity and the
Christian notion of the person as a living relation to this God: "The created being necessarily always has need of being united to God as to its first
cause and to receive his continual influences."

Bérulle writes on two fronts, and it is necessary that we have some understanding of them lest we miss the contemporaneity of his message. On
the one hand he writes to the Renaissance humanists, the precursors of our
more overdifferentiated isolated ego. It is this "isolated ego" that must be
annihilated: ". . . the soul should employ all its powers to lose itself and annihilate itself in God . . . so that God . . . may . . . bring about a sort of annihilation of the soul itself very different from that which the soul exercises
beforehand through its own power." In place of the self-saving ego, Bérulle
recommends adhering "to the movement by which God, creating and
forming all things, refers them and relates them all to himself. . . ." Although his categories are those of Neo-Platonism, it is a thoroughly Christianized Neo-Platonism. God is not the Isolated Monad—Plotinus's
"One"—but the Relational Being we have termed the Divine *Pathos:*
"[God] is more intimate to the creature than his own being itself." Bérulle's second front is that of the "spiritualists," who, under the influence of
an excessive Neo-Platonism, would bypass the humanity of Jesus in the
spiritual life. This should remind us of the earlier patristic struggle with
Arius. It was Arius's excessive Hellenism that made it impossible to come
to terms with the Incarnation. His implicit God-concept was that of the
God of *apatheia,* transcendently removed from history. Bérulle's spiritualists are repeating the same error, and this leads Bérulle to assert the permanent role of Jesus Christ in God's relationship with man: ". . . Jesus is
the true Center of the world, and the world must be in continual movement toward him."

One does not normally think of the seventeenth century as an age of
Christological exploration. On the one hand, the intellectualism promoted
by the Renaissance simply strengthened the theologians' resolve to carry
on late Scholasticism's intellectualistic trend, without breaking any new
ground. On the other hand, the recent problem of the Reformation caused
theologians to concentrate on ecclesiology and revelation rather than
Christology. Yet, thanks to the recent research of Jean Dagens,[1] we now
know that a number of factors were at work among spiritual theologians
that would be quite stimulating to developments in Christology, and which
would crystallize in the remarkable theological spirituality of Pierre de
Bérulle, the founder of the French Oratory.

Sources of Christological Renewal

A first factor was a growing reaction to a degenerate Scholasticism. Already in 1379 Gerhard Groote, founder of the Brothers of the Common Life, was warning of the dangers of theology's excessive rationalism. Gerson likewise recommended: "We are forced . . . to place mystical theology and scholasticism in accord."[2] In Dagens's judgment, it was Gerson's more moderate program, the reunification of mystical and Scholastic theology, that the forerunners of Bérulle and Bérulle himself would attempt.[3] This "spiritualized" Scholasticism became, by the sixteenth century, the goal of Europe's major Catholic universities. Bérulle came under the influence of this reformist program at the Sorbonne, where already in 1600 it was officially endorsed by statute. Thus his predilection for Thomas Aquinas himself, rather than his commentators. He tells us that he follows Aquinas on the questions of the incarnation, grace, and everything else to the extent that this were possible.[4] But because, as we shall see, Bérulle's theology is personal and experiential, he does not strictly adhere to any school. The influence of Bonaventure[5] is also marked, and when Bérulle relies upon Aquinas, it is usually a case of those views that both Aquinas and Bonaventure share. Perhaps, as Dagens indicates, Bérulle's attraction to both of these masters stems from his love for Augustine, the key influence behind both.

A second factor, allied with the first, was the growing recovery of the scriptural and patristic tradition. This was, again, a critique of the prevalent Scholastic theology, an attempt at *approfondissement*. The sixteenth century was, thanks mainly to the work of the humanists, an age of biblical renewal. Thus we find Bérulle frequently citing Paul and John, and though his exegetical method was that of Augustine, he was aware of contemporary biblical studies and encouraged them.

Among the fathers, the first in importance was Denis the Areopagite. What possibly accounts for his popularity in the humanistic sixteenth century is more the fact that he was considered a kind of link between Christian revelation and Hellenistic culture rather than, as the earlier belief had it, that he was thought to be a disciple of Saint Paul. That belief was rejected by Erasmus and Cajetan, and it is entirely possible that Bérulle rejected it too.[6] Denis's mystical agnosticism appealed to both the reformed Scholastics and the more secular thinkers of the age. Bishop Zamet, in approving Bérulle's *Grandeurs,* said he found therein "the spirit of the great apostle of France, Saint Denis and his *Divine Hierarchy.*"[7] In any case, all the great Christian Neo-Platonic themes of Denis find their echo in Bérulle: the *exitus-reditus* theme, the earthly church as an image of the heavenly church, and the Christian life viewed as a mystical ascent to God.

Additionally, thanks again to the humanists, few ages had so many patristic texts available as did the sixteenth century. Practically all the major Greek and Latin fathers were available by 1562, and little doubt exists, both from Bérulle's own works and from his contemporaries, that Bérulle was one of the foremost representatives of this patristic renewal. He knew the major Greek and Latin fathers well, with a special predilection for Augustine:

> It is beyond doubt that he receives the tone of his elevations, of his contemplative meditations, from Saint Augustine. . . . The powerful speculations on the Trinity and Incarnation, which form the beauty of the *Grandeurs de Jésus,* are of Augustinian inspiration; in the sweeping view of universal history which is that of the *Vie de Jésus,* one perceives the vestiges of the *City of God.*[8]

A final factor expressing the sixteenth and seventeenth centuries' desire for renewal was a special interest in mysticism. For our purposes, this interest in mysticism becomes most apparent in Bérulle's part in the discussion over the place of Jesus' humanity in the Christian life.[9] In a sense, the controversy was a minor one, confined to the mystics themselves. From a larger perspective, however, what was at issue was both the meaning of the redemption itself, and further, whether it were possible to reconcile Greek philosophical speculation and Christian incarnationalism. Discerning the tradition to which Bérulle attached himself will afford us a particularly good indication of the dominant mystical influences upon his own Christological synthesis.

Toward the end of the sixteenth century, Denis's influence had led to an ideal of "abstract spirituality." The spiritual goal was understood as the pursuit of "contemplation without images," probably in reaction to excessive rationalism. This Neo-Platonic ideal was particularly strong among the German mystics, and represented a departure from the Jesus-centered contemplative ideal of Bernard, Francis of Assisi, and Bonaventure. A clear example of the abstract ideal is furnished by Eckhart. His commentary on John 16.7, "It is good for you that I go away," reads:

> He had in view not only his disciples then, but all who would eventually become his disciples, and would follow him toward a high state of perfection. For even for them his human form is an obstacle, of which they divest themselves with love. They must, in effect, follow God in all his ways. They must not then enlist in the way of his humanity, which guides us only toward the voice of the deity.[10]

In Eckhart we have the clearest formulation of the Neo-Platonic ideal in the domain of spirituality. The spiritual goal is the God beyond the Trinity, beyond all distinctions and separations, the primitive unity and absolute poverty. Perhaps Teresa of Avila had Eckhart in mind when she disapprovingly said: "For, they say, when one is already so advanced, even the humanity of Jesus becomes an obstacle and an impediment to perfect contemplation: as they cite . . . John 16.7."[11]

Closer to Bérulle, Benoît de Canfeld will somewhat modify Eckhart's view. A member of the Capuchin reform, he was deeply indebted to Francis of Assisi and Bonaventure. Thus, although he teaches supraconceptual contemplation, he makes an exception of Jesus' passion, a theme very crucial to Francis: ". . . the Passion of the Savior must be perpetually practised, held before the eyes and contemplated. . . ."[12] Canfeld offers the solution of Augustine and Aquinas, and Bérullian commentators consider this to be Bérulle's solution also: it is necessary to regard and adore Jesus "not only as God or as man, or in his separated humanity, but inasmuch as he is the God-man."[13] Benoît, Capuchin that he is and thus deeply influenced by the stigmatic devotion of Alverna, makes room for the enduring place of the passion. Bérulle, more systematic and consistent, makes room for all the mysteries of Jesus' life: in the God-man all human actions and dispositions have been "deified" (*G, 2, 3, 173*). Bérulle, then, sees, not precisely Jesus' humanity, but the person of Jesus, God and man, as the goal of the spiritual life. By thus spiritualizing Jesus' humanity he is able to preserve its enduring place and yet accept the Germanic mystical emphasis upon the God-beyond-images. For the God-man is beyond images, deified and glorified. Here Bérulle is echoing Augustine, Aquinas, and especially Teresa of Avila:

> When God suspends all the powers of the soul . . . it is clear that whether we wish it or not this presence [that of Jesus' humanity] is withdrawn. Be it so, then. The loss is a blessed one, because it takes place in order that we may have a deeper fruition of what we seem to have lost.[14]

This deeper, spiritualized presence of Jesus' humanity, which William Johnston describes as "that 'sense of presence' of which all the mystics speak, the deep awareness of Another without thought or concept or image," seems to be the God-man of John of the Cross who is capable of entering all souls, just as he entered the upper room when the doors were locked.[15] In any case, here we have exactly the Bérullian sense of the presence of Jesus and his enduring place in the spiritual life.[16]

Thus, while in the realm of dogmatics the situation was not a particularly favorable one for developments in Christology, Bérulle may be taken as the foremost representative of a more creative undercurrent, in whom the critique of Scholasticism, the recovery of the biblical-patristic tradition, and the "mystical invasion" converged. All three factors would enable him to produce an impressive Christological synthesis.

Bérulle's "Conversion" to Christocentrism

The Bérulle that is of most interest in the history of Christian thought is the "later" Bérulle, so called after his "conversion" to Christocentrism, around 1605–1606. It is this later Bérulle that Urban VIII had in mind as the "apostle of the incarnate Word." And it is also this more mature Bérulle who was the founding genius of what Bremond would call the "French School": "incontestably the richest, the most original and fertile, of any born in the Golden Age of our religious history. . . ."[17] Among his followers were Vincent de Paul, De Condren, Louis de Montfort, Jean-Jacques Olier, John Eudes; and more recently, Mersch, Marmion, Vonier, and even Karl Rahner.[18]

Bérulle was born at Cérilly in 1575, eight years after Francis de Sales, and we can, from a Christological perspective, end his "early" period around 1605. During this time he came under the influence of Madame Acarie, and through her circle of mystically oriented friends, began his own long mystical interest. It was during this period that he published his *Bref discours de l'abnégation intérieure* (1597) and *Traité des energumènes* on discernment and possession (1599), both characterized by an "abstract spirituality." What perhaps accounts for his transition to Christological interests was his appointment as one of three superiors for the French Carmelites in 1603. This would argue for some influence of Teresian spirituality upon him. In any case, in his correspondence of 1606 to a Carmelite he claims that he knows "no treasure after God other than this holy and glorious humanity which is our well being," a notion remarkably similar to Teresa's thought: ". . .our whole well being and medicine is the most sacred humanity of our Savior" (*CB,* 1, 84).

The precise and immediate source of Bérulle's Christocentrism is a matter of some debate among Bérullian experts. I personally would follow Jean Orcibal, who sees the catalyst for Bérulle's Christological synthesis in the controversies that increasingly occupied him from 1608 onwards.[19] As a leader in clerical reform, and as the founder of the Oratory, he was a natural leader in the controversies of his time. On Orcibal's account, the debates with the Huguenots over the mystical body and the Eucharist led him toward Christology. His eucharistic tract especially encompasses all his later Christological interests: "The Incarnation is the original prototype of this mystery and our Eucharist is as the copy and the extract of it"[20] According to Orcibal, the Christocentrism here is so great and marks such a departure from the Areopagite and Germanic mysticism that we should see the influence of Teresian spirituality. This opinion seems confirmed when we realize that 1614 is the year in which he is named a canonical visitator to the Carmelites and the year in which he inaugurates the feast of the Solemnity of Jesus, proclaiming, against the Areopagite, a "reversal of the hierarchies": namely, the fact that "all the angels adore" the God-man.[21]

The second controversy to engage Bérulle, and the one immediately responsible for the synthetic *Grandeurs,* was that over the "vow" of servitude, which he introduced among the Oratorians and Carmelites between 1615 and 1618. The *Grandeurs* is definitely an apologetic work, occasioned by the attacks on the vow.[22] Bérulle had evidently first encountered the tradition of a vow to Mary, the perfect example of servitude to God, while on a mission in Spain in 1604 for the Carmelites. In any case, such a vow does date back to Ildephonse of Toledo in 667 and seems to be the inspiration of Bérulle's famous formulations of the vow.

It is difficult to precise exactly Bérulle's attraction to a vow of servitude. For one thing, it seemed congenial to his own "Dionysian" mind-set, which in turn reflected the structured situation of monarchical France. As the kingdom of France was composed of various orders—the clergy, nobility, and lower estates—so these orders corresponded to the Dionysian seraphim, cherubim, and thrones. Perhaps the vow more dramatically expressed one's position within this hierarchy. Further, it gave expression to Bérulle's new Christological concerns. For as the human nature of Christ is totally dependent upon the Divine Person, so the mystery of this hypostatic union could be the exemplar and archetype of total servitude to God. Bérulle's vow to Jesus expresses this aspiration very well: "Je vous supplie, âme sainte et déifée de Jésus . . . que vous me rendiez votre esclave en la manière que je ne connais point et que vous connaissez."[23]

Bérulle proposed two vows of servitude, one to Mary as a kind of mystical initiation into servitude, and one to Jesus, and those in both vows, in Paul Cochois's words, "would form a choir and an order, capable of diffusing upon the inferior hierarchies the deifying light that they themselves received by means of the Virgin and the incarnate Word from the fontal deity of the Father."[24] To be sure, when Bérulle initiated these vows among the Carmelites, his enemies tried to see in them a fourth canonical vow. When opposition mounted, mainly for what now appear to be political motives,[25] and when Bérulle was charged with heresy, the issue of the vow became the more fundamental one of Christology itself. The Jesuit theologian Lessius advised Bérulle to present the vow as a renewal of the baptismal promises. Saint-Cyran contributed his valuable knowledge of the patristic and Scholastic sources. Finally, in 1623 Bérulle's masterpiece, the *Discours de l'estat et des grandeurs de Jésus,* appeared.

Bérulle's "Christic Universe"

It is in the Bérulle of the *Grandeurs* that the sources for renewal, essayed above, manifest themselves most clearly and converge in perhaps the greatest synthesis of Christology written in the seventeenth century. To be sure, the *Grandeurs* is not the whole of Bérulle's work, and needs to be complemented by the later and more serene *Elévation à Jésus* (1625), the *Elévation sur sainte Madeleine* (1627), and the *Vie de Jésus* (1629). Still, the *Grandeurs* does contain, at least seminally, all the great Bérullian insights in the realm of Christology. However, presenting Bérulle's thought systematically is a difficult matter. He writes more in the manner of Augustine and Cyril rather than Aquinas. His preference is for the desert and Greek fathers, rather than the deductive reasoning which makes summarization easy. In what follows, I will attempt an overview, relying upon the best Bérullian scholars, and supplementing the *Grandeurs* with Bérulle's other works where that seems helpful.

In beginning, however, I would like to suggest that there is something of a hermeneutical key that seems to permeate Bérulle's work and perhaps forms the thread of continuity throughout the whole. To understand this "key" we must understand something of the larger development that Western man himself was undergoing at the time of the Renaissance. It seems valid to say that the predominant concerns of an age tend to foster a corresponding consciousness. We customarily describe our own age as scientific, in contrast to the medieval period of belief, and we are aware that the methodology of science permeates to some extent the consciousness of almost everyone today. Thus, utility, efficiency, competition, success, technique, experiment, organization, and analysis are implicit values to most in our Western culture. We speak of an analytic or scientific consciousness, and thereby recognize to what an extent an age actually shapes human consciousness. Now Bérulle stood at the turning point in Western history when this new analytic consciousness was coming into its own, and I am convinced that his own theological spirituality represents a creative attempt, not to reject, but to critique and integrate into a higher synthesis the concerns of this new, man-centered mind set. Adrian van Kaam has well described this new consciousness as "introspective":

> The rise of the Renaissance, with the growing emphasis on science and technology, made the knowledge and perfection of this world the focus of attention. . . . The living awareness of the sacred dimension of reality was lost. Man no longer experienced his interwovenness with his fellow men, with nature, history, and the cosmos as constantly originating from the Divine Presence. His self-in-isolation, facing a competitive society, became the nucleus of his personal concern. This heightened fascination with his own world, and his ego at the center of it, led him to concentrate excessively on what happened in his isolated interiority. He became obsessed with the need for ethical and psychological self-realization.[26]

Now Bérulle's theology might be understood against the horizon of this new, introspective consciousness. What Bérulle was searching for was a more wholistic view of human consciousness, one not viewing man in an isolated state, but seeking to find him in his totality; not as cut off from his ground and source of meaning, but in his fundamental relationship to God. This seems Bérulle's fundamental intuition, and the key to his thought.

First, a knowledge of this background aids us in understanding the exemplarist framework of the *Grandeurs,* a constant in Bérullian thought.[27] M. Dupuy has explained well Bérulle's predilection for this facet of the Areopagite's Neo-Platonism:

> We know the great theses: resemblance is the fundamental relation between beings thanks to which they become intelligible. To explain . . . to know causes . . . is to discern the similarities. A creature is situated in the hierarchy of beings when one knows what it imitates. To be a cause of a category of beings, this is to be the archetype upon which they are modeled.[28]

Now Bérulle's choice of this framework for his own *Grandeurs,* uniting him thus to Augustine and Bonaventure, is not to be understood as a simple nostalgia for the past, but rather as the expression of a wholistic anthropology, in which man is viewed, not in an isolated state, but rather in terms of his full reality, as a creature-in-relationship-to-God. Bérulle's anthropology is "relational," and thus motivated by the insight that man can only be understood when seen in relation to his source and ground of meaning. Already in 1612 he had said: ". . . we should adhere to the movement by which God, creating and forming all things, refers them and relates them all to himself, which is a movement . . . so forcefully imprinted in the being of the creature by the Creator's power, that it is more intimate to the creature than his own being itself."[29] This exemplarist emphasis is forcefully echoed in discourse eleven of the *Grandeurs,* where Bérulle is writing of the *seconde naissance de Jésus:*

> This is the birth of the order and state of the hypostatic union, which carries outside of God the highest and most eminent holiness that is possible. . . . And we receive from this mystery a grace, a holiness, a light, a life of light, a light of life in Jesus, as proper effects . . . (*G,* 11, 4, 345–346).

It is this exemplarist framework that led Bremond to speak of Bérullism as theocentric, and indeed as the purest example of theocentrism in Christian history. Perhaps the purity of Bérulle's theocentrism is directly proportionate to the depth of his critique of the Renaissance man-in-isolation.[30] But I believe that Louis Cognet is more correct in speaking of Bérulle's thought as a "trinitarian exemplarism." In fact, Bérulle's tendency to view the trinitarian relations as the analogous archetypes of the universe accords very well with his relational anthropology. It is as if "being itself could not but be trinitarian."[31]

Secondly, the critique of introspectionism is essential in understanding the passionate negativity that characterizes the *Grandeurs.* This "constant" in Bérullism is possibly the key element accounting for the seeming lack of popularity of the French school. Just as the element of theocentrism is accentuated in Bérulle, so, too, the element of man's nothingness is highlighted.

> Oh marvel, oh grandeur, this man who is nothing but . . . a cinder in his origin, according to the word . . . "You are dust and unto dust you shall return" (Gn. 3.19); this man who is nothing but impotence and feebleness in his state and progress, and nothing but a vapor, and a momentary one at that. . . . it is this man, I say, who is living and subsisting in the Divinity (*G,* 4, 6, 221).

Bérulle's awareness of man's contingency and sinfulness is simply a theological truism, and every balanced spirituality must come to terms with it. But Bérulle has an accentuated awareness of it. Man is so sinful that nothing less than an *anéantissement,* an "annihilation," will do:

> ... the soul should employ all its powers to lose itself and annihilate itself in God ... so that God ... may employ his divine power upon the soul to annihilate it by his intimate and secret workings, which bring about a sort of annihilation of the soul itself very different from that which the soul exercises beforehand through its own power (*Oeuvres de piété,* hereafter *OP,* 150, 1028).[32]

Yet Bérulle does not teach the total depravity of man. As if he were aware of his own passionate attempt to express himself, he once said that one must "use some metaphors ... no one understands the language of love but only love itself understands, or someone educated in its school."[33] He intends to say that man's sinfulness is something more than peripheral and yet less than total; it affects the deepest aspect of man, as Saint Paul so vividly said in Romans, without ruining him. We meet the same intuition in the anonymous *The Cloud of Unknowing,* where the author states: "He alone feels authentic sorrow who realizes not only *what* he is, but *that* he is." William Johnston's comment on this text is instructive:

> One can experience one's incompleteness emotionally or economically or culturally or sexually; and all that is painful. But how terrible to experience it at the deepest level of all, that of existence! For all these other sorrows are partial experiences of one root experience of existential contingency. And this, I believe, is the sorrow of the man who knows not only *what he is* but *that he is.*[34]

This notion of sorrow *that one is* approaches rather closely the Bérullian notion of *anéantissement.* When Bérulle and the author of *The Cloud* are speaking of man in his existential contingency, they have in mind the "incomplete" and isolated man, man-as-separated-from-God, his only true end. Bérulle's target is the isolated man fostered by the Renaissance. A representative text from the *Grandeurs* exemplifies this:

> For God dwells in the world by nature and by grace. ... God is more intimately in each thing ... than the spirit which rules and animates the body. This led St. Paul to say, *In ipso vivimus, movemus et sumus.* ... if it [i.e., the creature] is ever separated even for a moment, it loses at that very instant its being and existence (*G,* 6, 6, 250).

Thirdly, however, we reach the heart of Bérulle's critique of Renaissance introspectionism only with his Christocentrism. Although the Neo-Platonic and Dionysian exemplarist framework is already a critique of an isolated view of man, separated from his ground and source of meaning, Bérulle also critiques the Areopagite: ". . . reversing the dionysian hierarchies, he does not regard the celestial orders as the archetype, but Christ, whose state of Manhood-Godhood is for him the recapitulation of the 'visible, intelligible, and archetypical' world."[35] That Bérulle intends his Christocentrism critically is clear in the following:

> An excellent spirit of the age has wished to maintain that the sun is the center of the world, and not the earth. . . . This novel opinion, little followed in astronomy, is useful, and must be followed in the science of the saints. . . . Jesus is the true Center of the world, and the world must be in continual movement toward him. Jesus is the sun of our souls. . . . And the earth of our hearts must be in continual movement toward him . . . (G, 2, 2, 171–172).

What he is revolting against, as we have seen, is an excessive Neo-Platonism or Hellenizing of doctrine, in which the humanity of Jesus is considered an obstacle in man's relationship with God. For these Neo-Platonizers—or "spiritualists" as they were called—God is beyond matter, beyond the flesh and human history. Thus the humanity of Jesus was to be bypassed in one's spiritual assent to God. Here we should see the echo of the Arian problem, treated earlier. The difficulty of the spiritualists is, of course, the late Hellenic one of a God of apathy, of uninvolvement in human history. Bérulle's critique of Neo-Platonism, his Christocentrism, was a highly original recapturing of the Christic God-concept, God as the Divine *Pathos,* and thus a God present in the humanity of Jesus. What would be worthy of further study is the attraction of the spiritualists' point of view in the time of Bérulle. Could one speculate that the Renaissance man-centeredness, in which man was severed from his divine ground of meaning, generated its underside: a desire to flee from this world, to bypass its meaninglessness, and to be directly absorbed in the Divine? Being "absorbed in God" or "lost in God" is one of the perennial ways in which man seeks to escape from the isolation of his own existence. I personally would understand Bérulle's Christocentrism as his attempt to avoid this danger. His answer to the problem of the isolated ego is not absorption in God but relation to God through the deified humanity of Jesus Christ.

First of all, in Bérulle's exemplarist and relational world, the Man-God is the "perfect idea by which the entire work of God is accomplished" (*G,* 4, 4, 215). As Bérulle succinctly states it, "For God produces all things by his Word, and the Word is the principle by which the creation of the world is accomplished . . ." (*G,* 4, 10, 227). Bérulle is so emphatic that the Man-God is the true archetype of the world that he speaks of the incarnation as a "Second Trinity": "By these admirable unities, we have two holy trinities, divine and adorable in our mysteries: a trinity of essence in a unity of subsistence in the sacred mystery of the incarnation, in the essence of the soul, in that of the body, and in the divinity of Jesus" (*G,* 3, 8, 207).

And to underline further the role of the Man-God, he introduces his unique notion of the "fertile sterility of the Holy Spirit":

> Because he is sterile in the divinity by the condition proper to the mystery of the Trinity, it is necessary that by a new mystery he be fertile in another ineffable manner, in giving a new being to one of the subsistent persons in the plenitude of the Most Holy Trinity. . . . This third person, producing nothing eternal and uncreated, produces the Word incarnate (*G*, 4, 2, 212–213).[36]

Secondly, if we search Bérulle to discover why the Man-God is this archetype of a relational world, it is because his very being is relational: ". . . it is his proper work and state in eternity to be an eternal and substantial rapport with himself and consequently of everything which proceeds from him to the eternal Father, as toward the principle and source of his being and of every original being" (*G*, 5, 8, 236). What justifies Bérulle in this is his notion that in Jesus the Divine Word assumes the human nature in such a way that the humanity is "deprived" of its own human "personhood." The very personhood of Jesus is constituted by a relation to the Divine Word: it *is* this relation: "And as the person of the Word is divine and infinite, it possesses a wholly extraordinary and inexplicable relation to the human nature, which, being deprived of its subsistence, has need of that of the eternal Word; which . . . is actuating and penetrating this humanity, in its essence and in its powers, and throughout its whole being" (*G*, 4, 5, 218).

It has become clear with proper research that Bérulle was not a monophysite who denied the proper humanity of Jesus. In fact this would destroy the key point of the *Grandeurs*. Bérulle is simply dependent here upon Cyril of Alexandria, Aquinas, and Cajetan, and as Orcibal claims, he is attracted to the subsistence of the humanity in the Word greatly by his Neo-Platonism: "The created being necessarily always has need of being united to God as to its first cause and to receive his continual influence . . ." (*G*, 6, 6, 251).[37]

But Bérulle's Christological originality manifests itself clearly, not so much in its metaphysical aspects, but in its transposition into the area of spirituality. His notion of the privation of the human subsistence in Jesus affords him a way of dogmatically grounding the vow of servitude in the incarnation itself. But more importantly it is the basis for Bérulle's answer to the problems connected with Renaissance introspectionism.

As we have already seen, the importation into France of particularly the mystical theology of the Germans had promoted the notion that the goal and summit of the spiritual ascent was a contemplation of the divine essence, and thus a transcending of the humanity of Jesus. We have already seen how Bérulle had encountered this notion, particularly through the influence of the Carmelites and of De Canfeld. Bérulle's originality consists in the consistent manner in which he drew spiritual consequences from his theology of the incarnation. On the one hand, his entire program is an attempt to critique the one-dimensional view of man fostered by the Renaissance, the view that man is somehow complete in himself apart from his relationship to God. Thus, Bérulle must safeguard man's ultimate relationship to God and so in some way agree with the German mystics. On the other hand, he must avoid the danger of pretending to absorb man in God, of falling into the pretense that it is possible to surpass man's created nature. This, too, would destroy the relational anthropology that forms the heart of Bérulle. His position, original because of the consistency with which he drew consequences from it, has been well expressed by Louis Cognet:

> From the beginning it is above all necessary to consider the Man-God as a unique being, and one must not make any dissociation in him, even hypothetical. Because the humanity of Jesus does not subsist in itself, because it is, following the Bérullian formula, "united to the divine essence," one cannot attain it without simultaneously attaining God, and it is in this sense that Bérulle will speak of this humanity as "that which no one can see without seeing God." But then a further consequence follows: because the Word is inclined by his "perfections and proper conditions" toward the Incarnation, toward this humanity deprived of subsistence, because there is a kind of congeniality between the Second Person of the Trinity and the human nature to which it is united, one cannot attain the divine essence without finding in some manner the humanity of Jesus in the same perspective. . . . One does not attain the divinity by the intermediary of the humanity, but the divinity *in* the humanity.[38]

Thus, Bérulle's "universe," his anthropology, is neither isolationist, against the Renaissance humanists, nor pantheist, against his view of the German mystics, but *relational*. The glorified humanity of Jesus "in his state and subsistence . . . is the center, the circle, and the circumference of all the emanations of God outside himself" (*G,* 2, 5, 174). It is in this way that Bérulle is able to found his "Christic universe." He, as it were, prolongs his Christology into man himself.[39]

Bérulle's technical term for expressing his conception of a "Christic universe" is *"estat"* or "state." This term is a terribly subtle one in his thought, and apparently he did not always employ it consistently before writing the *Grandeurs*. In his later writings, especially the *Vie de Jésus,* the term appears less frequently; his focus seems to be less speculative and more personal and psychological. It is as if the later Bérulle, his theological grounding assured, has decided upon a more practical working out of his spirituality. Thus, it is to the *Grandeurs* and the works roughly contemporaneous with it—his *Collationes* and *Oeuvres de piété*—that we must primarily go for an understanding of the Bérullian "state."

The term "state" was not, of course, wholly original to Bérulle. The spiritual tradition spoke of "states" within the spiritual journey; canonical tradition knew of various "states" within the Church; and the theological tradition would speak of the different "states" of grace. But Bérulle had a predilection for this term, both because it conformed to his own love of the Dionysian tendency to hierarchize, and because it mirrored the stratified and monarchical society in which he lived. The term carries several derivative meanings in the Bérullian corpus, but generally its most fundamental sense seems to be that of *the perenniality and contemporaneity of the risen Jesus in the universe:*

> It is necessary to reflect upon the perpetuity of these mysteries. . . . They are past in regard to their execution, but they are present in regard to their virtue, and their virtue is never past, nor will the love with which they were accomplished ever cease. The spirit, then, the state, the virtue, the merit of the mystery, is always present. The spirit of God, by which this mystery has been accomplished, the interior state of the exterior mystery, the efficacity and the virtue which renders this mystery active and operative in us, this state and virtuous disposition, the merit by which he has acquired the Father for us and merited heaven, life, and himself; even the actual stirring, the living disposition by which Jesus has accomplished this mystery, is always active, actual and present in Jesus. . . . Thus we must consider the things and mysteries of Jesus not as things past and over, but as living and present, and even eternal, from which we can also receive a present and eternal effect (*OP,* 76, 1, 886).[40]

Because of the subsistence of Jesus' humanity in the Word, the human Jesus participates in eternity itself, and this in such a way that he is able to be a contemporaneous and active influence in the universe even now. Here Bérulle, in his very original manner, has given us Aquinas's teaching on the instrumentality of the humanity of Christ:

> If we regard his humanity, it is still a life and source of life, in a way proper to it, emanating from and dependent upon the mystery of the Incarnation, which unites the human and divine natures in one person, and makes this human nature alive and vivifying, by the spirit of the divinity which reposes and dwells in it as a primordial life. . . . And Saint Thomas views not only this nature, but the passion which is but an accident of this nature . . . as not only a meritorious cause, but even an efficient cause of life (*OP,* 29, 3–4, 795; cf. *Summ. theol.,* 3, 48, 6c.).

Bérulle's Christ, then, is the glorified humanity of Jesus, the risen Jesus, still present and operative in the universe. Karl Rahner, in another context, has caught the meaning of Bérulle:

> The purpose of His life is perfectly accomplished in His Resurrection. . . . This is so true that everything that He was in the course of His history has entered into the glory of the Father. . . . When He meets us now as the resurrected Lord, He is Who He is because of His past. What

He experienced during His life now shows, as it were, its absolute and final face. He took His whole life and everything in it with Him into glory.[41]

From this highly active and contemporaneous notion of the glorified Savior, Bérulle is able to derive his Christic universe. In brief, the deified, risen
Lord founds a "divinized" universe.[42] The "state" of the glorified humanity of Jesus is the "origin of the various states of grace and glory" (*OP*, 99,
1, 941). In this sense, "We are a capacity, a pure capacity, for Christ; he is
the only one who can fill and fulfill us' (*OP*, 143, 3, 1015).

The Christification of Life in Bérulle and Olier

The later writings of Bérulle reflect a desire to work out, in a less
speculative and more personal manner, the implications of his Christological spirituality. In particular, while the *Grandeurs* concentrates on man's
universal participation in Christ, his later reflections turn upon the *unique*
ways in which this participation is accomplished. But a treatment of Bérulle would be terribly inadequate if it did not indicate how he *practically*
envisioned the implications of his Christology. To this effect, then, I will
briefly indicate Bérulle's master insights, and then turn to Jean-Jacques
Olier, the founder of Saint Sulpice, and the one to formulate most succinctly the *praxis* of the French school.

In Bérulle's mind, the Christic universe has a "Christic character."
The state of the glorified humanity of Jesus renders, in some way, every
human state "Christ-conforming." Thus, the great spiritual task is not to
become something we are not, but to surrender ourselves to what we already are, in our very being, because of Jesus. Bérulle particularly likes to
underline the states of *servitude* and *adoration* that characterize his Christic
tic world. Both are ontological characteristics of human reality, capable of
being personally intensified only through surrender to them:

> I know the state in which you exist. This is God's way for you, and a
> way which honors the sacred mystery of the Incarnation, and the *anéan-*
> *tissement* of the creature which is in this mystery, and the absolute de-
> pendence of the humanity upon the divinity. . . . This state creates
> various states in people and creates in you this dependence in which you
> exist (*CB*, 3P, 686, 333–334).

Likewise, the entire eleventh discourse of the *Grandeurs* celebrates the
state of adoration of Jesus, "alone adoring by his state," because the humanity of Jesus is nothing but a "regard for God." Bérulle's conclusion is
obvious: "This Man-God has the power of rendering men gods in infinite
manners, all regarding, honoring, imitating, and dependent upon that by
which he is God and man at the same time" (*OP*, 147, 5, 1025). Again,

Bérulle is giving expression to his own relational anthropology. As the Man-God is constituted by relationship, so this same Man-God creates a relational characteristic in man himself. Servitude and adoration are but expressions for man's relational makeup. The true definition of man himself is not to be found in considering man as complete in himself. Man is relational, a "servant" and an "adorer," and thus can only be seen in his totality when viewed in the context of God, his source and ground of meaning.

To my mind it was Olier, among Bérulle's followers, who both preserved in his own poetic way the full richness of Bérullian thought, and formulated a sort of Christological *mantra* for the French school. Other followers, such as De Condren, Eudes, and De Montfort, concentrated on specific Bérullian themes—servitude/sacrifice, devotion to the crib, and devotion to Mary, respectively—and in some way sacrificed the full depth and balance of Bérulle. Not so Olier. As Bremond put it, "His special grace and mission was, not exactly to popularize Bérullism, but to present it with such limpidity, richness of imagination and fervour that its apparently somewhat difficult metaphysics are placed invitingly in the reach of most readers."[43] What I have found most helpful in Olier is his formulation of Bérulle's Christocentrism into a sort of *mantra* for the Christian life. It is appealing both because of its simplicity and because Olier discovered it through his own rich mystical experience.[44] It was this Christological *mantra* of Olier's that later led to the famous Sulpician method of meditation. Unfortunately, however, this method lost much of Olier's simplicity and was greatly elaborated and mechanized.[45]

Olier has provided us a neat formulation of his *mantra:* "We really believe that we are here giving a method which will make this exercise much easier. . . . It consists in *having our Lord before our eyes, in our heart and in our hands.*" And bringing out this method's Bérullian character, Olier adds:

> Christianity consists in . . . regarding Jesus, uniting ourselves to Jesus, and acting in Jesus . . . joined to the power of Jesus Christ. . . . The first is called adoration; the second, communion; the third, cooperation.[46]

The simplicity of this method is entirely appropriate to its Bérullian inspiration. Here we are not in the realm of the tedious, analytical, and dissective forms of prayer fostered by an overemphasized rationalism, but in the calm atmosphere fostered by a consciousness aware of its relation to its ground and source of meaning. The method is suprarational and intuitive, in the tradition of Augustine and the Greek fathers. The focus is not introspective and narcissistic, but relational and unitive: "joined to the power of Jesus Christ." What Olier seeks to foster and deepen is the relational man of Bérulle, united with the glorified and risen Savior.

As a method, the technique is one of "centering" and "localization."

Olier, like Bérulle, wants us to center ourselves on Jesus, and thereby free ourselves from our isolationism. As Van Kaam put it in another context:

> This reflection is not divisive but unitive. It is transcendent. It makes whole; it attunes us to a mysterious totality that already is; it is a healing reflection . . . a gentle preservation of all things as given and as tenderly held in the splendor of a Divine Presence. . . . When a person is always looking at himself merely introspectively he cannot help but become mesmerized by all the limiting dimensions of his person, life, and situation.[47]

Such centering, if continually entered into, can lead to an inner calmness, a sort of "localization," freeing the individual to experience the *fond de notre âme,* as Olier puts it, the deepest self-as-related-to-Christ. *"Fond"* is, of course, the consecrated term of the mystics for this deepest self, in contrast to the isolated and more artificial self. The method's purpose, then, is to foster and regain one's deeper, Christic consciousness. That is the meaning of "Jesus before our eyes," or "adoration," that Bérullian state of relationship to one's ultimate ground of meaning.

While one gets the impression that the method should lead immediately to its next movement—"Jesus in our heart"—Olier's text makes it clear that he is really describing the work of an entire life: *de faire un coeur nouveau* through the *onction divine* of Jesus' spirit. What Olier means is that as one more fully summons forth this deeper, Christic consciousness, the entire quality of one's life begins to change and take on a Christic character. The Christic consciousness becomes a principle of self-determination, penetrating more deeply the levels of one's "being," a word which is a modern equivalent of Olier's more biblical and mystical "heart." Olier is giving us here a Bérullian rendition of the Eastern "prayer of the heart." The image of the *onction divine* makes it clear that Olier has in mind a *healing (onction)* process, reaching ever deeper levels of the self. He has synthesized here the Bérullian teaching on Christ as "the only one who can fill and fulfill us," the risen Christ who is "still a life and source of life." In line with this the third movement—"Jesus in our hands"—describes the Christified person's ability to Christify all he touches. In another work Olier makes it clear that this form of prayer is oriented to a transformation of one's world: "There is in prayer a third part, which some people call resolution, but which may more properly be called cooperation, which is the fruit of prayer and extends throughout the day."[48] Olier is envisaging here the gradual Christification of the universe itself, thereby neatly recapitulating Bérulle's Christic universe.

Olier, then, neatly sums up the Bérullian teaching, as well as the entire patristic and medieval tradition that converges in Bérulle. Peter Faber, interestingly, was already aware of this: "The method of St. Sulpice . . . is faithfully based upon the traditions of the ancient fathers and the saints of the desert. . . . And in confirmation of this he quotes Ambrose, whose own method of prayer consists in *"Signaculum in fronte ut semper confiteamur* [adoration]; *signaculum in corde ut semper diligamus* [communion]; *signaculum in brachio ut semper operemur* [cooperation]."*[49]*

Bérulle and the Evolution of Christian Thought

Erich Neumann has recently conjectured that the basic crisis confronting today's person is the overdifferentiation and exaggeration of man's own rational consciousness.[50] It is as if, in discovering his own mind's ability to understand and control reality, man has absolutized reason and reduced himself to rationality alone. What ensues is that the fullness of man is lost. On the one hand, all of reality is judged by the court of reason, and realities that were once thought to transcend reason—God, for example, and the supernatural—become mere "projections" of man's rational consciousness. Furthermore, this reduction of man to reason forces the nonrational and suprarational aspects of man, such as the unconscious and supraconscious, "underground," where they remain uncontrolled and unbalanced. At a certain point they erupt, in defense against reason's repression. Should this occur, and Neumann thinks it has in our own time, the way is clear for mass neurosis and social irrationality. Neumann reminds us of Nazism to bring home his point.

This brief use of Neumann's more subtle psychoanalytic exploration of society serves as an excellent background for assessing the contribution of Bérulle and his French school to Christian thought. For Bérulle stood at that turning point in Western history when man was discovering his own rational consciousness in a heightened way. The new sciences, the new philosophy, the new awareness of history turned man's attention increasingly to himself and his rational ego. What began as a fascination for man became a fixation on man. The ideal of the "individual," complete in himself, slowly emerged and fascinated Western society. What distinguishes Bérulle from the *devotio moderna* and much of the Scholasticism of his time is that he creatively dealt with these new developments, seeking not to reject anthropocentrism, but to integrate it into a more complex Christian synthesis. The *devotio moderna,* on the other hand, unwittingly capitulated to them.

On the one hand, Bérulle sought to discover a more wholistic view of man. His early writings evidence a sort of capitulation to the Renaissance individualism. Yet the exigencies of his own personal experience led him to search the wealth of the Christian tradition for a fuller, relational view of man, man-as-originating-from-a-divine-source-of-meaning. The superb *élévations* of the *Grandeurs* reveal an individual attuned to a Divine Source of meaning. On the other hand, and here we encounter the greatest originality of our author, Bérulle knew the danger of the irrational, which already had erupted in his own time against the excesses of an overdifferentiated rationalism. We are referring here to the exaggerated mysticism of the seventeenth century, the attempt to escape from a life cut off from a Divine

Source of meaning through a pretended absorption in God. It is here that I would place what was later to be called "Jansenism." Bérulle's "conversion" to Christocentrism *is* his humanism, if you will. It is the manner in which he integrated the new man-centered concerns of the Renaissance into a higher Christian synthesis. It is the way in which he showed that there is no escape from man's created, human nature, no surpassing of the human. Because man remains man, his only access to the Divine Meaning is and forever remains human: the risen humanity of Jesus, which sums up the earthly Jesus and the human road he traveled to the Father. Bérulle showed himself to be a "humanist," too. But not any meaning of the "human" would do. For Jesus' humanity is the true archetype of humanity. In this original way, Bérulle recaptures what I have called a "Christic God-concept," in which God remains mankind's dialogical partner through the risen Christ.

Yet, difficulties exist in appropriating Bérulle for today. *One is personal.* By this I mean that Bérulle is thoroughly altruistic. His focus, at least in his mature thought, is away from the self and toward the risen Jesus. He is convinced that one will find himself by losing himself, as it were, in the Other, in Jesus. There is little room in Bérulle for the spiritual adolescent, concerned for himself. Olier's *Mémoires* are perhaps the only "nod" of the French School to the genuine needs of Christian adolescence. Yet, we must all pursue adulthood, and Bérulle can be a guide along the way.

A second difficulty is cultural. Bérulle, as Bremond warns us, is thoroughly French, from the era of the "magnificent monarchy." A cultural distance separates us from him. His work is filled with the passion of the French, whether in describing man's weakness—*anéantissement*—or his greatness—"We are a pure capacity for Christ." The *Grandeurs* reflects the magnificence of the court, and his Christ, the "Sun King." His predilection for dionysian hierarchies and his love of the word *estat* echo the highly structured society of pre-revolutionary France. Bérulle's man of *anéantissement* calls to mind the perfectly controlled servant of the court, or the nobleman totally dedicated to the monarch. Of course, this should not surprise us, for the greatness of any theological synthesis is partly measured by its ability to resonate with the cultural needs of the day. John of the Cross, after all, has much of the Andalusian *Conquistador* in his rugged *nada, nada.* Yet, when all due allowances have been made, perhaps too much of monarchical France is echoed in the nobility of Bérullism.

A final difficulty is theological. There is the problem, already mentioned, of the image of Christ fostered in Bérullism. The idealized and noble Christ of Bérulle is thoroughly Johannine, yet without the balance of the synoptics. The thoroughly human nature of Christ does not always come through, and thus ultimately neither does the Divine *Pathos.* The privation of human subsistence in Jesus, although thoroughly inspired by Aquinas and Cajetan, and found even today in De La Taille and Rahner, hinders a full appreciation of the human Jesus. Bérulle's intention was, of course, to bring home the enduring relevancy of Jesus' humanity, the glorious and risen Jesus, who sums up his past and introduces it as a salvific force within the universe even today. Yet his excurses on Jesus' desert experience and passion seem too noble and idealized. This idealized image of Jesus is linked with the Neo-Platonic exemplarism permeating Bérulle. James Mackey has recently written that exemplarism involves

> . . . a divinity conceived as a transcendent mind which is the locus of the exemplar plan according to which this empirical universe and all that is in it is structured and functions. Such a concept of divinity . . . gave a tremendous boost to the confidence with which Christian teachers could talk about the content of divine revelation.[51]

Bérulle's Christ is within this exemplarist tradition. He is too much the exemplar plan, and not sufficiently human and historical, subject to the randomness and contingency of history itself. What needs to be done is, with Gordon Kaufman, to reinterpret the doctrine of exemplarism, to view the *imago Dei* in terms "of man's historicalness, his historicity. Thus, the very characteristic that makes man unique among finite beings, lifting him above all others, is his historicity, his being created in the 'image of God.'"[52] That such a reinterpretation of the *imago Dei* tradition is possible makes sense in terms of the historical view of the God-concept we have developed throughout these pages.

In the end, however, Bérulle remains an important guide and witness within the Christian tradition. His critical method, his refusal simply to capitulate to the *Zeitgeist* of the times, is still a relevant method. And further, his great ability to synthesize and probe the implications of the tradition is terribly needed now in an increasingly complex age. With Bérulle as a guide, one can know that he is meeting the enduring values of Christianity.

Notes

1. Cf. Jean Dagens, *Bérulle et les origines de la restauration catholique (1575–1611)* (Paris: Desclée de Brouwer, 1952), upon whom I am relying.

2. Cited by Dagens, *ibid.,* pp. 39–40.

3. Fr. Vandenbroucke, "Le Divorce entre Théologie et Mystique," NOUVELLE REVUE THÉOLOGIQUE 72 (1950), 372–389, traces the direct cause of the split between theology and spirituality to the fifteenth-century rationalism of the schools, and the spiritual reaction against this primarily in the *devotio moderna.*

4. Cf. *Correspondence de Bérulle* (hereafter *CB*), J. Dagens, ed (Paris: Desclée de Brouwer, 1937–1939), 3, 20–21.

5. Bonaventure's *Itinerarium* and Bérulle's *Grandeurs* are remarkably similar. The popularity of Bonaventure at Paris was in part due to Gerson, who saw in him a corrective to the rationalism of the schools. Further, Bonaventure had been proclaimed a doctor of the Church in 1587. A pontifical edition of his works appeared between 1588 and 1596, and his thought greatly penetrated two influences upon Bérulle: Denis the Carthusian and Harphius.

6. Dagens, *op. cit.,* p. 31, cites *Discours de l'estat et des grandeurs de Jésus* (hereafter *G*), 4, 1, 211–212, as perhaps an indication of this: "Et comme selon le grand auteur que l'on nomme Aréopagite. . . ." A careful work on Denis is R. Roques, *L'univers dionysien: structure hiérarchique du monde selon le pseudo-Denys* (Paris: Aubier, 1954). My citations from Bérulle are, unless otherwise noted, from *Oeuvres complètes,* P. Bourgoing, ed. (1585–1662; reedited by Maison D'Institution de L'Oratoire, Villa Bethanie, Montsoult Seine-et-Oise, 1960, 2 vols., being the *editio princeps*). The Migne edition (1856) is a less accurate and less critical one.

7. Dagens, *ibid.*

8. *Ibid.,* p. 36. Cf. also for the sources of Bérulle, J. Huijben, "Aux sources de la spiritualité française du XVIIe siècle," LA VIE SPIRITUELLE 25 (1930), 113–139, 26 (1931), 17–46, 75–111, 27 (1931), 20–42, 94–122; Emile Mersch, "The French School: The Mystical Body and the Spiritual Life," in his *The Whole Christ* (London: Dennis Dobson, 1962), pp. 531–555; and Eugene A. Walsh, "The Sources of the French School's Teaching," in his *The Priesthood in the Writings of the French School: Bérulle, De Condren, Olier* (S.T.D. diss., Washington, D.C.: Catholic University of America, 1949), pp. 24–34.

9. Well explained by Dagens, *ibid.,* pp. 308–321. For the controversy on the place of Jesus in the Spanish mystics, see Tomas de la Cruz, "The Carmelite School: St. Teresa and St. John of the Cross," in *Jesus in Christian Devotion and Contemplation* (St. Meinrad, Indiana: Abbey, 1974, pp. 86–101.

10. Cited by Dagens, *ibid.,* pp. 307–308. Perhaps William Johnston's interpretation is closer to what Eckhart intends, although it surely was not understood in this way in the sixteenth and seventeenth centuries: "The Church fathers loved to quote the words of Jesus: 'It is to your advantage that I go away' (John 16.7); and they would comment that by his departure and the ensuing separation Jesus was liberating the disciples from excess absorption, leading them on to the cosmic dimension of his risen existence" (*Silent Music,* p. 163).

11. Cited by Dagens, *ibid.,* p. 308.

12. *Ibid.,* p. 311.

13. P. Bourgoing, "Préface des oeuvres de Bérulle," p. xix (Montsoult ed.). For Augustine, cf. *Sermo* 143 (*PL* 38, 786) and *In Joan. evan.* 94 (*PL* 35, 1869); for Aquinas: "We ought not to rest in it [i.e., Jesus' humanity] as an end in itself, but through it we should reach out to God" (*In Joan.* 7, 32; cf. *Summ. theol.,* 2–2, 82, 3, 9).

14. Teresa of Avila, *Life, Written by Herself* (London, 1916), 22, 12, as cited by William Johnston, *The Mysticism of the Cloud of Unknowing* (New York: Desclee, 1967), pp. 75–76.

15. Johnston, *ibid.,* p. 76, citing John of the Cross, *Ascent,* 3, 3, 6.

16. Cf. Bérulle's famous "second birth of Jesus in time" in *G,* discourse eleven.

17. Henri Bremond, *A Literary History of Religious Thought in France* 3, *The Triumph of Mysticism* (London: SPCK, 1936), p. 1.

18. Cf. Karl Rahner, *On Prayer* (New York: Paulist, 1958), pp. 20–21.

19. Jean Orcibal, *Le cardinal de Bérulle: évolution d'une spiritualité* (Paris: Cerf, 1965), esp. pp. 58–84.

20. Bérulle, *Oeuvres de controverse,* 1, 5, 686.

21. Bérulle, *Collationes,* 245, as cited by Orcibal, *op. cit.,* p. 80.

22. Orcibal, *ibid.,* pp. 113–114, has well brought out the apologetic nature of

the *Grandeurs.* Cf. Paul Cochois, *Bérulle et l'école française* (Paris: Seuil, 1963), pp. 30–43, for an overview of the vow controversy.

23. Cited by Cochois, *ibid.*, p. 32.

24. *Ibid.*, p. 33.

25. The chronology is as follows: As perpetual visitator of the Carmelites, a position that he received because of his Teresian leanings, he prescribed the vow to Mary in 1615 for all of the nuns at their solemn profession; Duval, a co-superior of the Carmelites, considered it a "fourth" canonical vow and alerted Rome. Madame Acarie, who had entered the Carmelites, disapproved of the vow and lent her influence against Bérulle. Meanwhile, Bérulle acted more prudently, and allowed only those nuns to take the vow who wished. However, the success of the Oratory seems to have antagonized the Jesuits. In any case, a number of Jesuits lent their influence against Bérulle, and when an unfortunate wording (seemingly monophysitic) of the vow was found in 1620, Bérulle's opponents convinced the universities of Louvain and Douai to condemn it. Interestingly, the Jesuit Lessius admitted having been misinformed and came over to Bérulle's side.

26. Van Kaam, *op. cit.,* pp. 78–79.

27. Cf. Julien-Eymard d'Angers, "L'exemplarisme bérullian," REVUE DES SCIENCES RELIGIEUSES 31 (1957), 122–132.

28. M. Dupuy, *Bérulle et le sacerdoce: Étude historique et doctrinale* (Paris: Bibliothèque d'histoire et d'archéologie chrétiennes, 1968), p. 151.

29. Bérulle, *Collationes,* 1151, as cited by Orcibal, *op. cit.,* p. 104. For Bérulle's relational anthropology, see Orcibal, pp. 102–113, and the excellent study of R. Bellemare, *Le sens de la créature dans la doctrine de Bérulle* (Paris: Desclée de Brouwer, 1959).

30. Bremond, *op. cit.,* p. 17, and pp. 22–25, n. 1; cf. also p. 26: "Is not this the purest theocentrism?"; and p. 32, citing Gilson, in reference to another Oratorian: "One feels in him, as in the Cardinal De Bérulle, a constant anxious care to exalt God over all else, a sort of ardour to withdraw Him as far as possible into infinity." Michel Dupuy, *Bérulle: une spiritualité de l'adoration* (Tournai: Desclée, 1964), pp. 51–52, describes the difference in accent between Bérulle's and Loyola's theocentrism: "Bérulle s'efforce de découvrir le créé à la lumière de la relation à Dieu qui le fait exister; ce n'est pas cette relation qui doit être découverte dans l'object [as for Loyola], mais l'object qui doit être découvert grâce à cette relation antérieurement connue comme pensée et volonté divines."

31. Louis Cognet, "Bérulle et la Théologie de l'Incarnation," XVIIe SIECLE 29 (1955), 331.

32. Cf. the whole of discourse two of the *Grandeurs,* which celebrates Jesus' own *anéantissement.* This latter term possibly comes from Ruysbroeck and the German mystics. Cf. Dupuy, *Bérulle: une spiritualité,* p. 81, n. 28.

33. *M* 233 (unpublished archive material at the Oratory), as cited by Cochois, *op. cit.,* pp. 77–78.

34. William Johnston, translator, *The Cloud of Unknowing* (Garden City, N.Y.: Doubleday Image, 1973), introduction, p. 12.

35. Fernando Guillen Preckler, "*État" chez le Cardinal de Bérulle: Théologie et spiritualité des "états" bérulliens,* Analecta Gregoriana 197 (Roma: Università Gregoriana, 1974), p. 63, referring to *G,* 9, 4, 316–317. The entire structure of the *Grandeurs* is Christological: an introduction to the incarnation (discourse one), a Christological grounding of the vow of servitude in the form of an elevation (dis-

course two), the unity (discourses three and four) and the communication of God in the incarnation (discourses five through nine), and three discourses on the three "births" of the *Logos,* in eternity, in time, and in glory (discourses ten through twelve).

36. Perhaps here Bérulle is following Cyril of Alexandria's notion of the Spirit as the *sumpleroma* of the Trinity (Cf. Cognet, *art. cit.,* 336). He also approaches the Greek notion of the epiclesis, which he alludes to in *G,* 6, 2, 246.

37. Cf. Orcibal, *op. cit.,* p. 101, and Thomas Aquinas, *Summ. theol.,* 2, 17, 2.

38. Cognet, *art. cit.,* 351.

39. To paraphrase Orcibal, *op. cit.,* p. 108: ". . . Bérulle prolonge sa christologie par la perspective de la naissance spirituelle en l'âme de la seconde personne de la Trinité."

40. Here we have the Bérullian equivalent of Aquinas's notion of the perennially efficacious *antiqua caritas* of Christ (Cf. *Summ. theol.,* 3, 22, 2, 3), and the redemption understood not *in facto esse* but *in fieri* (Cf. *Summ. theol.,* 3, 50, 6).

41. Rahner, *Spiritual Exercises,* pp. 245–246. Cf. William Johnston's helpful thoughts in his introduction to *The Cloud of Unknowing,* p. 17: "Now the Christian, following St. Paul, does not pray just to a historical figure but to the now existing risen Christ who contains in himself all the experience of his historical existence in a transformed way, as he indicated by showing his wounds to his disciples. As for the way of talking about the Christ who lives in our midst today, Teilhard de Chardin . . . speaks of the 'cosmic Christ' who is co-extensive with the universe. By death the body is universalized, entering into a new dimension and into a new relationship with matter. It is in this dimension that the risen Christ is present to us."

42. In general, as Preckler, *op. cit.,* pp. 153–159, notes, Bérulle speaks unqualifiedly of the deified humanity of Jesus. Although he will speak of the divinization of the individual Christian, particularly in his *Elévation sur sainte Madeleine,* he prefers terms like "divine" or "effects from God."

43. Bremond, *op. cit.,* p. 393. Works on Olier are presently in a state of flux, as the Sulpicians engage in an attempt to reconstruct his authentic works. Gilles Chaillot particularly, through a careful study of the authentic and still unpublished *Mémoires,* is enabling us to retrieve the original Olier. Textual analysis reveals that Olier's published works have been emended so as to mollify his mysticism. Cf. Chaillot, "La pedagogie spirituelle de M. Olier d'après ses 'Mémoires,'" BULLETIN DE SAINT-SULPICE 2 (1976), 27–68.

44. Cf. Gilles Chaillot, "Les premières leçons de l'expérience mystique de Monsieur Olier," BULLETIN DU COMITÉ DES ÉTUDES 40 (1962), 501–543, thus correcting Bremond, *op. cit.,* pp. 359–391, who averred that Olier was more of a neurotic than a mystic.

45. Cardinal Lercaro, "Sulpician Prayer," in *Methods of Mental Prayer* (Westminster, MD: Newman, 1957), pp. 107–130, has traced the various accretions to Olier's method. It is traditional to oppose the intuitive Sulpician method to the more discursive Ignatian one. Cf., for example, "Remarques de P. Faber sur la méthode de S. Ignace et sur la méthode de S.-Sulpice," in G. Letourneau, *La méthode d'oraison mentale du séminaire de Saint-Sulpice* (Paris: Victor Lecoffre, 1903), pp. 286–320. Contemporary Ignatian studies are nuancing this somewhat; cf. Hugo Rahner, *Ignatius the Theologian* (New York: Herder and Herder, 1968), esp. pp. 181–213.

46. Jean-Jacques Olier, *Introduction à la vie et aux vertus chrétiennes* (Paris: Migne, 1856), Chapter 4.

47. Van Kaam, *op. cit.,* pp. 175, 185.

48. Jean-Jacques Olier, *Catéchisme chrétien pour la vie intérieur* (Paris: Migne, 1856), lesson 8. Exemplifying his Bérullian theocentrism, Olier prefers "cooperation" to "resolution" because it emphasizes the Spirit's power in prayer.

49. Cf. Letourneau, *op. cit.,* pp. 286–287, and pp. 304–305. The citation to Ambrose is unfortunately unreferenced.

50. Neumann, *op. cit.,* pp. 363–394.

51. Mackey, *The Problems of Religious Faith,* p. 157.

52. Kaufman, *Systematic Theology,* pp. 330, 349.

IX

EXPLORING THE CHRIST-EXPERIENCE IV: THOMAS MERTON'S TRANSCULTURAL CHRIST

Transculturalization and the Need for a Unifying Myth

A notable number of scholars have called attention to the fact that our world is currently undergoing a process known variously as "world unification," "cosmification," or to use Thomas Merton's term, "transculturalization."[1] Karl Jaspers's formulation of this phenomenon is most helpful: "What is historically new and for the first time in history decisive about our situation is the real unity of mankind on the earth. The planet has become for man a single whole dominated by the technology of communications; it is 'smaller' than the Roman Empire was formerly."[2] Jaspers does not mean that this new experience of worldwide unity has yet been satisfactorily integrated by modern man. His work gives one the impression that this new experience is summoning humanity to a new understanding of unity and simultaneously a new, less provincialistic mode of existence. John Dunne probably gives us a more realistic estimate of how modernity is coping with our new planetary situation: he speaks of the world wars as the most obvious signs that a new transition is occurring in history. But those wars have come from a failure to enter into this new transition, and they illustrate just how deadly this failure can be:

> As for the massiveness and inevitability of the events, it is perhaps only the massiveness and inevitability that always makes its appearance when a journey of the spirit is called for and does not occur. There are two ways of going through life, Jung has said. One is to walk through upright and the other is to be dragged through. . . . The transition . . . to world history is something man can walk through upright on a journey of the spirit, or it is something he can be dragged through in a series of world wars.[3]

What are some of the indications that one is being dragged through this process? One such, for Jaspers, is that the "masses have become a decisive factor in the historical process." What he seems to mean is that our new planetary experience entails a constant exposure to conflicting cultural experiences, world views, ideologies, and counterclaims among the world's nations. While this could be the necessary precondition for a new and richer kind of identity for nations and individuals, it often fosters the loss of identity. The "masses" is Jaspers's term for a people losing its identity. Such a loss spawns an experience of doubt on a democratized scale. This in turn leads to the formulation of ideologies in the sense of dogmatic systems that legitimate a sectarian or ghetto-like insularism. For Jaspers, what is new about this ideological strategy is its planetary extensiveness: "But perhaps the formation of ideologies really is particularly great in its compass today. For in hopelessness there arises the need for illusion, in the aridity of personal existence the need for sensation, in powerlessness the need to violate those who are even more powerless."[4] Thus the stage is set for what Jaspers calls the tendency toward simplification: the use of easy slogans, simplistic solutions, the seeking out of scapegoats—all simply easily discernible defense mechanisms cloaking a basically disintegrating identity.

I have begun with Jaspers's somewhat negative appraisal lest we approach the phenomenon of planetization too naïvely, without an awareness of the profound development in human consciousness being called for in our times. In fact, Jaspers is even more ominous: "For whereas all previous periods of crucial change were local and susceptible of being supplemented by other happenings in other places, in other worlds, so that even if they failed the possibility of the salvation of man by other movements was left open, what is happening now is absolutely decisive."[5] Yet Dunne has told us, following Jung, that it is possible to walk through upright on a journey of the spirit, and it is here that I would place the contribution of Thomas Merton. Raimundo Panikkar tells us that this second approach is forging a new, unifying myth for our times:

> In fact, many people today clearly sense the insufficiency of their particular cultures and religions, and see further that no one has a monopoly on goodness or truth, but cannot yet discern what is emerging even as their own life-patterns disintegrate. We still lack a universal horizon, a reference point accepted because it is acceptable, a unifying myth for our times. But it is being born; it is dawning on the horizon.[6]

Here we have a certain disintegration of identity occurring too. But whereas our first identity-corrosion stemmed from a neurotic regression from growth, this one seems to be the necessary precondition for the "rebirth" of a richer, more universalized consciousness. This is a consciousness in search of a "myth" to give it orientation and meaning. Presumably a person whose life could be illuminated by such a unifying myth would possess the psychic capacity to undertake the planetary journey upright.[7] The question, of course, turns on how we should realistically expect such a myth to emerge. Historically one would expect the great religions to be a natural source, since they are the guardians of mankind's mythical inheritance. Panikkar seems to hope this will be the case: "If the venerable traditions of mankind do not collaborate in forging a new consciousness, this latter will emerge without their direct contribution."[8] It is here that I would place the contribution of Thomas Merton, for few thinkers within the Western Christian tradition have done more than he to draw upon the rich resources of the Christian heritage to forge a new unifying "myth," or, to speak of its psychological correlate, a new unifying consciousness. Although this is an estimate of Merton's work widely shared, perhaps it would be well to specify in an introductory way why I think Merton's work is worthy of special merit.

First, in line with Merton's view of the monk and solitary as one who takes the chance, as he put it, "to explore, to risk, to abandon himself sagaciously to untried possibilities,"[9] Merton viewed himself somewhat paradigmatically as forging a new planetary consciousness:

> If I can unite in myself the thought and the devotion of Eastern and Western Christendoms, the Greek and Latin Fathers, the Russians with the Spanish mystics, I can prepare in myself the reunion of divided Christians. From that secret and unspoken unity in myself can eventually come a visible and manifest unity of all Christians. If we want to bring together what is divided, we can not do so by imposing one division upon the other or absorbing one division into the other. But if we do this, the union is not Christian. It is political and doomed to further conflict. We must contain all divided worlds in ourselves and transcend them in Christ.[10]

Secondly, Merton accepted Karl Rahner's thesis of the diaspora situation of contemporary Christianity.[11] This means that the inherited form of "Christendom"—in which Christianity is the dominant religious institution of Western culture—no longer prevails today. In other words, Christianity is undergoing a process of detachment from its inherited Western forms—it is being summoned to a form of transculturalization. Merton feels we may lament this but nonetheless it is a divine summons to us in Christianity. All this is worth saying. It confirms Merton's view that Christianity does not possess an answer ready-made for today's planetary world. It should further confirm the conviction that the collective consciousness Merton was attempting to forge was not yet another subterfuged form of Christian imperialism.

Thirdly, and perhaps most importantly for those of us in the Christian West, Merton was remarkably faithful to the Christian tradition precisely while forging his new transcultural vision. While I could easily supply citations, perhaps the following suffices:

> I think, then, that in our eagerness to go out to modern man and meet him on his ground, accepting him as he is, we must also be truly what we are. If we come to him as Christians we can certainly understand and have compassion for his unbelief. . . . But it would seem a bit absurd for us, precisely as Christians, to pat him on the arm and say: "As a matter of fact I don't find the Incarnation credible myself. Let's just consider that Christ was a nice man who devoted his life to helping others!"
>
> What is the use of coming to modern man with the claim that you have a Christian mission—that you are sent in the name of Christ—if in the same breath you deny Him by whom you claim to be sent?[12]

This Christ-fidelity in Merton, which as we shall shortly see is a Christ-mysticism, deserves careful consideration with respect to its potential contribution to Merton's transcultural consciousness. Here I think we reach the heart, the ultimate foundations, of Merton's insights into man's possible transculturalization. Recall our earlier citation and note the stress on Christ: "We must contain all divided worlds in ourselves and transcend them in Christ." Christ's role is equally stressed in Merton's "Eastern" works. In the context of his exploration of the similarities between Zen and Christianity, Merton affirms: "But Christian experience always has a special modality, due to the fact that it is inseparable from the mystery of Christ and the collective life of the Church, the Body of Christ."[13] And further, after pointing to the similarity between monastic "purity of heart" and Zen "emptiness," Merton adds:

> Purity of heart establishes man in a state of unity and emptiness in which he is one with God. But this is the necessary preparation not for further struggle between good and evil, but for the real work of God which is revealed in the Bible: the work of the *new creation*, the resurrection from the dead, the restoration of all things in Christ. This is the real dimension of Christianity, the eschatological dimension which is peculiar to it, and which has no parallel in Buddhism.[14]

We of the Christian West can draw at least two helpful consequences from Merton's Christocentrism. First, it suggests to us that Merton's transcultural consciousness was a genuine outgrowth of his own Christian experience, and thus a genuine development in his consciousness, and not a heterogeneous reality superimposed upon him from without and unintegrated into his life. Jung quite some time ago[15] emphasized the need for Western man to develop a collective consciousness *in his own way* and through his own tradition. Not only would this mean that such a consciousness would mark a genuine and integrated growth in Western man, but it would also keep that same Western man from "snatching" from the East and thus only further appeasing his own already over-fed ego. Perhaps this is what Bramachari was trying to teach Merton when he told him, not to immerse himself first in the East but to "turn West": "There are many beautiful mystical books written by the Christians. You should read St. Augustine's *Confessions* and *The Imitation of Christ*."[16]

Secondly, this fact that Merton's transcultural consciousness was a genuine outgrowth of his own earlier Christian experience illustrates what might be the most useful aspect of his vision for us at large. What I mean can be explained by drawing upon Eric Weil's perceptive insights on the nature of breakthroughs in history. As he put it, "A breakthrough happens only where and when it is admitted that the old way has led to a wall; but even then it will happen only if a turning is discovered that can be considered as prolonging the old way so that it does not become meaningless." For Weil a genuine breakthrough prolongs the authentic values of the past rather than negating them. Because it builds on the past, it avoids an esoteric character and is in principle "accessible and acceptable to everyone." As he further states it, "Breakthroughs are never total ruptures with the past; accommodation is not a sin but a characteristic of breakthroughs that change the outlook of humanity or great parts of it."[17] Now if Merton's transcultural consciousness is indeed a genuine outgrowth of his *Christian* experience, surely we are dealing here with a breakthrough that is in principle relevant for all Christians and indeed a genuine possibility for them. Let us then begin our exploration of Merton.

Merton's Transcultural Consciousness

Merton's most sustained treatment of the transcultural consciousness is to be found in his provocative essay "Final Integration: Toward a 'Monastic Therapy.' "[18] Accordingly we will first dwell on this essay, drawing upon Merton's other writings where helpful. Then we will explore the philosophical and theological foundations for his view, concluding with some observations on what this might imply for Merton's and our own Eastern pilgrimage.

The "Final Integration" essay is a monastic and theological commentary on A. Reza Arasteh's *Final Integration in the Adult Personality*,[19] a work which draws upon and critiques the psychoanalytic literature on identity formation especially in the light of Buddhism, Taoism, and Persian Sufism. "Final Integration" is Arasteh's term, not for the limited cure that results from adaptation to society and may take the form of a "useful" role in society, but for a far more radical and complete cure: "the final and complete maturing of the human psyche on a transcultural level."[20] Arasteh thinks that societal adaptation does not liberate the full personality, but rather fosters a *modus tolerandi*—or, as we would say, a way of coping—with one's illness and/or limited development. This is particularly true if the society to which one adapts is itself "unhealthy because of its overemphasis on cerebral, competitive, acquisitive forms of ego-affirmation,"[21] as Merton expresses it. Oftentimes the healing profession itself only unwittingly produces conformists, all the while thinking it is liberating the individual. Arasteh quotes E. Knight to this effect:

> For the moment . . . what is important to remark is that the Western individual, while opposing integration of the Russian and Chinese models, not only accepts the herd values of his society, but has invented psychoanalysis to prevent him from straying from them. . . . The stresses that modern life often produces in sensitive and intelligent people are no longer considered to call for a change in society; it is the individual who is wrong, and he consequently becomes a neurotic, not a revolutionary. No more remarkable device than psychoanalysis has ever been devised by a society for preventing its superior citizens from giving it pain. Even when, as in the case of Karen Horney, the values of a society are disapproved of, it is suggested that the best course open to the individual is to conform. . . . [22]

Accordingly, Arasteh distinguishes between a "neurotic anxiety" which accompanies capitulation to societal adaptation and "existential anxiety," essentially the refusal to so capitulate and the yearning or summons to further, if painful, growth and development. In Merton's words:

> . . . this anxiety is a sign of health and generates the necessary strength for psychic rebirth into a new transcultural identity. This new being is entirely personal, original, creative, unique, and it transcends the limits imposed by social convention and prejudice.[23]

Thus Arasteh would further distinguish between the normal "birth" from infantile symbiosis into socialization—which much psychoanalysis stresses—and a further "birth," normally occurring after socialization, into the transcultural state. A number of factors might foster this second birth; Arasteh highlights the following:[24] (1) dissatisfaction with society (as with Rousseau); (2) the inadequacy of reason as a sufficient guide in one's life (Al-Ghazzali); (3) the experience of intercultural pluralism (Nietzsche); (4) religious conversion (Rumi); (5) radical self-scrutiny (Socrates); (6) constant inner conflict and effort ('Attar); (7) aesthetic development (Khayyam, C. P. Snow); (8) meditative sensitivity to life's tragedies (Buddha); (9) the stimulation of a creative environment (Goethe); (10) and as the fruits of companionship and intimacy (Gilgamesh).

While all of this brings home the fact that the transcultural state is not unknown to prior ages, Merton, following Arasteh, thinks that our age is especially characterized by a need for it: "Birth on this higher level is an imperative necessity for man." And again:

> . . . whereas final psychological integration was, in the past, the privilege of the few, it is now becoming a need and aspiration of mankind as a

whole. The whole world is in an existential crisis to which there are various reactions, some of them negative, tragic, destructive, demonic, others proffering a human hope which is yet not fully clear.[25]

Perhaps I am not wrong to see in these observations Merton's awareness of the phenomenon of planetization with its simultaneous spectre of the masses being dragged through this process rather than walking through upright.

What, then, is the transcultural state? Since I find Merton's description, even if somewhat lyrical, more compact and centered on the essence than Arasteh's, I will begin with the former's.

> Final integration is a state of transcultural maturity far beyond mere social adjustment, which always implies partiality and compromise. The man who is "fully born" has an entirely "inner experience of life." He apprehends his life fully and wholly from an inner ground that is at once more universal than the empirical ego and yet entirely his own. He is in a certain sense "cosmic" and "universal man." He has attained a deeper, fuller identity than that of his limited ego-self which is only a fragment of his being.[26]

Several aspects demand our attention. First, I should indicate that Merton's transcultural personality is no merely syncretistic mind, something like the Renaissance image of the "universal man" who supposedly possessed universal knowledge, grasping the totality of truth presently available to mankind. This would be to think in terms of quantity while Merton is on the level of quality. Quite apart from the question of whether such a Renaissance individual ever actually existed in the first place, the contemporary reality of pluralism and the increasing specialization of knowledge would indicate that no one individual could any longer possess such "knowledge." In fact, one could make a case, I think, that as "knowledge" continues to specialize and complexify, we grow more ignorant, not less, at least in the quantitative sense of informational knowledge. What Merton has in mind is the emergence of a person of such inner calm and personal and cultural detachment that she is capable of recognizing and perspectivizing the genuine values present in every person and every culture.

Note Merton's further elaboration: "He has attained to a deep inner freedom—the Freedom of the Spirit we read of in the New Testament."[27] Narcissistic self-absorption and attachment are the problems. To the extent that one gains detachment from these she experiences the freedom of savoring and appreciating the values of others. Here we have something analogous to Ignatius Loyola's gift of *indiferencia,* that ability to be interiorly free from an excessive attachment to the partial so as to be sensitive to the greater whole. Merton tells us that this state should call "to mind the theology of St. Thomas on the Gifts of the Holy Spirit which move a man to act 'in a superhuman mode.' "[28] Following up this clue perhaps I would not be wrong to view the transcultural person as the wise man in Aquinas's sense. Inner freedom results in perspective, and perspectivizing is Aquinas's view of wisdom: "It is the wise man who orders, for the ordering of things is possible only with a knowledge of things in their mutual interrelations as well as in reference to something above and beyond them—their end."[29] In another context, Merton will refer to this state as the recovery of paradise and lost innocence, Adam and Eve's "purity of heart," in which "the individual has 'died' with Christ to his 'old man,' his exterior, egotistical self, and 'risen' in Christ to the new man, a selfless and divine being, who is the one Christ, the same who is 'all in all.' "[30]

Secondly, the transcultural person is not a-social but transsocial. Perhaps Merton's stress on social adaptation as always implying partiality and compromise might give the impression of a radically a-social attitude in Merton, which indeed some would claim does characterize the thought of the Merton of *The Seven Storey Mountain*. In any case, Merton scholars now generally agree that such an attitude was considerably modified by Merton in his middle and later periods, and he himself repudiated it.[31] The transcultural person, then, does not repudiate society but lives and acts within it from a standpoint higher than any limited society itself can offer. Again let us hear Merton's description:

> He is in a certain sense identified with everybody: or in the familiar language of the New Testament . . . he is "all things to all men." He is able to experience their joys and sufferings as his own, without however becoming dominated by them.
> He has embraced all of life. . . . He has experienced qualities of every type of life: ordinary human existence, intellectual life, artistic creation, human love, religious life. He passes beyond all these limiting forms, while retaining all that is best and most universal in them. . . . He accepts not only his own community, his own society, his own friends, his own culture, but all mankind.[32]

This transsocial perspective manifests itself dialectically. On the one hand the interior freedom from individual and social attachment fosters a critical awareness of self and society. This is, as it were, a deidolization and deabsolutizing of self and society: "He does not remain bound to one limited set of values in such a way that he opposes them aggressively or defensively to others."[33] While this critical awareness is perhaps a constant in Merton's later writings on the eremitical vocation, it is his superb "Notes for a Philosophy of Solitude" which reveals to us his polished view of the matter. While admitting and even praising society's role in lifting the individual above his own narrow interests and thus enabling him to achieve a certain measure of self-transcendence, Merton cautions that societies also "tend to lift a man above himself only far enough to make him a useful and submissive instrument in whom the aspirations, lusts and needs of the group can function unhindered by too delicate a personal conscience."[34] Merton especially singles out the fact that many a crime which no individual would commit on his own is easily committed in the name of the "common good." It is "arbitrary social imagery"[35] which is being deidolized. But on the other hand, the result of critical deabsolutizing of the partial and limited is the ability to perspectivize reality in its proper limits: ". . . he is able to bring perspective, liberty and spontaneity into the lives of others."[36] The problem, if you will, is neither the individual nor society, but fixation and absorption in either.

Merton's Transcultural Anthropology

Thirdly, then, and coming to the heart of the matter, Merton's vision of the transcultural state is grounded in a Christian theological anthropology. Here our focus should be the attempt to more clearly decipher that "inner ground that is at once more universal than the empirical ego and yet entirely [one's] own." We can gain a first, psychological approximation to what Merton means by noting his use of C. G. Jung's notion of the self:

> [the development of the person to full ripeness] is at once a charisma and a curse because its first fruit is the conscious and unavoidable segregation of the individual from the undifferentiated and unconscious herd. This means isolation, and there is no more comforting word for it. Neither family nor society nor position can save him from the fate, nor yet the most successful adaptation to his environment.[37]

Jung is telling us that the self is more than family, society, or position. Hence their inability to actualize the full potential of the self. Here we seem to meet the characteristic Mertonian distinction between the Cartesian, isolated self of modern man and the Christian relational self.[38] We have seen how the isolated self conforms well to the kind of technological society in which we live, in which stress falls upon out ability to master and harness the forces of reality. This is then idealized in the cult of the "independent" Western individual, wholly sufficient unto himself. Normally historians of thought would date the most extreme emergence of this kind of ego with the Renaissance and the rise, since then, of industry and technology. Now this seems to be what Merton has in mind when he claims: "Modern man, insofar as he is still Cartesian . . . is a subject for whom his own self-awareness as a thinking, observing, measuring and estimating 'self' is absolutely primary." But once this stress on self becomes primary "the more one tends to isolate himself in his own subjective prison, to become a detached observer cut off from everything else in a kind of impenetrable alienated and transparent bubble which contains all reality in the form of purely subjective experience."[39]

Merton differentiates from such a solipsistic view of the self one that is grounded in the New Testament, patristic, and mystical experience of selfhood, and which he variously calls the self "as a self-to-be-dissolved in self-giving," the self of "letting-go," or of "ecstasy." More fully:

> The self is not its own center and does not orbit around itself; it is centered on God, the one center of all, which is "everywhere and nowhere," in whom all are encountered, from whom all proceed. Thus from the very start this consciousness is disposed to encounter "the other" with whom it is already united anyway "in God."[40]

Here we meet, as we recall, not the isolated ego, but relationality as the image of full personhood. "Intimacy," "letting-go," "ecstasy"—these are all ways of speaking of self-development through relationships. This is the kind of self fostered by radical quests, adventure and surrender, in which the person delivers herself up to something/someone beyond herself and in so doing finds herself on a higher plane. Further, this self of surrender and relationality does not suppress the sense of individuality which is the hallmark of the ego. In one sense, it presupposes a basic ego-identity, for one must be somewhat self-assured to have the confidence to let go. On the other hand, it builds up or enriches the sense of individuality, insofar as one learns to differentiate the self precisely through relationships. We have here an exemplification of the Teilhardian principle that in the realm of persons union differentiates rather than annihilates the person. Union or relationality does not lead to merging and absorption in the other. There is rather "at once a total unity and a total alterity."[41] For Merton, this relational notion of selfhood is grounded in man's fundamental relationship to God. Man is a being-unto-God, and since God is a God-with-a-creation, a being-unto-others. The self is "centered on God . . . in whom all are encountered," as he put it.

All this must mean that the Mertonian self is co-constituted by a transcendent Self. The epistle to the Romans will express this as "The Spirit gives witness with our spirit that we are children of God" (8.16). Merton will say that the self finds his identity "not in the individual self as a separate, limited and temporal ego, but in Christ, or the Holy Spirit 'within' this self."[42] In summary, then, to return to our transcultural state, because Merton's self defines itself in terms of a transcendent source of identity, he is potentially able to relativize all things finite. But the other side of relativizing is totalizing. Refusing to define oneself in terms of partial aspects of reality allows the full range of human selfhood to emerge. Jung felt we would discover this through isolation. Merton placed his stress on solitude as the privileged means of coming to this fuller awareness of the self:

> The shallow "I" of individualism can be possessed, developed, cultivated, pandered to, satisfied: it is the center of all our strivings for gain and for satisfaction, whether material or spiritual. But the deep "I" of the spirit, of solitude and of love, cannot be "had," possessed, devel-

oped, perfected. It can only *be,* and *act* according to deep inner laws
which are not of man's contriving, but which come from God. They are
the Laws of the Spirit, who, like the wind, glows where He wills. This
inner "I," who is always alone, is always universal: for in this inmost "I"
my own solitude meets the solitude of every other man and the solitude
of God. Hence it is beyond division, beyond limitation, beyond selfish
affirmation. It is only this inmost and solitary "I" that truly loves with
the love and the Spirit of Christ. This "I" is Christ himself, living in us:
and we, in Him, living in the Father.[43]

Merton's Transcultural Christology

While a transcultural capacity has always been at least more compact-
ly and latently present within the Christian notion of the self—and analogously present within the self of the great religions, as Arasteh shows—and
even actually realized in certain individuals in history, Merton, under the
pressure of our current planetary situation, has been able to explicate its
reality in a more differentiated manner. But I think we can go further, and
here we come to our final point, and maintain that Merton's view of the
transcultural personality provides us with the creative underpinnings of a
deeper view of Christology itself, and thus, if you will, with a new Christ-
vision capable of fostering in the Christian West our transcultural consciousness.

What has Jesus Christ to do with our transcultural person, with what
Merton has called "the growth of a truly universal consciousness in the
modern world"?[44] I am persuaded that we must pursue the few hints that
Merton has left us on the relationship between Christ and transculturalization, for few Christian scholars would deny that Christology remains the
one real stumbling block to an authentic transculturalization of Christianity. One may, of course, deny the problem at the outset, by rationalistically
denying the "continued existence" of Jesus in the first place, viewing the
lofty claims for Jesus as nothing more than imperialistic projections onto
Christ on the part of Western Christendom. Nor would Merton deny that
this contains a partial truth, for he spoke of the "medieval temptation . . .
an integral part of 'Christendom' " which believed that "because the
Church is the Body of Christ, then the world owes the Church absolute
submission in everything."[45] Here we might especially think of the "imperial" term *Pantokrator* used by much of the tradition for Christ, of how
much it owes to the Roman-Byzantine court, and how it fostered or at
least legitimated a certain form of Christian imperialism.[46] Yet Merton
would not be congenial to a theological solution which would dismiss the
continuing centrality of Christ: "There are differences that are not debat-
able, and it is a useless, silly temptation to try to argue them out. Let them
be left intact until a moment of greater understanding."[47] I might further
add that this Christocentrism in Merton forms the central core of his importance for those of us in the Christian West. On the one hand, a rational-

istic dismissal of Christ may very well be another example of Western projection, the projection by the Cartesian self of Western Reason into an absolute. Such a view would not foster a genuine rapprochement with the East, which remains largely committed to the suprarational. On the other hand, while such a view might appeal to a small intellectual and esoteric elite, it might well fall under the heading of one of those "breakthroughs" in history that is so discontinuous with the Christian past that it becomes virtually meaningless to those formed by that past. Could one say that it shrinks or truncates the full depth of Christian experience? One of the characteristics of our transcultural person is precisely the absence of such truncating: "He passes beyond all . . . limiting forms, while retaining all that is best and most universal in them."

In any case, Merton draws an intrinsically direct connection between the transcultural state and Christ:

> For a Christian, a transcultural integration is eschatological. The rebirth of man and of society on a transcultural level is a rebirth into the transformed and redeemed time, the time of the Kingdom, the time of the Spirit, the time of "the end." It means a disintegration of the social and cultural self, the product of merely human history, and the reintegration of that self in Christ, in salvation history, in the mystery of redemption, in the Pentecostal "new creation." But this means entering into the full mystery of the eschatological Church.[48]

To understand this, I think it necessary to distinguish two levels of Christological reflection in Merton's work. The one, which with many scholars we can term a "Christology from above," takes the form in Merton of the traditional patristic *Logos* Christology. Perhaps most fully articulated in his *The New Man*,[49] this views Christ as God's very Image, in whom all creation is oriented, both as source and as goal. This is the Christological legacy of the fathers and of St. Bernard's Cistercian tradition. While this view has the strength of emphasizing our ontological relationship with Christ and thus would imply more for Christ than simply the limited historical role of a great moral example, it suffers from a number of defects and needs to be enriched and corrected by what scholars would call a Christology from below. I say this because the *Logos* Christology does not clarify the role of the humanity of Christ in the life of mankind. Its focus is "from above," the divine level, and it does not dwell upon an attempted this-worldly clarification of the role of Christ in terms of his humanity. Further, the *Logos* Christology tends to foster an a-historical view of the Divine dealings with mankind. It too easily thinks in terms of an a priori, eternally decreed blueprint for man—the "Divine Image"—and comes to terms neither with the contingent vicissitudes of real human history nor with the role of Christ's humanity in all of this.

If we then pursue a Christology from below, what connection can we draw between Jesus Christ and the transcultural state? Merton has clari-

fied, in an important essay, that when we speak of the humanity of Christ
now, it is of the *risen* humanity that we are speaking. It is in the context of
the controversy over the role of Christ's humanity in monastic prayer that
Merton makes this clear. In response to the claim of some "spiritualists"
that the highest form of contemplative prayer is one that rises beyond Jesus' humanity to wordless, imageless prayer, Merton responds with the
monastic tradition that such a view overlooks a fundamentally Christian
distinction; namely, "that between Christ, God and man, as He was before
His Passion and Resurrection, and Christ, God and man, as He now is in
the glory of the Father."[50] It is the risen humanity of Jesus that forever remains a present object of monastic prayer, and to whom Merton refers
when he speaks of transcultural rebirth as "in Christ."

Might I suggest, then, that Merton is asking us to view Jesus' resurrection as an event in which Jesus himself became the "finally integrated
man." This would require that we move beyond thinking of the resurrection in an extrinsicist manner, as an event which only "vindicated" Jesus,
and think of it as one which marked a decisive development in Jesus' very
own being. We have seen how the scriptures imply such an interpretation.
Luke's Jerusalem motif (Lk. 24.47) presents Jesus' death as a culminating,
rather than as a destructive, event. John's notion of Jesus' death as "the
hour" (Jn. 17.1) echoes a similar meaning. Similarly the biblical attempt to
differentiate carefully Jesus' resurrection from a mere resuscitation points
to some decisive transformation in Jesus' life.[51] Jesus' death, then, seems to
lead to what could be called a "final integration." Biblically speaking, Jesus' death is viewed not simply in destructive terms but as an "expansive
experience," perhaps because through it Jesus makes a final and decisive
surrender to his destiny into God.

This view of the matter would clearly correspond to Merton's Christian anthropology, as well as to our own view of the relational self. When
the person is viewed as destined for the Unlimited God, death then ceases
to be only a terrifying experience and can be viewed as an expansive one,
rendering us radically open to God. Accordingly, the biblical texts speak
of Jesus' death and resurrection as a "universalizing" experience: it leads
not to a world-absence but to a participation in God's universal worldly
presence. To quote John 12.32: "If I be lifted up from the earth, I will
draw all things to myself."

On the level of our own experience, William Johnston, we recall, suggested that we view the resurrection event as a movement "away from self-
centeredness towards cosmification,"[52] or as Merton would say, away from
the partial ego-self to the fully transcultural self. Johnston likens this to
what occurs in the experience of deep friendship: "a strange combination
of affection and detachment, of sincere, personal love for another and lim-
itless personal love for the universe, of deep emotional attachment without
self-centered clinging."[53] The aging process also comes to mind here. Often, this too is a process of disengagement and detachment, from self, from
others, from possessions, releasing new energies, a less limited love, a love

and care freed from clinging and partiality. We might recall how William Johnston brings this idea home:

> The Church Fathers loved to quote the words of Jesus: "It is to your advantage that I go away" (Jn. 16.7); and they would comment that by his departure and the ensuing separation Jesus was liberating the disciples from excess absorption, leading them on to the cosmic dimension of his risen existence. They might well have added that in all friendship separation plays an important role in leading friends away from absorption to an even greater universality.[54]

On this view, then, Jesus Christ would become the paradigm and the cause of final transcultural integration. The paradigm, for this view clarifies why Jesus is considered by Christians *the* revelation of God, for the finally integrated person is precisely the most complete way in which God could possibly reveal himself to mankind in human terms. The cause, because Jesus is now a principle of universalization in our midst, drawing us from partiality and compromise towards cosmification and universalization. This would not mean that as we grow in our relationship with Christ our other human relationships disappear, nor that our human brethren and our earthly world are mere means to a better relationship with Jesus. Rather, as a co-present principle of universalization Jesus draws us from that self-clinging which makes authentic relationships impossible.[55] Could Merton have had this in mind when he stated (?):

> ... the familiar phrase "seeing Christ in my brother" is subject to a sadly superficial interpretation. How many Christians there are ... who do not hesitate to assert that this involves a sort of mental sleight-of-hand, by which we deftly do away with our neighbor in all his concreteness, his individuality, his personality ... and replace him by a vague and abstract presence of Christ.
> Are we not able to see that by this pitiful subterfuge we end up by trying to love, not Christ in our brother, but Christ *instead* of our brother?
> Our faith ... is the needle by which we draw the thread of charity through our neighbor's soul and our own soul and sew ourselves together in one Christ. Our faith is given us not to see *whether* or *not* our neighbor is Christ, but to recognize Christ in him and to help our love make both him and ourselves more fully Christ.[56]

Merton's "Eastern Pilgrimage"

In conclusion, let me briefly note the implications that come to mind from Merton's transcultural vision for the progress of the East-West encounter. Here I should clarify that I am speaking primarily of the encounter of the world's great religions, since this was generally Merton's focus. As Merton was fully aware, our planetary situation is even further complicated by the reality of modern secularism in its many forms, which is itself a factor now transcending the West and entering the East. Although this goes beyond the limits of this essay, one might speculate that the future of secularism will be radically determined by the ability of the venerable religious traditions to forge a genuine transcultural consciousness. This should not necessarily mean the simple negation of all the values of our secular world by the religions. Would a consciousness be genuinely transcultural if it simply negated such values as the secular sense of the individual as an autonomous and free being, the Western sense of historicity and self-creation, the technological and medical accomplishments of modernity, the critical scholarship made possible since the decisive breakthrough of the Enlightenment? Rather should one expect the integration and relativization of these values within a wider, more comprehensive religious context. It would be the fixation on these secular values that the transcultural person would transcend, not the values themselves. One senses that Merton would have been comfortable with this solution, for did he not say of the transcultural person that she "has experienced qualities of every type of life . . . retaining all that is best and most universal in them"? A similar integration on a higher level should also be our approach to the remaining primal cultures and religions in our world, such as the Native and South American Indian cultures represent.[57]

Moving to our implications, the first I would note is that Christianity can be an authentic partner with the venerable East in the forging of a transcultural consciousness, not in spite of, but precisely because of its conviction of the centrality of Christ. Briefly, to celebrate and confess faith in the risen Christ is to commit oneself to that passage from absorption to universality, from partiality to final transcultural integration, which the Easter faith proclaims. Here it is useful to remind ourselves that faith is not only the result of experience but itself creates experience. After all, our experience is not ready-made, but in part the result of our prior convictions and aspirations. One whose prior horizon has been shaped by Merton's vision would be in a position, not to be dragged through, but to walk through upright, in our planetary world. Further, the experience of planetization is in and by itself ambiguous. The world wars, which Dunne so masterfully sees as signs of our failure to develop a collective consciousness, are also signs to us that in this process authentic values must not be lost. But how are we to adjudicate these? Some norm of discernment is needed, the wisdom of which Aquinas speaks, and it is precisely this which Merton's vision may foster within the Christian West. But perhaps we can go further too and maintain that if transculturalization is genuinely a creative process in which all cultures need to be transcended, must this not require ultimately some transcendent principle operative in history, and drawing mankind toward a greater universalization? It is this which Merton names "the Christ," and while such a conviction might wrongly inspire in some a worthless passivity, it should rather inspire a certain confidence that transculturalization is indeed a possibility.

Secondly, Merton's vision more sharply focuses for us the theological/

philosophical issues involved in the East-West encounter. To quote Clarke and Burkel in their illuminating essay on the Eastern and Western self, the basic issue is "whether or not in its ultimate depths the human self is—and will always remain in any future mode of existence—finite, determined, and ontologically distinct from the Absolute Ground of all reality; or whether at its deepest level the human self is really identical (or at least continuous) with the Absolute, hence in its ultimate root indeterminate, infinite, nonmultiple."[58] No doubt exists that on the psychological/experiential level Merton is of one accord with the East that the transcultural self transcends the determinate and particular notion of selfhood characteristic of Cartesian, Western-man—achieving self-identity by means of excluding others. For the Cartesian it is the principle of contradiction that takes priority; for the transcultural person, the principle of identity. In Merton's words, "Christian contemplation must be able to show the Asian contemplative that the Christian too . . . does not confuse the person with the individual, and does not consider his relation to the ground of Being as a purely subject-object relationship—that he is not confined to the fussy and materialistic individualism of purely ethical and practical concerns."[59]

Yet Merton does not seem to be committed to the ontological view that all distinction of selves is merely illusion. He is of one accord with Burkel and Clarke "that it is possible also to have distinction not merely through determination and exclusion of the other but through affirmation of the other in love."[60] This seems to be implied in his assertion that the transcultural person "apprehends *his* life . . . from an inner ground that is at once more universal than the empirical ego *and yet entirely his own.*" Further, he views the transcultural state not only as a disintegration but as a *reintegration* of the person on a higher level. Here we encounter the precisely Christian and biblical notion of selfhood, which is often wrongly identified with the post-Christian Cartesian notion of selfhood. We can express this as at once *union and differentiation.* Paul in Galatians puts it this way: "The life I live now is not my own; Christ is living in me" [union]. Yet he adds, "I still live my human life, but it is a life of faith in the Son of God, who loved me and gave himself for me" [differentiation] (Gal. 2.20). It is common for Christian thinkers to view the Trinity as the classical example of such distinction through affirmation. On the level of history we could perhaps view the risen transcultural Christ in the same terms. His passage from partiality to cosmification did not annul his personality: the wounds are still present, but they are transformed (Jn. 20.27). Perhaps this is also why, in the greater part of the Christian mystical tradition, the contemplative never surpasses the humanity, albeit risen, of Christ himself. We have already noted Merton's view on this matter from his essay on the place of Christ in monastic prayer. Teresa of Avila agrees: ". . . to withdraw completely from Christ or that this divine Body be counted in a balance with our own miseries or with all creation, I cannot endure." Of course, she speaks of the *risen* Jesus: "The Lord appears in the centre of the soul . . . just as he appeared to the Apostles, without entering through the door, when He said to them: 'Pax Vobis'. . . ."[61] William Johnston suggests that this is how the Christian contemplative keeps his feet on the ground and remains in touch with reality: "by remaining with Christ he remains close to the heart of the universe."[62] We could say that the risen Christ insures that the individual is neither "absorbed in" nor "annihilated by" the Divine Presence. Rather that Presence relates to us in a way that accords with our humanity, and with God as a dialogical God.

Finally, Merton tells us that the transculturalizing process "for the individual, and for the community lies . . . beyond the dictates and programs of any culture ('Christian culture' included)."[63] It is eschatological, in other words. While this inevitably introduces a healthy relativization of every individual and every religion, it is not often noted that it therefore also implies the partial validity of every religion. History is open-ended under God's providence, and that providence admits of many, although partial, historical realizations. Only if the Christian fails to see that his allegiance to Christ implies transculturalization need he fear that his identity is called into question. Individuals who would identify final integration with any this-worldly realization of it run the risk, it seems to me, of either fanaticism or despair. Fanaticism, because they inevitably are absolutizing what is actually relative. Despair, because after the realization of this relativity comes "the fall."

Merton and Theological Reflection on the Religions

We can usefully conclude this final chapter by indicating how Merton's approach to the world religions coincides with other approaches advanced in the theological tradition relative to the religions. At the same time this will serve as a positioning of our own tentative view, since Merton's transcultural Christ seems to me simply to be a further development of our own view of the Christ as a co-present principle of universalization "present" within humanity's midst. In what follows, I will outline five "typical" Christian approaches to our problem, following and augmenting the useful analysis already provided by Charles Davis and H. Richard Niebuhr.[64]

A first view, hardly advanced today except by fundamentalist groups, is that called after Niebuhr "Christ against the religions." Here the non-Christian religions are rejected as false and the Christian mission is one of simply converting the "pagans" from an unsalvific existence to a salvific one in Christ. We can bring, of course, several objections to such a view. It seems contradictory to God's universal Lordship over history, isolating that Lordship only to the select few known as Christians. Further, it springs from a "ghetto" mentality and cannot prove itself credible in light of what is now known about the various world religions.[65] But specifically from a Christological point of view, it ultimately denies Christ's transcultural presence throughout the world.

A second position, that of "the Christ of the religions," is the relativist solution, and thus the extreme contrary of the first view. There can be no doubt that societal factors tend to favor this form of thinking, given the modern reality of pluralism and our new awareness of human historicity and conditionedness. One might recognize the relativist view in the following expressions: ". . . each religion appropriately expresses its own culture; there is not absolute truth in religion, only truth for us; all religions are different paths to the same goal."[66] No doubt this is the most difficult position to contend with, and our own observations here must be tentative. On a more general level, one wonders whether a relativism of this kind, while motivated by a deep respect for the plurality of the religions, might not end up fostering a kind of indifferentism toward the various claims advanced by the religions. Theologically there are serious differences between the religions, some of which we have sought to point out above. Could it be said that such a view is actually based on an ignorance of the claims of the various religions? Christologically it denies Christ's universal mediatorship and God's decisive disclosure as Divine *Pathos* in Jesus. In an earlier chapter we indicated that Ernst Troeltsch was the great pioneer of this view, but I also tried to propose that perhaps his view of God was more pre-personal and a-historical, and that it was this that kept him from understanding the incarnation. It does seem to me that the uniqueness of Christianity does consist in its dialogical, personal view of the Divine manifesting itself fully in Jesus. At this stage of my reflections I do not see how one can maintain this unique element in Christianity on the relativist view. But, and this should be emphasized, I do not see how one can maintain the possibly unique elements of the other religions on the relativist view either. The relativist view is simply not attuned to the manner in which the religions understand themselves. Perhaps it was more an outgrowth of nineteenth-century relativism rather than of theological reflection upon the religions.

Thirdly, one can speak with Niebuhr of a "synthesis between Christ and religion." While maintaining Christ's presence among the other religions, against view one, and repudiating relativism against view two, this solution would maintain that the Christ is most definitively manifest in the historical religion of Christianity. Hence, Niebuhr's claim that this third view "fuses" Christ with a particular religious and cultural expression of him. Historically examples of this would be the medieval fusion of Christ and Christendom or the Eastern Orthodox fusion of Christ and Byzantium. I am inclined to think that the Second Vatican Council espouses a form of this solution, at least in its document on the non-Christian religions. This latter document maintains, for example, that the non-Christian religions "often reflect a ray of that Truth which enlightens all men" but which the Church itself fully proclaims in Christ.[67] Here we encounter, of course, the untenable position of absolutizing a finite, cultural mode of expressing and understanding the Christ and the way is open to the kind of Christian imperialism against which we have seen Merton inveigh. This view absolutizes the cultural instead of the transcultural Christ; Merton's transcultural Christ is much more subtle.

Fourthly, one may speak of "Christ and the religions in paradox." Recognizing the inability of a definitive fusion between Christ and any cultural expression of him, this view argues for an "insurmountable polarity and tension between the Christian revelation and every concrete religion, including empirical Christianity, which itself is emphatically distinguished from the Christian revelation."[68] Christ, who transcends any concrete religion, stands in judgment over religion with its human institutions, corruptions, and sinfulness. Such a view would make room for the non-Christian by disembodying religion from its cultural forms and making the Christ-relationship a purely inward, privatistic affair. On these grounds, someone is saved in spite of his religion, not because of it.[69] But it is surely questionable whether any cultural form of religion can simply be written off with this negative caricature. It can be persuasively argued that humans are essentially historico-cultural beings and that all religious experience needs some cultural embodiment and mediation. The Christ-experience does not exist "in the abstract" but is co-present within and mediated by particular cultural religious expressions. Christologically this view is not that of the transcultural Christ but of an a-cultural Christ.

Our final view, and the one with which Merton's transcultural Christ is most congenial, is that called after Niebuhr "Christ the Transformer of religions." On this view, Christ is truly envisaged transculturally as present to and yet transcending all the religions. Thus, the varied world religions are viewed positively. But not naïvely, for the transforming Christ summons every religion to a continual conversion and regeneration, and thus the finitude and sinfulness of every religious expression is clearly recognized. Now let us explore this view somewhat more carefully.

We might indicate, first, that belief in a transcultural Christ is able to grant religious and salvific validity to every form of religion and to every authentic religious experience. The transcultural Christ is co-present wherever the Divine *Pathos* is authentically mediating itself, whether through some cultural form of religion or through some more "personal" religious experience. To say that the transcultural Christ "transcends" the cultural religions is not to maintain that he is a-cultural. As transcultural he is co-present in and yet not simply identified with every experience of the Divine *Pathos.*

Secondly, belief in a transcultural Christ opens the possibility of truly discovering religious insight from the non-Christian religions. It is simply not the case that Christians already know in a supposedly explicit manner what is only implicit among the non-Christians. As the transcultural Christ, the possibility opens up of Christians learning from non-Christians authentic religious values that are either unexpressed or underexpressed in the Christian tradition. This is already happening in the area of religious and mystical experience, and in any case one must say that for Christians truly to develop a transcultural consciousness, a real historical dialogue with the East must occur. It is preeminently the transcultural dialogue that will foster the transcultural consciousness. But, further, the possibility is also present of the non-Christian religions enjoying the Christ-experience in their own cultural manner. It is simply not true that one can only "know" Christ by way of the cultural form of Christianity. This would land us in an untenable fusion of Christ and culture. Merton, I think, put what we are trying to say in a most daring way in one of his later writings. During his visit to Ceylon, he drove up to the old Buddhist shrine of Pollonnaruwa, where he encountered two colossal Hinayanist Buddhas carved from natural rock about eight centuries ago. One figure was in the lotus posture; the other, in the samadhi; with the smaller figure of Ananda, the faithful disciple, near the latter's head. Merton exclaimed:

> Looking at these figures I was suddenly, almost forcibly, jerked clean out of the habitual, half-tried vision of things, and an inner clearness, clarity, as if exploding from the rocks themselves, became evident and obvious. The queer evidence of the reclining figure, the smile, the sad smile of Ananda standing with arms folded (much more "imperative" than Da Vinci's Mona Lisa because completely simple and straightforward). The thing about all this is that there is no puzzle, no problem, and really no "mystery." All problems are resolved and everything is clear, simply because what matters is clear. The rock, all matter, all life, is charged with dharmakaya . . . everything is emptiness and everything is compassion. I don't know when in my life I have ever had such a sense of beauty and spiritual validity running together in one aesthetic illumination. Surely, with Mahabalipuram and Pollonnaruwa my Asian pilgrimage has become clear and purified itself. I mean, I know and have seen what I was obscurely looking for. I don't know what else remains but I have now seen and have pierced through the surface and have got beyond the shadow and the disguise. This is Asia in its purity, not covered over with garbage, Asian or European or American, and it is clear, pure, complete. It says everything; it needs nothing.[70]

Was Merton merely being poetic when he, a Christian, maintained that the Buddha "says everything; it needs nothing"? Or was he trying to get us to see that the Orient, too, knows the Christ, on its own terms, in its own way?

Thirdly, belief in the transcultural Christ does not imply that one should indiscriminately swallow any and everything offered by the various religions, including Christianity. It does not land us, in other words, in a religious relativism. Niebuhr stresses that Christ the Transformer calls for a never-ending process of conversion. Not only is culture open-ended and subject to an ongoing revision; so too is religion in all its forms. Merton, we saw, spoke of the need to transcend "partial views" stemming from the "partiality and compromise" of cultural adaptation.

In more concrete terms, this would mean for Christianity that it must undergo transculturalization through detaching itself from a simple identification with the Western culture. Merton noted that an important indication of the passage from cultural adaptation to transcultural integration is anxiety, the necessary disillusionment with cultural partiality. We should expect just such an anxiety as Christianity undergoes the very difficult process of cultural detachment.[71] And it is not difficult to isolate some of the more important elements from which the West must be detached. One might point to the tendency to stress Western cultural stability, which legitimates the hereditary faith at the expense of a genuine world dialogue. Further, a conception of faith that stresses unanimity of thought and expression in its inherited Western form. And most importantly, we must learn detachment from the many defense mechanisms we employ to legitimate our failure to undergo cosmification.

Similarly for the non-Christian faiths one suspects that the process of cultural detachment will foment enormous anxiety. On the most general level, the great religions must not succumb to a neo-ghettoism in the face of the challenge brought before them by the West. They must not call a "religious renaissance" what is really a refusal to undergo planetization. Similarly, as Hans Küng has suggested,[72] although perhaps not carefully enough, there is a great need for the elaboration of a critical and scientific theology among the religions, so that the interreligious dialogue can really be fruitful. Just as in the West, this will bring enormous challenges to the East on the philosophical and historical levels. More specifically one can point to at least problematic areas among the great religions, needing more complete treatment: (1) Islam's unhistorical dogmatism and belief in the Koran's inerrancy; (2) the cyclical world picture of Hinduism, Buddhism, and Jainism, and how this might relate to the Western historical consciousness; (3) the problem of the Hindu caste system and to what an extent this is allied with Hindu thought; (4) the possibility that Hindu and Buddhist conceptions of the world as illusion (*maya*) perhaps excessively devalue external reality; and (5) the traditionalism of Confucianism.

Fourthly, believing in the transcultural Christ does not devalue the non-Christian religions by leading to the view that these have no function any longer under "God's providential ordering of history," as Davis has pointed out.[73] This would again presuppose that Christianity is the exclusive cultural medium of the Christ, again an untenable fusion of Christ and culture. It would further presuppose that cultural and religious diversity is in all respects evil, to be replaced by some "super-unanimity." Davis puts the issue very well:

> Can we assume that the unity of all men in an explicit acknowledgment of Christ is a goal to be reached in this historical order? Christians undoubtedly regard such unity in Christ as a hope to be fulfilled in the eschatological order to come. But is it also going to be achieved in an earthly fashion in history? I do not see that this must be so. Since even under the sovereignty of God history is open-ended, offering a manifold of possibilities for actualization by men, I should not exclude a universal acknowledgment of Christ as impossible in history, though I should regard it as achieved in history as essentially impermanent.[74]

Following Merton one might surmise that religious diversity in some respects is at least grounded upon the transcultural Christ and is perhaps the necessary manner in which this transcultural Christ can indeed come to be experienced and known.

Fifthly, such an understanding of Christ does not devalue the role of Christianity in God's providential ordering of history. Such a view still calls upon Christians to witness to Christ as the revelation of God's very own *pathos* in history. Through such witness the Christian trusts that that *pathos* is itself more completely mediated to the world. Yet it is a witness that recognizes its limited, albeit necessary, role under God's sovereignty in history.

Finally, let me close by commenting briefly upon what Davis regards as the one real difficulty of Niebuhr's "Christ the Transformer" model, a model that he himself seems to adopt, despite this difficulty. He says: "If . . . one refuses to suppose that a pure essence of the Christian revelation can be extracted and formulated apart from any cultural embodiment, then Christ as motivating a conversion is Christ as presented in the Christian religion of a particular time and culture."[75] Thus, Davis thinks that this necessarily lands us in the difficulty of really being unable to transcend cultural particularity. Here, I think, Merton's view of the transcultural Christ offers us some aid. While it is true that one cannot "extract" the Christ from his cultural and historical embodiment—for us culture-bound creatures there is no "pure" Christ—it is also true that one cannot "identify" him with any particular embodiment. As transcultural, the Christ is a principle of transculturalization, drawing us toward the transcultural state. If this were not the case, Christianity would always be tied to its particular cultural form, and this is plainly not the case. But with this, we come to the end of our *zetema,* our search. I am confident, however, that as we pass to this new planetized standpoint, our vision of the Christ will be substantially deepened and clarified.

Notes

1. Cf. my "The Risen Christ, Transcultural Consciousness, and the Encounter of the World Religions," THEOLOGICAL STUDIES 37 (1976) 381–409, and *Christ and Consciousness,* pp. 128–159, for a more complete treatment of planetization.

2. Karl Jaspers, *The Origin and Goal of History* (New Haven: Yale, 1953), p. 126. Cf. pp. 126–228.

3. John Dunne, *op. cit.,* p. 151. This is balanced by a more optimistic trend in human development, as Andrew Greeley relates, "Sociology and Theology: Some Methodological Questions."

4. Jaspers, *op. cit.,* p. 133.

5. *Ibid.,* p. 140.

6. Raimundo Panikkar, "The Emerging Myth," MONCHANIN 8 (1975) 8–9.

7. "Myth" is being used here in the Greek sense, as explorations of our destiny.

8. Panikkar, *art. cit.,* 11.

9. Thomas Merton, "Christian Solitude," *Contemplation in a World of Action (CWA)* (New York: Doubleday Image, 1973), p. 258.

10. Thomas Merton, *Conjectures of a Guilty Bystander (CGB)* (New York: Doubleday Image, 1968), p. 21.

11. Cf. Thomas Merton, "The Christian in the Diaspora," *Seeds of Destruction* (New York: Farrar, Straus and Giroux, 1961), pp. 184–220.

12. Merton, *CGB,* p. 336.

13. Thomas Merton, *Zen and the Birds of Appetite (ZBA)* (New York: New Directions, 1968), p. 46.

14. *Ibid.,* p. 132.

15. C. G. Jung, "The Difference Between Eastern and Western Thinking," in Joseph Campbell, ed., *The Portable Jung, op. cit.,* p. 490.

16. Thomas Merton, *The Seven Storey Mountain* (New York: Doubleday Image, 1970), pp. 241–242. Here I would not want to leave the impression that Merton could have developed his view of the transcultural consciousness without actually going to the East. I agree with Panikkar, *art. cit.,* 10: "It is all very well for zealous preachers to insist that we (Westerners, Christians, Hindus, Japanese, Russians, etc.) have in our own tradition what we pursue elsewhere, but they preach in a vacuum . . . because the peoples of the world tend to look *outside* for a solution, a complementarity, a way, a savior, a salvation. But a great wind is blowing across all the boundaries, bearing with it the seeds of dialogue and genuine tolerance." My stress here is only to note that this outward tendency must be truly integrated—a development from within—before it can mark a genuine development in consciousness.

17. Eric Weil, "What Is a Breakthrough in History?," *Daedalus* 104 (1975) 26–30; cf. p. 30: "But it is impossible for us totally to reject our inheritance. The new meaning must have a positive significance for us; we are what our past has made us. . . . This is why intellectual purists are so often scandalized when they look at the development of new ideas; they want them to be radically new and they want them to remain so. They are looking for breakthroughs that would come into the world without parents; that would spread without being accessible to any larger public—in other words for breakthroughs that are essentially destined to be abortive."

18. Merton, *CWA,* pp. 219–231.

19. A. Reza Arasteh, *Final Integration in the Adult Personality: A Measure for Health, Social Change, and Leadership* (Leiden: E. J. Brill, 1965). A second edition, with a preface mentioning appreciatively Merton's use of the first edition, appeared under the title of *Toward Final Personality Integration* (New York: John Wiley and Sons, 1975).

20. Merton, "Final Integration. . . . " p. 222.

21. *Ibid.*

22. Arasteh, *op. cit.,* p. 173, citing E. Knight, *The Objective Society* (New York: George Braziller, 1960), p. 127.

23. Merton, "Final Integration . . ." pp. 223–224.

24. Arasteh, *op. cit.,* p. 91.

25. Merton, "Final Integration . . ." pp. 224, 230. Interestingly Arasteh's Chapter 10, pp. 303–312, is an analysis of Kamal, whom Arasteh views as the image of the future planetary man.

26. *Ibid.,* p. 225.

27. *Ibid.*

28. *Ibid.*

29. Thomas Aquinas, *Summa contra gentiles,* 2, 24. Cf. Conley, *op. cit.,* and, for the notion of indifference, Rahner, *Spiritual Exercises,* pp. 23–27.

30. Merton, *ZBA,* p. 117.

31. Cf. John J. Higgins, "Merton's Attitude toward 'the World,'" *Merton's Theology of Prayer* (Spencer, Mass.: Cistercian Publications, 1971), pp. 91–101; and cf. Merton's own comments on his *The Seven Storey Mountain:* "I was still dealing in a crude theology that I had learned as a novice: a clean-cut division between the natural and supernatural, God and the world, sacred and secular, with boundary lines that were supposed to be quite evident. Since those days I have acquired a little experience, I think, and have read a few things, tried to help other people with their problems—life is not as simple as it once looked in *The Seven Storey Mountain*" (in Thomas P. McDonnell, "An Interview with Thomas Merton," *Motive* 28 [1967] 32–33).

32. Merton, "Final Integration . . ." pp. 225–226. Arasteh, *op. cit.,* clearly formulates this interest in the social: "[the transcultural state] requires insight into conventional realities—cultural realities which not only help the integrated man become aware of stations which he has passed through but also helps him develop insight into the life of others" (p. 117). Yet linked to this is a simultaneous critique of society: ". . . he has two impressions about the reality of the cultural world: the socio-cultural realities which exist seem meaningless, valueless, and arbitrary in comparison to his state. Yet he can also appreciate how these meaningless contributions are meaningful and necessary in previous states and in the life of others" (pp. 119–120).

33. *Ibid.,* p. 226.

34. Thomas Merton, "Notes for a Philosophy of Solitude," *Disputed Questions (DQ)* (New York: Farrar, Straus and Cudahy, 1960), pp. 182–183.

35. *Ibid.,* p. 187. Neither are we dealing here with a regression to a crude individualism: "The individualist in practice completely accepts the social fictions around him, but accepts them in such a way that they provide a suitable background against which a few private and favored fictions of his own can make an appearance. Without the social background, his individual fictions would not be able to assert themselves, and he himself would no longer be able to fix his attention upon them" (*ibid.,* p. 185).

36. Merton, "Final Integration . . ." p. 226.

37. *Ibid.,* p. 228, as cited by Arasteh, *op. cit.,* p. 86.

38. Cf. Han Fortmann, "The Dangerous Ego," *Discovery of the East,* pp. 83–91, and Lewis Mumford, *The Transformations of Man* (New York: Harper Torchbooks, 1972).

39. Merton, *ZBA,* p. 22. Cf. Higgins, *op. cit.,* pp. 25–47, for Merton's anthropology.

40. *Ibid.,* p. 24. Cf. Raymond Bailey, *Thomas Merton on Mysticism* (New York: Doubleday, 1975), for the biblical, patristic, and mystical background of Merton.

41. William Johnston's phrase from his *Silent Music,* p. 147.

42. Merton, *ZBA,* p. 74. Here he also refers to this as "a matter of superconsciousness," a notion nicely explored by Roberto Assagioli in his *Psychosynthesis: A Manual of Principles and Techniques* (New York: Penguin, 1976), esp. pp. 192–224. For the Pauline view of the self, cf. my *Christ and Consciousness,* pp. 48–84, 175–187, and Krister Stendahl, "The Apostle Paul and the Introspective Conscience of the West."

43. Merton, "Notes for a Philosophy of Solitude," p. 207.

44. Thomas Merton, *The Asian Journal of Thomas Merton (AJ)* (New York: New Directions, 1975), p. 317.

45. Merton, *CGB*, p. 318.

46. Cf. Hans Schmidt, "Politics and Christology: The Historical Background," *Concilium* 36 (1968) 72–84.

47. Merton, *AJ*, p. 316.

48. Merton, "Final Integration . . ." pp. 229–230.

49. Thomas Merton, *The New Man* (New York: Farrar, Straus and Cudahy, 1961), esp. pp. 131–223. This *Logos* Christology is predominant in all of Merton's works. Cf. Higgins, *op. cit.,* pp. 12–18.

50. Thomas Merton, "The Humanity of Christ in Monastic Prayer," *Monastic Studies* 2 (1964) 9. Here Merton's view is echoed by Karl Rahner's "The Eternal Significance of the Humanity of Jesus for Our Relationship with God," *Theological Investigations* 3 (Baltimore: Helicon, 1967), pp. 35–46, esp. p. 44: "Jesus, the Man, not merely *was* at one time of decisive importance for our salvation . . . but—as the one who became man and has remained a creature—he is *now* and for all eternity the *permanent openness* of our finite being to the living God . . ."; and p. 43: "We may speak about the *impersonal* Absolute without the non-absolute flesh of the Son, but the *personal* Absolute can be truly *found* only in him, in whom dwells the fullness of the Godhead in the earthly vessel of his humanity." For the controversy to which Merton refers, cf. Irénée Noye *et al., Jesus in Christian Devotion and Contemplation* (St. Meinrad, Indiana: Abbey, 1974), esp. pp. 86–101. As for the pre-Easter Jesus, Merton (*ibid.,* 18) says: ". . . the Fathers reflected on the life of Christ much as they reflected on the Old Testament: that is to say, as on something which has been radically changed in achieving its final fulfillment and perfection." Note the similarity in view to Karl Rahner: "The purpose of [Christ's] life is perfectly accomplished in His Resurrection. . . . This is so true that everything that He was in the course of His history has entered into the glory of the Father. . . . When He meets us now as the resurrected Lord, He is who He is because of His past. What He experienced during His life now shows, as it were, its absolute and final face. He took His whole life and everything in it with Him into glory" (*Spiritual Exercises*, pp. 245–246).

51. Indicated by Jesus' unrecognizability as risen (Lk. 24.16); by the "third day" motif, which is a standard biblical one for some profound religious transformation (Ex. 19.11, 16; Hos. 6.1); and by the alternate description of the risen Jesus in terms of "exaltation" and "ascension." I have been greatly stimulated by Karl Rahner, *On the Theology of Death* (New York: Herder and Herder, 1961), and Édouard Pousset, "La resurrection," and "Croire en la resurrection."

52. Johnston, *op. cit.,* pp. 160–161.

53. *Ibid.,* p. 161.

54. *Ibid.,* p. 163.

55. As suggested by Johnston, *ibid.,* p. 160. The question can rightly arise as to why Christians need to invoke Jesus as a principle of universalization when God might seem to do well enough. But the issue is not precisely *whether* God is such (which, of course, as transcendent, God is) but *how* God is to be such a universalizing factor within history. It is this latter issue that Christology seems to clarify.

56. Thomas Merton, "The Power and Meaning of Love," *DQ*, pp. 123–125.

57. Cf. Thomas Merton, *Ishi Means Man: Essays on Native Americans* (Greensboro, N.C.: Unicorn, 1976), for Merton's appreciation of primal religions and cultures. He notes these characteristics of the primal: ". . . the indifference to

technological progress, the lack of history, and the almost total neglect of the arts of war. The three things go together, and are rooted in an entirely different conception of man and of life. That conception, of which we have already spoken as a network of living interrelationships, can be called synthetic and synchronic, instead of analytic and diachronic. . . . it is a difference between a peaceful, timeless life lived in the stability of a continually renewed present, and a dynamic, aggressive life aimed at the future. We are more and more acutely conscious of traveling, of going somewhere, of heading for some ultimate goal. They were conscious of having arrived, of being at the heart of things. Mircea Eliade speaks of the archaic concept of the sanctuary or the sacred place as the *axis mundi*, the center or navel of the earth, for those whose lives revolve in the cycles of its liturgy" (p. 63). And further: ". . . there is some advantage in remembering that after all peace, tranquillity and security were once not only possible but real. It is above all salutary for us to realize that they were possible only on terms quite other than those which we take for granted as normal" (pp. 69–70). Merton's view of the primal is similar to Carl Starkloff's: "When we speak of 'the primitive,' we ought literally to take off our shoes. If we lightly dismiss all elements of the supernatural with such a term, intending it to mean any quality that belongs to a benighted, bygone age or a backward society, we sadly misconceive ourselves and our own world. The notion of the primitive is not chronological or geographical, but existential: it explains those hidden forces in individuals and collectivities that call for expression and interpretation. . . . it is only prudent at least to suspect that the primitive is deep within each one of us" (*The People of the Center: American Indian Religion and Christianity* [New York: Seabury, 1974], p. 22). The best study I have seen is Jean Cazeneuve, *La mentalité archaïque* (Paris: Armand Colin, 1961).

58. W. Norris Clarke and Beatrice Burkel, "The Self in Eastern and Western Thought," in Heaney, *op. cit.*, p. 165. The Islamic tradition seems to span both options: monistic (Sufism) and dualistic (orthodox Islam).

59. Thomas Merton, *Mystics and Zen Masters* (New York: Delta, 1967), pp. 213–214, a view held even by Aquinas in his *De Veritate*, 2, 2.

60. Clarke and Burkel, *art. cit.*, p. 169.

61. Teresa of Avila, *The Book of Her Life*, Kieran Kavanaugh and Otilio Rodriguez, transls., *The Collected Works of St. Teresa of Avila* 1 (Washington, D.C.: Institute of Carmelite Studies, 1976), p. 144; and *Interior Castle*, E. Allison Peers, ed. and trans., *The Complete Works of St. Teresa of Jesus* 2 (London: Sheed and Ward, 1975), pp. 334–335.

62. Johnston, *op. cit.*, pp. 87–90. Suzuki, following Zen Buddhism, does not think this is radical enough; cf. *ZBA*, p. 133.

63. Merton, "Final Integration . . ." p. 231.

64. Charles Davis, *Christ and the World Religions* (London: Hodder and Stoughton, 1970), pp. 49–60, who in turn creatively follows H. Richard Niebuhr, *Christ and Culture* (New York: Harper, 1956).

65. See Friedrich Heiler, "The History of Religions as a Preparation for the Co-operation of Religions," M. Eliade and J. M. Kitagawa, eds., *The History of Religions: Essays in Methodology* (Chicago: University of Chicago, 1959), pp. 132–160.

66. Davis, *op. cit.*, p. 50.

67. W. M. Abbott, ed., *The Documents of Vatican II* (New York: America, 1966), p. 662.

68. Davis, *op. cit.*, p. 55.

69. This was characteristic of the older, Roman Catholic notion of baptism of desire. Here one's intention, and not one's religion, was given a salvific efficacy.

70. Thomas Merton, *AJ,* pp. 233–236.

71. See Wilfrid Desan, *The Planetary Man* (New York: Macmillan, 1972), pp. 143–151, for this notion of detachment.

72. Hans Küng, *On Being A Christian* (Garden City, N.Y.: Doubleday, 1976), pp. 104–109.

73. Davis, *op. cit.,* p. 128.

74. *Ibid.,* p. 129.

75. Ibid., p. 59.

INDEX OF NAMES

277

SUBJECT INDEX

Abba, in Jesus' ministry, 65–66
Agape, see "love"
Alexandrine Christology, 178–179
Androgyny, the divine, 141, 174–175, 182–183
Antiochene Christology, 178
Apathy, the divine, the problem of, 124–126, 158 *n*97
Apocalyptic, 76, 138, 172, 216
Appearances, of the risen Jesus, 92–94, 95–96, 195–197, 209 *n*5
Archaic cultures/religions, 264
Arianism/Arius, 124–125, 152 *ns*38–40, 227, 236
Ascension, 93
Assumptus-Homo theory, 189 *n*51, 190 *n*52

Biblical Citations, see text; the translations are either from the New American Bible or my own
Biblical Criticism, difficulties in, 34–39
Buddha/Buddhism, 84–85, 133, 254, 255, 269, 270

Cappadocians, 125–126, 152 *n*44, 178
Chalcedon, Ecumenical Council of, 3, 175, 177–179, 183
Christ-mysticism, in Bérulle and the French School, 226–245, in Thomas Merton, 253, 260–263, 265–266, 274 *n*50, in St. Paul, 195, 200–202, 208–209 *n*2
"Christ of Faith," as hermeneutical category, 45–49

Christology, and God-Concept, 113–149, as transcultural, 253, 260–263, as Trinitarian, 148–149, 160–161 *n*101, basic kerygmata of, 78–83, 101–102, biblical approach to, 5, comparativist explanation of, 83–87, cross- and passion-centered, 114–115, dialectic approach to, 5–9, dogmatic (conciliar) approach to, 3–5, from above, 16–17, from before/ahead, 16–17, from below, 16–17, functional vs. ontic, 83, Hellenization of, 87–88, implicit in Jesus' historical ministry, 63–71, implicit vs explicit, 100–102, incarnation-centered, 113, Jewish "no" to, 83, 117–122, ministry of Jesus-centered, 113–114, of New Testament, 71–83, 89–102, reflection on Jesus' person within, 162–185, resurrection as the basis of, 89–102, resurrection-centered, 115–116, theopathic, 17, titles of Jesus within, 71–75, 79–83, types of, 113–116, undifferentiated and differentiated, 48–49, 63, 77–78, 100–102
Conciliar Christology, importance of, 3–5
Confucianism, 270
Constantinople, Ecumenical Councils of, 3; 125 (I), 179 (II), 179 (III)
Cosmification, 204–205, 220, 250–271
Critical theory/theology, 143–144, 156 *n*88

John the Baptist, 64
Judaism, 83, 117–122, 137–138

Kenosis/Kenoticism, 147–148, 158
  *n*97, 160 *n*99, 190 *n*51
Kingdom of God, Jesus' preaching of,
  60–61, 63–71, 171–173, as apocalyptic, 76, as present and future,
  66, as prophetic, 75–76, as universal, 137–138, 154–155 *n*78
  *n*78

Lateran, Fourth Ecumenical Council
  of the, 224 *n*16
Liberalism, Protestant, 16
Literary Criticism, 37–39
Logos-anthropos, 16, 178
Logos Christology, 197–198, 203, 261
Logos-sarx, 16, 178
Love, and Christology, 86–87, 118,
  132–133, 140, 147–148, 153–154
  *n*61, 157 *n*92, 169, 190 *n*51, 204–
  207

Mediator, Jesus as the, 77, 195–207,
  220
Messiah, as title for Jesus, 71–75
Middle Platonism, see Greek theology
Miracles, of Jesus, 61
Modalism, 124
Modernists, 181
Monarchianism, 124
Monophysitism, 158 *n*97, 177–178,
  188 *n*49
Monotheism as affirmed by Christian-
  ity, 117–118, as Trinitarian, 149,
  types of, 149
Montanism, 149
Mystery Religions, 27, 84, 200–202
Mystici Corporis, 191 *n*53
Mysticism/Mystics, and Christology,
  146, 158 *n*96, 166, 187 *n*28,
  200–202, 210 *n*17, 227, 229–230,
  260–263
Myth, the nature of, 13–15, 18–19 *n*15

Neo-Platonism, see Greek theology
Nestorianism, 177–178, 188 *n*49
New Quest, 16, 29–34, 43, 45–49

Nicaea, Ecumenical Council of, 3,
  125, 158 *n*97, 178

Old Quest, 26–27, 43, 45–49
Ontic vs Functional Christology, 83
Orphic Mysteries, 123
Ousia, 125

Panentheism, 144–148
Pantheism, 144–148
Parables, 64–65
Passion/Death, of Jesus, 61–63, 69–
  71, 114–115, 137–139, 149 *n*2,
  173–174, 230
Pathos, the Divine, 134–149, 158 *n*97,
  160 *n*99, 162–185, 198, 204, 218,
  220, 222, 236
Paul, Saint, 79–81, 114–116, 119,
  126–129, 146, 150 *n*18, 167–169,
  200–205, 208–209 *n*2, 212–213,
  214, 218, 219–222, 235, 265
Pharisees, 35, 60, 67–68, 79, 93, 119,
  137–138
Pluralism, 7–8, 164
Prayer, in Jesus' ministry, 170–171
Preexistence, 83
Process Philosophy/Theology, 98,
  114, 157 *n*94, 159 *n*98
Prophet, as title for Jesus, 71–75
Prophets/Prophetism, 134–136, 172,
  200–202, 216
Proverbial Sayings, in Jesus' ministry,
  65

"Q" Source, 96–98

Rabbinic Judaism, 138; see Pharisees
Redemption, see Soteriology
Redaktionsgeschichte, 34, 37, 44, 91
Religionsgeschichte, 34–35
Renaissance Humanists, 226–245
Resurrection, 33, 48–49, 63, 78–79,
  89–102, 107–108 *n*73, 108
  *n*s81–82, 108–109 *n*83, 109
  *n*s85–86, 109 *n*92, 139–140, 174,
  202–207, 210–211 *n*22, 235–240,
  260–263
Resurrection, of the flesh, 206
Roman Theology, 138–139